THE JESUS CONSPIRACY

Holger Kersten studied theology and pedagogics at Freiburg University, Germany. He is an author who has specialized in religious history, and his best-selling *Jesus Lived in India* (also published by Element) has been translated into fifteen languages.

Elmar R. Gruber studied psychology, philosophy and ethnography in Vienna, Freiburg and Los Angeles. A scientific adviser for German TV and radio, he is also the author of several books and has had more than sixty articles published in major scientific journals.

D1322816

The Jesus Conspiracy

THE TURIN SHROUD AND THE TRUTH ABOUT THE RESURRECTION

Holger Kersten and Elmar R. Gruber

ELEMENT

Shaftesbury, Dorset ● Rockport, Massachusetts
Brisbane, Queensland

© 1992 by Albert Langen/Georg Müller Verlag in der F.A. Herbig
Verlagsbuchhandlung GmbH, München
English translation © Holger Kersten and Elmar R. Gruber 1994

First published in Great Britain in 1994 by
Element Books Limited
Shaftesbury, Dorset SP7 8BP

Published in the USA in 1994 by
Element Books, Inc.
PO Box 830, Rockport, MA 01966

Published in Australia by
Element Books Limited
for Jacaranda Wiley Limited
33 Park Road, Milton, Brisbane, 4064

First hardback edition 1994
First paperback edition 1995
First mass market edition 1995

Cover design by Max Fairbrother
Designed by Roger Lightfoot
Typeset by Footnote Graphics, Warminster, Wiltshire
Printed and bound in Great Britain by
BPC Paperbacks Ltd, Aylesbury, Bucks

British Library Cataloguing in Publication
data available

Library of Congress Cataloging in Publication
data available

ISBN 1–85230–756–0

Contents

Acknowledgements

Many people have assisted us in the course of our research, and without their strong support, their readiness to talk to us and their valuable advice it would not have been possible to get this comprehensive work finished in such a short time. Special thanks are due to Susan Brown, Elizabeth Crowfoot, Père Daniel Weber, Ian Wilson, Claude de Cointet, Prof Gilbert Raes, Helen Leynen, Dorothy Crispino, Dr Alan Whanger, Dr Manfred Gessat, Dr Trevor Lloyd Davis, Dr Roger Caron, Prof Hermann-J. Vogt, Prof Andreas Resch, Basilius Grolimund, Prof W. Wölfli, Tristan Grey Hulse and Karl Herbst.

For their technical assistance we extend our gratitude to Matias Heidemann, Word Perfect GmbH, Michael Hahn, engineer at Projectina AG, the Institut für Textil- und Verfahrenstechnik and Sick Optik/Elektronik GmbH.

For the reading of the German manuscript and their critical comments we have to thank Dr Arnol Stadler, Dr Anneliese Schumacher, Dr Christian Lauermann, Gerda Huchthausen, Hannah Samtleben and especially the editor Ria Schulte.

Our special thanks go to Dagmar Neff-Westrick, Elmar R. Gruber's companion, without whose dedication the project could neither have been taken up nor brought to a close.

Preface

Ever since the existence of the Turin Shroud became known, opinions about it have differed. The discussion had long seemed to favour its authenticity when, in 1988 at the order of the Vatican, three groups of experts, using the so-called radiocarbon method, dated the linen cloth to the fourteenth century. For many that was final. And yet so much was left unanswered. As we seek to show in this book, the Shroud is not a fake. And there is good evidence to prove it.

One of the authors, Holger Kersten, commenced his investigations as soon as the dating results were released. Following his previous work on the Shroud, the medieval date looked extremely suspect to him. And in due course it became clear that behind the scenes of the ominous dating experiment things were in something of a muddle.

In the course of a discussion the authors discovered to their surprise and delight that they were both working on the same subject, albeit from two different standpoints. Elmar R. Gruber had come across the Shroud in the course of his studies about the mysterious Order of Templars. His historical research had also indicated that the cloth, which is preserved today in Turin, was in existence long before the Middle Ages. During our discussions Kersten strongly stressed the importance of the Shroud. Its importance did not, as many assume, lie solely in the fact that it may represent the only surviving piece of original evidence for the existence of Jesus. The special feature of this unusual image of a crucified man on a cloth is that *it is the image of a living person!* This obviously throws quite a different light on the circumstances under which the cloth was, under Vatican supervision, stamped as a medieval forgery. It forces us to modify all prior conceptions: yes the cloth is not just an unusual object, it is one of the most sacred relics of Christianity, and yet it is this very relic which may prove to be dangerous, even catastrophic, for the institutional Church. Should it be confirmed that the man on the Shroud is actually Jesus, it means Jesus survived the crucifixion. But what of the 'salvation' which Jesus is supposed to have vicariously obtained for all by his 'death on the cross'? In short, what would become of the crucial sentence written by Paul in his letter to the Corinthians, 'And if Christ be not risen, then is our preaching vain, and your faith is also vain'? (1 Cor. 15:14).

Only then did the enormous implications of the facts dawn on us. We immediately resolved to pool our energies and fields of expertise, to carry out a thorough investigation into the mysterious circumstances of the radiocarbon dating and the secret of the Shroud. Hardly a day passed without exciting new discoveries being made as, little by little, we uncovered a carefully planned act of deception. Beyond this, even the Bible was seen to reveal a long-guarded secret: Jesus had survived the crucifixion. And a silent witness of the events had also survived, preserved to this day by a lucky turn of fate – the enigmatic linen cloth.

It is not easy for a person brought up in a Christian culture to distinguish between the man Jesus and the Christ of dogma. One may take the easy option and just avoid the historical facts entirely. Or alternatively one can view the historical facts from the standpoint of the current teachings of the Church and fit them in somehow. In the first case one follows a speculative path, a kind of religious conviction, outside the confines of which no historical facts are required. In the second case the tinted glasses of dogma prevent an unbiased view of the true circumstances. And yet to be able to discriminate between myth and truth, one just needs to keep one thing in sight: the facts. It is the facts that decide. And it has been the historical, scientific, philological and exegetical facts which have determined the content and conclusions of this book.

We are well aware that we have touched upon a delicate subject, and perhaps may even have offended the religious feelings of some of the faithful. We thought long and hard about how best to present the facts, and we avoided rushing to any premature conclusions. Where the ground was uncertain, we constantly pursued our inquiries, sparing neither journey nor expense, in order to see things at first hand; hunting in the remotest archives for documentary evidence, and even setting up our own experiments to explore the process of image formation. We have invested a great deal of time in this project, in the conviction that the truth may help to bring to light the treasure of the true teaching of Jesus, buried under 2000 years of accumulated ecclesiastical rubble.

Part One

THE OLD RELIC
AND MODERN SCIENCE

Holger Kersten

Traces in the Linen

There it rests, in the dim light of the chapel's baroque cupola, high over the altar, protected by trelliswork, toughened glass and alarm systems, sealed in its precious shrine, hidden from the view of mortals: the alleged Shroud of Christ, which seems to have preserved in some miraculous manner an impression of his supine body. Rare are the occasions when the pontifical guardians of this most precious relic of Christianity ascend the heights of the angel-ringed altar, to bring out the linen cloth. Up there it rests securely (see Plate 1). Rare things have an aura of mystery about them, a breath of the numinous. Over a century ago, scientific curiosity had begun to try and draw even this object into the sober world of facts and figures. The path to demythologizing the riddle was opened, and the Church was in danger of losing its most impressive document of the historical Jesus.

Yet the cloth confidently stood up to all the measurements and weighings, the irradiation, the close-up macro-photographs peering into the core of every fibre, the major test projects, and surrendered nothing of its secret – that is until that momentous day, 13 October 1988. On that day a statement was issued by the experts of three laboratories, all specializing in the dating of old materials, announcing that their experiments had shown that the cloth originated in the Middle Ages. At one stroke it looked as though a centuries-old secret had been exposed and this revered relic had been branded a forgery. Had hope in the truth of the extraordinary finally been destroyed? If this were so, it would mark the end of the story of the Turin Shroud, and the start of the search for the most ingenious forgery of all time.

But who would want to perpetrate such a forgery? Was it even possible? Could a forger have taken into account all the facts which have been brought to light only recently in the course of minute precision work by numerous researchers using all the latest technology? When one looks more closely, the result of October 1988 gives rise to more questions than answers. We have been careful to look at the matter objectively. What we discovered is in some ways more amazing, exciting, incredible than the whole previous history of the cloth.

The Turin Shroud is 4.36 m long and 1.1 m wide, and shows in surprising detail the impression of a male body: on one half the back view, on the other half the front view of a crucified person. The cloth is folded in the middle above the head of the man. One easily recognizes head, face, arms, hands, legs and feet. The image is mainly in a sepia colour, with some areas in grey. Additionally, clear traces of blood are visible, bearing a faint crimson tint in the original image.

Looking at the cloth one's attention is first drawn to two darkened stripes running the length of the fabric, widening at some points to form larger trapezoid regions (see Plates 2 and 3). These are burn marks, which have been patched over by the lighter-coloured pieces. The cloth, folded in forty-eight places, was lying in a silver shrine in the castle chapel of Chambéry, France, when, in 1532, it was nearly lost to fire. Fortunately it was saved, but only after one side of the precious container had already begun to melt in the heat of the flames. Fire and molten silver left these geometrically shaped burn marks, later to be repaired and patched.

At some stage a strip was sewn on down one side, for aesthetic reasons; today this is somewhat shorter than the main cloth, and measures about 3.6 m long and 8 cm wide. With this added the image is shifted to the centre of the cloth, restoring the symmetry. The side strip is made of the same fabric in the same weave. This suggests that the addition was made soon after the main cloth was produced.

This 4.8 m² piece of cloth is one of the most extensively examined and researched single objects known to science. A whole range of specialist journals are devoted to the single topic of the Turin Shroud. Since 1898 the greatest authorities from a variety of scientific disciplines have taken up the challenge of this phenomenon. Applying the latest techniques they have been able to identify a great number of details regarding the history of the 'Man of the Shroud'.

In 1978, the 400th year of the cloth's presence in Turin, it was once again displayed to the public, forty-eight years after its last showing. Reports of the event echoed around the world, and it was then that I set out on a thorough study of this alleged linen of

Christ. Although many books and specialist articles had already appeared, doubts were constantly being voiced as to the authenticity of the relic. To many it seemed just too perfect to have simply arisen by a lucky chance some 2000 years ago. For centuries the parties for and against its authenticity had confronted each other. Only a definite chronological placing of the time of origination of the cloth could finally clear the matter up. In the 1950s the invention of a new method of dating objects provided for the first time a means of putting an end to this debate. What is known as the radiocarbon technique rapidly became the favourite of the archaeologists. Anything that could be dated by this method was brought along to the radiocarbon laboratories, and piece by piece the annals of ancient and classical history were filled with the dates – even if at first with an accuracy that was less than encouraging.

Calls for a radiocarbon dating of the Turin Shroud were made at a very early stage. But for a long time the minimum size of the sample which would have to be sacrificed from the cloth for the dating test was too large. It was only towards the end of the 1980s that the techniques of radiocarbon dating had advanced to the point where a fragment the size of a postage stamp would suffice to obtain a precise figure for the age.

In March 1988 the newspapers reported that in the next three months the Vatican would release a sample of the precious textile to allow several institutes the opportunity of doing a C-14 test. For security reasons the precise date was to be kept secret. Then on 22 April the press was able to announce that 150 mg of the Shroud had been handed over to three scientific institutions in Great Britain, Switzerland and the USA.

At the end of August I was to fly to India, via Amsterdam. The plane arrived *en route* from London, and on my seat I found a copy of *The Times* with a short article bearing the heading 'Turin Shroud 14th Century Fake, Don says'. My eyes rapidly ran through the text of the article:

TURIN SHROUD 14TH CENTURY FAKE, DON SAYS

A Cambridge University academic said yesterday that scientific tests had proved the Turin Shroud, in which the body of Christ was supposedly wrapped after the Crucifixion, was a fake, probably dating from the fourteenth century.

However, Oxford University scientists taking part in the project to date the shroud said they had no idea of the basis of the claim, made by Dr Richard Luckett, Fellow of Magdalene College, Cambridge, and the Cambridge University's Pepys librarian.

The British Museum said the results of the carbon dating tests made by Oxford University and laboratories in Switzerland and Arizona had all been received and were being collated.

Signor Luigi Gonella, Italy's leading expert on the Turin Shroud, accused British scientists of leaking details of the tests. 'Frankly, we in Italy we have been taken for a ride,' he said.

I found this news quite astonishing. So many genuine investigations had previously shown that the relic was in fact a good deal older. I found it hard to believe that Dr Luckett's result would be corroborated by the official announcement.

I passed several eventful weeks in Kashmir and the Himalayas, until I was forced to cut short a trekking tour in Ladakh because of disasters caused by the weather conditions. When I was finally able to leave the country on the first plane out, I found myself stuck fast in Kashmir: the sole connecting road to the Indian plains was buried for three weeks under a landslide. Back in Europe at last, I felt the need to rest after the rigours of the journey. I relaxed for a while in Sardinia and the Shroud had almost slipped from my mind when, at a small beach café on the south of the island, I came across a copy of the Italian paper *La Repubblica*. The front-page headline read 'Cardinal Ballestrero of Turin announces scientific results: "The Shroud a forgery", the "holy cloth" is medieval!'

So that was it: the Turin Shroud was a medieval forgery, and whole generations of researchers and experts had been taken in! Were all the previous research results on the Shroud really wrong? Had the scientists with their modern analytical instruments been duped by a medieval forger?

Let us survey the research on the cloth carried out prior to the radiocarbon test, so that we are in a position to form a proper picture of the whole subject.

Revelations of Photography

In 1898 the young state of Italy celebrated the fiftieth anniversary of the Italian Constitution, which is based on the Sardinian *Statuto*.

This occasion was thought important enough to justify another public showing of the holy Shroud, following its previous exhibition in 1886.

The invention of photography was still quite recent, and now for the first time in history a photograph of the cloth could be taken. In this way the mysterious portrait could be made accessible to the wider public. Everyone would have a chance of viewing a true likeness of the relic.

The owner of the cloth, King Umberto I of Italy, was not entirely enthusiastic about the idea. In those days the new technique of photography was viewed with considerable scepticism, and he did not wish to show disrespect or irreverence to the Shroud by profane handling. However, Baron Manno, the organizer of the festivities, succeeded in winning the King over. Still Umberto was concerned that the work should be performed by a Christian lay person, so that the photographic image of the relic would not pass into commercial hands.

The baron proposed as photographer a real amateur – in the best sense of the word – a man who had already won a series of major awards for his photographic work: Secondo Pia, forty-three-year-old barrister and Mayor of the north Italian town of Asti.

In those days photography involved a far greater outlay than it does today. Pia was in possession of a huge box instrument with a precision lens manufactured by the firm Voigtländer. One can still see this camera in the little Shroud museum of Don Piero Coero Borga in the Via San Domenico in Turin. Pia had laboriously to coat the light-sensitive glass plate, a full 50 × 60 cm in size, himself and develop it in his own laboratory. He was only permitted to illuminate the cloth set in its frame, high above the altar of the Turin chapel. There were no electric lights, and it was very dark just round the altar.

On the evening of 25 May, the first day of the eight-day exhibition, after the last of the numerous pilgrims had left the cathedral, Pia appeared with several assistants and a mass of materials and equipment. First he erected a scaffolding, to be able to work with the camera directly in front of the cloth high up where it hung. Then he had to position two powerful floodlights with electric arcs producing the maximum intensity then available. He had to provide the current himself with two generators he had brought.

Just when everything was finally assembled and arranged in place, the glass covers of his lamps shattered in the tremendous heat given off. These glass covers served to spread the light diffusely and softly, and now the lamps were unusable.

Pia had only the evening of 28 May for a second, final attempt. But in the meantime the King's sister, Princess Clotilde, had had a sheet of glass inserted in the frame securing the cloth, to serve as protection against the incense and candle smoke. Now the poor photographer had reflections off the glass to contend with as well. Secondo Pia was obliged to move the scaffolding with the camera to a distance of 13 m. The electric voltage of the generator fluctuated so severely that the whole operation became risky and unpredictable.

Towards 11 pm everything was sufficiently ready for Pia to take the first picture, with an exposure time of fourteen minutes, and then a second one with twenty minutes' exposure. Shortly before midnight he rushed the plates to his laboratory, to see the results of his efforts at once. What he then saw, he described in a report that is both moving and informative. His initial feeling was one of great relief, as he actually beheld, appearing on the glass plate in its bath of ferropotassium oxalate, the outline of the linen portrait. As the picture emerged more and more distinctly, his astonishment mingled with growing excitement. Still he let the plate lie in the developer bath a few seconds longer, and suddenly he was seized with amazement: this was not the familiar mask-like shadow of a face that he knew from the Shroud and which looked more like a skull than a real face. The picture which emerged from nothing before his eyes in an almost miraculous manner, appeared as natural and living as a normal photographic portrait. The grotesque mask had been transformed into a well-formed and expressive face.

There before him lay, as photographic negative, what seemed to him to be the true-to-life photograph of the real Jesus with natural-looking tones of shading. A tremor of wonder passed over him at the thought that he might be the first person permitted to look into the face of Jesus himself after nearly two millennia (see Plate 5).

News of the marvel spread like wildfire, and soon Italian nobles and dignitaries of the Church were pressing into Pia's studio to wonder at the negative plate with the positive image of Jesus, which the lay photographer had impressively set up illuminated from behind in a darkened room.

On 13 June 1898 the Marquis Filipo Crispolti wrote in the Genoa paper *Il Cittadino*: 'The picture leaves an unforgettable impression! The lean, noble face of our Lord, the wounded body and the long slender hands are quite clearly visible. They are revealed to us now after the lapse of centuries, unseen by any since the time of the Ascension. I have not lost a minute in passing on the news to the whole world.'

In the wake of Pia's discovery, scientific discussions about the cloth began. While up until then all the arguments had been based only on painted copies or eyewitness accounts, it had now become possible to reproduce the portrait thousands of times and make it accessible to all. The negative was a striking proof of the authenticity of the relic. No painter, however ingenious, would have been able to produce the perfect negative of a picture before the invention of photography. And in any case what would have been the point in producing such a picture? If the cloth were meant to be an object of reverence, one would surely have produced a distinct portrait, not this strangely diffuse, ethereal figure which is only gradually visible to the untrained eye. The natural rendering of light and dark tones, *in reverse*, as found on the cloth, is to this day possible only by some sort of photographic technique, and all the artists who have tried since 1898 to paint a copy of the Turin Shroud portrait, using a variety of techniques, have produced very unsatisfactory results.

Later the proponents of the forgery hypothesis were even to accuse Pia of retouching the plates. Because the cloth had immediately been enclosed in its silver shrine again, with a seal set upon it, only the two photographs remained as objects for research. So it is understandable that both parties were set on edge. It was only after the cloth had been photographed again in 1931 that the seventy-five-year-old Pia was vindicated.

Authenticity Doubted

At the threshold of the twentieth century, relics of saints were classed simply as relics from the age of magical thought. One of the exercises of reason-guided thought was the exposure of many relics as medieval or later forgeries. The excessive demand for sacred objects had produced a flourishing market for them. In former times excavations were specifically carried out at sites where saints were supposed to have lived, and every bone that was brought up instantly became a precious holy relic. As late as the sixteenth and seventeenth centuries the Vatican was engaged in a considerable trade in skeletons from the catacombs under the Eternal City, posthumously 'baptized' to be on the safe side, and then installed as baroquely ornamented martyrs and catacomb saints behind uncounted numbers of glass cases in the churches of Christendom, revered to this day.

From the Age of Enlightenment, sceptics and ever more incisive interpreters began to come forward, putting forward a severe criticism of the old stories and representing them as fables and legends. Then for the first time reports were printed in which doubts were raised about whether a Jesus of Nazareth had ever lived at all. With the faith in science that characterized the nineteenth century, educated people wished to show their supposed knowledge by trying to be rational and by rejecting all cults of miracles and relics as mere superstition. There were even some office-bearers of the Church among them.

Among these we find the towering figure of the Catholic priest and canon Ulysse Chevalier. His *Summary of Primary Sources of the Middle Ages* is rightly considered one of the major scholarly works of the nineteenth century. This voluminous documentation of practically all the available medieval sources appeared in 1883 and was at the time the most extensive work of history by a single author. It is still valued as a standard work of medieval historical research. Chevalier was a marvel of industry and scholarship. In 1862, at the age of twenty-one, he was ordained a priest, and while still at the seminary was selected as member of the Societé Nationale d'Histoire, then considered a very great honour. He was constantly publishing scientific essays, and his work was officially honoured by the National Congress of History. At thirty-six he was made a Knight of the Legion of Honour. Later some of his colleagues lauded him as 'the most learned man in France and perhaps in the world'.

Contemporary portraits of this learned man do not show him as the sort of person one would choose to confide in: they show a tight-lipped mouth, with thin lips, a shadowy gaze from dark, piercing eyes set under a wrinkled brow in a round, broad skull. He almost gives the impression of a fanatical inquisitor right out of the Middle Ages.

He had the amazing gift of rummaging through old archives and libraries and stumbling across source materials in which nobody had shown any interest during previous centuries, with a quite incredible tracker's passion. To take one example: for his *History of the Dauphiné* he had in a short time viewed more than 20,000 documents.

He came across the Turin Shroud by chance, while researching his monumental work about the Middle Ages, and he located sources in which the cloth was described as a painting from the fourteenth century. When all the newspapers in Europe were reporting about the photographs of Secondo Pia, and the discovery of the negative image was being extolled as a true marvel at the threshold of the twentieth century, the scholar, now nearly sixty years old, was shaking his head in blank incomprehension. And before the old century was out he had published a first critical study of the problem of the linen's authenticity, followed in the autumn of 1900 by his extensive *Critical Source Studies*. In the latter, he included fifty documents in a sixty-four page appendix, so that the interested reader could check at first hand that the references allowed just one conclusion: the Shroud was quite definitely a fake and was painted by an artist around 1350!

Arguments against the authenticity of the Turin Shroud can indeed be made from the published references, and to a reader knowing nothing of the history of the relic except this information, that may seem to settle the matter once and for all. The documents presented offer an interesting glimpse into a bizarre controversy, when a bishop urged that the Pope put a stop to the exhibition of the cloth in the church of Lirey, near Troyes, France. Although relics were highly treasured and revered in the Christian world at that time, and there was such a demand for sacred articles that questions of authenticity were not looked into too closely, this man tried everything he could to stop the display of the holy Shroud.

All the arguments turned on a letter of the Bishop of Troyes, Pierre d'Arcis, to the Anti-Pope Clement VII in Avignon. According to this so-called memorandum, it appears that in the year 1389 d'Arcis called for a ban on further exhibition of the cloth in the small wooden church of Lirey. He claimed that the cloth was displayed there not out of piety but merely for greed and profit.

D'Arcis claimed to be in possession of evidence that a predecessor in his office, the bishop Henri de Poitiers, had already carried out a thorough investigation into the matter over thirty years previously, and had discovered the deception. Allegedly Bishop Henri had even been able to question the painter who had painted it. But Clement VII did not prohibit the display; instead he imposed an order of perpetual silence on the bishop. And there are reasons for believing that the 'memorandum', which had always served as the main basis for disbelieving the authenticity of the Turin cloth, is not as important as is claimed. In 1991, in a brilliantly researched article, Bruno Bonnet-Eymard showed just how fragile the evidence of the letter really is. Chevalier spoke of a dated parchment, probably wishing to enhance the importance of the document. In fact it is simply a paper, and the title page at the beginning informs us that it is a narrative of a story and not the original memorandum at all – should such a thing ever have existed in the form described in this paper. The document is in Latin, but at the end is written '*1389 fin*', in French. Chevalier presents this as '*1389 exeunte*', that is, in Latin, and thereby avoids the obvious inconsistency – the date is a later addition. One has to leave aside the question of whether the narrative of the 'memorandum' of Pierre d'Arcis was in fact written at this date. In his criticism of Chevalier, Bonnet-Eymard goes so far as to say that Chevalier had never actually seen the document himself. It is quite clear that he tried to bolster its extremely shaky value as evidence.

In those days the proliferation of relics which ended up in the churches and monasteries of medieval Christendom, often as the loot of campaigns and crusades, was quite astonishing. Once a Church authority had pronounced its blessing on such relics, no one normally thought of questioning the authenticity of the sanctioned shrines thereafter. Thus some barons were able to amass sizeable fortunes from the lucrative pilgrim trade, as each year there were thousands of the faithful wishing to see new relics. In such circumstances it seems particularly strange that in the town of Troyes two bishops in succession fought vigorously against the display of the Shroud. What could the true reason have been for this vehement attack on the genuineness of such a unique relic?

We will return to this question in some detail in the second part of this book. For the present, suffice it to say that, in the period around 1900 Chevalier enjoyed renown as the greatest authority in all questions of medieval history, and his judgement on the authenticity of the cloth meant practically all interest in the relic was nipped in the bud. No serious person would study the cloth now, and only religious enthusiasts or fanatics could still find the matter of interest.

The opinion of Chevalier was generally accepted by historians, and in 1903 the German historical scholar M. Baumgarten wrote: 'The Sindon (Shroud) of Turin was born amidst festivities in the fifties of the fourteenth century; it was carried to its tomb under great persecution and with few mourners in the year 1903. There can be no resurrection for it any more.'[1]

Nonetheless an attempt was soon to be made to restore the honour of the 'exposed false relic', and it was not based on appeals to questionable medieval documents about the cloth, but rather on the examination of the object itself.

The Beginnings of Scientific Research

Paul Joseph Vignon was born in 1865, the son of wealthy parents in Lyons. He studied biology, and his consuming passion was mountaineering. He was often accompanied on his bold climbing tours in the French Alps by his student colleague, Achille Ratti, a young Italian priest. Many years later the Shroud was to bring the two friends together again. In the meantime Vignon had become in a sense the father of scientific research on the Shroud, and Ratti had successfully moved up within the ecclesiastical hierarchy all the way to the rank of Pope, and as Pius XI he stood openly for the authenticity of the relic.

Vignon's life-work was to be an extremely thorough and intensive examination of the cloth. He was already able to offer quite satisfactory answers to many of the questions which were to be raised again and again in later decades. Especially commendable were his test procedures and his explanation of the question of the formation of the image and the cause of the peculiar phenomenon of the impression on the linen.

Once Vignon turned his hand to a thing, he did it thoroughly and with great zest. Excessive mountain climbing had brought the thirty-year-old to the limit of his bodily powers, and he suffered a mental and physical breakdown. While convalescing in Switzerland for a year, he taught himself to paint, and went at the task with such ardour that he was soon exhibiting his work in famous Parisian galleries as a member of a well-known group of painters. About a year after his stay in Switzerland he became acquainted with one of the most important biologists in France, Yves Delage, professor at the Sorbonne in Paris and director of the Museum of Natural History. In 1897 Vignon obtained a position on the staff of the biology journal published by Delage, and soon thereafter the dedicated young man became the Professor's assistant at the University and in the Museum. Vignon had at last found his calling in life and felt deep gratitude for this fatherly friend, whom he always called his master.

It was Professor Delage who in 1900 first acquainted his assistant with the Shroud photographs of Secondo Pia. Two years later Delage was to present a highly appreciated lecture at a session of the French Academy of Sciences, defending the authenticity of the Turin Shroud. Delage's scientific work was in biology, zoology, physics and mathematics, but his special field of interest was anatomy.

An agnostic, he opened his lecture with the admission that he did not believe Jesus to be the sole incarnation of God, but did consider him to be a historical person. Delage had studied Pia's photographs thoroughly and had come to the conclusion that it would have been impossible for a medieval artist to paint the picture on the Shroud, as Ulysse Chevalier had claimed in his publications. Vignon was encouraged by his professor's doubts to approach the problem from the scientific front. Over 1000 verifiable details could be identified on the cloth, and it should be possible with the aid of precise scientific methods to clear away all doubts and contradictions and decisively settle the question of its authenticity. Such a task was just what Vignon was looking for, and he resolved to take up the challenge. Delage assured him of his support and put at his disposal the technical assistance of his laboratory.

In early 1900 Paul Vignon travelled to Turin and immediately secured from Pia two plates with negative copies of the Shroud.

Pia informed him that two further photographs existed – previously unknown – made unofficially during the exhibition of 1898: one was a snapshot which a priest had secretly taken, the other had been made by a police officer who had been given the task of guarding the cloth. Neither picture was comparable in quality to those of Pia, but comparison of the plates showed that Pia had not tampered with his originals.

Proponents of the hypothesis that the cloth was genuine had two explanations for the formation of the image. One was that it could have been formed by a 'transfusion of blood', but they did not say precisely how this could happen. The other explanation was that a kind of supernatural electrical radiation, emanating in some unknown way from the body at the Resurrection, could have projected the picture onto the cloth. Being a clear-thinking rationalist, Vignon was convinced that the formation of the image must have taken place by some scientifically explicable means. He felt his task was to study and explain this natural process of origination.

To be able to form as objective a judgement as possible, he mentally rejected the idea that this piece of woven linen had anything at all to do with the person Jesus. He treated it simply as an old sheet of cloth and tried to forget all he had been told about it. Then he divided the investigation into two distinct categories: the first was simply the origination of the image; only secondarily would he turn to the question of whom it portrayed.

Vignon first turned to the problem of the negative character of the cloth image. In Delage's laboratory he placed enlarged prints of the positive picture and the negative picture next to each other, so that he could better compare them. He quickly saw that the original positive picture showed few human contours, that it was almost unsettling to an observer and had no aesthetic effect. Only after the photographic technique reversed the tonal values of light and dark did a recognizable body appear on the negative, with natural proportions and contours. It was quite different from the schematic collection of unconnected spots on the positive image. It is clear that the representation on the cloth is a negative image, and indeed one of a refinement and perfection that could only be approached by a photographic process. Being a painter himself, Vignon could draw as a first, most important conclusion, that the cloth could certainly not be the work of an artist of the fourteenth century, as had been claimed in the documents published by Ulysse Chevalier. How could a painter even have had an idea of a negative before the invention of photography, and how could he then have portrayed such a picture in such perfection? Even a genius commanding skills and talents greater than those of a Leonardo da Vinci would clearly have been incapable of such a masterly feat. It was photography which first provided the magic key as it were, to unlock the secret of the cloth. It seems almost as if there were some kind of divine plan behind it, as if the secret of the Shroud was meant to lie buried in the shadows of history down the centuries, until the time was ripe for its revelation in the twentieth century.

Critics may counter that some colours can be altered in their chemical constitution by external influences such as humidity, sunlight, heat or similar factors, leading to a reversal of hues. Thus pigments containing lead or zinc oxide, in combination with ochre, burnt earth or bitumen compounds, can in fact become more opaque or darker. One can sometimes see this effect on very old oil paintings. But all the tests Vignon made along these lines resulted in very coarse, reversed and false images, which could not be compared with the fine contours on the negative of the Turin linen. Moreover the pigments applied to the cloth would have had to be preserved over the centuries, but all witnesses who had been allowed to handle the cloth agreed, when questioned by Vignon, that the material was extremely soft and pliable and bore no traces of applied pigment.

These finds led Vignon to surmise that the impression must have arisen by direct contact with the body. Therefore he set up a series of different experiments along these lines. He used himself as the test subject, stuck on a false beard and had two assistants powder his face with a reddish lime, which he lay on an operating table in Delage's laboratory. Then his assistants placed a linen cloth coated with egg white over him and carefully pressed it on to the raised contours of his face. When after a while they took the cloth off it was found to bear a clearly visible impression. But it was deformed into a grotesque caricature. The face looked about twice the width of the normal view. It is the same phenomenon one finds when one cuts open a cylinder and unrolls it. Even a negative photograph of such an imprint does nothing to make the picture more harmonious. But the image on the Turin cloth does not exhibit any distortions of this nature. This demonstrates with certainty that one cannot speak of an *imprint* formed simply by direct contact of cloth and body. Vignon thought that a forger in the Middle Ages would most probably have had far greater difficulties than he did in obtaining such a contact imprint from a human body. In a number of test sequences, for which he had at his disposal modern technical aids and qualified assistants, he was not able to produce a picture which came anywhere near the perfection of the Turin cloth.

Vignon found by measurements and comparisons that the form of the man on the cloth corresponded in all details to the normal proportions of an average person. The position of all the recognizable limbs agreed with the corresponding natural posture of a test person in his laboratory. Thus he was able to deduce details of the size of the person portrayed: the height of the man on the cloth was close to 1.82 m (almost 6 ft). There is a widespread notion that the people of 2000 years ago in the Mediterranean area were shorter on average than people today. In contrast to this, more recent studies have established that the bodily sizes of people in the ancient world were quite comparable to those of today. The man on the cloth was indeed quite tall, but not exceptionally so.

In the course of his research, Vignon noticed that the intensity of the shading of the image varied in proportion to the distance of the sheet from the bodily extremities. The colour was stronger and darker at the places where the cloth lay directly on the skin, and the picture took on brightness with increasing distance above the depressions in the surface. The incomparable contoured reproduction of the portrait is due to this gradation. It makes the negative copy of the picture appear like a sculpture. Systematic analysis of this phenomenon showed the scientist that there was a consistent plan across the whole image: only those areas of the body directly touching the cloth or less than a centimetre from it left any colouring at all; everything at a greater distance was not imaged. One important result of this connection is the fact that large areas of the body are not imaged at all. Thus on the front view the neck region is missing. The omission of certain regions of the body is further evidence, not only that the cloth was definitely not painted (almost all the painted copies of the cloth show all regions continuously modelled with solid contours), but also that this is not an intentionally produced imprint of a body but a unique chance effect.

Vignon formulated the following conclusions from all these findings:

1. The picture was evidently produced by direct contact, but it also involved some kind of projection.
2. Vapours coming from the body itself must have been the cause of the formation of the image.
3. The warmth of the body had transferred the vapours on to the fabric in an exclusively vertical emanation following the physical law of gravity (because warm air rises).

But the young researcher needed to perform more experiments to find out just how all this happened.

There existed in France at that time a scientific discipline, still new, which was specially concerned with such chemical phenomena. A small team of researchers was investigating the effect of various gases on light-sensitive plates, under the name *action à distance*. Vignon approached the director of the experiments, Prof René Colson of the École Polytechnique in Paris, and succeeded in interesting him in his ideas. Colson had been working with zinc vapours, and he suggested that they try an experiment with them. They applied zinc powder to a small plaster head and then placed it thus prepared under a photographic glass plate, so that the relief touched the plate at forehead, nose and beard. After twenty-four hours they developed the photographic plate. The result was a happy surprise for both of them: an image of the bearded head of a man was distinctly visible! In fact the image was so excellent that Vignon thought this technique of projection could be developed further and perhaps later used commercially. After only the first attempt, both scientists were sure that they had discovered the process whereby the image on the Turin Shroud had been formed.

Now it remained to identify what chemical substances on the cloth had reacted together to produce the image. Vignon and Colson went on to experiment with ammonia vapours in reaction with powdered aloe (*aloe medicinalis*), applied to cloths of linen. According to St John's Gospel large quantities of aloe and myrrh were used at the entombment of Jesus. 'And there came also Nicodemus, which at the first came to Jesus by night, and brought a mixture of myrrh and aloes, about an hundred pound weight. Then took they the body of Jesus, and wound it in linen clothes with the spices, as the manner of the Jews is to bury.' (John 19:39–40.)

The form and colour of the resulting images were so astonishing that based on them the researchers derived their 'vaporgraphic' theory of image formation: humid vapours bearing ammonia from urea secretions, found abundantly in sweat caused by injury and fever, had, in combination with the mixture of aloe and myrrh, caused an oxidation process in the cellulose of the flax fibres, leading to a change in colour of the surface of the material. This change in colour was finally caused by the reaction of the solution of aloe and myrrh absorbed by the cloth, with the formation of ammonium carbonate, the vapour of which, in the humid atmosphere between skin and sheet, had darkened the colour of the fibres in direct proportion to body contact. Thus the colouring is strongest where the cloth touches the body, and becomes fainter as separation between cloth and body increases. This also explained why the image is like a photographic negative (see Plate 6). Even in tests with a very short exposure time of just forty-five seconds, faint imprints were formed which resulted in distinctly recognizable positive pictures on the photographic negatives. The visibly darker colouring of the blood traces was explained by a stronger chemical reaction.

In 1933 Vignon's experiments met with strong criticism, because the body salts needed for the chemical reactions, and the bodily warmth which brought about the evaporation process, could not occur in sufficient amounts in a corpse. Still it had been proved that an aloe-myrrh mixture in humid conditions leaves permanent body imprints on cloth very similar in hue to the Shroud's image. Interestingly, aloe was used in former times in the manufacture of dyes, because the polychromatic alterations in colour it causes were considered to be extremely durable. Detailed comments on the origination of the image will be given in the final section.

New Photographs – New Finds

The researchers' meticulous search for clues was given a fresh boost in the 1930s by new, technically improved, photographs made by Giuseppe Enrie. The pictures once more confirmed that there was nothing to indicate that the image had been produced by any kind of painting: the picture of the body gradually blends into the cloth background without any outlining, and no clear contours can be made out. All attempts by artists over the centuries to copy the Shroud image have led to poor results. Even the copy ascribed (surely incorrectly) to Albrecht Dürer, preserved in Liers in Belgium, does not even approach the original, and can at once be distinguished as a panel painting from the true Shroud image.

Let us have a look at the picture of the 'Man of the Shroud', as revealed to the scientists on Enrie's quality photographs. The first noticeable feature is the unclothed state of the body. In fact under Roman law criminals were beaten and executed while naked. It would, however, have been an unforgivable sacrilege to show the completely naked Jesus in an artistic representation. The second thing that immediately strikes the eye, is the severe wounding which clearly shows the man to be a victim of a crucifixion. He was not bound to the cross with leather thongs, as was often the practice, but nailed by hands and feet to the cross-beam and vertical post. This appalling type of capital punishment was abolished under emperor Constantine I (306–37). Thus one can be fairly certain that the image on the linen comes from a person who had been laid in the linen sheet before the year 330.

The distinct details allow us to recognize six of the Stations of the Cross reported in the Gospels. First, expert medical studies have discovered a severe swelling under the right eye and other surface face wounds, which are obviously related to the blows to the face inflicted by the soldiers.

Secondly, a large number of small, very conspicuous, dumbbell-shaped markings are visible on the front and rear of the body – they are particularly distinct on the shoulder and back regions. In total over ninety of these wounds can be counted, and their shape allows a reconstruction of the kind of instrument used to inflict them. The wounds are clustered in groups of three at a certain fixed angle to the body, so one has to assume it was a whip. The characteristic form of the individual wounds points to the Roman *flagrum*. One often encounters this terrible instrument of torture in stories of the early Christian martyrs. It was especially feared because it was fitted at the ends of the three leather thongs with small lead dumbbells, called *plumbatae*, and sometimes bone pieces, which could cause painful wounds.

Thirdly, in the shoulder region the whip wounds appear smeared with blood. This observation tallies with the custom of making the person sentenced to death on the cross carry the cross-beam (*patibulum*) to the place of execution himself.

Fourthly, the irregular course of the streams of blood on the forehead and the back of the head allow us to infer a crowning with thorns. The way these wounds are distributed over the head is interesting. It shows that what the 'Man of the Shroud' wore was not the ring of thorns familiar to us from the whole Christian iconography. It was rather a cap covering the whole head. This corresponds exactly to the oriental crowns which were widespread in those days.

Fifthly, the nail wounds are striking, especially one of the hand wounds. The course of the larger streams of blood indicates that the arms were stretched out on the cross at an angle of 55–65° to the vertical. The hand wounds supply a surprising piece of information: in art it is only the palms of the hands that are pierced, but the blood flows on the cloth clearly show that the nails were actually driven through the wrists – a fact which was to be supported by later investigations.

The final Station of the Cross is evident from an oval wound on the right side about 4.5 cm in length, situated between the fifth and sixth ribs. Quite a lot of blood appears to have flowed from this wound, the dispersal of which is best made out on the rear view. As is well known, the text of John mentions an injury to the side caused by a lance, saying 'blood and water' immediately flowed from it.

One does not find any sign of major injuries to the upper or lower legs, suggesting that the legs were not broken, again as confirmed by the Bible.

A precise study of the cloth picture itself suffices to rule out totally a forgery along the lines of a kind of art object. Besides the technical impossibility, to which we have referred, of producing such a picture in medieval times, there is the evidence provided by all these details which would have set a forger completely outside the iconographic tradition. In art the crown of thorns was always a ring, so the cap-like blood marks would be inexplicable;

and the hand wounds are always put in the middle of the palms and never in the wrists.

The anatomically precise representation of the body is similarly inexplicable. Anatomical knowledge up until the sixteenth century was based on the works of the Greek physician Galen (129–201), and was not modified until the pioneering studies of the Flemish anatomist Andreas Vesal (1514–64). One only has to glance over the medical codices from the end of the fifteenth century to be confronted in a striking manner with the paucity of the anatomical knowledge then available for iconography. As an example, I can refer you to the manuscript of the famous *Monumenta Medica* of John of Ketham of 1491, now kept in the National Library in Paris.

There can be no doubt that the picture on the cloth shows the imprint of a man which really has been impacted on the sheet of fabric. Moreover the evidence of the details proves that it could not have been just any crucified person. The agreement in so many details with the reports of the Gospels about the Passion of Jesus, and with other historical data about his crucifixion, is so impressive that even the Jesuit and historian Herbert Thurston, who considered the linen to be a forgery, wrote in 1903: 'If this is not the impression of the Christ, it was designed as the counterfeit of that impression. In no other person since the world began could these details be verified.'

The Surgeon and the Cloth

The study of Enrie's photograph had a stimulating effect. Many found the data so intriguing that they started to examine the facts of the Crucifixion as evident on the cloth picture in more depth. One of the most active in this field was the chief surgeon of St Joseph's hospital in Paris, Pierre Barbet. His numerous experiments with amputated arms showed that when the nails go through the palms a body weight of 40 kg would suffice to tear them through. As the wounds on the cloth picture show, the nails went through the so-called space of Destot at the base of the hands. Barbet found from his experiments on amputated forearms that this gap, which he had thought too small, did allow a thick nail to be easily driven through. The ring arrangement of the bones of the base of the hand provides great stability so that the body weight can be supported – albeit with great pain. In a similar way Barbet found the place where the nails had pierced the feet. This was located in the second metatarsal spezium. Neither the nails through the hands nor those through the feet had damaged larger blood vessels or bones. A person hammered to a cross in this way could support himself by the feet, and his body weight would not tear through the hands. It achieved two things; first, nails could quite easily be pushed through at these places; and secondly the agony of the victim could last for days as he supported and pulled up his torso. This was the basic reason for crucifixion: the horrifying drama of the death throes of a person over a long period.[2]

Barbet and others after him have also attempted to explain the details of the side wound. It is situated on the cloth near one of the patches used to repair the holes after the fire. On closer examination the actual wound is seen to be an oval 4.4 cm long and 1.1 cm broad. The blood marks from this wound, which can be traced further on the rear image, were described in detail by the British physician Dr David Willis. Willis observed that the inhomogeneous dispersion, broken up by clear areas, indicated the 'mixture of a clear fluid with the blood'.[3] This interesting find was confirmed by several other doctors, and may be seen to agree with the Gospel report, according to which 'blood and water' flowed from the side wound (John 19:33ff). However, opinions differ as to the explanation for this find. Barbet supposes that 'water' refers to pericardial fluid from around the heart, normally present only in very small quantities, but increased by mistreatment. The German radiologist Hermann Mödder of Cologne supposes that it was fluid from the pleural sac, again increased by the whipping. The American doctor Anthony Sava presented a similar view. By clinical studies with the victims of severe violence to the thorax, he was able to establish that a bloody fluid collected in the pleural cavity as a result of the injuries to the lung surfaces. The quantity of fluid that builds up can be considerable. In view of the many whip wounds to the chest, such an explanation seems quite plausible.

The Linen Tested

A new phase, one could say a new era in Shroud research, began in 1969. On 16 June the Turin Cardinal Pellegrino called together a commission of experts, who were for the first time to be given the chance to examine not just the photographs but the cloth itself.[4] The Cardinal could easily have invited scientists from around the world, and they would certainly have accepted his request. But the commission members under whose alert gaze the first scientific examination of the precious textile took place were mostly Piedmontese. Of the eleven observers invited, only six were scientists: Prof Enzo Delorenzi, head of radiology at the Mauriziano hospital in Turin, Prof Giorgio Frache, director of the Institute of Forensic Medicine at Modena University, Prof Giovanni Judica-Cordiglia, head of the Institute of Forensic Medicine at the University of Milan, the professors Lenti and Medi, and finally Prof Silvio Curto, curator of the Egyptian Museum of Turin. Without wishing to play down the attainments and abilities of the individual researchers, considering the uniqueness of the task at hand one has to describe the investigative commission as provincial.

One should not underestimate the diffidence and reserve with which the first scientists probably confronted the relic. They were in a sense explorers in *terra incognita*, where the paths and taboos were unknown. It is unfortunate that the harvest of finds was accordingly small. The first colour photographs, taken by a son of Prof Judica-Cordiglia, were also disappointing. They could not compare in quality with Enrie's black and white exposures of 1931.

For two full days the experts were able to study the cloth under the microscope, and in ultraviolet and infrared light, in strict privacy away from the public. The preparations for this quaintly *ad hoc* 'examination' were patently disastrous. Hardly any of them knew the first details about the history of the cloth, and thus seemingly endless discussions arose beside the exposed relic, while precious time which could have been used for gathering scientific data slipped by. The commission's results were predictably meagre. The single tangible result worthy of further consideration was the recommendation of Monsignor Caramello, curator of the Shroud, to allow more extensive scientific investigations in future, including the removal of 'minimal samples'.

The Incision

In 1973 the stage was set for a new round of experts to be allowed access to the Shroud. From his exile in Cascais in Portugal, ex-King Umberto II had given the go-ahead for the removal of the smallest possible samples – on the condition that they be restored to the reliquary later. Several of the 1969 commission members were again present. Among those who were newly appointed one should specially mention: the Turin physicist Prof Cesar Codegone, who was to study the feasibility of a radiocarbon test; Prof Guido Filogamo, a blood specialist from Turin University; Prof Mario Milone, director of the Department of Chemistry at Turin University, Prof Gilbert Raes of the Institute of Textile Technology in Ghent, and the Zurich forensic scientist Dr Max Frei. This time the researchers had three days to examine the linen in a planned and purposeful manner. Afterwards it was shown live on television to an audience of millions, while Pope Paul VI made a speech.

From the 'minimal samples' removed on 24 November 1973, Prof Raes was given a piece of cloth from the lower right-hand edge 40 × 13 mm in size, and a sample of 40 × 10 mm from the right side strip, together with a 12 mm long weft thread and a 13 mm long warp thread. Prof Mari and Rizzatti took with them a total of ten threads from various blood stains for Prof Frache. The longest measured 10.5 mm, the shortest just 4 mm. Profs Filogamo and Zina each received a thread from the right foot of the rear image.

Gilbert Raes was the first person ever to be given a sizeable fragment of the Shroud, although the sample came from a region containing neither image nor blood marks (see Plate 11). Raes is a textiles expert, whose speciality is cotton. He was to examine the cloth just as a textile. Naturally the characteristic herringbone pattern had long been known, using the three-to-one technique where each weft thread is passed under three warp threads, then over one, and so on. (The weft or woof threads are the ones running across the weave, the warp yarn passing lengthwise, as it is woven on the loom.) This complex and demanding technique of weaving is known from the first century almost exclusively from specimens of silk fabric, although this does not in any way preclude the possibility of linen having been woven in this way. There are some extremely good examples of linen fabrics from the Neolithic period, especially from Egypt. The Turin Egyptian Museum possesses a perfectly preserved Egyptian robe of linen. The special way in which the linen threads of the Shroud are spun, together with the herringbone weave, has led textile experts to postulate a Syrian rather than an Egyptian origin.[5]

On close inspection Raes found traces of cotton present on the cloth. These cotton fibres obviously came on to the fabric by chance and were not intentionally woven in. From their location Raes was able to rule out the possibility that they came on to the cloth in the course of time as a result of soiling. It seems probable that they come from the workshop where it was manufactured.

The various types of cotton fibres can be distinguished by their characteristic twists. Cotton grows in two distinct phases. In the first thirty days the exterior coat is built up, and in the second phase the twists develop, and these distinguish the species. Three species exist, clearly differing in the number of twists per centimetre. Raes only found fibres of the species *Gossypium herbaceum*, which has 8–9 twists per centimetre (see Plate 9). *Gossypium herbaceum* has been cultivated in the Near East from very early times. The inference is clear. None of the other species of cotton, which are native to America, were found; and cotton was not cultivated in Europe. This confirmed that the cloth material came from the Middle East. Of course this tells us nothing about its age, but nevertheless another piece has been fitted in the puzzle.

On examining the piece from the side strip, woven in the same manner, Raes could find no trace of cotton. The difference in the thickness of the threads is not itself sufficient to differentiate the two parts of the textile clearly. However the complete absence of cotton fibres is a clear distinguishing feature. The side strip, obviously intended to shift the picture on the Shroud to the centre of the complete cloth, was probably sewn on quite soon after the manufacture of the linen. This alone explains how such a linen strip, matching so well in colour, texture and weave, could have been obtained. One interesting fact in this context is that there are sections missing at the upper and lower ends of the side strip; it is not the same length as the rest of the cloth. Examination has shown that the end pieces were not cut off later; the strip was already shorter to start with.

In Modena and Turin the blood analysis experts worked on the threads they had been given, on which blood appeared to be present. In the laboratory of Prof Frache in Modena, who had many threads to study, fine microscopic examination showed that the 'blood traces' were not formed of a heterogeneous material which would be the case with artificial pigments, but fine, yellowish-red granules, which were found only on the upper fibres of each thread. Inspecting the reverse side of the cloth, the commission members confirmed that the picture is not visible there, nor the blood areas, even though the cloth is quite thin. This again speaks against the hypothesis of forgery by the application of paints: they would not be restricted solely to the uppermost fibres, and they would certainly be visible when viewed from the rear.

However, neither Prof Frache's research group, nor Prof Filogamo's who examined the fibres under the electron microscope, managed to identify the granules definitely as blood. On the other hand there was just as little indication of substances which would have suggested a forgery. The investigators were interested by the fact that the blood, if it was blood, did not penetrate through the fibres. The process which led to the image, the scientists then concluded, must have somehow been 'dry'. Several years were to pass before more precise data about the true nature of the blood-like areas could be presented.

Pollen Traces Lead to the Holy Land

In the meantime the criminologist Dr Max Frei had a brilliant idea. Frei, head of the Zurich police laboratory, was asked to test that the photographs taken by Judica-Cordiglia in 1969 were genuine. Frei had been involved with the falsification of photographs in the past and this was the reason he had been invited by the commission. His real interest, however, was in quite a different field – the analysis of microscopically small samples of biological substances.

In 1938 Frei had already written a book about the geography of flora of Sicily, and later he developed a forensic technique from his work in this special field. Crime-fighting with the magnifying glass was followed by investigation with the microscope. Frei had made an interesting observation on the photographs: the cloth appeared to him to be covered with very small dust particles. If one were to examine these, a whole world of micro-organisms, dust, bacteria, moss spores, fungal spores and pollen would be discovered. Frei chose to focus on the pollen. Although the precise identification of pollen is a laborious task, it might possibly provide information about the origin and geographical movement of the cloth.

Frei was allowed to remove samples from twelve different locations, using his surprisingly simple method: he used clean strips of adhesive tape, 10–20 cm^2 in size, pressing them on to the cloth. Under the scanning electron microscope Frei found, besides dust and fibres, about 1–4 pollen grains per cm^2. Pollen has an average diameter of 0.0025–0.25 mm and so most of them cannot be distinguished individually with the naked eye. The minute bodies are surrounded by a double layer, whose chemical composition has yet to be completely unravelled. This outer shell is extremely resistant and enables the pollen to survive under certain conditions for many millions of years. The tiny grains from different plants have different characteristics, so one can say which plant each comes from.

By March 1976 Frei had been able to identify forty-nine different species of plant whose pollen he had found on the Shroud.[6] Many of these plants are now found in most of the regions where the cloth is presumed to have been in the course of its history, such as for example the cedar of Lebanon (*Cedrus libani*). Of special interest, however, is the pollen of eleven kinds of plant which do not occur in Central Europe, but are halophytes of the Middle East. Halophytes are plants which only live in soil having an extremely high salt content, such as is typical for the region around the Dead Sea. These included for example special desert varieties of tamarisk (*Tamarix nilotica bunge*), suaeda (*Suaeda aegyptiaca zoh.*), bassia (*Bassia muricata asch.*) and artemisia (*Artemisia alba turr.*) (see Plates 22 and 23). To buttress his discoveries scientifically, Max Frei undertook extensive research trips in the countries where the Turin cloth may have passed during its history: France,

Italy, the eastern Mediterranean countries, Istanbul, Urfa (Edessa) and Jerusalem. He collected flower pollen at these places and meticulously compared them with the tape samples from the Turin Cloth. Little by little it became clear that on the cloth were a large number of pollen grains from plants that grow in the Jerusalem area. A total of forty-four of these plant species were found in the immediate geographical vicinity of Jerusalem, fourteen of them exclusively there. Besides this, twenty-three of the plant species were discovered in the region around Urfa, the former Edessa, including *Prusus spartioides spach.*, a plant which has been found only there. Around Istanbul, the ancient Constantinople, Frei was able to find fourteen kinds of plant whose pollen was on the cloth, one of them indigenous to this area (*Epimedium pubigerum*).

Of course this does not mean that all the plant species discovered *can only* grow in these areas. However, some are only found in limited areas, notably the typical desert plants and those from the steppes of Asia Minor. Furthermore, it was found that some of the pollen grain types found on the cloth were present in a relatively high concentration in the sedimentary layers of the Sea of Galilee from the time of Jesus. Before drawing any conclusions from this most interesting line of research, one would have to look at the local flora in its entirety. For the rest of his life Frei tried to cover this in his work. But the Zurich criminologist had taken up a task which would have kept even a large team of researchers busy for years. He left behind a priceless collection of pollen and the original tape samples from the cloth, as well as many pages of unpublished analytical data. American sindonologists (Shroud experts) have purchased the material and are intent on continuing this important research.

Investigations that attract a lot of attention always face the same fate: they run into the crossfire of criticism. Frei's palynological studies were no exception. Some people were surprised that there was so much pollen present on the Shroud, as if it were a regular pollen trap; certain arrangements were criticized; and, not least, the question was raised why of all things the pollen of olives or of the many varieties of *Gramineae* (grasses) were absent, although these plants were typical for the region around Jerusalem.[7] It has to be admitted that so far no proper answer to this question has been found.

Most of the critics, however, present their doubts in cautious terms, mainly because they concede that Frei's work as it stands is entirely convincing. If Frei had really wanted to prove that the Shroud is genuine, and to this end placed fraudulent pollen on his adhesive tapes – an accusation that was also levelled – then he would have 'discovered' pollen from plant species that had since become extinct. Frei, as he himself wrote, found it unfortunate that he had located no such pollen, which would of course have provided a rock-solid proof for the age and authenticity of the cloth.

Nonetheless the pollen analysis, especially the concentration of Jerusalem flora, does show that the linen has been in Palestine. To explain the large number of pollen grains from Palestine, it has been suggested that they landed on the fibres during the manufacture of the cloth.[8] This process involved washing the new textile and then bleaching it for a long period on an open field. The Turin cloth, which is of exceptionally good quality, was most probably subjected to a lengthy bleaching process, with repeated dampening to speed it up. This long process provided ideal conditions for collecting many pollen grains from the region.

During later showings of the cloth in Europe the biochemical conditions were not as favourable as during the bleaching with constant moistening, and therefore not so many of the locally typical pollen grains were left on the cloth. One interesting example, which probably indicates an exhibition of the cloth in Europe, is the discovery of rice pollen. The cloth was displayed on a balcony of the castle of Vercelli in 1494 and 1560. This castle is situated in what was then the most important region of rice cultivation in Europe.

State of the Art Technology Exposes Secrets

In 1978 the cloth had been in Turin for 400 years, and to mark the occasion it was shown to the public once more. Between 28 August and 8 October more than three million people made the pilgrimage to Piedmont to see the precious relic. Until then the linen with the image of the crucified man, despite its immense significance, was known only to a relatively small number of people. All that suddenly changed. Newspapers, radio and television broadcasts around the world reported the event. What for some was the chance to catch a glimpse of the Incarnation of the Lord, was for others at least the challenge of an unsolved riddle. There were few who were unmoved by the image on the cloth. For many it has still lost none of its fascination.

On the evening of the final day of the exhibition, the linen was removed from its bullet-proof fastness and placed on an adjustable board. In a chamber of the Palazzo Reale, adjoining the cathedral, two teams of scientists were waiting expectantly. This time the selection of investigators was more international. Leading scientists in their fields, many from the USA, joined the remaining members of the original commission. The Americans numbered twenty-five, and brought with them an extraordinary range of equipment, some of it constructed specially for the analysis of the Shroud. Among them were specialists in photography, spectroscopy, X-ray analysis, computer technology, organic chemistry and physics. Then there was the Turin researcher Luigi Gonella, physicist and scientific adviser to the Cardinal, and Giovanni Riggi, specialist in microscopy, and also the Milan pathologist Prof Pierluigi Baima Bollone. This time the research team had a unique opportunity to carry out an intensive research programme running to a full two weeks.

The preparations had been well made, and they went to work very systematically. They started by dividing the cloth into sixty sections, to provide a reference grid. Vernon Miller, of the world-famous Brooks Institute of Photography in Santa Barbara, California, photographed each of these fields using a whole range of different filters. Sam Pellicori, working with the specialist in picture analysis Don Devan, took countless microphotographs from very close to the surface, recording every square centimetre of the textile. Along with various other photographic techniques, this provided the basis for a large number of optical experiments.

This is a good point at which to describe an earlier result obtained by using high technology on pictures of the Shroud. Some years prior to this, in 1976, John Jackson and Eric Jumper had tried storing Enrie's pictures on an image-processing computer, NASA's VP-8. The VP-8 was designed to transform image intensities into depth contours; at the time it was the most advanced device of its kind. Jackson and Jumper wanted to determine how the change in intensity of colouring depended on the distance between the body and the cloth. For this purpose they had to set up an experiment in two phases. First the brightness values of a black-and-white photograph of the cloth picture were digitized. The computer was set to put raised points where the areas were dark, elevations of less height where the colouring was less intense, and where there was no image no data at all. In a second phase the aim was to measure the distance between cloth and body at various points. For this purpose the director of the test laid a cloth over a man lying in the same posture as the one crucified, and photographed him from the side, so that the contours of the material could be precisely shown. They then compared this photograph with one of the man in the same position without the cloth. Comparing the two profiles superimposed, average distances between the sheet and the particular body regions could be derived. The computer then calculated the reconstruction formula for the whole body from the correlation between cloth distance and colouring intensity.

Then, as the program slowly transformed the image into a three-dimensional form, the result was another sensation, like Secondo Pia watching the positive image of the man emerge for the first time in a bath of developing fluid. Now the figure was made somehow tangible, visible as a three-dimensional body. The image on the cloth even contained this information, information which is neither visible to the human eye nor achievable by painting or photograph![9]

Later the mathematical formula coded in the shading intensity could be refined. This allowed Jackson and Jumper, and the Italian physicist Giovanni Tamburelli, to reconstruct the 'Man of the Shroud' fully in three dimensions. Impressive modelled forms emerged. They make the onlooker wonder at the possibilities of modern science, and yet they also evoke a peculiar feeling of awe, as once faces the tangibly resurrected person of the crucified man. One even feels that one is perhaps on the point of crossing a limit which must for ever be shrouded in veils of mystery.

Science, with its nonchalant common sense, drives all such thoughts away. The discovery of the key to the coding of three-dimensional information in the cloth image was an incomparable triumph. Now there could be no more doubt: a man had once lain in the cloth. It is the features of this man that have, in a mysterious way, survived the centuries. From the relief image it was even possible to work out the measurements of the body: about 1.82 m (almost 6 ft) in height and some 79 kg (12½ stone) in weight.

Jackson and his colleagues were also present at the 1978 tests, which were greatly assisted by the Americans' discovery. It was no longer necessary to concern oneself with proof that the cloth was not a forgery. Now one had to examine how the image was formed, and perhaps find clues as to how old the image might be.

In the days following the public exhibition, dust and fibre samples were taken, a large number of photographs and special images were prepared, tons of the latest analytical instruments were moved into position, and countless pieces of data were recorded, to be evaluated over a lengthy period with the help of computers. The processing of all the material has still not been finished, but since 1980 the institutions taking part have published reports in the scientific journals at irregular intervals, allowing a glimpse of the extent and significance of the investigations.

Is it Blood on the Cloth?

While examining fibres from the image-bearing regions under the electron microscope, it was first established that the image was not caused by any extraneous substance: there was simply a darker coloration on the surface of the top fibres of the cloth, not found on fibres outside the coloured areas. One experiment that was performed directly on the cloth was the analysis of its X-ray fluorescence spectrum. This method is based on the knowledge that by using X-rays of certain energies every atom can be made to emit its corresponding radiation, that is to say it will fluoresce. The fluorescence spectrum produced in this way reveals information about the atomic structure of an object. The blood marks, such as those on the side wound and on the feet, were found to contain a particularly high concentration of iron.[10] Iron is one of the main constituents of blood. For the American chemist Dr Walter McCrone, however, the presence of iron was reason enough to declare before the world press, at the 1981 session of the American Association for the Advancement of Science, that the Turin Shroud could not be genuine. McCrone claimed that iron in the marks was a clear indication of an iron oxide pigment, in use only since the fourteenth century.

This theory, from a man who had never seen the cloth himself, was decisively refuted by further tests.[11] In these later experiments dust particles from the blood marks on the linen were treated with vapours of hydrazine and formic acid and then irradiated with ultraviolet light. The red glow of porphyrin molecules was seen under this radiation. Porphyrin occurs in a stage of haem synthesis and is considered a sure proof of the presence of blood, even where the haem itself has been destroyed by the effect of heat. By a detailed spectrographic analysis Sam Pellicori of the Santa Barbara Research Center in California could clearly show that the marks on the cloth which appear to be blood are in fact blood. The spectrum shows that it is a denatured metahaemoglobin. Metahaemoglobin comes from the oxidation of the haemoglobin iron in blood. It can no longer combine with molecular oxygen.

Moreover, McCrone had not mentioned the traces of manganese, cobalt and nickel which are always found in the iron oxide pigments used by artists, and are absent in the blood marks of the cloth. Finally Profs Heller and Adler of the group STURP (Shroud of Turin Research Project) – the main forum of scientists for the study of the Shroud – using techniques for identifying haematic micro-traces which are accepted as legal evidence in the USA, were able to prove that the reddish brown marks of the wounds are indeed blood.

Nowadays it is relatively easy to identify even the tiniest amounts of blood by a chemical reaction in a laboratory. The usual method is the so-called peroxidase reaction: even the minutest traces of the red blood pigment haemoglobin liberate oxygen from hydrogen peroxide, and this in turn oxidizes the colourless chemical benzidine, turning it blue. Haemoglobin and its decomposition product haem have very stable molecules, which normally retain their reactivity even after centuries. The pathologist Prof Baima Bollone has continued the analysis using several fibres extracted from the blood regions.[12]

The ancillary sciences of archaeology have in recent years developed new ways to carry out a detailed analysis of blood that dried thousands of years ago. Using the method of fluorescing antibodies, Baima Bollone was even able to prove that it is *human* blood. And in sensational tests using an immuno-histochemical technique with monoclonal antisera, he could even find out the blood group of the 'Man of the Shroud: the crucified person was AB![13]

The studies of the STURP members with fluorescent photography also revealed that two different types of burn mark are found on the linen. It seems that in 1532, during the fire in the chapel of Chambéry Castle, the cloth smouldered in an environment low in oxygen. The smouldering fire in the chest of silver that history records matches the reddish fluorescence of some of the singe marks. Other burn marks have another fluorescence spectrum and suggest a second burn in an open fire.

The various spectrographic studies can also help us to understand how the image was formed. Of course a final explanation for the origin of the image is still a long way off. But at least certain hypotheses can be dismissed as highly improbable. Many sindonologists thought that the image on the cloth may have originated by some kind of unexplained radiation: the body of Jesus emanated a powerful energy at the time of the Resurrection, which 'burnt' the image of the entire body into the fabric. Pellicori tested this and similar hypotheses by comparing the fluorescence spectrum of the cloth with that of images artificially produced on linen. He found that a superficial singeing of the cloth produced an image which was quite similar to that on the Shroud. In both cases only the outer fibres were turned brown by loss of humidity and alterations in the chemical structure of the cellulose. He investigated the fluorescence spectrum in two phases: first after the singeing and then after he had additionally baked the cloth for a period of five hours at 150°C.

By the baking process the cloth was artificially aged and assumed an overall yellowish hue similar to that of the Turin cloth. The fluorescence of a cloth treated in this way was very similar to that of the linen in the image-free areas. However, it was found that the images formed by singeing on linen after it had been baked fluoresced with a reddish-brown glow under ultraviolet (UV) light. But the body image on the cloth did not fluoresce under UV radiation. If the body image had originated by a kind of heat radiation, it ought to have fluoresced a reddish-brown colour in the same way.

The Problem of Image Formation

How, then, did the image arise? Further experiments have shown that the sepia-coloured shading of the image is caused by a change in the chemical structure of the cellulose of the linen. It was possible to produce the same colour gradations in the laboratory by decomposing the cellulose of linen with various oxidizing substances. These oxidation images even became more distinct as time passed, due to the ageing process. Pellicori achieved particularly interesting results with aloe, myrrh, olive oil, sweat and skin oils. In these tests the scientist followed the reference in the Gospel of St John to an anointing of the body with such a herbal mixture. Comparison of the spectra of aloe, myrrh, sweat and skin oils before and after the baking process showed that all these constituents individually applied became darker, and the myrrh, sweat and skin oils also became redder. In a way these tests came close to the theories of Vignon. But the formation of an image by a kind of vapour process, as proposed by Vignon and Colson, was rejected, for such an image would also be found between the fibres and not only on the surface.

Another interesting find came from a test in which one coating of sweat and skin oils applied with pressure was compared with another made with just light contact with the linen. At first the two imprints differed considerably; the former appeared dirty and the latter was not visible at all. But after the baking process the spectral characteristics of both imprints looked very similar. Obviously, Pellicori concluded, the chemical process of image formation was not affected by the different pressure of the front and rear sides of the body on the cloth. That explains why the images of both sides have about the same intensity, although the pressure in each case must have been very different. Thus the picture would have been formed by the transfer of substances exuded from and applied to the skin, while the ageing process, that is the effect of heat, brought about the fixing and darkening.[14]

These findings led to some interesting lines of inquiry. It seems that in theory the cloth image could have been formed by applying the herbs mentioned in the Biblical report. Vignon had already set up tests to support this, and so too had the Turin forensic doctor Ruggero Romanese in the 1930s. The Institute of

Forensic Medicine at Turin University today holds about eighty pieces of cloth bearing the imprints, prepared by Romanese, of faces of bodies coated with aloe and myrrh. None of these images, of either Vignon or Romanese, approaches the quality of the Turin picture, undistorted and precise in detail, but they do help one to form hypotheses about the possible process of formation. Baima Bollone, who continued Romanese's tests even before the examination of 1978, was able to show that even briefly touching a cloth to a face coated with a mixture of aloe and myrrh in solution and blood, was sufficient to obtain permanent, clearly visible imprints, showing a distinct contrast between image and blood.[15] When the opportunity later arose for him to examine several threads of the Turin cloth at length, he made a decisive discovery: six different microscopic analyses and an examination by the so-called X-ray energy dispersion spectrometer (EDS), showed the presence of substances having optical characteristics and organic composition like those of myrrh and aloe (as well as blood). To check his results, Baima Bollone examined comparable threads from Romanese's test cloths, which he knew to be formed from aloe-myrrh solutions, and threads from mummy cloths placed at his disposal by the Anthropology Institute of Turin University. Romanese's threads closely matched the optical and electronic features of the original threads of the Turin cloth, while no such similarity was found in the case of the mummy threads.[16] Independent of this, Pellicori's experiments showed that, like the Turin cloth, aloe and myrrh imprints also do not fluoresce under UV rays.

The researchers had done a good job. Forgery was excluded, data from the fields of textile science and palinology linked the cloth closely with Palestine and the region of Asia Minor. The first clues about the formation of the image had been found. The 'Man of the Shroud' was being tracked down. Even without drawing on historical sources, there were several indications that the strip of fabric might be 2000 years old. Certainty, the investigators unanimously agreed, would only come from a radiocarbon dating.

The Relic in the Laboratory

In the decade following the Second World War, the American chemist Willard F. Libby developed the radiocarbon method for determining the age of organic material. This method relies on the production of the carbon isotope carbon 14 (also called C-14, and sometimes written as ^{14}C) in the atmosphere: neutrons released by the impact of cosmic radiation combine with the nitrogen isotope ^{14}N to form C-14 atoms (which then join with oxygen to form more of the gas carbon dioxide). Isotopes are atoms of the same chemical element (number of protons) with different atomic mass (number of neutrons). A distinction is made between stable and unstable, radioactive isotopes. C-14 is a radioactive isotope, a more exotic, heavier variant of the common carbon C-12. Radioactive isotopes decay to eventually form other, stable isotopes, half the quantity decaying in a period of time known as the half-life. The radiocarbon dating method makes use of this fact. It is known that the C-14 isotope decays back to N-14 over a half-life period of 5730±40 years. There is a constant equilibrium of creation and decay, so that the total proportion of C-14 in the carbon in the atmosphere is always constant. In living organic material the small percentage of constantly decaying C-14 is replaced all the time by new intakes (both isotopes behaving the same chemically for the organism and being taken in with the carbon dioxide). But as soon as the organism dies, this intake stops and the C-14 clock slowly ticks away. From the proportion of C-14 found remaining one can infer the age of the object.

Libby himself suggested that the Shroud could be dated by his new technique. The cloth consists of linen, which as we know is obtained from the flax plant, and so has an organic basis. One could find the date on which the flax for the linen was cut. But at that time no less than 870 cm^2 of the precious material would have had to be destroyed. Understandably such a plan was rejected. But here, as in other fields, science progressed with great strides. In 1977 the radiocarbon laboratory at Rochester, USA, and that at Toronto, were able to announce that it was possible to date test samples of just a few milligrams. This was made possible by a new technique in which the isotopes were separated by accelerator mass spectrometry (AMS). In this method the entire quantity of C-14 present in an object is measured, and not just the decaying portion. One of the pioneers of this new method was Harry E. Grove. Another procedure was also developed, which uses small gas counters, working with samples that have been transformed to carbon anhydride. With this method even a single thread 20 cm long can be dated.

Calls were again made for a radiocarbon dating of the relic. Before it actually was done, almost ten years later, however, the plans and proposals followed a fairly odd, often baffling, course of development. With many of the decisions and events covered under a cloud of concealment, the run of events can only partly be traced. Nevertheless, what we have is enough to gain a glimpse into the play of personal interests and power, a play which was to turn the search for truth into a vanity fair. Or were there perhaps motives of quite another kind hidden behind these theatrical scenes, motives which were somehow meant to be concealed by the whole comedy?

In the mid-1970s, the Reverend David H. Sox of Britain was the secretary of the British Society for the Turin Shroud. In 1976 he presented himself to Gilbert Raes, the textiles expert, in Ghent, and offered to have the piece of cloth still in Raes' possession dated by Walter McCrone, a specialist in the radiocarbon technique. Here we already come up against the first inconsistency. So far Sox had been a vehement supporter of the genuineness of the Turin cloth. His close collaboration with McCrone, who was later to figure as a convinced defender of the forgery hypothesis, seems strange. In fact Sox was soon to switch sides, and today he is considered one of the most embittered opponents of the authenticity hypothesis. His proposal to Raes was put aside. Sox then turned to Harry Gove and tried to fire the enthusiasm of the co-inventor of the AMS technique for a dating of the linen. Gove did not need much persuading, and immediately took on the project. He contacted Teddy Hall and Robert Hedges of the Oxford Radiocarbon Laboratory, who were also working with his technique. Hedges responded coolly to the idea, while Hall showed great interest. In 1979 an informal committee for the dating test took shape, including, besides Sox, the two STURP chemists Ray N. Rogers and Robert H. Dinegar.

Arguments About Who Gets the Job

In July 1979 Gove and Garman Harbottle of Brookhaven University, USA, approached the Archbishop of Turin. Together they had developed the so-called proportional counter technique. They asked to be allowed to date half of the Raes sample, but received no reply to their request. Later it was claimed that the proposal could not be agreed to because it was no longer possible to check whether the Raes sample was really the original piece from the cloth.[17] McCrone and Sox became more and more outspoken in pressing for a dating test.

In 1982 the STURP members formed a committee to deal with the possibility of a C-14 dating test. They were of course spurred on by the fruitful results of the investigations of 1978. Dinegar led the committee. Including Gove there were six institutions specializing in the dating of minute samples which were interested in the enterprise: Rochester, Tucson, Oxford and Zurich, all working with the AMS technique, and Brookhaven and Harwell, which favoured the gas counter technique. Under the supervision of the British Museum, the feasibility of a dating experiment on the Shroud by the six laboratories was to be examined. The directors of the institutions all agreed that no single laboratory should be allowed to perform the dating test, and that a variety of techniques should be used. Then the laboratories were each given two cloth samples of about 100 mg, without being told their age; one was Egyptian from 3000 BC and one Peruvian from AD 1200. The Zurich institute was 1000 years off the mark, because the cloth was not cleaned properly. This showed how critically dirt and other contamination can influence a reliable dating test. All the laboratories gave far too recent a date for the Peruvian sample. Without any explanation it was just swapped for another one.

These preparations for a 'water-tight' determination of the age of the Turin cloth were not exactly encouraging. The dating results of the six laboratories for this 'test run' were announced in June 1985, at the 12th International Radiocarbon Conference Dating in the Norwegian town of Trondheim.

In the meantime the STURP members worked out an extensive research programme. A total of twenty-six researchers was proposed, to obtain definite answers to eighty-five crucial lines of inquiry. Besides the C-14 dating a diverse range of physical, chemical, optical and other valuable experiments was offered. The race to the best start positions for a new analysis of the linen began. Everyone wanted to take part. Many different interests were involved. There were some who wanted nothing to do with a radiocarbon dating test: hardened sceptics pointed out that some 20 per cent of the entire material consisted of biologically foreign matter, which could influence the sensitive dating result considerably. The STURP researchers intended the dating to be just *one part* of their comprehensive, interdisciplinary analysis. Yet other researchers wanted just the C-14 test, and this at any price.

The tug-of-war began. Sox calumnised the STURP researchers as 'militarily organized religious fanatics'.[18] In fact they were respectable scientists of the most diverse convictions, even numbering some agnostics. But it was no longer a case of fair treatment or balanced argument. Here motives were at play which were not always transparent, and all too often revealed their less noble origins. At the Trondheim congress Gove spoke the lines fed to him by Sox, proposing that the STURP group be entirely excluded. The six laboratories agreed. Perhaps the STURP people seemed suspect to them. After all, they had already laid out a whole range of results that spoke for the authenticity of the cloth. Could preconceived judgements have been at play in this phase of the decision-making, which found a cloth in which Jesus lay unacceptable for science? It is difficult to understand. The STURP researchers carried out their investigations in a perfectly neutral manner and based their judgements on the facts. Science itself does not doubt the historicity of Jesus. So there should be no need for mental dislocation before being able to accept an object that was connected with him. After all, it was not a question of some paranormal object, things occult or even a miracle, with which science as we know currently has its problems. On closer inspection the decision of the radiocarbon lobby against the collaboration of STURP seems to be based on professional vanity.

While at Trondheim the representatives of the six laboratories drafted a protocol, which was accepted by all:

1. The British Museum would assume the co-ordinating role in the investigation, and act as 'guarantor' for a correct performance.
2. STURP members could cut the specimens from the cloth, so that they would not feel completely excluded.

3. The British Museum would provide two control specimens from cloths of known age. All three specimens, including those of the Shroud, were to be unravelled, so that they could no longer be identified.
4. The British Museum would receive a written assurance from the laboratories that they would inform no one of the results except those authorized by the Museum.
5. The laboratories could use the methods they considered best for preparing the samples, but were to keep a precise record of all the details.
6. The results were to be communicated to the Holy See before publication.

Dinegar of STURP, who was present in Trondheim, insisted that the radiocarbon dating should only be done after the analysis of the fibre components proposed by the STURP researchers Heller and Adler. The C-14 specialists threw out his suggestion, claiming that any further examination would be absurd as long as the age of the cloth was not settled. Obviously the STURP people were to be portrayed as fantasizers and undermined. Sox was even angry that they were allowed to be present at the sampling, while Gove declared in a polemical speech that he would abandon everything if STURP had any role other than the one allotted. At least now it was clear where the lines were drawn. Nothing remained of the team spirit for which scientists are often praised, nor of their dedication to the pursuit of knowledge, or the search for a variety of techniques to do justice to a complex problem. At Trondheim the declaration of war was on the table.[19]

The next stage was the involvement of the Pontifical Academy of Sciences.

It is not clear who approached the scientific experts of the Vatican, but their involvement is only logical when one considers that after Umberto's death in 1983 the relic passed into the hands of the Vatican. What is strange is the unconvincing role that their president, Prof Carlos Chagas, was to play. The Vatican agreed to a conference between the Academy and the scientists who were interested in the dating test. Chagas was to organize it. Strangely enough he delegated this task not to a member of the Academy, but to Vittorio Canuto, an astrophysicist at the NASA Institute for Space Studies in New York, who was his private adviser. Together they decided against the STURP proposals and in favour of the Trondheim protocol.

At this point one has to ask what possible motives could have lain behind this. STURP members had already presented a lot of excellent research, their dedication and their thorough command of the subject matter were known. Their own proposals included a C-14 dating test as part of a more comprehensive project, and this would certainly have increased the significance of the individual experiment. As far as the Turin cloth was concerned, Gove and the radiocarbon specialists were considered to be complete amateurs. Most of them did not even know the general facts about its history and the research already done. The 'test run' under the watchful eye of the British Museum had turned out to be a disastrous farce, leading one to expect any number of problems, and the behaviour of the researchers themselves had so far been marked by pride and conceit.

The developments over the ensuing period were accordingly muddled. In spring 1986 Canuto committed the indiscretion of passing Gove a confidential letter from Prof Luigi Gonella, the scientific adviser to Turin's Cardinal Ballestrero. Gove passed it to his friend Sox, who actually published it. In this letter Gonella accused Gove of trying to secure research funds for his institute in Rochester from the National Science Foundation, the largest science funding trust in the USA, by posing as the director of the six laboratories. In the midst of these intrigues Dinegar announced to Gove that the Vatican Secretary and the Pontifical Academy of Sciences had accepted the STURP project! To complete the confusion, on 13 April an article by the journalist Peter Jennings appeared in Britain claiming that Chagas had personally spoken out against a radiocarbon test.[20] After the diplomatic tug-of-war between the parties, probably themselves not knowing by now who was on who's side, the conference of carbon experts – 'the conclave of the carbonists'[21] – took place in late September 1986. Representatives from the six radiocarbon laboratories and other scientists, including some from STURP, took part. But no one was invited from the Turin Centro Internazionale di Sindonologia, the largest association of sindonologists.

While Gonella continued to insist that the taking of specimens should be integrated with the whole STURP programme, Gove was adamant. The carbon test could not be postponed any longer, and any further undertaking would just delay things. The representatives of the institutions pointed out that the test should be a so-called blind test. In a blind test the researchers do not know which piece is the actual test object and which samples are control specimens. In this way conscious or unconscious manipulation, or prejudicial treatment of the different specimens, was to be prevented. Gonella made it clear that it was not Turin but the laboratories which were insisting on a blind test, 'so they would feel protected from the press'.

After three days the participants came to the agreement that seven institutions should be involved in the dating, with five using the AMS technique and two using the other methods. The British Museum was to supply a control sample. Original cloth and control samples were to be handed over to the individual laboratories after being unthreaded so as to be unrecognizable. Three institutions were to assume the supervision: the Pontifical Academy of Sciences, the British Museum and the Archiepiscopal Ordinariat of Turin. At a certain date after the examination all the laboratories were to pass on the data from their experimental results to three institutions for statistical analysis: the Pontifical Academy of Sciences, the British Museum and the Istituto di Metrologia G. Colonnetti (IMGC) in Turin. In this way stringent scientific criteria were to be ensured, guaranteeing the credibility of the enterprise.

These proposals appear to have been well thought out, although the additional STURP projects were still not out of the way. But the C-14 lobby had won priority for themselves.

The 'Radiocarbon Mafia'

In early 1987 things came to a head. STURP presented a final programme of analysis, to be run concurrently with the sampling for the date test – STURP still hoped to participate in the examination. Gonella was annoyed about the harsh way in which the radiocarbon team had discredited STURP and himself personally. As scientific aide to the Turin Cardinal he was kept well informed, and on 27 April he dropped a bombshell by announcing in the respectable Turin daily *La Stampa* that only two or three laboratories were to perform the dating test. By this act he sowed a seed of division in the phalanx of the 'radiocarbonists'.

Chagas' adviser, Canuto, again violated his obligation to be silent, and told Gove that the Vatican did in fact plan to entrust three laboratories with the task. The laboratory directors were infuriated, suddenly feeling misled themselves, but they could not of course reveal the indiscretion of their 'agent' Canuto. Gove then suggested that they protest against Gonella's article in a telegram to the Pope and the Archbishop of Turin. Of course such a thing was unheard of among the higher echelons of the Vatican, where the infallibility of the decisions tends to be the rule. When asked by Gonella about their intentions in sending a protest note to the Pope, Prof Wölfli, the director of the Zurich radiocarbon laboratory, gave the terse reply: 'Well physicists are never good diplomats.'[22]

On 10 October 1987 Cardinal Ballestrero wrote to the seven laboratories and told them that he had received the go-ahead from the Holy See for the experiment. But now suddenly the procedure looked completely different. All that was left of the agreement made a year before was the role of the British Museum as procurer of control samples. The most interesting and certainly the most unexpected change was the total exclusion of the Pontifical Academy of Sciences. Chagas was now only to be admitted to the sampling as personal guest of Cardinal Ballestrero. There was not a word about precautions to prevent the specimens being swapped; and this even though this precise danger had been addressed in an article which appeared shortly before, which had excited a lot of attention – accusations, discussions and apologia – and must still have been fresh in the organizers' memory.[23] No mention was made either of the Swiss textiles expert Flury-Lemberg, who was originally to have taken the specimen from the relic. Only Tite of the British Museum was left as guarantor of the correctness of the procedure. Neither the Pontifical Academy nor the IMGC would take part in the analysis of the final data. This too was to pass exclusively into the hands of Tite. Only three laboratories – Tuscon, Oxford and Zurich – were selected; a decision which had apparently been reached as far back as May. All three worked with the newer AMS technique.

Harry Gove, who had assumed the role of sole leader of the radiocarbon investigation, was furious. He fired off letters to the

Pope, the journal *Nature* and the British Museum. His colleague Harbottle at the Brookhaven laboratory also aired his disappointment. They had both worked to develop the classical technique further as a method for small samples. The exclusion of the Harwell laboratory baffled the others, because it had the most experience of them all, and was renowned for the most precise datings. In their joint letter to the Pope, Gove and Harbottle classed this decision as scientifically short-sighted. The original Turin protocol with the seven laboratories would eradicate errors like those at the Zurich laboratory during the 'test run'. it would be better to do nothing at all, they added, rather than dare to go ahead with such a truncated experiment. In another letter of protest Robert Otlet of the Harwell laboratory voiced the suspicion that someone in Italy wanted to obstruct the course of science. Reducing the number of laboratories to three would lead to a scientific catastrophe. 'It is,' he wrote, 'like ordering a bulldozer to run over an archaeological dig site before you had examined it.'[24] The rumour spread that the Vatican had restricted the test to three laboratories in the hope of obtaining contradictory results. Gove accused the Archbishop of having a false advisor. He said Gonella was not qualified for the post, he was nothing but a 'second-class scientist'.[25] Gonella countered that they were dealing with a real 'radiocarbon Mafia', who were seeking their own advantage.[26]

One thing emerges clearly from these reactions. The excluded parties felt deeply offended, and did not hesitate to speak out against these decisions, taken by anonymous backroom men at the Vatican, and to attack their 'adversary'.

What had happened since the meeting with the seven laboratories in Turin? What had made the Church authorities alter the Turin agreement so drastically and against all scientific advice? The samples needed for the full dating test could be so small that their removal would not present any problem. Why the rejection of the second method, and what is particularly serious, why dispense with the two additional controls? It is all very confusing, and the real motives are difficult to discern. When we started our investigations they were totally incomprehensible. But gradually the scandalous meaning of it all was laid bare.

On 21 April 1988, under the gaze of delegates from the selected laboratories, Riggi cut off a section of the cloth, and Prof Testore

put it on a precision balance. Then it was divided up (see Plate
20). Dr Tite took the pieces and, accompanied by the Cardinal,
disappeared into the adjoining sacristy to put the cloth specimens
into the metal containers they had brought, in total secrecy. Then
he appeared again with nine small tubes on a tray – the smiling
waiter serving up an extraordinary, a unique dish (see Plate 17).
Three cylinders were intended for each laboratory: one with the
specimen of the Turin cloth and two with control samples. Nearly
half a year later it was announced that the laboratories had dated
the Turin cloth to the Middle Ages. For science, it was the end of
a legend, the end of a myth.

I had already studied in some depth the scientific investigations
and facts from the more recent history of the Shroud research, the
reports about the fate of the linen in the Middle Ages and the
iconography of the portrait, when during my stay in Sardinia I
learned from the Italian press that radiocarbon dating tests had
exposed the cloth as a medieval forgery. By that time I had
concerned myself with this remarkable textile for a good ten
years, and naturally I felt that I was well informed about it. So I
was relatively sceptical about this result. While still in Sardinia I
resolved to go into all the facts behind the radiocarbon dating.
I wanted to examine every detail as minutely as possible, and
question all the participants about the events. From *La Repubblica*
I obtained the names of the institution which had performed the
C-14 dating tests. Zurich is only two hours' drive from the town
where I lived, so at the top of my list of priorities came a visit to
Prof Wölfli, head of the Zurich radiocarbon laboratory.

Returning from Sardinia in early November, I at once wrote a
letter to the Zurich institute, presenting myself as a journalist. On
16 November a prompt reply came from Switzerland by telephone.
The friendly voice at the other end of the line was Prof Wölfli: a
full report was in preparation for the journal *Nature*. It had originally been scheduled for November, but due to difficulties among
the three laboratories composing it, publication was being delayed until December. *Nature*, of course, is the Rolls Royce among
scientific journals. Only those who have had something published there can be counted among the scientific high society,
and anything printed in *Nature* has to run the gauntlet of strict
vetting by independent critics, and can thereafter be counted as
scientifically accurate. No wonder that Prof Wölfli sought to

appease me with the article: it would surely answer all my questions. But in an official report one could only expect a sober stocktaking of results, a test design based on orderly foundations, all methodologically acceptable, making the results and conclusions appear unchallengeable. It is an open secret in the research business that the blunders in an experimental run are covered up. The finished product is always a faultless experiment by faultless researchers. Such a report was hardly going to provide answers to the questions I was interested in: those little episodes at the fringe, those inconspicuous facts which would never find their way into a scientific essay. Wölfli promised to contact me again as soon as he had had the chance to check his schedule.

Thus the first step had been taken. But I was too fired by the problem to just sit at home and wait. Soon I was on my way to Belgium to see Prof Gilbert Raes. Before his retirement, Raes had been Director of the Laboratory for Textile Technology in Ghent, and was the only person who had ever received a sizeable fragment of the Turin Shroud. So he knew it better than anyone else. Should I ever manage to obtain photographs of the specimens examined, Raes would be the only one who could compare them with the Shroud cloth. And then I never had been able to find out what became of the Raes sample. Did the professor perhaps have a specimen of the Turin Shroud still in his possession? One could have the cloth piece dated by a neutral laboratory under supervision, although I hardly dared imagine such a lucky chance.

Conveniently enough, I had to visit Amsterdam for discussions with a film producer, so the visit to Prof Raes would be just a short trip from there.

The Textile Researcher and the Holy Cloth

Gilbert Raes lived alone on the top floor of a large block of flats in the middle of town. He was a very agile and bright man of over 70. He had kept the whole morning free for my visit. Quickly coming to the point, I told him I had serious doubts about the correctness of the Turin Shroud dating. He rummaged out a small photocopied journal from the piles of paper on his desk – a

number of the *Shroud News*, which he had just received from
Australia. Rex Morgan, the energetic editor of this lively and
informative pamphlet obviously held an opinion similar to my
own, and gave full publicity to his doubts. Then Prof Raes
showed me his report on his examination of the cloth fragment in
1973, and drew my attention to the photographs printed in it.
One could clearly see where his sample was cut. Raes told me that
the side strips differ from the main cloth in the closeness of the
weave. Moreover no traces of cotton could be found on the side
strips, unlike the rest of the fabric. He suggested that the molecular structure of the fabric might have been affected by the great
heat of the fire in 1532, leading to incorrect results in the C-14
date. But he was quick to add that he was no expert in that area
and so could only speculate.

When I finally came to ask the whereabouts of his specimen, he
embarked on a lengthy narrative: 'Yes, the fragment of cloth was
indeed in my possession for some years. In the report on the 1973
investigations prepared by Turin it was stated that all the pieces
handed out to the various researchers should be sent back to
Turin. All the other researchers taking part were Italians, and the
report was written in Italian. Unfortunately I do not understand
Italian, and I did not know what I was supposed to do with my
piece. So I kept it, and nobody seemed to mind. But one day I
received a letter from the Rev David Sox, then secretary of the
British Society for the Turin Shroud. He asked me to receive a
certain Dr Walter McCrone, a "radiocarbon specialist" from
Chicago. This McCrone then visited me in September 1974, telling
me that he could even date minute pieces of cloth, and asked me
to give him the specimen. I was not particularly enthusiastic
about this idea, and wanted to consult a specialist first. Since I
knew little about radiocarbon dating tests, I asked the Belgian
expert Prof Daniel Apers of the University of Louvain for advice.
He and his assistant said they were willing to receive McCrone.
But the outcome was that they advised me against handing the
sample to McCrone, because with his method the expected in-
accuracy in dating a 2000 year old object would be ± 700 years. In
other words no useful result could be expected.'

I interrupted to ask if he knew that McCrone was always
strongly of the opinion that the cloth was not genuine. Raes
thought this might be because McCrone had not been able to get

the piece from him, and that Sox had changed his whole attitude for the same reason. The professor could recall that McCrone belonged to the group of Americans who were involved in the 1978 investigations in Turin.

'After the visit,' continued Prof Raes, 'I felt somehow uneasy about having the cloth piece, and I wrote to Prof Sylvio Curto, the Turin archaeologist at whose recommendation I had been brought in to do the textile examination, asking what I should do with the sample of material. Curto said I should send the piece back to Turin right away. On 15 November 1976 I sent it by registered post direct to him. Just after that I received another letter from David Sox telling me that the owner of the cloth, ex-king Umberto of Italy, had officially agreed to my handing the sample to McCrone. To my relief I could now reply that the specimen was no longer in my possession.'

In his book about the Turin Shroud, Ian Wilson wrote that Prof Raes had casually and neglectfully just kept the precious fragment somewhere among the papers on his desk. This remark seemed so strange to me that I mentioned it to Raes. He rejected it out of hand, and ventured the opinion that Wilson must have heard this from Sox as, on the occasion of Sox's visit, Raes had placed the specimen in readiness on his desk.

But what interested me more than this episode was the question of what had become of the sample. This must have been of interest to many people, because it was then, and still is, next to impossible to obtain pieces of the Turin Shroud. But nobody seemed to know what happened to the Ghent specimen after it had been returned. Raes shrugged: 'I too don't know what has happened to it. I was led to understand that they would join the piece back to the main cloth in its shrine, as previously agreed. The King had only given his permission under that condition. There has been so much speculation about it. Statements which I never made are constantly being attributed to me. I merely stuck to the results of our examination, and never speculated that it had been proved that the cloth really was 2000 years old. I had only been able to determine that the fabric was linen and that there were fibres of cotton present in it. Our laboratory actually specializes in the examination of cotton.'

I was interested to know whether this type of cotton was later also cultivated in Europe. The professor's reply was emphatic:

'No, never in Europe! The cotton woven here is usually Opland and comes from America, Africa and some Arabian countries. Cotton of the type *herbaceum* does not come from Egypt, but mainly from other Arab countries.' To the question whether there was another variety in the Middle Ages, Raes assured me that other kinds were found only in Russia and Greece, and just recently in limited amounts in Spain. But none of them are of the type *herbaceum*. In his final report he therefore came to the conclusion that the *herbaceum* could only have come from the Near East.

Could a forger in the Middle Ages have taken these facts into account, I asked him. Prof Raes replied: 'No, I have already said that it is quite impossible. Just recently I publicly rejected it, when I was questioned about it by both Flemish and French television in Belgium and also a channel from France. I really don't know why everyone wants information from me just now.'

I had to clarify one point that Raes had obviously not thought about: 'Well, after all you are the only person who has ever had a fair-sized piece of the cloth to look at.'

Prof Raes replied, 'That is true, I have held it in my hands and had it in my laboratory.' Then he added thoughtfully: 'I cannot understand why representatives of the dating laboratories were present during the sampling in April. As I heard, everything was to be kept in strict secrecy, to avoid influencing the researchers. But the weave of the Turin Shroud is so characteristic that it can be recognized immediately. I think they should have taken the specimens apart to leave only the individual threads; then they really would have been unrecognizable. But as they were anyone could recognize the Shroud specimen at once. That is not a blind test! And then they probably talked among themselves too. If there were differences of 600–700 years, they had to harmonize the results so that the public was not suspicious. I am fairly sure they compared notes. Finally there is still the question why the four other laboratories from the seven originally selected were suddenly excluded! I find more and more reasons to make me doubt the correctness of this dating procedure. What makes me most suspicious is that the laboratories were in contact with each other. I personally do not believe that the cloth can be a forgery, for how could anyone in the Middle Ages have produced a perfect negative?'

I added: 'And nobody at that time knew that the nailing was really done through the wrists and not through the palms. Furthermore nobody knew that the crown of thorns was not a ring but a kind of cap.'

Raes agreed: 'Until someone can explain the formation of the image, it will remain a mystery!'

After four hours of intense discussion, I took my leave of Gilbert Raes, with the assurance that I would try and question all the participants in this mysterious dating test, to shed light on the many dark areas. He offered any assistance he could give in answering any questions that might arise. Confidently I set to work, encouraged by the willingness of the Ghent textile expert to help me in solving the puzzle.

Friends from Ireland had sent me a video cassette of a film about the research on the Shroud. It was a production by the BBC, famous for its excellent documentary reports. The film was broadcast in July 1988 on British television in the *Timewatch* series, and carefully shows the full sampling procedure in Turin and the preparations for analysing the cloth fragments in the laboratory of Prof Wölfli in Zurich. In the film David Sox, the priest who was for several years secretary of the British Shroud society, talks about the history of the cloth. His name is in the credits as adviser.

For some time this film became my constant companion. I no longer know how often I watched every scene, in slow motion, with notepad and stop-watch. At the end the scenes were fixed so well in my memory that it was as if I had been there myself. The Turin Cardinal Anastasio Ballestrero spoke twice. On both occasions he said that if the cloth turned out not to be genuine it would present no problem for him and the Church. It struck me as odd, to put it mildly, that the curator of this most precious of all relics had obviously entertained the thought that the treasure he guarded was not genuine; and this at a time when no serious sindonologist could doubt the authenticity of the cloth. Who, after studying the history of the Turin Shroud, could still not have known that there were hundreds of indications that made it possible to trace the cloth back to its origins? What had made him assume that the Shroud of Jesus, which lay in the care of his cathedral, was perhaps just a kind of unusual religious painting? On two occasions the churchman stated in the full light of publicity that it would not be detrimental for the cloth should it now turn out to be a 'work of art'. Then it would no longer be a relic, but an icon worthy of reverence. It was that simple! It would all be fine for the Church. Or did the Cardinal wish to prepare people for the disappointing result even before the investigation was concluded? I could not help feeling that for him everything was settled long in advance: the cloth simply came from the Middle Ages.

The film was intended for the general public and only showed brief glimpses of the events at the sampling. This was understandable enough but disappointing for me. Nevertheless, one could observe how Prof Riggi cut off a strip parallel to the long edge. One could also see how the separate pieces into which the rectangular strip was cut were weighed before being placed into small metal containers by Dr Tite. But how the experimental and control specimens were distributed, who was involved and how long the whole procedure had taken, remained a secret. The second part of the film showed Prof Wölfli with his precious textile specimens in a limousine on the way to the airport, and shortly thereafter the container seals being broken to take out the little cloth patches. The process of radiocarbon dating was explained with the aid of animated graphics. The BBC team managed, as they so often do, to present obscure scientific relationships in a simple and understandable way. Odd though, that the film team did not film on their doorstep in Oxford, where the radiocarbon dating laboratory was also working on a specimen of the Turin Shroud. Instead it was decided to film, inconveniently and at great expense, in distant Zurich. Did Prof Hall in Oxford perhaps not want any curious journalists around him? The film left more questions than answers.

Shortly after this an invitation arrived from Prof Wölfli to meet him on 19 December in Zurich. The investigation could begin.

Zurich: A Laboratory Visit

The new section of the *Eidgenössische Technische Hochschule* (ETH, the prestigious technical university of Switzerland), is a large modern building complex on the Hönggerberg hill, on the outskirts of Zurich. From the enormous basement garage, signs bearing strange acronyms led me through dim galleries and bleak lift doors. It took a while for me to find my way in this hieroglyphic maze.

Wölfli sized me up with a few quick glances and at once took the offensive. He enquired about my motives, wanted an explanation of my special interest in the matter. I countered by asking if it was all right if I ran my tape-recorder. At first he was suspicious. When I assured him that I would only use the recording as an aid to my memory, he finally agreed. Before our appointment I had decided to put all my cards on the table. So I told him about my research on the historical Jesus, and handed him a copy of my book on the subject. Wölfli's reaction was: 'Ah, now the penny drops. I have heard of your hypothesis, I have even read extracts from your book somewhere. It is based on certain properties of the Shroud I believe; it is quite interesting. But of course this evidence collapses if the cloth is medieval. I can say nothing about it, I have not tackled the pieces of evidence. But now over Christmas and New Year I will find time to study your book.'

I briefly explained to him that there were many lines of evidence which suggested the cloth was in existence before the Middle Ages, and mentioned the pollen analysis by Dr Max Frei of Zurich. Wölfli said thoughtfully: 'Yes, but sadly he has since passed on. I knew him well, for quite a long time. He was trained in the scientific department of the cantonal police, and when they examined the cloth in 1978 he was taken on as pollen specialist. I spoke to him about it, and he too thought that only the C-14 dating test could finally settle the age of the cloth. He himself did not lend such importance to the pollen analysis as various publications now make out. Yes, he sat there on your chair, and then I could even have obtained threads for the dating, but there was still the danger – ' Here quite suddenly he broke off in mid-sentence. Danger? What danger? I listened attentively as he continued: 'We have taken great care to ensure that no mix-up of the specimens could happen. But now we are accused of it, because naturally it is said that the test was not truly "blind". It was quite easy to recognize the cloth from the fabric photographs of 1978, because the type of weave is after all very special and quite rare.'

I remarked that Dr Tite obviously could not find any similar fabric, and consequently the whole procedure with the blind specimens was really quite unnecessary.

'Yes, but, the coding was needed at least because . . . shall we say for the journalists for one thing,' the professor said, trying to justify the way the investigators had acted.

It is interesting, I reflected, that experienced scientists apparently allowed journalists to dictate their methods, and so jeopardized the credibility of their work. This was something new to me, quite irrational; it did not sound like the customary self-confidence of science at all. I let Wölfli go on with his justification: 'But in the case of the British Museum specimens of course we did not know which was which, it was not obvious, and also we did not know their ages. The conditions were quite clear, we did not communicate among ourselves, each laboratory just sent on its results to the British Museum; there the results were evaluated, and then this paper was written.' With these words he placed a manuscript of some forty pages on the table and started to flick through it. 'So here we saw for the first time the figures compared. We are hoping that publication in *Nature* will now take place in January.'

I asked him if it would be possible to obtain a copy of the manuscript, to get the full picture. At once Wölfli's mistrust returned – and then the excuses: 'Now, the situation is this . . . at the moment I am not sure whether the paper will be accepted by *Nature*. You can imagine that it is not simple for what are in effect four competitors to write a common paper. We have struggled at it for quite some time! I do not mean about the results. That is . . . we have been able to check the statistical evaluation by the British Museum ourselves. Obvious errors have been recognized and corrected. It is rather the way the paper is written, we have argued about that for quite a long time. Here we could write as much as we liked, but for *Nature* we were allocated 4000 words, and there almost every sentence has to be struggled for.'

I reminded him that this examination had a very far-reaching significance. 'One should not overestimate it either,' Wölfli said. 'For certain people yes, but for humanity at large I do not think so. The paper is still just a draft, not the final version, and so I do not wish to give it out. Not because it contains something secret, but because it is possibly not the final version. To be more specific: it may be that a serious error still remains in it, which we have overlooked and which would still have to be eradicated. You see, I do not know you well enough, and there is the problem that if something still has to be changed in the text, and you published the earlier false version then one would have to withdraw it, because there would be some mistake in it which only the reader had noticed and none of us, then . . .' Again the sentence was left hanging in the air.

This set me thinking. So it was errors which had to be eradicated. I had a very simple idea of scientific work. One does a test, and at the end one obtains a result, which can be expressed as a numerical value. If everything was done correctly, there can be no mistake. Surely he could not have meant typing errors? For a practised team which had already composed many papers, writing down numbers correctly should not present any problem. What could he have meant by 'false version'? I asked him why it was that Oxford had taken so much longer to send its results to London. From the start, he said, no result was expected before September or October. In any case the matter was not as exciting for him as it was for the Church organizers. He had the general impression that too much had been read into the relic. He was not a Catholic and in general he had great doubts about the organized religions. I was surprised to hear this from a respected scientist. Or was there some truth in the popular prejudice, that scientists do not look beyond the confines of the ivory tower of their specialized discipline? Had not Wölfli seen for himself the scale of the outlay for the dating of the Turin Shroud, the extent of the literary and scientific interest. Could he really not see how profoundly the last 2000 years of Western history had been influenced by Christianity, what decisive importance the historical Jesus had in our understanding of this development, and what a unique position the Turin Shroud must assume in this context? It is not possible to have so little knowledge of things outside one's special field. But obviously his doubts about organized religion were the same as those which, in view of such attitudes, one must have about organized science.

'I do not wish to be too critical here,' he told me. Then he got out the laboratory diary to show me when he sent his results to the British Museum. I forestalled him by giving the date myself, 22 July 1988. 'You know it better than I do!' he said. Our laughter relieved the tension a little. Since he had the diary in front of him, I asked him about the precise weights obtained for his specimens.

'Oh yes, that is the simplest thing in the world. We have even got accurate photographs of the specimens,' he said and from the book took two large photographs. One of them showed three different pieces of cloth on a red background, and one a piece subdivided into smaller fragments. The photographs were labelled with Swiss thoroughness, bearing the title 'Shroud of Turin/Zurich', an identification for each sample and precise figures for the weight in milligrams to one decimal place. A scale was included, so that the exact sizes of the individual specimens could easily be seen. One glance at these photographs showed me that any lay person could easily distinguish the Shroud specimen from the other two. The Shroud piece was a cleanly cut rectangle, with the characteristic herringbone structure clearly visible, while the other two specimens were shapeless pieces cut from a simple twill fabric.

The whole procedure of secretly distributing the specimens in the small, screw-capped containers was a farce. This play-acting was of no use even for the benefit of the press and public. The BBC film team was present in Wölfli's laboratory when he broke the seals of his three containers and laid out the cloth pieces before him, and anyone could see which one belonged to the Turin Shroud (see Plate 17). It was rather poor play-acting, and unnecessary. It is astonishing that these crucial events were not better planned, if only to fool the public. Or had some crude blunder occurred during the planning? This secret distribution of specimens would only have made any sense if, as Prof Raes remarked, the fabric pieces had been unthreaded before being placed in the containers. Then the scientists in their laboratories could not have distinguished the experimental specimen from the control specimens.

I asked Wölfli why they did not do just this. His matter-of-fact reply was: 'We discussed this very question during our preparatory meetings in London in January this year. But finally we decided to leave the specimens intact. Even two years ago at the September meeting in Turin, attended by all seven of the selected laboratories, we discussed the sampling procedure. It was found that while cleaning the unravelled material too much waste was incurred. You can see this loss of material on our lab picture with the test sample separated into small pieces: if you add up the weight of the small pieces, a considerable quantity is missing. Besides, it was nice to be able to keep track of the specimen right up to the time of vaporization in CO_2, so that no swapping could take place. Yes, that was itself a good way to check that it was really the right specimen.'

I find this quite baffling. It seems that the decision to keep the Shroud specimen intact until its experimental destruction had been made long before, years before in fact. Nonetheless, control specimens were procured at great expense, and the shoddy farce of a secret distribution was acted out. All the participants knew it was totally unnecessary. If they wanted to date other textile pieces from different periods, they could just have been handed out to the researchers in transparent containers. Containers of different colours could have been sealed before the running cameras, and in the presence of a notary, and we would have been spared a lot of mystery. Instead Shroud and control pieces disappeared behind locked doors, until a nervously smiling Dr Tite reappeared with some tin boxes on a tray. Who was trying to fool whom? The researchers behaved as if they had only realized that the test was not quite 'double blind' afterwards, and then said their action was justified to avoid the danger of a switch. These same scientists spend their whole time analysing blind specimens, never asking whether they could have got their specimens mixed up. When it came to the Turin Shroud, they had agreed for obscure reasons not to perform a blind test, and still wanted to let the public believe it was one. Why had such a major undertaking, after years of planning, ended up with this contradictory test programme? Was it just sloppiness? That was unthinkable, when one considers the precision with which scientific tests are normally carried out, without the benefit of lengthy preparations. Such thoughts left me with a very uneasy feeling about the affair.

During my talk with Prof Raes in Ghent I had heard mention of a mysterious fourth specimen. I felt it was a good moment to ask Wölfli about this. He confirmed that this fourth specimen did exist, 'but it does not really count as one of the blind specimens' (I could not help smiling at the continued mention of 'blind specimens'). This additional specimen consisted of threads from a cope (a large ceremonial cloak worn by a priest) of the fourteenth century. 'About this the British Museum told us: "Here's something extra, if you like you can practise on it, the age is precisely known!"'

At the time I was not in a position to see the true significance of this 'extra specimen', and so I paid little attention to it. It was just one more strange fact to add to the string of other confusing things: these highly specialized laboratories were offered a chance 'to practise', although they were in the habit of dating hundreds of specimens month by month and were hardly in need of any practice.

I was occupied with another, more burning, question. I was very keen to find out just how long the Cardinal and Dr Tite had spent alone in the sacristy, to distribute the specimens among the nine small containers. After all, this procedure, both pointless and crucial, did take place in the presence of just two people; everyone else was excluded, the attending public and even the special video cameras. Here, away from the gaze of curious onlookers, the scientist from the British Museum had to take the nine little pieces of cloth from their glass dishes and place them in the containers, labelled with the initial letters of the labs (Z = Zurich; O = Oxford; A = Arizona) and the numbers 1–3. He did not have to apply the seals himself, as that was dealt with later in the chapel in full view of everyone. Wölfli's answer was: 'That is difficult to say; I did not look at the clock, because I finally had the chance to examine the cloth in peace. I would say about half an hour.'

Half an hour, to put nine pieces of cloth the size of postage stamps into small tubes. Incredible! In the BBC documentary of course this period of time was passed over by a cut, so it looked as though the whole mysterious procedure lasted just a moment. 'Theoretically an exchange of specimens was possible here,' I suggested.

Wölfli had to concur: 'Yes, that was the only phase in which we were excluded. But Dr Tite was our referee, it was after all his task to see that everything was done correctly.' Evidently Wölfli had not the least doubt about the integrity of the Briton. Now I asked a second time about the results of the weighing, the Turin weighings shown briefly in the BBC film. Wölfli was evasive, saying with a mischievous smile: 'Yes, I have recorded the data in my private notebook. I do not know if they have been noted elsewhere. But they must be visible on the complete video documentation. So if you are prepared to watch television for fourteen hours in Turin, you will certainly be able to see them.'

I assured him that I had already viewed and analysed the BBC report a dozen times, so I would be quite happy to view the fourteen hours of video. My gaze again came to rest on the photographs of the Shroud specimen Z1 lying before me. I now noticed that only half of the specimen was divided up further, the other half being left whole. The professor explained that he did indeed only use half of the cloth specimen for the dating. He stored the other half outside the laboratory for security. 'You know, there can always be a fire. It would not be the first time that there has been a fire here in our lab.' I was curious to know where the unused half of his specimen was now. The reply came with a secretive smile: only he and his wife knew that! I was disappointed at the mystery-mongering, but did not press him further.

I asked him a third time if he would show me the Turin weighing results in his diary. Finally he gave in and showed me the notes. He pointed to a column of three numbers and told me that they were the weighing results for the three specimens received by Zurich. The photographs were still lying in front of me on his desk. Thus I could easily compare the Turin figures with those which Wölfli later measured in his lab. While checking them I make one more unsettling discovery. The figures for the two blind specimens matched exactly; but when it came to the Shroud specimen the Zurich measurement differed appreciably from the Turin one. I pointed out the difference – nearly 2 mg – which the experimental specimen Z1 seemed to have lost since Tite had placed it in the tube in Turin shortly before. I asked how such a difference could arise. Now it seemed that I had managed to surprise him at last.

Wölfli nervously compared the notes once more, stuttered a little and then quickly said that he had noticed the discrepancy before. 'Perhaps loss of weight during the flight, due to the varying humidity of the air?', he suggested, shrugging his shoulders. Why only the Shroud piece suffered a loss in weight, while the two other specimens did not, is probably one of those little puzzles which official circles would rather keep quiet about.

We had been talking for some three hours, and Wölfli was

starting to look at his watch more often. He politely offered to show me the accelerator unit, the technical apparatus for radio-carbon dating. I have little interest in technology, and I would probably not have been able to follow the complex processes properly, so I declined with thanks, adding that I did not wish to take up any more of his precious time. Instead I would be very pleased if he would let me have the two photographs with the pictures of the cut specimens. As he hesitated, I added that he must have the negative and could have new copies made at any time. He had to accept this reasoning. He let me have them after noting his copyright on the back and expressly forbidding me to publish them.

The following day I turned my full attention to Wölfli's pictures. The scale included in the picture allowed me to measure with a ruler the exact size of the original, undivided Zurich Shroud specimen Z1. The piece of cloth was found to be precisely 18 × 14 mm. Apparently the whole piece was cut into three pieces of equal size. Starting with the Zurich specimen it was thus a simple matter to reconstruct the original piece. The complete piece would have to have measured 54 = 14 mm [(18 times 3) × 14]. But that is quite different from the size of the strip in the BBC film. There it was stated that the piece that was removed was 70 × 10 mm. This discovery disturbed me, and I was so concerned that again and again I measured, calculated and double-checked. The weave pattern was clearly visible on Wölfli's photograph, and I com-pared it with other detailed photographs of the Turin Shroud. I then found that the herringbone pattern which runs lengthwise along the small piece from Zurich, must have run at right angles to the long edge on the strip which was cut off lengthwise. That meant I had made a mistake, and the complete piece must have been 42 × 18 mm. But this is even less like the 70 × 10 mm mentioned by the BBC. I was stunned. That was just impossible! After repeated checks I came to the conclusion that the error could not lie in my calculations. Somewhere something must have gone wrong. There emerged the exciting and yet deeply disturbing possibility that the Shroud specimens had in fact been exchanged for another cloth similar in appearance. What a deception! And I held the proof in my hand. Well that was just the beginning of a meticulous search for more clues. Now every detail of the dating had to be gone over with a fine comb, to eliminate every last doubt.

London: The British Shroud Society

There were only a few people in the world who were able to compare the photographs of the Zurich specimen Z1 with the fabric of the original cloth. And no one was better qualified for the task than Prof Raes in Ghent. I telephoned him right away, and he agreed to examine the Zurich photographs. On 2 January 1989 he sent his views: 'First I am surprised about the size of the specimen.' He worked out the loss in weight when cutting up the specimen Z1 as 3.1 mg or about 6 per cent.

'I have compared the specimen which I received in 1973 with Prof Wölfli's photos. I must state that the general appearance is quite different. What could be the reason for this difference? In each case the main difference lies in the differing number of threads per centimetre in the directions of warp and weft. It is not easy to count the number on a photograph, but I did not find the same number as on the piece I received in 1973. I can find no explanation for this difference. I may conclude from it that the two specimens cannot come from the same item. That is my impression when looking at the specimens.'

Prof Raes was obviously of the opinion that the cloth fragment on the Zurich photograph must have been of a different fabric from the original cloth. This confirmed my suspicion that someone may have swapped the genuine cloth specimens for specimens of another, similarly woven cloth.

My next step was to visit London. The British Museum, which played a decisive role in the radiocarbon dating programme, was situated there, and the Oxford laboratory was not far away.

On 18 January I flew to London. Friends had allowed me to use their flat and for a while I made this my base. I had several acquaintances in London and felt quite at ease.

The author of the fascinating book *The Evidence of the Shroud*, Ian Wilson, was President of the British Society for the Turin Shroud (BSTS). I had a great desire to meet him because he is considered one of the best authorities on the history of the Shroud. Wilson was also editor of the *Newsletter*, the bimonthly journal published by the Society. I had already discovered a lot of valuable information among the pages of this small, simple journal. I first asked the Secretary of the Society, Susan Brown, for an appointment. She telephoned me and we arranged to meet in two days for tea in the lounge of the Charing Cross hotel, directly above one of the busiest railway stations of London. We would recognize each other by carrying the latest copy of the *Newsletter*.

When we met I told her frankly of my doubts about the cloth dating, and took her into my confidence about my plans. It was comforting to hear that she shared my doubts, but she did not think any intentional deceit had taken place, rather that some technical blunder had led to an incorrect interpretation of the date. In any case she offered me all the help she was in a position to give, and gave me the complete set of past issues of the *Newsletter* to study. Unfortunately she was not able to set up a meeting with Ian Wilson at that time, because he was staying for some weeks in Kenya for peace and quiet to finish a book about Christian icons. But she promised to visit me and bring all the material she had.

She appeared punctually and brought with her a suitcase full of books, journals, photocopied articles and letters. The most important news was a press announcement issued by Agence-France-Presse the previous November. It claimed that a secret radiocarbon test on a thread of the Turin cloth had already been done years before. A certain Prof William Meacham, an archaeologist at Hong Kong University, reported that a team of Americans who had taken part in the 1978 examination of the cloth had already done an unauthorized test in 1982. They had divided a single thread in two halves and dated it with the nuclear accelerator apparatus at the University of California. They had obtained two different results: approximately 1000 AD and 200 AD. Since the examination had been done without any official arrangement, and had also produced these conflicting results, the information had never reached the public, although it seems the specialists knew about it. Susan added that the experts thought this secret dating was of little value, because at the time the dating techniques were not refined enough to give an exact date for such tiny fragments. 'We had known for years that a secret radiocarbon test must already have taken place.'

I asked her if she thought the thread they had tested could have come from the Raes specimen. 'I had a strong suspicion it did, but I thought that the date showed "anti" because of the way David Sox behaved. When he was my predecessor [he had been general secretary] he was very, very pro the Shroud, very sure the Shroud was authentic. Then suddenly after he met with some American scientists at London Airport, Heathrow, when they were coming back from Turin in 1978, having done the initial tests, he changed his mind and he went completely the other way, and started issuing books and papers which said the Shroud was a fake. Very suddenly! I met him that evening, and he was shattered, he was destroyed! He knew something we didn't know. Later on he said it was the fact that they had done the X-ray luminescence tests on the Shroud – they had thought initially that they were proving it was a fake. But when they went over the tests again later in America, they realized they were wrong the first time and in fact they showed that it wasn't a fake. No, I think there was more to it than that, I think he was told something then, and later on also, which I assumed was in fact that someone had dated the sample. I doubt whether Gonella knew in 1982 that it was tested, and the date. If there had been a bad test, I doubt that they would have permitted it this time. But I don't know, I just don't know what happened.'

Finally we discussed the specialist articles she had brought. Among them was one by Noel Currer-Briggs, another member of the BSTS. This article described the case of a mummy whose linen wrappings were dated by the radiocarbon method to be far younger than the mummy itself. The Egyptologist Dr Rosalie David of Manchester University had shown that there was no evidence that the mummy had been rewrapped. She went on to mention the general difficulties encountered when dating fabrics with the radiocarbon method. Other texts dealt with the thesis that technical errors during the cloth dating had led to a false result. Apart from David Sox, no BSTS member appears to have agreed that the cloth was a medieval fake. Some authors believed the specimens were contaminated with foreign matter; others supposed that the molecular structure of the ^{14}CO had been altered by external influences; some thought that it was a piece of the side strip added later that was dated. Hardly a single specialist who had studied the cloth in detail seemed to have accepted the hypothesis of a fake.

Susan asked me in passing if I had really come to London just because of the cloth dating. When I confirmed this, she commended my commitment. I said that I was sure there was something wrong, I wanted to find out what went wrong, and I was considering the possibility that a manipulation may be at the bottom of it. Therefore I was firmly resolved to track down the cause of the false dating result.

Before contacting the British investigators personally, I asked Susan to give me a run-down of what sort of people the scientists were. Susan knew the two men from her work with the BSTS, and also had visited Prof Hall in his laboratory in Oxford. She described Hall as an arrogant careerist, not at all interested in the cloth itself. He was only interested in gaining publicity for himself and his institution, and he thought the members of the BSTS and all those interested in the cloth were mad. His powers of imagination seemed to stop at his laboratory doors. Now that the Turin Shroud has been dated to the Middle Ages, Hall claimed that he had known it all along. But really he knew absolutely nothing about the cloth, he did not have a clue, Susan told me, and added: 'This is a volte-face for him. I suppose if the Shroud had been dated to 100 he would have gone the other way – he would have said how wonderful it was and how he always believed it.'

Then, with a knowing smile, she warned me to be careful I didn't find myself hanging under Westminster Bridge one day, like Roberto Calvi the manager of the Vatican's Banco Ambrosiano who was involved in a scandal. She went on, 'Yes, you do have to be careful, seriously. There are some very strange religious groups around. We were approached once by a group who said they were Templars, modern Templars. Now the Masons, Freemasons, have a group of modern Templars too, but this is another group which was into all sorts of rather strange, questionable things. And Ian Wilson and David Sox – it was some years ago, 1978/79 – they started investigating this group. They thought they were very strange and rather dangerous. They had an interview with a woman who knew what was going on in this group, she worked in a bank. And she disappeared! From work, from her flat, with everything left there; no explanation, she just went, and nobody ever knew where she went. Subsequently when we had the exhibition at Westminster Cathedral, a journalist, also a very strange chap, he said he was a member of this group, and that he was a spiritualist also, and he had a Templar guide – you know a spirit – who said that he must tell me that I must go down to Templecombe, where there is a Templar preceptory; there is more to be found in Templecombe and there must be some digging and excavating at Templecombe.' And with a penetrating glance she added, 'I would be careful, you just don't know!'

Moving on such unsteady ground, one is never safe from mysterious groups and sects. Since others had already cautioned me, saying this was dangerous terrain I was covering, I had rented a safe deposit box in a bank vault behind steel doors a metre thick, to store the original documents which I had collected so far. I left the key for this deposit box with a lawyer. Should anything happen to me, the lawyer would see that the material was published.

We changed the subject to a matter no less obscure, David Sox's book. I assumed that he was back in America, but learned that he was living in Kensington. Susan explained that although Sox was an American he had lived in London for a long time and had taught at St Johns Wood American School. I asked her how it was possible for Sox to publish the results of the dating even before the official announcement.

'He was very unpleasant when we last spoke to him because we had just told Reuters or someone that we thought he was implicated in the rumours. So he is not very pleased with us . . . He is a very emotional guy . . . He tends to get very excited about things and then there is a big depression. . . . He knew the results then pretty well, he obviously knew what they were, but the book indicates that the only way he knew was from Harry Gove, who was with Paul Damon in Arizona. Harry Gove's laboratory did not get the sample that they wanted. They were the people who first asked Turin to do the sample, it was all their idea, and their original paper and everything else, and they were very annoyed when they didn't get a sample. It was because all the three laboratories chosen were using the same method, which again is very strange, it doesn't seem sensible at all. Paul Damon from Arizona is a terribly nice, gentle, very scientific man, who doesn't really understand all this kind of religious fervour, and Gove managed to persuade him to allow him to be in attendance when the result came through, that's how he knew. Harry Gove is very sociable, and Sox found out about the bet with Harry Gove's assistant, and that's what he based his whole premise on.

'I don't think he was there for all of the sampling. He likes to imply that he was, but I don't think he was. He's seen the film, I think that's probably where he's got the details from. And that's why he had to be vague about where the sample was taken from because obviously the film doesn't show it very clearly, he just says everyone assumed it would be near the Raes samples and that's all he says, which is very peculiar.'

Her description of Dr Tite was of particular interest to me, because he played a key role in the whole dating affair as co-ordinator at the British Museum. Besides the Cardinal of Turin, Tite was the only person who had the chance to switch the specimens when he was away from the public gaze, before they were packed in the small steel vessels. This is how Susan described Tite: 'He is almost a businessman; he is a scientist but he is obviously capable of avoiding the truth, because he certainly avoided telling the fact that the dates of the other samples were known.' To my direct question whether he might possibly be bribable, she replied evasively: 'Oh, I don't know about that. You just don't know, every man has his price, there may be something that I don't know.'

Could Tite have had access to the textile collection of the British Museum, I asked her. 'Certainly, yes, sure he would. There is no reason why he shouldn't do, he is head of the department there and he would be dealing with other textiles to test . . . In fact we couldn't believe that there wasn't another similar sample that he could take to the Shroud to add to the test samples; so similar they wouldn't tell the difference by eye, or microscope. He said there were one or two, there was one in Cambridge, one of the libraries in Cambridge, but they were reluctant to part with a piece of it. They weren't particularly important textiles, and it was not satisfactory to us that there was no other sample available with a similar twist.'

At this I asked: 'So you had the idea he is hiding something?'

'I had the idea either they didn't look very carefully, and they didn't really think it was very important, or yes he is hiding something, he doesn't want people to know that there are other similar samples, or where they are. He was very vague.'

I then resolved to attempt to find a comparable piece in the archives of the London museums myself. 'Perhaps,' I remarked to Susan, 'somewhere there is such a piece that is missing!'

Susan reflected for a moment and then turned to me: 'If your theory is right and they have something to hide then there's no way that we are going to get it looked at again, they will just simply lock it away. It would explain why they seem to have done it so badly, because it is unimaginably badly done for a scientific test of such importance. Everything that could have been done wrong has been done wrong, and none of the things that were suggested by the Harwell laboratory, which was an objective outside laboratory, were done at all. Something strange there!'

The discussion ended with Susan promising to get me a tape recording of the meeting with Dr Tite; there were certain facts in it of importance for me. That evening I did not know how right she was.

Dr Tite and the 'Indisputable Facts'

A couple of days later I was able to listen to this tape recording. It was shocking to hear how Dr Tite, this 'man the dating laboratories trusted', as Prof Wölfli had called him, could deal so capriciously with the truth. In a fairly short talk he presented himself to the assembled members of the British Shroud society: 'I should first of all emphasize that neither myself nor the British Museum laboratory actually undertook any of the radiocarbon dating. My role in the dating of the Shroud was as a sort of guarantor that the samples the laboratories were given came from the Shroud, and then subsequently as a co-ordinator of the results, providing an agreed result which we then transmitted through to the Archbishop Cardinal of Turin. I was asked to do this when the original offer was made by several laboratories in September 1986, and when Turin invited or selected three laboratories to do the dating in October 1987 they invited me to take on this role of guarantor and co-ordinator. And as a result I was present in Turin on that morning of Thursday, 21 April 1988 when the samples were removed, and I watched the cutting of the samples – ' here he corrected himself, 'of the sample and then the cutting into three pieces. I watched the weighing, and then together with the Archbishop Cardinal of Turin went to a separate room where we packaged the Shroud samples together with the control samples; we packaged them in aluminium foil and then into steel containers, and then they were more or less immediately handed to representatives of the laboratories.' He went on to declare before all those present: 'And so I am really able to fully guarantee that the samples actually came from the Shroud itself!'

Following this short explanation he showed about ten slides to illustrate the procedure and confirm his credibility. In those few sentences he twice stressed that he was the only person who could guarantee the genuineness of the cloth specimens.

In the remainder of his short speech he came to speak of the size of the specimen: 'The sample from the Shroud was a strip about 1 cm by 7 cm which was cut from just above the location on the bottom left hand corner, if that's the right way of describing it, where the Raes sample was removed in 1973. There was no doubt, I mean from myself seeing it and two textile experts seeing it, that it came from the main body of the Shroud, and it was away from any patches or any charred areas, and . . . not from the side strip which was attached at some other date.'

If one looks more closely at his statements, first he stated that the piece cut off was divided into three parts. As we were later to learn, it was in fact cut into four parts, that is it was first halved, and then one half was divided into three parts. Then he said that only he and the Cardinal took part in the secret packing of the specimens. He failed to mention that Prof Gonella was also present. He can surely not have forgotten whether there were two or three of them in the room? And if he had forgotten, so much the worse for his credibility! Thirdly he said that the strip removed was 1×7 cm in size. In fact it must have been almost twice as wide and over 8 cm long! This discrepancy must have been known to the 'co-ordinator' of the dating test, or at least he must have noticed it at some stage.

At that time none of the sindonologists of the BSTS knew the full details, and therefore no objections were raised from the audience to these assertions. He then explained where the two so-called 'blind specimens' had come from, and he mentioned that the laboratories had been given a third blind specimen as well, consisting of individual threads taken from the cope of St Louis d'Anjou. This vestment is kept in the Basilica of Saint-Maximin in the South of France. 'This is historically dated, I am told very precisely to about 1290–1310 AD, based on the date at which the chapel was built, for which there are records. So they had these three control samples in addition to the Shroud samples.

The labs were not told which of the samples was the Shroud.' Tite admitted here that it had not been possible to obtain a piece of cloth of the same appearance, and that the laboratories could have recognized the special weave of the Shroud in any case.

Finally the audience was allowed to ask questions. Besides various questions about a possible contamination of the cloth specimens, one of those present said that he was surprised to read in David Sox's book that Tite and the Cardinal had signed a document which expressly declared that the specimen of cloth really did come from the Turin Shroud. He asked: 'Does such a document really exist?' Tite's reply, in his exact words was: 'I don't know, I'd have to go back to the video.' The questioner said again: 'But according to him it was signed by yourself!' Tite replied: 'Well I was going to say I'd have to go back to the video, this is why we had a video taken, I mean I have a feeling that I did sign something, yes, which is why I had a video taken!' Laughter in the hall. One might consider it strange that the person guaranteeing the experiment could no longer remember anything about this extremely important detail.

Moreover it would be quite pointless to refer to the video on this point, since there were (according to Tite's statements) no witnesses present at the distribution of the specimens in the containers, and so that procedure was not filmed. Surely Dr Tite must at least have remembered that. Tite was obviously disturbed and somewhat ruffled. Chairing the discussion that evening was Ian Wilson, and he was polite enough to pass quickly over the embarrassment and ask if anyone had any further questions.

A member of the audience then raised the question whether the laboratories had been in contact with each other during the test phase. After categorically denying it at first, Tite admitted that there had probably been leaks contrary to the agreement, and in the ensuing unrest in the hall he conceded that the so-called blind test too was really no blind test! Surely he must have known this already before the sampling, when he was supposedly unable to organize the procurement of identical fabrics. Why then stage the whole show with the secret packing of the samples in the containers away from the public eye? What purpose could such play-acting have served? There is no reasonable answer to this question. The responsibility for the exchange of information among the laboratories, which Tite admits to, also rests on his shoulders. He was the guarantor, the referee so to speak, who was supposed to see that the agreed experimental procedure was exactly adhered to. In the event it was as if no agreement were followed at all.

Clue-Hunting in Museum Archives

The next day was a Sunday, and I had decided to pay a visit to the British Museum. I wanted to find out for myself whether a piece of cloth like the Shroud might just possibly be found somewhere. The Museum did not keep any special fabric collection, and so I had to sift through all the departments. In an English history room I was lucky. There in a glass chest lay a small fragment of dark cloth from the fourth century woven in the same herring-bone pattern as the Turin cloth. According to the label it was a wool fabric and not linen, but the object did provide evidence that this special weaving technique was already known in about 350 AD. It would be interesting to search in the archives, and I was resolved to do this if at all possible.

British museums are geared to serving the public, and usually have departments where members of the public can approach the experts for advice about their special queries and problems. A couple of days later I found my way to the Advisory Department of the British Museum, where first I had to enter a peculiar kind of waiting room. A row of people were already there, all of them carrying strange antique objects. I was asked to enter my name in a big book and note down my query in it. After a while a lady came, and I put my particular request to her. She asked me to wait a little longer, and finally a man of about fifty introduced himself. This was Dr John Cherry, who has among other things written a book about the history of the ring, which I chanced upon later while browsing in a bookshop. I told him that I was very interested in fabrics of the fourteenth century, whereupon, without a moment's hesitation, he led me through long corridors and many stairways to other floors, until coming through a door we arrived back in the public display rooms. Here he pointed out some medieval textiles to me, but none of them was woven in the herringbone pattern. I told him that I had already seen the fabrics on display and would much rather have a look at the storerooms and shelves, to see the items which are not on public display.

He eyed me with a somewhat uncomprehending look, but finally I managed to persuade him to let me into the archives, and again he led me, though hesitantly and reluctantly now, down endless passageways to rooms of enormous dimensions, in which stood numerous cupboards and work tables. He opened one of the smaller cabinets and indicated a pile of about thirty flat boxes and cardboard covers. One by one I took them out and carefully opened them. Here I found an enormous variety of cloths and cloth pieces, remnants, fragments small and large from a wide range of eras, all completely disordered and labelled only with inadequate little handwritten notes. A kind of stock list had been fixed to the inside of the cupboard doors; it had probably not been brought up to date for decades. Some of the boxes were empty, and no one could say what they had once held or what had happened to the exhibits. John Cherry did not seem to be very well informed about textiles, and I asked him if there was then no textile specialist within this massive institution. He told me that they did not specialize in textiles here and therefore only kept a small number of cloth articles. When special tasks in connection with textiles did come up they used the services of one of the greatest authorities in this field, Elizabeth Crawfoot, as a free-lance; but she did not live in London.

This visit had proved something of a disappointment. I had imaged that there would be a lot more suitable items to be seen here. At least I had been able to see that if any matching piece of material had been in the archives, practically any member of staff could have got hold of it without being noticed.

Oxford: The Vanishing Professor

Right at the start of my London visit, I had written to Prof Hall in Oxford, explaining my situation and asking him to let me see him for a short talk as soon as possible. As two weeks had passed without a reply from Oxford, I phoned his office, and I was told that the professor was abroad and would not be back for ten days. After the ten days had passed his secretary told me that my letter had indeed arrived at Hall's office, but the professor was out of the country and was not expected back for another ten days. Off again already? Obviously she was obeying some evasive order. I had learned that Hall was to give a public lecture on the Shroud radiocarbon dating in a few days, on the day of my departure, in a room at the British Museum, and so I decided to go to Oxford myself.

It was Wednesday, 10 February, at about 11 am, when I entered Hall's secretary's office. When I asked for the professor I received the same stereotyped reply: 'The professor has just gone abroad and will be returning in ten days.' If Hall's statement were not so important to me, I would probably have found the quaint little comedy amusing. I quickly worked out how I might avoid returning totally empty-handed. My main intention was to obtain a photograph of the Oxford specimen, and I thought I might be able to get one from Hall's assistant, Hedges, who had accompanied the professor on all his public appearances. I therefore asked to speak to him. The two secretaries had obviously been programmed for every eventuality and I learned that Hedges too was not available. Only when I told the lovely ladies that I had travelled specially from Germany to speak to one of the participants did they take the time to call Hedges in his laboratory. I was careful to ask them to say that ten minutes of his precious time would be enough and I was prepared to wait the whole day for him. But under no circumstances was the industrious assistant prepared to receive me unannounced; it would have to be after written application in advance if at all. I had already seen how written applications were dealt with. Perhaps the dutiful servant had only acted according to his master's order, but whatever the circumstances, the two efficient receptionists appeared to find my fruitless efforts highly amusing, and so nothing was left but to depart, disappointed and feeling low.

I decided that I could at least have a look at the institution from the outside, and I walked to the inner courtyard, where the staff parked their cars. Each car had a parking permit with the owner's name fixed to the inside of the windscreen. I wanted to know for sure whether I had been lied to, and started checking the names on the little labels to see if I might find Hall's car. Passing from car to car like this, I noticed that I was being watched through a window. Not wanting to be thought a car thief, I broke off my search. While leaving I was able to recognize Dr Hedges through the window in a room at ground level, standing before a large piece of equipment. His face with the conspicuous full beard which was known to me from various photos, was unmistakeable (see Plate 19).

Keen to find out whether Hall had really left or had got people to lie about his whereabouts, I looked his number up in the local phone book. I called the number and asked to speak to the professor. A young, friendly man at the other end of the line told me that Hall must be at work, but would certainly be back home that evening. Now it was quite clear I had been systematically lied to. Why was the Oxford professor so evasive? Was he afraid of uncomfortable questions? Or did he even have something to hide (see Plate 21)?

In a BBC film which was televised before the dating, there was an interview with the Victoria and Albert Museum's textile expert, Linda Woolley, in which she was asked about the Shroud's special weaving technique. I telephoned to arrange a time to meet her, and she proved to be both competent and very helpful. This time, changing my tactics, I told her directly that I was looking for a cloth which matched the Turin Shroud in age and type of weave. With an amused smile she said she had already been asked this once before, when the British Museum was looking for samples for comparing with the Turin cloth during the dating. For this reason she could now say straight off that no such cloth was to be found in her collection. She showed me a few examples of textiles from the twelfth to the fourteenth centuries so that I could see for myself. Along the walls of the enormous rooms were shelves, cupboards and chests of drawers, reaching to the ceiling some 10 m up. Half way up a raised gallery with railing led round the room. From this balcony we had to ascend a rather shaky ladder to be able to see into the topmost drawers. Mrs Woolley explained to me as we went that all the linen of that period was imported and was very rare, which meant there were very few examples of it in Europe.

To her knowledge only two small linen pieces in the herring-bone weave from the first century were to be found, and they were in Israel. She finally recommended that I approach Elizabeth Crawfoot, who was considered the best textile expert in Britain. Linda Woolley promised to arrange for me to contact her. As

Mrs Crawfoot often visited London, it was quite likely that I could be able to meet her there before my departure.

Another person I had contacted was Dr Tite. The only mutually convenient date was Tuesday, 14 January, the last day of my stay in London. When we met he seemed rather nervous, his face flushed with excitement. I made a mental note to be careful not to arouse his suspicions, and to keep my doubts about the conduct of the test to myself. Perhaps questions of a general nature would soften his reserve. He had been the central figure in the dating drama, organizing, supervising, distributing and analysing the tests and test objects. But he told me nothing new. Perhaps because of the many penetrating questions posed by Shroud researchers, he seemed to sense my misgivings and at the end of our talk was quick to assure me that he could personally guarantee that everything about the dating of the cloth was correct and in order.

Over lunch I met my 'accomplice' Susan Brown in the Great Russell Hotel, just round the corner from the British Museum. The scene had an amusing side to it, rather like a second-rate spy film. I pressed a tiny cassette recorder into her palm, so that she could record Prof Hall's lecture the following day. But I was unable to harvest the fruits of my plan. For some obscure technical reason the apparatus refused to work at the appointed time.

The Article in *Nature*

The next day I was back in Germany, awaiting publication of the article on the radiocarbon dating in *Nature*, the article which, Wölfli had assured me, would answer all my questions. Filled with expectation, I opened the journal. The extent of the article was itself disappointing: four sides, including all the addresses of the authors, tables and acknowledgements. Four succinctly composed pages, which, as the authors would have it, were to mark the end of a legend, a legend to which thousands of pages had been devoted over hundreds of years.

The report itself offered hardly any new information. Interesting details were missing. Under the heading 'Radiocarbon Dating of the Shroud of Turin', were listed the names of the authors, twenty-one in all, who had taken part in the experiment at the various institutions. Under these were three lines summarizing the content and conclusion of the article: 'Very small samples from the Shroud of Turin have been dated by accelerator mass spectrometry in laboratories at Arizona, Oxford and Zurich. As controls, three samples whose ages have been determined independently were also dated. The results provide conclusive evidence that the linen of the Shroud of Turin is mediaeval.' After this the basic facts about cloth, as previously known, were given in just half a page, and there was a brief description of how the specimens were removed. Then followed a description of the so-called control pieces in just twenty-four lines. The authors devoted half a side to the preparation of the samples and the actual measurements. At the end a summary of the results was presented, with a brief discussion of their statistical significance, followed by acknowledgement of thanks to sixteen named persons and institutions.

One obvious feature of the results immediately drew my attention. There were two tables, one giving all the individual measurements with their probable error ranges, and the other showing the average values of the ages derived experimentally. From the figures given in the tables, as well as those repre-

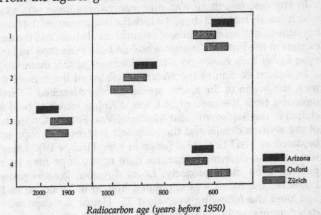

Radiocarbon age (years before 1950)

Fig. 1. *When one compares the mean values for the ages, one can at once see that the measurements of the three labs (A = Arizona; O = Oxford; Z = Zurich) for the specimens 1 (supposedly from the Turin cloth) and 4 (control specimen from the cope of St Louis) show a very good match.*

sented graphically, one sees that the samples from the Shroud and those of the mysterious control sample No 4 match almost exactly. Among a total of twelve sets of figures for the cloth there were such diverse average values as a minimum of 646 years (Arizona) and a maximum of 750 years (Oxford), compared with a lower limit of 685 years (Arizona) and the upper limit of 755 years (Oxford) for the control sample No. 4 (from thirteen separate measurements). Given such enormous fluctuations one can surely say that both textile samples are of the same age. If this is coincidence, then it is a remarkable trick it has played. The simplest explanation, though, and the one most in harmony with the scientific duty to look for the most obvious solution, is that both of the allegedly independent specimens must have something in common, which is not apparent from the test. Either they are identical or they are subject to an identical error. If an intentional deception was involved, the manipulation probably had something to do with the fourth specimen, so unexpected and contrary to every agreement. Could the fourth specimen simply have been passed off as the first? There was no evidence of this, and potential fraudsters would probably not have proceeded so clumsily.

In any case one thing was sure: somewhere there was a cloth which exactly matched the age which the proponents of the forgery hypothesis had set as the time of origin of the shroud, and the textile experts at the British Museum who had been consulted had managed to lay their hands on a few milligrams of this material.

In a short section of the *Nature* article about the control samples, the origin of the fourth specimen was described: 'Threads removed from the cope of St Louis d'Anjou which is held in a chapel in the Basilica of Saint-Maximin, Var, France. On the basis of the stylistic details and the historical evidence the cope could be dated at ~AD 1290–1310 (reign of King Phillipe IV).' Later we were able to determine that the date of the cope may be pinpointed even more precisely. Louis d'Anjou, great-nephew of Louis IX, the Saint, was appointed Bishop of Toulouse in 1296 and died the following year aged 23. Hence the cope may be dated more exactly in the years 1296–97. I was very keen to take a closer look at this cope. I could find no reference to the vestment in the art history books in the libraries. Perhaps it was woven in herringbone weave, and perhaps there was a little piece of material missing from some inconspicuous corner.

The Vestment of Saint Louis

The Saturday before Easter I had arranged to meet up with some friends at the foot of Mont St Victoire, the mountain made famous by Cézanne's painting. At midday we met in Vauvenargues, before the gates of a magnificent château, a former residence of Picasso. From our position east of Aix-en-Provence it was only 40 km or so to Saint-Maximin-La-Sainte-Baume, where the cope of Louis was kept.

Saint-Maximin is a small town with that special atmosphere which distinguishes the South of France. In medieval times it became an important place of pilgrimage. The legend goes that Mary Magdalene led a life of austerity here in the immediate vicinity of the town in a cave on the Baume massif, and died here too. Mary Magdalene was supposed to have landed here by boat together with her sister Martha, her brother Lazarus, Mary Jacobea (mother of the younger James), Mary Salome (wife of Zebedee and mother of the elder James and of John), and also their dark-skinned servant Sara and two more followers of Jesus, Sidonius (the man blind from birth whom Jesus healed) and Maximin. The Jews had not put these followers of Jesus to death, but left them adrift on the open sea in a boat without rudder or sail. By miraculous providence the little group came unharmed to the Provençal shores of the Mediterranean near Marseilles, at a place which is now called Les Saintes-Maries-de-la-Mer.

The town of Saint-Maximin is dominated by the imposing cathedral, which was erected in the thirteenth and fourteenth centuries above a fourth-century crypt, after excavations in the crypt in 1279 had uncovered the alleged bones of Mary Magdalene. Drawn by tidings of this event, streams of pilgrims visited the place of the discovery, so that soon a large church had to be constructed, and work on it started in 1295. King Charles II pushed ahead with the building work and in 1300 the first section of the building was consecrated. The long Gothic church seems strangely foreign in the bright landscape of Provence. The basilica with its nave and aisles has no towers and so looks austere and compact. The central space, a full 70 m long and almost 30 m high, presents an imposing sight to the visitor on entering. A dark, narrow stone staircase leads down to the dim vault of the crypt, lit only by the pale light of a few naked bulbs and some votary candles. Situated in this shady fifth-century tomb are the sarcophagi of the four saints Sidonius, Maximin, Marcella and Magdalene. At the rear of the crypt one can just make out a niche covered by a grille, from which there emerges the hint of a golden shimmer. As the eyes grow accustomed to the darkness, gradually the outline of a lifesize bust of pure gold takes shape, with a face that looks quite black. Only on closer study can one make out the ghastly features of a death mask, staring back from the shady sockets of the eyes – the mortal remains of the head of St Mary Magdalene, surrounded by long, golden hair.

Relieved to be back up in the friendlier surroundings of the cathedral, we continued our search for the relic. We found the artistically embroidered cope of St Louis d'Anjou hanging in a glass display cabinet nearly 4 m long, behind a folding iron grille. The cloak was in the form of a semicircle some 3 m across, and bore about thirty embroidered medallions illustrating scenes from the life of Christ and the Mother of God. Here too the lighting was not very bright, probably to avoid damaging the 700-year-old fabric, but the glass cover allowed me to get to within a few centimetres of the cloak and by close inspection I could see that the fabric next to the figures did indeed have the same herring-bone pattern as the Turin cloth.

I was very excited by this discovery. Was the embroidered linen vestment really made with the same weave as the Turin cloth? I needed to have a really good look at it. Two days later I was sitting with my companions in the office of Abbé Weber, the priest and curator of the cathedral. We had arranged to meet at 9 am, and he seemed already to be engrossed in his work. As is usually the case in France, Abbé Weber was wearing an ordinary lounge suit and, seated behind a large desk, he looked more like the director of some local government office. He was very friendly and helpful, taking the time to answer all my questions, and he had a strange tale to tell about the way the thread samples were taken.

He was not able to give an eye-witness account of the events, because he was not even present when the threads were removed from the cloak. Although he was the person responsible for look-ing after the treasures in the church, the local mayor also had a certain authority over the cultural property of the state. When on the morning of 12 April 1988 a group of people presented themselves to the mayor, the priest happened to be out on a visit in the neighbouring town. As he later found out, early that morning the mayor had received a call from the Church Authority for Cultural Possessions, announcing the visit of a delegation who wished to examine the cope of St Louis. Soon afterwards there appeared at the town hall seven or eight people led by the Church Administrator for Cultural Possessions for the district of Var. The Mayor, Monsieur Olivier, knew the place in the cathedral where the key was kept, and readily opened the barred display case containing the relic. As the priest later learned, the company then removed the precious pluvial from its case and spread it out on a table in the sacristy. Then someone obviously opened the stitches at one side of the lining material to remove a few loose threads from the rear of the embroidered cloth (see Plate 24).

Just as the group was about the leave the basilica, the priest returned from his trip. He was amazed at the scene before him, and not at all pleased that without his knowledge and in his absence strangers had been handling one of the best-guarded treasures in his cathedral. By way of appeasement they gave him an envelope sealed with red wax, in which the scientists said were five linen threads each 5–6 cm long.

The whole affair seemed extremely odd to Abbé Weber. Why had he not been informed in advance? After all he was the curator of the church treasures. Surely the scientists from Lyons and the official from the Draguignan prefecture could not just have decided on this action that very morning. One does not just march into a church on the spur of the moment to remove a piece of a relic, which is moreover a valuable art treasure. Such a thing requires some planning, and no one had more right to be told what it was all about than Abbé Weber.

When I told the priest that my interest in the cope was connected with the Turin Shroud, and I had my doubts about the correctness of the latest dating, he said that he was following the case and also had doubts about it. A fragment of the skull of Mary Magdalene from his cathedral had also been dated by the radiocarbon method. As regards the Turin cloth, the entire scientific apparatus had probably just served to confirm a result that had already been decided upon. He personally did not think much of relics; they were found in such quantity that one had to assume that the great majority were not genuine. At last he took his key from a cupboard and led us into the cathedral to the saint's garment. Opening the first lock, he pushed aside the heavy iron grille and opened the glass panel. Now we were able to examine the fabric properly. It was soon apparent that the herringbone pattern was only sewn with golden threads on to the quite ordinary linen weave. I had to abandon the nice theory I had formed. This cloth was out of the running as a possible substitute piece for the Turin cloth. And anyway the coat was decorated all over with embroidery, which would make it difficult to take any unembroidered fabric from it.

I then remembered that there had previously been some mention of a lining material, and I asked the priest if I might also inspect the rear of the cloak. He allowed me to touch the cloth and turn it over where I liked. Reluctant to take this precious article in my hands, I touched it with great care. The Abbe's confident smile told me that the material, despite its great age, was not at all as brittle as I imagined. Encouraged, I lifted up the lower part of the robe a little, so that we could comfortably view the other side. Now my last hope of being on the track of a possible manipulation vanished. The lining material of the rear side also turned out to be linen of very ordinary weave. Unlike the material of the front surface, however, this lining looked surprisingly new. The priest explained that the lining cloth was indeed new: the cope was restored some time before he took up his post, and the old lining material, weakened by age, was entirely replaced by a new one. This was an interesting detail, and I asked him about any literature on the cope, so that I could look more deeply into the matter. Back in his office I flicked through a dissertation written a few years before by an American, but found no reference to the restoration.

There are times when it takes many weeks to obtain a small piece of information, a piece in the puzzle, and often one does not know if it will be useful at all. But this is all part of the thrill, trying to get to the bottom of something and not knowing where the search will take you. When I was finally able to get hold of a copy of the dissertation for closer study, it still proved of no use in answering my question. The only glimmer of light it shed were references to further literature. One standard text it mentioned, which covered all the medieval embroideries in France, gave a detailed description of the ornaments but said nothing about the condition of the cloak. I contacted the author, who had since become curator of the museum of the *département* of Gers. At last I was able to chalk up a success: she gave me the name and address of Mme Classen-Smith, who had restored the cope of St Louis in Saint-Maximin in 1965. A lead at last.

Now, I hoped, it would not be too long before I knew what had been done with the original lining material and what type of weave it was in. Although twenty-five years had passed since then, I was very hopeful that Mme Classen-Smith could provide the missing information. One month passed without a reply to my letter, so I tried the telephone. The ringing had gone on so long that I was just about to replace the handset when a high-pitched voice responded at the other end of the line. As I quickly found out, the old lady was nearly deaf, and even when I shouted in the phone she could hardly understand what I was saying. She finally managed to tell me that she was ninety-six years old, could hear very little, was almost blind and could not remember anything any more. Then she hung up. In a last attempt I wrote a letter with large script and hoped that my persistence would win her over. Just ten days later I had her reply in my hands, written for her by a friend. She could no longer remember the weave of the cloth, nor whether she had replaced the lining material. One thing I did learn from her, however: if she had removed the old lining material she would have passed it on to the ministry in Paris responsible for historical monuments, together with the report about her work.

An Unexpected Letter from Oxford

I had in the meantime written to Prof Hall in Oxford and told him how surprised I was at the reluctance of the people at his laboratory to provide me with information. I said I would like to have a photograph of the cloth sample which he had dated in his laboratory. I added that I had already received such photographs from Zurich and Arizona (as far as Arizona was concerned this was not quite correct at the time), and that I did not think he had anything to hide. The criticism and doubt implied in my letter were quite intentional. Suspicious after what I had found out so far, I naturally wanted to know how much the specimens had weighed on arrival in Oxford. I explained to him that I wanted to publish a report about the investigations, and enclosed a blank cheque for his expenses.

What I had not dared hope for happened: just a week later I received Teddy Hall's reply. His answer about the weight of the samples was not specific: they had all weighed 'about 43 mg'. That was very unprecise and hardly scientific, and in the case of the Turin cloth sample the figure could definitely not be right. He enclosed what he said was a poor photograph of his cloth sample and photocopies of two different enlargements of this picture. On one very much enlarged picture he had marked by hand in red ink a protruding frizzy black thread, which he thought was a foreign body in the fabric. I had already heard of this foreign thread and contacted the laboratory where Hall had sent it for further examination. It was identified as cotton. Raes, who had been given the microphotographs of it, was unable to determine what kind of cotton it was because the piece was too short. Hall was kind enough to return my cheque. At the end of the short letter he added in his own handwriting: 'Apologies about the photographs, but we had nobody who could make copies of the polaroids.' That threw me a little, because to me it did not look as though one of the pictures had come from a polaroid camera, nor was the print with the cloth sample of poor quality. On the contrary, it was a black-and-white glossy photo of excellent contrast and in perfect focus, 11 × 16 cm, and I thought it might be a print from his original negative. Perhaps the coordination between Hall and his secretary was not running too smoothly. In any event I was satisfied with the fruits of my efforts, and the photograph gave me the chance to compare the sample with the original cloth (see Plate 12).

Looking at Sample O1 there are two very noticeable features which immediately stand out: there is a bunch of protruding fibres very near the centre of the cloth fragment, as if a knot had been woven into the threads during the weaving. Secondly, in the illumination coming from the side one can see that at one edge of the rectangular sample a fold of cloth has been bent to form a little ridge.

Now I was only missing the piece from Arizona and, most

importantly, a photograph of the complete section cut off in Turin. Without this photograph no comparison could be made.

Hunting for Evidence

I was very pleased to learn that in May an international Shroud conference was to take place in Bologna, with the cream of the sindonologists expected. Hoping to have the chance to question everyone who had taken part in the dating of the cloth, I made my way to Italy. The meeting took place in the theatre hall of an old palazzo. Golden cándelabras on the walls, red velvet curtains and splendid chairs provided a noble setting for the gathering. The list of speakers was impressive. Here I met many researchers whom I had only known through their publications, such as Paul Maloney, Alan D. Whanger, Werner Bulst, Pierluigi Baima Bollone and Giovanni Tamburelli. However, I saw from the list of speakers that the camp of the Shroud researchers had split into two parties. On the one side were those who had come to terms with the disappointing report of the C-14 results. In the other camp were those who doubted the result and were looking for the error which must have led to it. Obviously because of the competition between the two camps the first group had not appeared. This meant I missed the chance of questioning people such as the Profs Riggi and Gonella, who were prominent at the sampling but were not invited to the Bologna congress.

Among the speakers invited was the British author Ian Wilson, whom I had not met personally before, although Susan Brown had told him about my investigations and we had exchanged a few letters. In the interval we had a chance to compare notes. Wilson trusted the result of the dating test as little as I did, but he was unable to see how it could have come about. He was after all the first one who managed to trace the history of the cloth right back to the first century. He assured me that he would be pleased to support me in my investigations, and offered his assistance. I gladly accepted his offer. For some time I had tried to obtain the cloth sample photographs from Prof Damon at the University of Tucson in Arizona, but I had still received no reply, even after five letters. It transpired that Wilson knew Damon personally, and he said he was willing to telephone him and speed things up.

He kept his word, and soon the matter was settled at last: I had the photographs of all three cloth samples dated in the Oxford, Zurich and Arizona laboratories. Now only a photograph of the complete section cut from the Turin cloth was missing, to compare with the three test pieces. I hoped to get it from Prof Giovanni Riggi. Not only had he cut the specimen himself, it was under his supervision that the whole procedure was recorded on video and photographically documented. He controlled the documentation material, and anyone wanting photographs of the procedure had to go through him.

In the meantime I arranged with Elmar Gruber that we would undertake this report jointly. Elmar had been working on the history of the Turin cloth for some time, and we often discussed current problems in the field. Our first task was to be the visit to Riggi. We knew that as private individuals we had no chance of viewing the documentation, and so we presented ourselves as Elmar Gruber's film company, for which he had been working for years. Riggi proved to be very accessible. He said he was prepared to show us the whole film material of 10–12 hours' duration at his office in Turin. We were excited about what we might discover. Of course we wanted to take a very close look at the sampling, but the point that interested us most was to find out exactly how much time elapsed before Tite and the Cardinal reappeared from the sacristy with the sealed containers.

Our cases were packed as we telephoned to give our exact time of arrival. Then Riggi made a sudden U-turn. He said that we would not be able to see the complete material after all; they did not think this was necessary for a film documentary. After consulting with Gonella, he would only let us see an edited version. Yet again we were disappointed to find the doors slammed shut at the last minute, and only censored material could filter out to the public.

One has to ask, why an apparently uninterrupted video recording (excluding the episode in the sacristy) was made if people were not going to be allowed to view it as it stood. Would it not have been better to drop the documentation entirely, just as the verbal protocol had been simply dropped? What use was the assurance that everything proceeded correctly and was 'perfectly' documented, if no one was allowed to check? They had evidently also decided against having a notary confirm the events.

Turin: 'Journalists are Dangerous'

Our journey to Turin together was put off for the time being. But as I urgently needed a photograph of the cloth sample, I left for Turin on my own, unannounced. Riggi was away at a meeting about a planned Shroud conference in Paris, but would be back in two days. This at least gave me an opportunity to see the splendid town with its majestic buildings, and to visit the Chapel of the Holy Shroud in the cathedral, which I had not seen for over a decade. The relic sits enthroned in a shrine, locked behind a grille, at the centre of the baroque altar of the royal chapel built by Guarino Guarini, now the Capella della Santa Sindone. Perhaps this is the only right way to keep it. If the cloth were always on display, there would probably be no stopping the flood of the faithful and those believing in miracles.

Riggi was prepared to receive me on the evening of his arrival from Paris. He was Acting Vice-President of STURP, and first he wanted to know exactly why I had so many questions and was researching everything so thoroughly. I told him of my ten years' study of the Shroud, and the hopeless confusion which had arisen during the dating experiment because of the many inconsistencies. I told him that I wanted to get first-hand information to clear up the matter for an article I intended to write. Riggi's sibylline comment right at the start seemed very strange: 'Journalists are dangerous, you also are dangerous.' Any inquisitive person can seem a danger to someone who wants to concoct something unobserved. Danger is feared by those with something to hide. 'It is like the people at the Bologna conference,' Riggi explained. 'No one knows anything precisely. None of those who were in Bologna have ever seen the cloth, whereas we, we work and talk little.' By this 'we' Riggi, who was excluded from the Bologna conference, meant the STURP members. With an air of mystery he took from a drawer a booklet bearing the title *Formal Proposal for Performing Scientific Research on the Shroud of Turin*. It was the work compiled by STURP in 1984 about a number of urgent further experiments.

I was not allowed to handle the 'treasure' – only a dozen copies are in circulation and it is kept from the eyes of outsiders.

It had struck me as peculiar that Cardinal Ballestrero had retired just after the announcement of the dating results, and I asked Riggi the reason. He gave an evasive reply. The Cardinal had not seemed very ill or old. Riggi did not know the details. I next asked what had happened to the Raes sample. Riggi replied: 'I have a part of it myself, but it is unusable because . . .' He broke off mid-sentence and changed the subject. Why was it unusable? Riggi no longer answered the question. I was not satisfied, but I made a note of the strange reply and passed on to the radiocarbon experiment. In front of running cameras Riggi had cut off the cloth piece to be dated, from the region where the Raes sample had been removed in 1973. I asked him the size of the strip removed. 'Seven by one centimetres,' he replied. From the photographs of the specimens I knew that this could not possibly be right. But even when I repeatedly asked the precise size, Riggi stuck to these measurements.

He said the second half of the strip, which was retained as a control sample, was about 3–4 cm long, and he was looking after it himself. 'That is for the future,' he told me with a significant smile. I asked what that was supposed to mean. His mysterious reply was: 'There is always a future!'

He then inserted a video cassette into his recorder. The time had come, and I was allowed to see the film of the sampling, the edited version. One could easily see that the strip cut by Riggi was wider than 1 cm. The cloth was frayed along one edge. When I asked whether the frayed edge had been cut straight, Riggi's reply was vague.

I saw how the textile expert Prof Testore weighed the piece of cloth. The balance read 478.1 mg. In the background the radiocarbon experts were sitting expectantly: Hedges, Hall, Damon, Tite, Wölfli. Again I asked Riggi if the strip was not wider than 1 cm. 'About 1.2 cm, but not straight, uneven,' was his answer.

Then the film showed how the strip was divided in the middle. One half was placed to one side, the other half cut into three parts. Prof Testore placed the separate pieces on the precision balance with tweezers. I could clearly read the weights of the individual specimens on the digital display: 0.0520, 0.0528 and 0.0537 g. I showed Riggi a drawing of the section of the Shroud where he has cut out the piece. The Raes sample removed in 1973 was already marked on the sketch. I asked him to mark where he had removed his piece, Riggi completed the drawing and wrote the width measurement, 10 ± 0.2 mm.

After the removal of the length of cloth, the film showed how the lining was opened at three places. Riggi took dust from various regions behind the cloth with a special vacuum cleaner, to test the biological environment. Pollen was irrelevant, he told me; they had even found pollen from the Triassic era on the cloth. He was more interested in the search for minerals which are found only in a few places in the world.

As the film continued to run, I asked him about the loose threads of the fourth sample. Riggi played down their importance: 'The fourth sample is of no importance really, just an insignificant extra. I received them from Vial at the last moment and handed them over to the representatives of the laboratories.

The film showed nothing more of interest, and at the end of our talk I asked for some photographs of the pieces of cloth. He remarked that there were no less than 200 photographs, but then he brought me a pile of selected prints to look through. I chose nine interesting photographs and asked him to have copies made for me soon. To apply a little moral pressure, I insisted on paying for them right away. But Riggi made everything complicated; I should be very patient he said. As I took my leave of him, he mysteriously hinted that I could expect a publication of sensational import at some time in the future. 'We need another three years of quiet for it,' he said, 'then there will be an incredible disclosure.' He and certain STURP members still needed this time for their work. He pressed me not to publish anything until them.

By the end of August I had still heard nothing from Riggi. I reminded him about the photographs, and he wrote to say he had not thought there was such a hurry, as the pictures could not be used for publication, but merely for scientific study. He promised to try and send them before the Paris congress, but it started on 7 September 1989, and still the photos had not arrived.

Paris: The Symposium of Shroud Researchers

The International Scientific Symposium of Paris on the Turin Shroud took place in the Centre Chaillot Galliera, in the presence of many illustrious sindonologists and other researchers. In front of the conference centre, a stone's throw from the Champs d'Élysées, the members of the Contre-Réforme Catholique (CRC, Catholic Counter-Reformation) distributed pamphlets with the provocative title *The Carbon-14 Affair* and still more provocative contents. In this they accused Dr Tite of fraud, saying he had switched Shroud fragments in the sacristy. Shortly thereafter Tite was appointed to succeed Prof Hall as Director of the Oxford radiocarbon laboratory, which had been set up with a donation of £1 million 'from unknown benefactors'.

In the auditorium too the emotion was evident. Some speakers presented new facts from history, which confirmed the existence of the Shroud many centuries before the date given in the test. Among them were Prof Gino Zaninotto from Italy and Ian Wilson from Britain. Others including Dr Paul Maloney, Dr Allan Adler and Dr Gilbert Lavoie from the USA and Prof Pierluigi Baima Bollone from Italy analysed the image formation process and the physicochemical indications for an earlier dating of the cloth. The radiocarbon daters and those supporting their results were also heard, including Dr Michael Tite, Dr Gabriel Vial and Dr Jacques Evin; while Prof Teddy Hall, though announced, failed to turn up for the meeting, giving no apologies. When, towards the end of the congress, Dr Alan Whanger took the rostrum and tried to show slides to prove that a manipulation had in fact occurred during the dating, the committee refused to allow it. He was not on the speakers list. The unrest among the public, who were largely sceptical about the radiocarbon results, had no effect.

In the Brancion Hotel, where most of the speakers were lodged, I met Gilbert Raes again. We decided to have a coffee together. At that moment Riggi emerged from the lift and was about to storm past me. Not wanting to miss my chance, I greeted him. He stopped short a moment, then he seemed to remember me and said: 'Ah yes, your photos, Gonella does not want you to have them.' I was amazed and angry. Riggi seemed to notice this and pacified me: 'I have had the prints made for you anyway. Come to me this evening and I will give them to you.'

Relieved and calmed, I accompanied Raes to a café and exchanged news with him. I told him that I now had all the sample photographs, from Zurich, Oxford and Arizona. Raes was very keen to see them, and said he would examine and compare them.

Riggi was not in his room at the time agreed. I left the hotel disappointed. As luck would have it, I glanced through the open window of a neighbouring restaurant and saw Gonella, Wilson, Rex Morgan and Riggi all sitting at a table. It was now or never, I thought, although the inscrutable Gonella, the one who was trying to obstruct my plans, was with them. As I entered the restaurant the company were already on their dessert. Riggi greeted me, and Wilson, obviously pleased to see me again, at once asked me how far I had got with my book. Gonella and Riggi exchanged questioning looks, while I hoped Wilson would not ask me any more questions which could arouse the Italians' suspicions. The gentlemen invited me to coffee, and after a time Riggi asked me to walk round the corner with him to the hotel. He kept his word and handed me the slides I wanted. He again emphatically stressed that Gonella was against giving out the pictures, and made me sign a paper declaring that I would only use the photographs for purposes of private study. Under no circumstances was I to publish them (see Plate 14).

The main hurdle had been overcome. Now the photographs of each of the laboratories' cloth samples could be compared by scientific methods with the complete strip in Turin – that at least was what I hoped. The next day I was able to have a short talk with Vial on the steps of the lecture hall. He seemed to me to be a congenial gentleman, whose role in the whole affair was obscure. I really had just one question for him: how many threads had he removed from the cope in Saint-Maximin, for use later for the mysterious fourth control sample. Vial was not very precise. It must have been about 200 mgs. The threads were divided into four equal parts of 50 mg each. He himself received one part, the rest he placed in three envelopes, which were given to the laboratories. They were just threads which were hanging loose on the back of the relic, and were not tightly sewn to the cloth by the embroidery.

His statement was of some interest. Prof Wölfli had told me in a letter of 17 August 1989 that the weight of his specimen No 4 had come to 68.8 mg. But if the four parts divided were about equal that would give a total weight of nearly 300 mg. The figures always seem to be a particular cause for confusion. But let us not anticipate matters here – the figures were to lead to still greater confusion.

The Photographs Prove the Deception

I could hardly wait to be back at home, to make a start on the comparative study in which I had placed so much hope. I soon found, however, that even with the latest technical aids at one's disposal one always comes up against some limitations. To obtain usable results, I started making excursions to various institutes and specialists. It became a real Odyssey. The laboratory samples had been 'burnt' to carbon in the radiocarbon dating process and so were no longer available for comparing with the original. Therefore my plan was to look at the structure of the original fabric, as visible on one of Riggi's macro-photographs, and zoom in on a small area, treating it like a fingerprint; then I would try to see if an identical structure could be found on one of the fragments which the laboratories had been given. Of course one would have to focus on at least two such 'fingerprints', because half of the cloth strip was not divided up and stayed with Riggi.

It turned out that actually only two photographs were suitable for comparison, because they were the only ones with very characteristic features which allowed me to match up the sections. On the colour picture which I obtained from Riggi in Paris, showing the section of the Shroud just before it was removed, I could clearly see a fold in the fabric (Photograph A). Such a fold, or at least one that looked similar, could also be identified on the photograph which I obtained from Hall in Oxford (see Plates 25 and 26).

If a match was to be found, I would have to start from the fold which was visible on both photographs. No such conspicuous features could be located on the photographs from Zurich and Arizona, so they could not be matched to a specific point on the uncut cloth. Besides, the picture from Wölfli in Zurich showed only the reverse side of the sample and would have required demanding and extremely complex computer-aided calculations for a useful comparison to be made. The picture from Arizona showed only a 5×12 mm portion of the piece which the university had received (see Plate 13).

At this juncture I happened to see a film report about the methods of the Zurich Criminal Investigation Department, making use of the most modern technical equipment. I tried submitting an enquiry to the Zurich municipal police. On 20 January 1990 a reply came from Dr K. Zollinger of the Forensic Science Department. In principle it was possible to accept tasks from private individuals, provided there existed some public interest. Their department could analyse textile fibres, but did not usually deal with fabric patterns. However, they were prepared to make the attempt if the original textiles were presented. Of course I had no original textiles to offer, so I wrote back describing the kind of test that was needed. In this letter I pointed out that Dr Max Frei, who had done the famous pollen analysis for the Shroud, had been the director of this very scientific department of the Zurich police. Perhaps this would make them interested. But on 2 February they advised me that in view of the importance of the case I should only approach the top specialists in the field. It was a pity, as I had hoped they were the 'top specialists'.

I began my next attempt with a call to Wolfgang Goede at the editorial office of *PM*, a popular science magazine for young people published in Germany. I had read an article by him about the criminological methods of the Federal Criminal Investigation Agency (Bundeskriminalamt, BKA). He referred me to Dr Franz Peter Adolf at the BKA. Here too I met with a refusal; no expert opinions could be prepared for private individuals. They were only made at the request of courts and public prosecutors. Lawyers with whom I spoke advised me to file a charge of neglect, because it was only a non-material case and no crime against property was involved. In this way a comparative investigation could be forced through. But this plan seemed to me rather unsound, as the BKA had said they would need to compare the original materials to test if they were identical.

In the meantime I received some news from the Zurich cantonal police. I had asked them for the address of the manufacturer of their picture-analysis equipment. Dr P. W. Pfefferli recommended a macro-comparison projector for testing the identity of images on two photographs. The police used such an instrument for testing suspicious documents. It allows one to do what they call superposition and tangential comparisons. The instrument was made by Projectina in Switzerland.

The director of Projectina, Mr Werner Liechti, seemed quite confident when I told him my requirements on the phone. His technicians then tried to do a picture comparison using Projectina equipment. Unfortunately they ran up against technical difficulties, and Mr Liechti suggested I contact Prof Pierre Margot of the Institute of Forensic Science at Lausanne University, who had a lot of experience with Projectina instruments. However, Prof Margot was out of the country for several months.

The next stop on my search for a suitable laboratory was the Institute of Photogrammetry in the Geodesy Department of Stuttgart University. The director, Prof Ackermann, patiently listened to my plan during my visit on 13 March 1990, and referred me to his colleague, the engineer Michael Hahn. The latter, together with his colleagues, devoted a whole day to analysing the pictures. The photographs were read into the graphic program of a computer via a scanner, using a Zeiss Planicomp C 130, a high precision digitizing apparatus. Later the scientists even tried to modify the computer program to increase the optical contrast of light and dark values for the indistinct threads on the images.

The result, however, was not very satisfactory; they did not manage to bring out the individual threads. The analysis was delayed by Hahn's departure to China for several weeks, but at last, just before Christmas, his detailed opinion reached me.

The projective matching of digitized images is best done with flat objects. Unfortunately the photographs did not satisfy this condition. In particular the image of the cloth section exhibited a marked fold line, as we have seen. Despite this a quantitative comparison was able to achieve a surprisingly accurate correction for the distortion. This meant that the departure of the textural surface from an ideal plane could then be neglected. Identity of the two pictures could not be shown from the projective similarity of the specimen photographs.[28]

For the textural comparison, sections of the pictures were compared pixel by pixel (a pixel is a point on the grid of the digitized image). The information for the comparison was taken from the intensity value (grey level) of each pixel and its context, that is the pixels surrounding it with their intensities. However, problems arose with the present images, because the features to be used could not be influenced by the varying illumination, and not obscured by the differences in sharpness of focus of the two pictures. Features of this kind are not normally encountered in image processing. To get round them the scientist adjusted the pictures to get a better match, first by aligning the distance scales, then by approximating the sharp to the unsharp image (low pass filtering), by matching them geometrically while correcting for distortions, and by calculating the correlation with small correlation masks (correlation refers to a statistical method for matching two sets of figures). To obtain a significant correlation it is necessary not only to test the similarity with a compared object, but also that of the object with itself. This revealed something which the eye notices just by looking at the cloth samples: the structure of the weave on each piece is not regular, but varying, because of the manual workmanship. Hahn said that no definite correlation between the specimens could be calculated by this approach, especially because the similarities found are distributed at random.

Obviously the researcher, who had compelled me to reveal the origin of the specimens for analysis, found the case rather too hot. The zeal he displayed early on quickly changed to an attitude of great caution. I could tell he was not entirely happy about the task. This alone explains why he relied on the mathematically problematic correlation, and did not do a direct, visible comparison on the specimens. Photograph B (Plate 25) could be compared with the section on Photograph A (Plate 26) to the left of the clearly visible fold. Photograph A showed the selected part of the Shroud before being removed by Riggi. Photograph B was the alleged Shroud sample which the Oxford laboratory was given. This sample is excellently suited for a comparison because it is the only one known to show a fold on it. From the direction of the herringbone pattern and that of the fold it would be possible to determine precisely the section on Photograph A to which the specimen should be identical.

In the meantime I had approached a firm in Waldkirch which had developed an instrument which can precisely analyse the thread thickness, thread numbers etc. of a textile by optically running over a piece of the cloth. Would it also be possible to compare photographs of textiles in this way, using the video shrink image processor 1 (VSIP 1)? The attempt was made, but it was foiled by the surface of the photographs, which was obviously not suitable for extracting the information: the light beam was reflected, producing just black images.

In Waldkirch they referred me further to the Institute of Textile and Process Engineering in Denkendorf near Stuttgart. At this institute the staff attempted a precise optical analysis. In their expert opinion given on 19 December 1989, the investigators,

P. Ehrler and Z. Cai first said that the optical impression of the two fabric patterns was different. The reason for the difference was not clear though, since it might also be due to the photographic process or the reproduction. Sample A (colour photograph of the entire piece removed in Turin) had a looser structure (large gaps between the weft threads) and a shorter floating thread than Sample B (the Oxford sample). On both samples the researchers counted the same number of warp threads between the two 'peak' threads, forty-one. But they found a difference in angle of the peak. On Sample A it was about 59°, on Sample B about 65°. 'This difference may also have been caused by a difference in thread thickness, or by differences in tension which may arise when laying the sample out on a surface.'[29]

The Denkendorf scientists made a further observation of great interest: 'The impression of a matching type of weave contrasts with the impression of a dissimilar pattern of fabric.' The cause of the dissimilar pattern of fabric was the varying thickness of the warp threads of Sample B. 'This arrangement of thick and thin warp threads cannot be found on Sample A.' Finally the textile scientists come to the conclusion: 'The said differences cause us to state that the samples are not identical.'

So they noted a difference in optical impression, due to a looser structure in the Oxford sample compared with the original cloth, and due to a difference in thread thicknesses. This finding agreed with what Prof Raes had already said about the Zurich sample. Moreover, the two sections compared had a 6° difference in the angle of the herringbone structure. The threads visible differed in thickness, and there were certain differences in the relative thread thicknesses of warp and weft.

I had not dared hope for such a confirmation of my hypothesis. But still I could not be fully satisfied, because the photographic conditions for the two pictures were different and final certainty would only be attained after this difference had been cleared up.

I was constantly on the look-out for new ways of checking whether the specimens which the laboratories received were identical to the original section of the Turin cloth. I had counted on the photographs, and it was unfortunate that the Zurich laboratory's photograph showed the rear side of the sample, and was therefore unusable for the comparison. In my time of need I recalled that Prof Wölfli had used only half of his sample and still had the other half. If Prof Raes could be allowed to examine the *upper* surface of the sample, he would be able to compare the pattern and numbers of warp and weft threads with those on the piece he had received in 1973. In this way it could be established beyond doubt whether they were identical or different.

Of course I could not hope to be given the unused sample myself. So I asked Wölfli for a decent photograph of it. On 3 November 1989 I wrote to him describing the state of my research to date, as he had asked me to do. I made it clear that I could not of course rely solely on my own eyes for the comparative analysis but that I had drawn on computer measurement data. I also told him that I had managed to find a firm which could digitize photographs by video, to compare the data of different patterns of materials. I explained that the photographs which he had given me only showed the back of the cloth and were not suitable for a comparison. I urgently requested him to have a photograph taken of the front surface of the cloth sample which he had kept back, in as sharp focus and as enlarged as possible. I also asked him to tell no one of my investigations at this stage, so as not to put my efforts in jeopardy. I added that I was quite sure by now that the laboratories had had nothing to do with any manipulation that may have happened.

Although I had stressed the urgency of my request, no reply came from Zurich. Nearly four weeks later I wrote another polite letter to Wölfli, again asking him to send the photograph. I reported that all my efforts to make comparison had so far proved in vain. It had not been possible to locate the laboratory sample in the original section. I told him that the Institute of Textile Research and Process Engineering in Denkendorf had prepared an expert opinion to this effect.

This time Wölfli responded, but his reply appeared odd, even puzzling:

Dear Mr Kersten

I refer to your two requests of 3 and 28 November and can tell you that after some searching among 5000 specimens we have found the remains of our Z1 sample. There are just two small pieces of about 2 mg each, and they have already been treated chemically. Next week the micro-photographs will be taken, and then we will see how strongly the threads have been broken up by the cleaning. If the pictures are usable, I would be pleased to let you have them, but only if you

inform me of the latest state of your investigations. I am willing to
reserve another appointment for you for this. Please call me in about a
week, so we can fix a date.
Yours sincerely
Prof Dr W. Wölfli.

The photographs taken by Wölfli clearly showed that he only
used a 25.9 mg portion from the whole specimen which he had
been given in Turin (52.8 mg). He had according to his own
statement kept the remnant, a single 26.5 mg piece of cloth, 'in a
safe place outside the lab', known only to himself and his wife.
How is it then that he had to spend weeks searching for the
fragment among 5000 other samples, when he had supposedly
kept the Turin cloth remnant in this safe place? And why was he
left with just two meagre 2 mg threads, from which nothing much
could be seen, certainly nothing about the closeness of the
weave? One might suppose that he could have used the four
weeks to ask the 'powers that be' how he should proceed. The
carefully preserved back-up piece could not just disappear, that
would be too obvious. After a period of mutual discussion they
probably hit on the idea of 'conjuring up' some loose threads,
unusable remnants of a once useful sample. This ensured that all
comparison with the original cloth would be safely excluded. And
then there was the condition, that he should first be informed 'of
the latest state of my investigations'.

Until then I had considered Wölfli to be trustworthy, and
thought that he himself may have been the victim of a cleverly
arranged deception. But after these odd statements, the picture
looked somewhat different to me. It all suggested that the supposedly independent dating laboratories were bound by the
directions of a secret authority. Whether this was to be sought in
the British Museum, in Turin or even in the Vatican, was at the
time still not clear to me.

There was another strange thing. Wölfli knew that I could not
use his photograph of the rear surface of the sample for my
comparison, athough it would otherwise have been very suitable
because there was an exact scale included in the picture and the
weight was also known. In the meantime I had received another
photograph from the CRC, the Catholic Counter-Reformation in
France, showing the upper surface of the sample. So there were
after all other photographs taken in Wölfli's laboratory, which he

had intentionally withheld from me, not even telling me that they existed. Why had he not let me use this photograph, after his initial willingness to co-operate?

Finally, towards the end of 1991, I asked Wölfli for permission to print his photographs, which had already been published in the annual report of the ETH. He wrote back saying that he wanted to know in exactly what context the pictures were to appear. I complied with his request and wrote that these photographs had no value for me as proof, but they looked good in colour and so they would be nice in a book. Four weeks later, after I had repeated the request, the terse reply came: 'I did not like your answer at all. Therefore I cannot allow you to use our photographs of the Turin Shroud'.[30] I can find no explanation for such a strange reply; somehow the professor seemed to have become suspicious.

I could still not help feeling that more could be learned from the photograph. Luckily there was someone in my circle of acquaintances who specialized in the computer-aided processing of graphical information. He had spent more than a year working with the software of a leading manufacturer and was a virtuoso on all graphics programs.

In order to compare the two photographs, they first had to be digitized with a scanner (that is, divided up into a grid of image points), so that the computer could process the pictures as sets of light and dark values. The second step was to change the values of the individual image points to bring out the structure of the individual threads more clearly. One reason for this was the lack of depth of focus in some parts of the colour photograph of the complete strip. Then the values of all the points below a certain brightness were reduced a little, to make them appear darker, and the brighter ones increased in intensity, so that they appeared a little brighter. In this way the main lines in the image could be considerably enhanced. The size of the image and the scale were not changed at all; all the image points kept the same proportions to each other.

Even the tiniest sections, forming just a vanishingly small part of the whole cloth, appeared gigantic when magnified enough. They were much too large to be compared point by point. Thus we concentrated on the fold, visible on the complete strip and (apparently) also on the Oxford photograph; this became in a way our 'Archimedean point'. If we set up coordinates for the fabric, to allow precise orientation, the visible fold could form the X-axis. The Y-axis of the coordinate system was formed by the peak or zero-thread, running almost at right angles to the fold. This was the thread where the herringbone pattern turned, forming a pointed V shape. This zero-thread too was clearly visible on both pictures. In this way one could exactly locate the theoretical area where Specimen B would have been cut from the cloth strip A.

Of course the two photographs were not enlarged to the same scale to start with. We had first to face the problem of matching up the sizes so that a comparison was possible at all. Then we had to align and adjust the dimensions of the most similar structures on both photographs, so that they matched as closely as possible. These were structures such as the individual threads that are visible and the diagonal herringbone pattern. The diagonals, formed by the depressions between warp and weft threads, have a similar angle on both photographs, and so it was possible to project the smaller section B onto the larger one A. Each image could be given a different colour by pressing a key for the graphics program.

Thus the two images could be superimposed and each enlarged or reduced as necessary until the diagonal lines on the monitor covered each other in as close an alignment as possible.

Although the 'herringbones' on the two samples could be matched up together, it was found that the distances between the threads on the two sections differed. A definite find: the two cloth samples differed in the closeness of their weave (see Plate 27).

This result agreed with the observation Prof Raes made about the Zurich sample, that 'the general appearance is quite different' because there was a 'differing number of threads per centimetre in the directions of warp and weft'; from this he drew the conclusion 'that the two specimens can not come from the same item'.

Unfortunately the photograph of the Tucson sample was not suitable for a similar computer comparison, because it showed too small a section, and the zero-thread was not visible on it. We would have liked to analyse this photograph, as Prof Raes had in his detailed expert opinion come to the astonishing conclusion that the Tucson specimen showed a completely different type of weave, which was not in any way comparable with either the front or the rear surface of his cloth sample of 1973![31]

We went on to do a second comparison of the weave structure of the Oxford sample with the original cloth. In the first test we had tried to line up the obliquely running gaps in the fabric (which produced the typical herringbone pattern) on both sections, and then found that the individual threads could not be matched up one to one; in other words the two weaves had a different compactness.

In the second test we proceeded differently: we now wanted to line up the overall herringbone structure on both sections, to see whether the individual threads covered each other there. Again the original photographs were entered in the computer with a high-resolution scanner, and their relative sizes adjusted. We selected what should have been the same section on both images, aligning them by the coordinates formed by the zero-thread and the fold.

When we superimposed the two image sections on the monitor, with the zero thread, the sixth thread and the eighteenth thread lined up so as to form a continuous whole, the obliquely running herringbone structure no longer matched up. More discrepancies were clearly visible along the edges of the two photo sections (see Plate 28). This made patently clear for any lay person what the expert opinion had previously stated: that the two sections, which should have been completely identical, differed quite visibly in the closeness of their weave and in the thickness of the individual threads.

Summing up, one can establish the following differences in appearance between those samples which the laboratories were given and the piece of cloth actually removed in Turin:

1. The individual protruding fibres which were seen extending above the fabric in the middle of the Oxford specimen could not be located on the original piece. Prof Hall expressly assured us that this feature was already present on the fabric when he took the sample from its container.
2. While it is true that a fold similar to the one on the original cloth was found on the Oxford specimen, it had a much larger angle opening. The fold on the small section 1 should have been tighter (that is have had a smaller angle opening) without the tension of the larger surround.
3. The laboratory specimens differed in the closeness of their weave from the original piece.

4. The individual threads when compared were seen to differ in their thicknesses.
5. The angle of the woven herringbone pattern of the laboratory specimens differed significantly from that of the Turin original.
6. If one lined up the Zurich specimen Z1 so that it joined up exactly with the Oxford specimen O1, a complete piece resulted but it would extend beyond the border of the original Turin cloth. Hence the strip of fabric thus produced was much wider than would have been physically possible (about 20 mm instead of the alleged 10 mm).

Therefore, although the fabrics looked similar at first glance, they were not the same after all. The proof is conclusive: the laboratories were given pieces of the wrong cloth for dating, cloth which did not come from the Turin Shroud!

Part Two

THE CLOTH IN THE SHADOWS
OF HISTORY

Elmar R. Gruber

In Pursuit of the 'True Shroud'

Setting out on the search for the 'true Shroud', the first thing
we have to ask is what happened to the burial linen after it
was left behind in the empty tomb. Fortunately it is not just any
burial cloth we are looking for, but that of no less a person than
the Son of God himself. So we might still hope to find, even at
this distance of time, some clue which would make the quest
feasible. We are confirmed in this positive attitude when we
consider how even the early Christians soon came to develop a
great zeal for collecting relics. And right from the start the Passion
relics, of which the burial cloth is one, were at the top of the list of
sought-after items among the faithful.

Reports about the immediate fate of the burial linen are few,
and seem to be little more than speculations or legends. Most of
them are known to us only decades, often centuries, after the
event. In the apocryphal Gospel of the Hebrews we find it said
that after the Resurrection Jesus himself gave the Sindon (Shroud)
to the 'Servant of the priest', whoever that may mean.[1] St Nino
(who died about 335) says the burial linen remained for a while in
the possession of Pilate's wife. Then it passed into the hands of St
Luke, who kept it in a secret place. And the Sudarium (facecloth)
was 'found' by Peter. This account has to be taken in the context
of a certain legend which holds, contrary to all the known facts of
history, that a change came over the personality of Pilate and he
then did what he could to help the Jewish leaders who admired
Jesus. As far as our search for the Shroud's fate is concerned, the
value of this lead is just as small as that of a further reference by
St Hieronymus, because there are no reports to cover the subsequent movements of the cloth directly after these accounts.

Some centuries later, Bishop Braulio of Saragossa (631–51) wrote
that the linen and facecloth had been found and kept, but that
there were no clues as to their whereabouts. He also said he did
not think 'that the apostles neglected to preserve these and such-
like relics for future times.'[2] We have to bear in mind that this
statement was made at a time when relics were seen as visible,
tangible proofs for the truth of the Gospel narrative; and for the

simple populace drawing on their pagan religious origins, they were also counted as magic talismans for protecting and healing. With such attitudes as these, the pious churchman must have thought it absurd that anyone would not want to preserve a relic, especially one connected with the Passion of Jesus. But at the time of Christ itself this was not at all a common idea.

One has to imagine the circumstances of Jesus' crucifixion and burial, the shock at seeing the empty tomb. Had the body of Christ been stolen? What were the disciples to make of its disappearance? There must have been great confusion as they suddenly found themselves on their own. Those were dangerous times. Their leader had just been crucified, and it was unlikely their persecutors would remain inactive after such a triumph. The followers of Jesus had to go underground. They were extremely worried. Many of them chose to return to private life; when Jesus met them later he found them pursuing their former trades. After the stoning of Stephen those who remained steadfast began to face open persecution (Acts 8:1–4). Many were forced to leave the country. They probably had little time for or interest in relic collecting, and anyway it would be dangerous to be caught with one.

Things look quite different if we start by assuming that the impression of Christ was seen on the Shroud, as we see it on the Turin cloth. This fact would immediately have transformed the relatively unimportant burial clothes into a unique sign: the incarnate Logos leaving behind a mysterious picture in a miraculous way, a divine parting gift for the faithful. The apostles would hardly have left such a cloth lying unattended, even in the dire straits they were in. But did they notice any impression? We now know that the features of the man did not take shape on the Turin cloth by a slow biochemical process over a long period, but appeared immediately. Even then could they have made out such a faint picture in the dimly lit tomb chamber? Was the linen not rather so steeped in spices – about 100 lb of them according to St John's Gospel – that no image could be made out?

If no one did notice the picture, the cloths would probably have been left lying there for the time being. Burial clothes were considered ritually impure by the Jews. Therefore it would, under normal circumstances, be unthinkable for someone to take and keep them. It is not only conceivable but highly probable (given a certain precondition which we cannot go into just now, although we will deal with it in detail later), that the linen was taken from the tomb at a later time, without anything unusual about it being noticed. Conventional burial cloths were very plain, inexpensive fabrics. The Turin cloth was no ordinary winding-sheet, it was certainly very costly, and it may have been intended for reuse after washing. When the spices loosely adhering to the fabric were washed off, the 'miraculous' image, which could not be washed out, came to light. In this case again one would presume that the followers of Jesus looked after the cloth in their care. But we are again unable to follow up the clue. No references to a place of keeping are made; we find no reports about any place of concealment in the early centuries. In 670 we find the Frankish Bishop Arculf of Périgueux telling the story of his pilgrimage to Palestine. On this trip, he says, he saw the Shroud displayed in a church, where, along with a large crowd of others, he kissed it. Was this 'our' Shroud? The Bishop makes no mention of a picture on the cloth. Besides, he reports that the cloth had a length of 8 ft, which makes it much shorter than the Turin cloth. The shroud which Arculf had seen was most probably the one given to Charles the Great in about 797. A century later it was taken to the Abbey of St Cornelius in Compiègne. The holy shroud of Compiègne was the goal of countless pilgrims up until the time of the French Revolution, when it was destroyed.

Whatever the origin of such 'burial clothes', we hear no reference to any image on them. And if we want to trace back the history of the Turin Shroud it is references to this clear distinguishing feature that we have to look out for.

The obvious course was first to focus my attention on the relic treasures of medieval Constantinople. In this flourishing metropolis on the Golden Horn there was at that time not only an incomparable number of splendid palaces, but also by far the most important collection of relics in Christendom. By the time of Constantine the basis for this collection had already been gathered. Empress Helena, the mother of Constantine, was piously busying herself on her travels throughout Palestine, uncovering Golgotha, tracking down the relics of the Passion and shipping them from the Holy Land to Constantinople. By doing this she set a trend which was to be followed with growing fervour in the ensuing centuries. The import of relics reached its first peak when the 'genuine' cross of Christ was rediscovered at the end of the fourth century. During this period the first pilgrims were arriving in the Holy Land. With the Bible for their guide-book, they visited the sacred places, said prayers on consecrated ground and brought home relics as mementoes. In this way there soon developed a brisk trade in the more easily transported sacred objects of Christianity. Many found their way to the local churches of the European pilgrims, while the majority of them, and the most important, ended up in Constantinople.

In the fifth century Theodosius II (408–50) had the imperial capital adorned with beautiful churches. He ordered the rebuild-ing of the burned Hagia Sophia and restored the church of Our Lady at Blachernae. The numerous sacred buildings were con-secrated by installing all these valuable relics in them. It was said that Theodosius' consort, Athenais-Eudokia, passed on the burial clothes of Christ to his energetic sister, the empress Pulcheria, and she had them permanently installed in the Blachernae church. Athenais-Eudokia apparently brought the cloths back with her from her visit to Jerusalem in 438. We can no longer trace whether these were in fact burial clothes.

Endless lists of sacred objects have come down to us from the tenth to the thirteenth centuries, especially the Passion relics which were treasured above all other types and displayed to visitors of high standing in the capital of the Byzantine empire. These reports give us some idea of the importance and compass of the collection. One can judge from this the status Constantinople was accorded within Christendom, for the city was in a sense under the protection of a whole army of silent witnesses to the activity of the Lord.

In some inventories we do find mention of a 'shroud' of Christ.[3] But it would not be right to conclude from the documents that they definitely referred to the linen known today as the Turin Shroud. Actually the information given about burial clothes in Constantinople is often quite confusing. The reasons for this are many. For one thing we are faced with the problem of finding a clear translation for the terms used. In those times there was no sort of clear rule of speech which allowed a cloth to be un-ambiguously identified as a burial cloth. Then there is the fact that according to the Gospel reports there were at least two and maybe even more cloths left behind in the tomb, all of which could be classed as burial clothes. So it is quite possible that there were a number of burial clothes, each authentic. Another problem is the widespread custom of giving out copies of relics as originals, not to mention the outright forgeries which were slipped to the enthusiastic collectors, Christian emperors and pious pilgrims, by hardened swindlers.

Be that as it may, there is one text which stands out from all the others, and is viewed as evidence by sindonologists around the world that the cloth which is now kept in Turin was being exhibited in Constantinople at the beginning of the thirteenth century. This is the account by a Frankish knight, Robert de Clari, who describes the splendours of the city as a member of the unfortunate Fourth Crusade. He tells of his visit to a church 'which they named Our Lady Holy Mary of Blachernae, where was kept the shroud in which Our Lord was wrapped, which was held up on display every Friday so that the figure of our Lord could be clearly seen.'[4]

This important piece of information, from someone who was obviously an eyewitness, is indeed remarkable. It shows that in August 1203 a shroud of Christ was exhibited in the Blachernae church, which was put on display every Friday in a way allowing one to see the form of Jesus on it. Many sindonologists see this as a clear proof of the presence of the true Shroud in Constantinople, before it resurfaced in France 150 years later.

But how did the linen come to Constantinople, and why had no one referred to the remarkable image on the cloth before that? Answers to such questions are not easily come by. After all we face no less a task than to reconstruct the whereabouts of a linen cloth over a period of nearly 1000 years, during which time we find, mysteriously, hardly any mention of it in the records.

The Story of King Abgar

We have seen the tangible presence of the Shroud with the image of the body in Constantinople. Now we have to uncover the tracks of this unique item of fabric as it passed on its way to Byzantium.

Our search starts with the following scenario. Somehow or other the mysterious image of the front and rear view of Jesus was discovered on the cloth. It was looked after by followers of Jesus. They were not apostles, because the apostles had already gone into hiding during the crucifixion. It was Joseph of Arimathea and Nicodemus who saw the removal of the body from the cross and the burial, two respected councillors of the Jewish Sanhedrin who were part of the clandestine following of Jesus.

At first the cloth was held in hiding; but they were keen to display it when the time was right, so that the people would 'see and believe' like the favourite disciple, who 'saw and believed' when he looked into the empty tomb (John 20:8). But Palestine was in turmoil. Many conflicting religious and political groups were confronting each other, and added to this there was the constantly mounting tension with the foreign Roman rulers, which was to culminate in the final destruction of the Temple of Jerusalem in 70 AD and the fall of the Masada fortress in 73. Finally in 135 under Hadrian the Jewish insurrection of Bar Kochba was quashed. Further north, especially in towns such as Antioch, Corinth and Ephesus, the teachings of the apostles found fruitful soil. Jewish-Christian and pagan-Christian communities formed strong groups which were able to flourish far from the sites of Jesus' activity, in relative security among coexisting Messianic sects. If they wanted to get the Shroud out of the country, the only areas worth considering were towns to the north with strong Christian communities. Edessa was one such town.

Today we know of a tradition, commonly classed as a legendary cycle, which has in the course of time been subject to a great variety of changes. At first sight it may seem to have little bearing on our problem. But when we look closer a fascinating episode comes to light, behind the veil of anecdote, in which the Shroud of Christ plays a central role. I refer to the narratives involving a certain correspondence of Jesus with Abgar, King of Edessa. So to continue our search for the key to solving the puzzle, let us wend our way to ancient Edessa.

Edessa, today the Turkish provincial capital Urfa in south-east Anatolia, lay on the border between the Greek and Oriental worlds. The town was apparently mentioned in Sumerian, Akkadian and Hittite cuneiform documents dating back as far as the third millenium BC. At the time of the Roman emperor Tiberius the royal court of Medzpine was transferred to Edessa in the Osrhoene province, an event conferring a great importance on the town and soon drawing people from all directions. Edessa was situated near the old royal road which, stretching from Ephesus in the west to Susa in the east, had traversed the old kingdoms of the Lydians, Medians and Persians, and was connected with Antioch, Persia, Armenia, even with India and the regions of eastern Asia. It was not only goods that were transported through the gates of the city on these important trade routes, but above all ideas, world-views, myths and legends. As a flourishing intellectual centre Edessa can perhaps best be compared with Alexandria. Its character was marked by the variety of nationalities and creeds which here found a mutually fruitful coexistence. It was favoured in this regard by the peculiar location of the town, which through its long history always lay in the outlying areas of the various political fields of influence, and never at their centre: at the borders of the Seleucid empire, then the Parthian empire, the Roman empire, the Sassanian empire, finally the Byzantine empire.

Politically, Edessa was subject to the Abgar dynasty from 132 BC to 216 AD. Towards the end of the second century the Christian community gained greatly in importance, and Abgar IX bar Ma'nu, Toparch of Edessa, was converted to Christianity. At this time, to grant the young Church a special weight – so the ortho-dox history runs – a legend was prepared which set the origin of Edessan Christianity back to the time of Christ: the Abgar story.[5]

The earliest confirmation of the Abgar tradition is considered to be that given by Eusebius (260–340), the father of ecclesiastical history. We have him to thank for reporting the following events. Abgar V of Edessa (15–50), named Ukkama, on hearing of the miracles of Jesus, sent a messenger to Jerusalem. He was to invite Jesus to visit Edessa, to heal him of a disease. Thereupon Jesus sent the prince a handwritten letter informing Abgar that he had important tasks to perform in Palestine and could not come him-self. But he promised to send a disciple who would heal him. Eusebius conscientiously reports the correspondence between Abgar Ukkama and Jesus. He mentions old Syriac texts from the archives of Edessa as his sources (Syriac is a kind of Aramaic, the old dialect of Hebrew which Jesus spoke).[6]

If this report were an isolated one, it could be dismissed as a yarn invented simply to lend special authority to the Edessan Church of the second century. In fact the correspondence is viewed by most authors in this way: the acceptance of Christianity, which they say actually happened much later, was subject to a legendary backdating, and the Edessan Christian community was placed under the special protection of the Lord, with Jesus saying in his letter that the presence of his epistle would shield Edessa from misfortune and attack. But the story of the correspondence has been passed down in many different variants, and is obviously so intimately bound up with the religious beliefs of early Christianity that one has seriously to ask whether there were not some actual events behind it which led to its being handed down as a tradition. There can be no doubt that an organized Church did not take shape here until the middle of the second century. It is quite possible, though, and after thorough study of the historical sources I even consider it quite likely, that there had been a 'Christian interlude' in the Osrhoene even at the time of Jesus.

The report of Jesus' activity was soon carried beyond the borders of Palestine. It is to be expected that talk of his miraculous cures and his teachings was heard, especially in a trading centre such as Edessa, through which the spice and silk caravans passed. There were Jews of the Diaspora living in Edesssa, who as merchants had an important share in the trade with lands to the east. Batne in the province Osrhoene, a day's journey from Edessa, was host to a famous market which in early September drew together the merchants of distant lands, especially Indians and Serians from Turkestan. It was mainly a place of exchange for silk. The Edessan Jews were busily engaged in this trade. And in Edessa they spoke a local dialect of Aramaic which differed little from the language of Jesus. Given these circumstances it is quite possible that a disciple of Jesus came to the town, shortly after his Passion, to spread the word of the Lord, after hearing that its ruler was interested in the miraculous cures of Christ. Perhaps he saw a chance of quickly getting the Christian teaching established in the protection of a small but not insignificant kingdom. The meagre historical information available about Abgar Ukkama is not enough for us to decide definitely whether he did actually have a leaning to Christianity.

But the report of Eusebius does not stand alone – and this is the crucial point, which takes us on a journey where we discover an exciting and extraordinary set of events. In the West the legend of the correspondence of Abgar with Jesus became known from the

Latin translation of Eusebius' history of the Church by Rufin of Aquileia (345–410). Rufin was the main source from which many later authors drew, although the story must have been known before. The Aquitaine pilgrim Aetheria, who journeyed to the Holy Land in around 383, already knew it.[7] After the obligatory stops in Palestine she went on to visit Edessa, the town in which according to one legend the apostle Thomas was martyred, and made inquiries about Jesus' letter, which was kept in the archives. She brought a copy back with her, because the one known in the West was not complete.

At some time towards the end of the sixth century a form of the Abgar narrative was circulated, in which a new element emerges. According to this tradition, which was first mentioned by Evagrius Scholasticus (527–600),[8] not only did Jesus send a letter to Abgar, he sent a picture as well. The picture was a portrait of himself, but a special, miraculously formed one. As we now know, the oldest version of the portrait story goes back to the *Doctrina Addai*, which was written down as early as the end of the fourth century in Syria, although it obviously found a limited circulation at the time. Until about 150 years ago the story was known only from later written versions. But in the 1840s, when a sensational discovery of numerous manuscripts was made in the Natron valley in Lower Egypt, these early Syriac versions of the Abgar story were found.[9] And it can be safely assumed that the oral traditions were much older yet. It has been speculated that Eusebius, who had access to the archives of Edessa, and the author of the *Doctrina Addai* were also aware of the portrait, but avoided mentioning it because of their disapproval of religious images.

Later we again find a detailed report about the Edessa Portrait in a commemorative sermon which was to become famous, held at the court of Constantine VII Porphyrogennetus (913–59) in the year 945; the author says he is using old Syrian sources.[10]

This sermon is worth dwelling on here, because it is of special importance for the whole context of our historical reconstruction. In August 944 a picture of Christ 'not made by human hands' (*acheiropoieton*), the so-called Mandylion, was brought to Constantinople from Edessa. In Edessa it had been most highly revered since the sixth century. It was so important that many copies were prepared, and all were claimed to be the original. The decisive point, however, is that the Mandylion was linked with the Abgar story: it was said to be the portrait of Christ which he had presented to Abgar via one of his followers.

From the sixth century onwards the correspondence between Abgar and Jesus recedes into the background, while in its place the miraculous portrait gains more and more in importance. The picture even comes to assume the function of protecting the town, which had previously been attributed to Christ's letter alone. In 944 the Emperor Romanus I Lakapenus won Edessa from the hands of the Arabs and had the Mandylion brought to the imperial capital. It arrived in Constantinople still in the golden casing in which it had been found in Edessa.

To celebrate the installation of the sacred picture in the imperial chapel at Pharos, on 16 August 945 a sermon was read, and this has come down to us with the title 'Narratio de imagine Edessena' ('The Story of the Edessa Portrait'). The author certainly belonged to the circle of co-regents around Constantine VII Porphyrogennetus. Constantine was an enthusiastic researcher with a keen interest in history, little suited to the craft of statesmanship. His passion lay in the field of art and literature. Indeed, many authors have been led by this fact to suppose that he may have written the sermon himself. The complete text has been preserved and it provides the most comprehensive view of the Mandylion story as linked with the Abgar episode. Especially noticeable is the candour of the author, who is particularly keen to present as authentic a report as possible. No attempt at all is made to offer a consistent and tidy story. Instead the compiler shows that he was aware that after the time that had elapsed since the events it was no longer possible to test the validity of the reports in detail. Where he himself is not sure about which version is the right one, he passes both traditions on to the reader.

The Miraculous Portrait of the Saviour

According to one version of the Abgar story, as presented in the sermon, after the demise of Jesus the disciples sent a proclaimer of the glad tidings, as promised by the Lord in his letter, to Edessa. He was to hand on the portrait of the Saviour not made by human hands. The Greek texts refer to the emissary as Thaddaeus, the

Syrian Addai. One point in favour of the authenticity of the account is the express mention that he came from Paneas and was not the Apostle Thaddaeus, but 'one of the seventy' (Luke 10:1) whom Jesus chose and sent out ahead of him in pairs. In Edessa Thaddaeus went to the prosperous Jewish community and found lodging with the Jew Tobias. The rest of the account also reads more like a factual report than a legend.

Thaddaeus did not then immediately present himself before Abgar, as one would expect in his role of messenger, but prepared his mission with great care. He set about healing the sick, 'calling only the name of Christ. Therefore, talk about Christ became widespread (as happens in such situations; when things happen unexpectedly, there are always plenty of people to announce them).' It seems that the healings of Thaddaeus came to the notice of a noble called Abdu, who enjoyed great influence at court. Perhaps he hoped for a healing for himself, for it is said that the disciple later freed him from gout. Abdu informed Abgar in detail of the miracles, and the latter at once concluded 'that this was the man whom Jesus had promised in his letter that he would send to him'. He had Thaddaeus called to his presence.

When he was about to appear before him, he placed the portrait on his own forehead like a sign and so entered.

Abgar saw him coming in from a distance, and thought he saw a light shining from his face which no eye could stand, which the portrait Thaddaeus was wearing produced.

Abgar was dumbfounded by the unbearable glow of the brightness, and, as though forgetting the ailments he had and the long paralysis of his legs, he at once got up from his bed and compelled himself to run. In making his paralysed limbs go to meet Thaddaeus, he felt the same feeling, though in a different way, as those who saw that face flashing with lightning on Mount Tabor.

And so, receiving the likeness from the apostle and placing it reverently on his head, and applying it to his lips, and not depriving the rest of the parts of his body of such a touch, immediately he felt all the parts being marvellously strengthened and taking a turn for the better; his leprosy cleansed and gone, but a trace of it still remained on his forehead. Having been instructed then by the apostle more clearly of the doctrine of truth, and concerning the amazing miracles by Christ and his divine passion and burial and resurrection from the dead and his taking up into heaven, and having confessed that Christ was the true God, he asked about the likeness portrayed on the linen cloth.[11]

That is the description given in the sermon of 945.

The historical sources clearly show that shortly after Abgar received the portrait it vanished, to be rediscovered only centuries later. Only a faint memory of the picture remained in the oral tradition. It is found for example in the early *Doctrina Addai*, according to which Abgar's messenger Hannan (or Ananias), who apart from being a highly placed diplomat at the Edessan court was a painter as well, painted the portrait of Christ and brought it to Edessa. Certain features of the story of the letter can also be traced back to the portrait tradition. For example the vision of splendour which in Eusebius' report Abgar beheld on seeing Thaddaeus arrive, is found as a mysterious light which radiates from the messenger of Jesus himself: 'As he came up and the dignitaries of the king were standing there, at the moment he entered a wonderful vision appeared to Abgar on the visage of Thaddaeus.'

The accounts of this event in the early centuries seem incomplete and obscure. The picture itself gradually faded from the tradition, leaving just the vision of light, with the context missing. From observations of other *acheiropoieta* we find clear indications that this vision of light is attributed to the miraculous picture of Jesus and not to Thaddaeus. To take one better-known example I will just mention the account by Antoninus of Placentia, who was said to have seen an *acheiropoieton* of Christ in Memphis in about 570, dazzling him by its brilliance so that he was unable to discern any details.[12]

The miraculous image of Memphis belongs to a whole series of *acheiropoieta* which sprang up everywhere after the reappearance of the Edessa Portrait in the sixth century. The best-known picture is that of Camuliana, a small town to the north-west of the capital of Cappadocia, Caesarea Mazaca, today's Kayseri.[13] The respect paid to this picture allows us to form some idea of the status of miraculous images of Christ in this period. The older version of the Camuliana legend (between 560 and 574) tells of the heathen lady Hypatia, who found the image of Christ on a canvas submerged in a cistern of water. When she removed the picture she found it was quite dry. On the way to her teacher, who wanted to convert her to Christianity, she pressed the picture to her dress. When she came to show her find, she saw that the face had been imprinted on her garment. We are further told that one of the two pictures was brought back to Caesarea (evidently the miraculous imprint on the dress), the other remaining in Camuliana. The Camuliana image was carried in festive processions through the whole region from 554 to 560.

In the sixth and seventh centuries the image of Camuliana was highly revered. Justin II (565–78) had it brought to Constantinople in 574, together with fragments of the sacred cross from Apameia in Syria. Even then it was probably considered to offer protection, like the Edessa Portrait, the helping presence of Christ being guaranteed by its miraculous origins. Justin, who did not hesitate to end the 'everlasting' peace which his predecessor had negotiated with the Persian emperor Chosroes I Anushirvan, by stopping the tribute payments to Persia, thought he faced a hard and long drawn-out war. A *palladium* (protective talisman) for the empire would be most welcome, not only for protecting the country but also to stir the army's fighting spirit. Ever since the time of Constantine miraculous signs of the Lord were considered to be an excellent means of inspiring courage in battle. Constantine himself had his standard, the *labarum*, led as a sacred sign against the enemy and had it protected by a special guard. (In the First World War Russian troups still carried the image in their campaigns as their battle standard.)

The arrival of the picture in the capital was celebrated with great pomp and enthusiasm. As with all great *acheiropoieta*, copies were soon produced, and kept in various churches. In subsequent years the Camuliana image had plenty of opportunities to prove its protective power. The war against the Persians raged for twenty years with varying degrees of success. Under Maurikios the general, Philippikos, showed his men an *acheiropoieton* to fire their courage before the battle at Arzamon in the year 586. If this was not the Camuliana image itself, it was most probably a copy of it. The same holds for the image 'not made by human hands' which was brought to the Persian wars under Heraclius (610–41).

One might ask whether it was the Camuliana image, which after all definitely did exist, which triggered the other stories about miraculous images of Christ which suddenly sprang up everywhere. One might accept this if the Edessa Portrait had only appeared afterwards. But the opposite is the case. The image of Christ which the Byzantines were later to call the Mandylion was very well known in Edessa in the middle of the sixth century. It was at once linked to the Abgar narrative, and the half-forgotten episode of the picture in the oral tradition saw a renaissance.

The sudden appearance of an image of Jesus must have been an exciting event for the Edessan Christians, confirming the old tradition which was known only in fragments. Considering the importance of the Abgar story for Christianity in the region, news of the discovery of the miraculous image must have spread like wildfire. It was a period when relics and miraculous apparitions were highly valued. So it is not surprising that very soon one finds other *acheiropoieta* appearing in various towns in the region around Edessa, in a sense competing with the important original.

These miraculous images of the countenance of Christ, known in the sixth century mainly in eastern Asia Minor, also form the basis for a legend which has been preserved to this day in the pious folklore of the West. This is the legend of Veronica. It is one of those tales which every Catholic child knows and remembers throughout life because of its simple appeal. Put briefly, it runs as follows: a lady named Veronica heard the laments and cries of a crowd of people as they passed her house in Jerusalem. Worried, she ran to the gate and saw Jesus being led to the scene of execution, covered in blood and under the burden of the cross. She pressed her way through the mass of people until she finally came to stand before Jesus. Taking her veil she wiped his face, covered in blood and sweat, for him; and on the veil there remained an imprint of his face, the most precious gift of the Saviour.

The event finally grew to become an integral part of the Passion story, being included as the sixth Station of the Cross until in 1991 Pope John Paul II had it replaced by another one. Today this story has become so taken for granted, even by poorly informed Catholics, that many think the Veronica tale is found in the Gospels. In reality it is the product of a slow transformation of legends circulating since the appearance of the Edessa Portrait. The story of Veronica as we know it today goes back to the medieval mystery plays, which included the events of the Passion.

It is probably the dramatized version of a tale composed by Petrus Mallius, canon of St Peter's, in about 1150. This tells how Veronica possessed a face-towel (*sudarium*) of Jesus which he had used to dry his face during the agony in Gethsemane. There is no mention here of the scene when he was carrying the cross along the Via Dolorosa. Mallius' story is a reworking of legends which came into circulation from the sixth to eighth centuries. The most recent of these is known as 'The Death of Pilate'.[14] In this Veronica wished to have the portrait of her master painted, knowing that he would soon leave her. On the way to the artist she was met by Jesus, who asked her for the canvas, pressed it to his face, and so left the impression of his features on it. The two older legends are the less important 'Vindicta Salvatoris' ('The Vengeance of the Saviour'), and the very influential 'Cura Sanitatis Tiberii' ('The Healing of Tiberius'). Both derive directly from the tradition of the Edessa Portrait.[15] It is interesting to note that in 'The Healing of Tiberius' Veronica was equated with the *haemorrhissa* of the Gospels, the woman with the issue of blood who wanted to touch the hem of Jesus' robe to be healed.[16] Veronica, so it was said, had the portrait of Jesus painted because of her love for him. The emperor Tiberius, being afflicted with leprosy, sent the temple priest Volusian to Palestine to bring the woman and the image of Christ. Just as Thaddaeus came before Abgar, Veronica came with the picture before Tiberius, who then dropped to the ground in awe, and tearfully worshipped Jesus, freed of his illness.

Just as the Mandylion of Edessa led to a series of similar *acheiropoieta* of Christ, such as the Camuliana image, so the two tales of Abgar and of the *haemorrhissa* gave rise to the legend of Veronica and the face-towel. The fact that in the course of this transformation the *haemorrhissa* finally came to bear the name Veronica, is due solely to the image of Christ on the face towel. Because it is an image 'not made by human hands', it is naturally the true image of the Lord. 'True image' in Latin/Greek is *vera icon*, which became 'Veronica'. The key to understanding the essence of the two narrative cycles is not the miraculous image itself – it is absent in the original version of the healing of the *haemorrhissa* – but the *touch* of a cloth, the link with Jesus. It matters little here whether the cloth is the robe of Jesus or a towel on which he dried his face. The crucial thing is that it can be associated with Jesus. This means it can heal others who touch it or who are touched by it – in the figurative as well as the literal sense. The work of healing and salvation, which is the basis for the whole Christian message, gains here a concrete, tangible form, striking chords of resonance at the archetypal, myth-forming levels of the soul. The ramifications and reworkings of legend which have been the fate of the stories of both Abgar and Veronica, are eloquent examples of that basic trait of the human psyche, the tendency to take intuitions of existential meaning and fashion from them vivid graphic events, often allegorical in nature.

The Discovery of the Mandylion

The original model for all the *acheiropoieta* of Christ is the Abgar image in Edessa, and this is where we have to take up the threads of our search. The first person to report its reappearance after a gap of centuries was Evagrius. In his *Church History* it is said that the Mandylion was used in May 544 as a protective *palladium* when Edessa was under siege by the Persian King Chosroes I Anushirvan. Chosroes, who suffered from rheumatic facial pains, wanted to make a third attempt to take the town, which was defending itself bravely, by means of a rapid blow, although his magicians tried to warn him against it because of unfavourable omens. Chosroes had an enormous rampart of wood and earth erected, and it was pushed up to the walls of the town. His troops were to use it to climb the walls and so take the town. This type of siege attack was typical of those days. As a counter-measure the Edessans decided to dig a tunnel under the town wall, in order to set fire to the rampart from underneath before it could be finished. The tunnel was soon ready, but the ventilation in the subterranean chamber was not sufficient to feed the flames.

> In these dire straits they [the Edessans] brought up the image fashioned by God, which human hands had not made, which rather Christ, the God, had sent to Abgar because he fain had seen him. This most holy image they then brought into the tunnel, washed it with water and sprinkled this water on the heap of firewood. And lo, at once the divine Power answered the faith of those who did this, and what had before been impossible for them, was now achieved. For the sticks at once burst aflame, and turning to glowing embers in a flash, they spread it to those above them, so that the fire devoured everything around.

The interesting thing about this report is the matter-of-fact way in which the newly discovered Mandylion is linked with the Abgar story. Evagrius refers in his account to the records of the highly reliable historian Prokop of Caesarea (about 500–62); Prokop makes no mention of the miraculous image. Rather, according to Prokop, the Edessans managed to get the subterranean fire going after initial difficulties. They then distracted the attackers by catapulting fire-vessels and flaming arrows, so that Chosroes arrived at the embankment to see the danger too late, and his rampart succumbed to the flames. So how did Evagrius come to write about the Mandylion being shown as if there was no question about it? The miraculous image is introduced in his text as if it must have been immediately clear to his contemporaries what he was talking about. He must have been aware of a connection which was generally accepted in his day, linking the Abgar story and a miraculous image of Christ, 'not made by human hands', kept in Edessa.

It is interesting that Prokop presents Chosroes' assault on Edessa as a religious campaign. It was intended to show the folly of Christ's promise that the town would not be taken, as given in his letter to Abgar. This gives us some idea of the importance which was attributed to the Abgar story in the sixth century in the regions of the Middle East. If it could lead to a campaign on such a scale one can see how strongly the faith in divine protection was rooted in the native populace, and how greatly it could inflame the emotions of those of different beliefs. But we have to ask whether Prokop's interpretation of the siege as a religious campaign can rest solely on the letter of Christ. The fact that his description was written down just two years after the events speaks in favour of Prokop as a key witness to the actual events.

As we have said, Evagrius wrote after the year 593, that is at a time when the Camuliana image was known throughout the empire, having long since been transferred to Constantinople as an imperial *palladium*. And if my assumption is correct, that the origination of the Camuliana *acheiropoieton* of Christ depended on the appearance of the Edessa Portrait (which could lay claim to the highest authority because of the old Abgar tradition), then the Mandylion must have been known at the beginning of the second half of the sixth century. Whether it really was, as Evagrius says, used in action at the siege of Edessa as early as 544, must be left undecided. Wilson tried to give out Evagrius' version as historically correct, without consulting the conflicting account of Prokop,

which Evagrius expressly refers to.[17] Evagrius first followed Prokop's version in describing the Abgar story, but then introduced
the image during the events at the siege. That means that either
Evagrius was consulting a more complete version of the Prokop
text than the one that has come down to us, or that the Mandylion
had surfaced in the meantime. The latter seems to be nearer the
truth. With the image in Edessa being automatically linked with
the Abgar story, which went back to the time of Jesus, Evagrius
assumed that the miraculous image of Christ had been in the
town for centuries.

If the Mandylion was the prototype for the Camuliana image,
then it must have been discovered before 554, the time when the
Camuliana *acheiropoieton* appeared. St Ephraim (died 373), known
as the 'Syrian harp', who was living in Edessa, has not a word to
say about the Mandylion, although he reports the Abgar story in
his *Testament*. The chronicle of Josua Stylites, which was composed in Edessa in 507, makes no mention of the miraculous
image. Similarly the Edessan author Jacob of Sarug (452–521) has
nothing to say about it. We will probably not be far off if for the
time being we cautiously date the appearance of the Mandylion to
the period between 521 and 554.

But where did the picture come from? If it really was the Christ
portrait of the Abgar narrative, it must have been in the town for
centuries. Why was there no mention of it by anyone over this
enormous length of time? Why was only the correspondence
remembered, with just a dim memory of a striking vision of light
which overpowered Abgar as Thaddaeus approached? The solution to this puzzle can only be that the Mandylion was withdrawn
and concealed at some early date. Just such a thing is reported in
the sermon to have happened during its transfer to Constantinople.
Apparently the sources the author of the sermon was using offered
no chance of showing how the Mandylion was known prior to the
siege of Edessa. Probably the connection between the image and
the religious campaign seemed to him such an important turn of
fate that he shifted the discovery of the long-hidden Abgar Portrait to the time of the siege itself. In this version of the story[18] it
was the Persians who built a tunnel to get into the town. Their
ploy was discovered when a smith's copper pots started to rattle.
In their hour of need the Edessans turned to God for refuge. That
night a superhuman lady figure appeared to Bishop Eulalios, and

asked him to go and bring the 'divinely fashioned image of Christ'; the Lord would then surely work a miracle.

The bishop replied that he did not know if the image existed, and if it did, whether it was in their possession or someone else's. Then the lady of the apparition said there was such an image concealed at a certain place above the gates of the town, which she described. The bishop, convinced that the vision was genuine because it was so clear, reverently made his way to the place described, in the dawn twilight. Pushing aside the stone above the archway, he discovered the portrait of Christ. In front of the picture was a lamp, still burning, and on the stone which had been placed there for protection they found a miraculous imprint of the image of Christ.[19] The Edessans dug their own tunnel under the house of the smith where the enemy tunnel had been discovered. Just before it joined that of the Persians, the image and the holy lamp were brought into the passageway, and some oil from the lamp was sprinkled on the fire which the Persians had set against the town. The fire turned and consumed the aggressors.

It is highly unlikely that the Mandylion really was discovered during the siege in the way the sermon describes. Wilson rightly points out that if that were the case Evagrius would not have neglected to describe the dramatic scene of the discovery. The historian Ian Wilson, who relies on the Evagrius account, presents the following reconstruction. The picture was in fact walled in over one of the gateways to the town. During a devastating flood in 525 large parts of Edessa were destroyed. The river Daisan breached its banks and washed away the finest buildings and a large part of the outworks and the town walls. In a very short time the town was reduced to a scene of desolation. Justinian I, obviously recognizing the importance of the town in the south-east borders of his sphere of influence, had Edessa rebuilt immediately afterwards. As Prokop points out, it was not only the flood which damaged the town walls; they had been in a critical condition for a long time anyway. It was said that in the course of these building works 'the old Parthian gateway, which concealed the Mandylion' was to be 'moved away and its astonishing content brought to light'.[20]

One must admit this does sound plausible, and perhaps the discovery did take place in this very manner. But then Prokop would most probably have emphasized the role played by the picture during the siege, if it was already at that time been known. But this reliable contemporary witness does not mention the picture. Therefore one has to assume that the Mandylion only came to light after the retreat of the Persian troops. In any case the Edessans had another chance to carry out improvements to their protective walls. The siege itself and the assault ramps had probably caused damage to the wall at several points. Perhaps the Christ picture was discovered in the course of these new restoration works. In this case we can place the rediscovery of the Abgar Portrait in Edessa in the period between 546 (Prokop's account) and 554 (when the Camuliana picture appears). Perhaps Evagrius found it astonishing that Edessa could not be taken after so many Persian attacks, and so assumed that the Mandylion was known at the time of Chosroes' siege, with its protective influence being effective even from its place of concealment.

Abgar and the Messenger of Jesus

But how did the picture come to be hidden in this unusual place? Who could have wanted to conceal it? After all at the time of the discovery there had been an important Christian community in Edessa for over 300 years, and they certainly preserved the Abgar tradition. Why would they have had to hide the picture? The answer can only be that it had already been hidden many years before the establishment of the early Christian community at the end of the second century, and even then was only known from the stories. To explore the reason for the picture being walled up in the gateway and the time it was done, we have to go back to the time shortly after the Passion of Christ, when Thaddaeus went to visit Abgar Ukkama in Edessa.

According to the sermon, Abgar removed the statue of a Greek deity from in front of the gateway and replaced it with the Mandylion, which he mounted on a panel decorated in gold. All who passed through the gateway on entering Edessa were meant to honour the new Faith symbolized by the *acheiropoieton* of Christ. Abgar remained steadfast in the faith and his son after him, but it is said that Abgar's nephew reverted to primitive demigod worship and pagan customs. Fearing that the Mandylion might be destroyed by this nephew, the bishop of the diocese lit a lamp before the picture, which was in a semicircular, cylindrical hollow, and concealed picture and lamp with a stone.

> Then he sealed the entrance from the outside with bricks and mortar, and made the wall appear smooth again . . . Then there passed a long time, and the origins of this sacred image and its place of concealment both vanished from the memory of the people.[21]

If Edessa did in fact revert to paganism just a short time after the Christian interlude, then it is quite possible that such a precious picture would be brought to safety in this or some similar manner. That would indeed explain why there was so much confusion in the Abgar story through the following centuries; why the theme of the image only survived in a garbled form in various diverging traditions; and why only the vision of light remained and the true story of the picture came to disappear almost totally. Of course one has then to ask how it came about that the story of the correspondence was handed down, while that of the image went under. The picture must surely have left as great an impression as that of the letter of the Lord.

From all that we have ascertained so far, we can say that the correspondence between Abgar and Jesus does belong to the tradition of the early evangelizing of Edessa. According to the *History of Armenia* by Moses of Khoren, Abgar received word of the activity of Jesus from his messengers, the high dignitary Mar-Ihap, Shemashgram and his close friend Hannan. Abgar's envoys had to meet with the Roman Governor in Eutheropolis in southern Palestine, to explain the reason for a journey Abgar was planning to make to the east. In the course of their mission they had to traverse the whole of Palestine, and here they heard about the activities of Jesus. On their way back they stopped in Jerusalem and witnessed his miracles at first hand.

It is certainly possible that Abgar's attention could have been drawn to Jesus in this way. The news of the interest shown by the envoys from Edessa, and later that of their ruler, may have then spread among the disciples. They would then probably have wanted to sow the seeds of the Faith in such fertile soil as soon as the chance arose. And they could expect security for the precious image of Christ in that distant town. The contact with the messengers and the subsequent visit of a disciple to Edessa may then have been transformed into a correspondence through the embellishments of the oriental art of story-telling. Besides, it was a current theme of early Christianity to represent the Gospel itself as a heavenly letter. It is not necessary to assume that Jesus actually sent a letter to Abgar.' The exchange of messengers was made into a correspondence and included as such in the traditional story. Then what the emissary of Jesus was really carrying came to be forgotten.

It was not unusual for the early Christian Jews to go to foreign lands. The scattering of the people of Israel had already reached an advanced stage in Jesus' day. The Jewish Diaspora was dominated in many places by an intensive tradition of religious propaganda to recruit proselytes in the community of the Law. The same approach was taken by the first Christian Jews outside Palestine for the Christian mission. Thaddaeus was following this tradition when he met a community of Diaspora Jews in Edessa and set about winning them for the Christian cause. The community of Antiochia, prominent in Eastern Syria, was formed in a similar way at about this time. The picture which Thaddaeus carried with him was, however, too precious to him personally for him to show it at once to all comers. It was a time of shifting beliefs. New prophets and teachings were continually making their appearance among the people, including an increasing number of those claiming to offer the 'true' teaching of Christ; and it was not uncommon for the officially acknowledged creed to be changed with the current ruler.

It was a clever move on Thaddaeus' part to secure the confidence of influential citizens before taking up the real purpose of his mission in earnest. Through Abdu he gained admittance at the ruling house. One can imagine that after a long stay in Edessa and discussions with his close friends Tobias, Abdu and a certain Aggai, Thaddaeus decided to hand the picture to Abgar at a private audience, after he had assured himself of the man's honest intentions. Abgar, deeply moved by the *acheiropoeton* of Christ, would have gladly taken it to keep safely. Thaddaeus, who knew the picture's secret, would have made him promise to guard the picture and preserve it for posterity. It is extremely unlikely that Abgar did actually have the Mandylion put into the niche above the archway. As a new convert he would certainly not have allowed such a priceless sacred object to be exposed to the danger of being destroyed or stolen. Abgar would surely had hidden the picture in his palace, well guarded. But as a token of his new faith he may have had a tile bearing a relief of the Christ of the cloth, in the current style, inserted in the arch above one of the town gates. This was in harmony with the custom, common in the Parthian Empire, of posting figures of gods and demons at certain points on gates and walls, where they were meant to provide protection against evil spirits. A characteristic feature of these figures is their frontal aspect. The best examples of such stone reliefs in the form of a face can be found on the great temple in Hatra or on the Baalshamin temple in Palmyra, where the guardian deities Nebu and Bel are portrayed in frontal view.

Taking these events into account, one can see why special protection for the town was later attributed to the picture and also to the letter: Abgar was dealing with the 'new god' as with the indigenous guardian deities. Probably only a few learned of the presence of the Mandylion in Edessa. Still, the gateway that is mentioned does seem to have played an important role. In 383, a bishop who was showing the sights of Edessa to a pilgrim lady from Aquitaine, showed her a town gate through which the envoy had passed with Jesus' reply to the Toparch Abgar. Since that time no person who was unclean or in mourning was allowed to pass through the gate, and no one was allowed to carry a corpse through it. Other traditions say that, when an enemy appeared before the town walls, Abgar brought the letter of Christ to the gateway of the town and held it up to display it, whereupon the attackers turned and fled. Prokop reports that Christ's letter was inscribed on the town gate instead of the normal phylactery.[22] Whatever the story behind the gateway was, a vague memory linked with it remained, surviving just as a vague silhouette through the mists of time – a silhouette, though, that persisted in relating it to the story of the Mandylion.

The sermon which Thaddaeus delivered at the Beththabara square on the day after the meeting with Abgar falls, according to the *Doctrina Addai*, in the year 343 of the Edessan reckoning; that corresponds to 32 or 33 AD of our calendar. Recent studies have indicated that Jesus was crucified in 33. This would mean that Thaddaeus came to Edessa that same year.

We can identify the historical Abgar Ukkama as the fifteenth King of Edessa, the fifth of his name.[23] His reign of thirty-seven years lasted from 13 to 50 AD (according to Gutschmid's revised chronology). Even after his conversion to Christianity Abgar does not seem to have been a particularly noble chap, as far as one can tell from the scanty reports about his life. Tacitus tells how in 49 the Parthians requested that Rome send Meherdates (Mithridates) to depose the Parthian King and tyrant Gotarzes II and rule in his place. Meherdates arrived accompanied by a Roman army. Abgar, who was secretly in league with Gotarzes, received Meherdates at Zeugma, pretended to be friendly and loyal, but delayed him in Edessa with festivities long enough to give the enemy a chance to gather his troops. When the army, exhausted after the march, confronted its rivals, Abgar abandoned it. Gotarzes conquered Meherdates and crippled him to make him incapable of ruling again.[24]

Of course one should not read too much into such reports and banish Abgar's conversion to the realm of legend because of them. Tacitus was writing from the standpoint of Rome, whose protégé suffered a severe defeat, and was probably not without resentment. Besides, the fact that Abgar was converted does not mean that he immediately gave up all his old habits in the political arena. What is more, it is fair to assume that the authors describing the Abgar story were trying to show Abgar's personality in a way acceptable to Christianity for propaganda purposes.

An analysis of the major figures and events at the time of Abgar Ukkama – as mentioned in the sermon of 945, the *Doctrina Addai* and the writings connected with it – confirms the great historical reliability of the Abgar tradition. If we were dealing with a vague and mostly legendary or anecdotal tradition, we would expect certain events presented as facts to turn out to be untenable. This is certainly not the case. The statements relating to Abgar agree with those of the reliable early historiographers, such as Moses of Khoren's *History of Armenia*. The most diverse sources refer to Abgar's epithet Ukkama. Eusebius writes that Abgar V had suffered from an incurable disease. His epithet 'Ukkama' means 'the black' and this has led to speculations about the nature of his disease. Prokop saw Abgar's disease as gout – apparently basing this on the cure of the Edessan noble Abdu. The Syrians supposed it was black leprosy or, contrary to his epithet, white leprosy. It seems Abgar had made use of his illness in his attempts at arbitration in Persia. After such diplomatic intervention he struck an alliance with the King of Petra, Aretas IV, providing troops to support him in his war against Herodes Antipas, who had been disowned by Aretas' daughter because of Herodias.

The early conversion of Edessa to Christianity proved to be short-lived. After Abgar's death in 50 his son Ma'nu V ruled Edessa, and his sister's son, Sanatruq, Armenia. In 57 Ma'nu VI succeeded Ma'nu V on the throne, reverting to paganism and restoring the old sun and moon gods Nebu and Bel to their original sites.

The Portrait is Rescued

At this time there must have been an alert observer of the turn events were taking, who was also a Christian and an old confidant of Abgar V and his son Ma'nu V, and who arranged for the image of Christ to be brought to a safe place. In view of all that we have learned we have to assume that he had access to the royal house up till the time when Edessa reverted to paganism, and knew where the Mandylion was being kept. Thanks to his close contacts at court he had heard that the image of Christ above the archway was going to be destroyed and replaced by a local deity. He at once resolved to hide the Mandylion in the niche above the arch. Out of reverence to the picture he installed a lamp before it, then he simply turned the stone with the relief of the portrait of Christ round and sealed the outside of the cavity with bricks; perhaps he had the image of a heathen deity placed in front of it. The hiding place was ideal in many ways. No one would think of looking for the sacred picture there. And there was some guarantee that the picture could be preserved undamaged for half a millennium in the massive archway, which was to survive many floods and enemy onslaughts.

Who could this mysterious saviour of the Mandylion have been, the one whom the sermon of 945 calls 'the bishop of the region'? And why had he told no one of the hiding place, not even anyone in the Christian community? It cannot have been Thaddaeus, because he died while Abgar was still alive; he was buried in Abgar's ancestral tomb.[25] Whoever it was, the person obviously had to act fast. Because the picture had been a present for Abgar, it is unlikely that it was in the possession of the municipality. It is more likely to have been kept at a place to which Abgar had convenient access and which only those with special privileges could visit. The town leaders were certainly allowed to enter the room. Ma'nu VI, who brutally persecuted the new Faith, would have been out to destroy the 'hated' image of his grandfather's deity; the image which was famed for granting divine protection. A Christian leader must have got to it first, and it is not unlikely that the brave man's determined action meant the sacrifice of his life.

The Syrian and Armenian traditions mentioned, besides Addai (Thaddaeus), a certain Aggai, who played an important role in Edessa in connection with the Mandylion. We have already encountered Aggai as one of the close friends of Thaddaeus. In the tradition Aggai is described as 'a maker of golden chains and the one who made the royal headdress'.[26] As such he appears to have been not only rich but influential as well. Doubtless he came and went freely at the court and was a respected man in Edessa, on friendly terms with the ruler and the nobles of the town. Aggai became the leader of the Christan community in Edessa after Addai. A chronology of the Chaldaean patriarchs[27] allocates a twenty-three-year episcopate in Edessa to Aggai. One can assume that Addai (Thaddaeus) did not lay claim to leadership of the Edessan community. As a foreigner he would have found it difficult to exert a lasting influence on the native population. Following the initial intake resulting from his cures in the name of Christ, he would soon have chosen to entrust the leadership of the community to a respected Edessan who had converted to Christianity. Aggai was the ideal man for the job. It is likely that Aggai was made 'bishop' of Edessa just a few years after the arrival of Addai.[28] In this way his twenty-three-year episcopate would indeed have reached up to the assumption of power by Ma'nu VI. At the end of the fourth century some people were shown 'the grave of Aggai below the arch in the middle of the church, between the men and the women' in Edessa. Even Tixeront, who otherwise treats the Abgar story as a mere legendary embellishment for the founding of the Edessan Church in the second century, sees in this a genuine detail; not an invention but rather an indication that Aggai was a historical personality. We find an interesting statement in this regard in the apocryphal

Gospel of Nicodemus. This says that among the three witnesses
of the Ascension of Jesus there was a doctor named Adas and a
Levite called Aggaios.[29] Evidently the author of the Nicodemus
Gospel intended to link the Syrian tradition of the Abgar story
closely to the following of Jesus. Presenting Addai (Adas) and
Aggai (Aggaios) as witnesses of the Ascension lends the Christianity of Edessa a special authority; and it was probably also
meant to highlight these two men as the first important leader
figures of the Christian community there.

Thus Aggai was the Christian leader in Edessa whose privileges
would have enabled him to gain information about the intentions
of Ma'nu VI early enough, and quickly get the Mandylion to
safety. Ma'nu, who felt he had been cheated out of his triumph of
destroying the Christ picture, had Aggai, the only one under
suspicion, cruelly executed. The tradition says that Ma'nu demanded that Aggai make the royal headdress for him; the latter
refused his services to the apostate ruler and so was put to death.
I suppose that this rather trivial reason for his murder was a later
invention, when people no longer knew the role of the Christ
acheiropoieton. It was far more likely that Ma'nu wanted Aggai to
tell him where the picture was hidden. Aggai did not reveal his
secret; nor did he confide in anyone in the community, to avoid
endangering the priceless relic. According to Mares Salomonis he
suffered martyrdom on 30 July one year, after the rogue Ma'nu
had broken his legs.[30] Thus Aggai took his knowledge to the
grave with him, probably trusting in the divine Providence to lift
the veil and reveal the secret when the time was right.

How the Shroud Became the Mandylion

Now we have seen the whole story of the Edessa Portrait, and it is
time to ask how it is connected with the cloth now kept in Turin.
Let us recapitulate the elements of our puzzle: a shroud in Constantinople in 1203 with a 'figure of our Lord' on it; an unusual
account of a linen portrait of Christ 'not made by human hands'
which arrived in Edessa shortly after the Passion, only to remain
hidden for hundreds of years; and finally the absence of clear
reports about an image-bearing shroud throughout the whole

long period from the entombment of Jesus up to at least the end of the first millennium. In a hypothesis that is both exciting and provocative, Wilson claims[31] that the Mandylion of Edessa is none other than the Shroud itself folded so that only the face of Christ is visible! The complete cloth then only came to light in the years following the transfer of the Mandylion to Constantinople.

Wilson's reconstruction has split the Shroud researchers into two camps. Some see in his thesis a constructive contribution towards solving a historical enigma in an unusual manner; others think the thesis is just too far-fetched and devious. I have looked into the pros and cons of Wilson's arguments in some depth. Apart from several weak points and questionable conclusions, not only does his thesis remain by far the most plausible, it can actually be supported by documentary evidence. In what follows I will trace out the path of the cloth from Jerusalem to Constantinople, working on the basis of what we have described so far.

We have already seen the problems which the cloths left in the tomb must have posed for the disciples. First there was the difficulty in even picking up the linen cloths: according to Jewish custom they would have made anyone touching them impure. And then there was the image on one of them. What confusion the disciples must have been thrown into, for they belonged to the world of late Judaism, and in the Mosaic Law it is said that one should not make any image of God or man (Ex 20:4). Even the evangelists were later to abide by this, so that today we do not even have a description of Christ's appearance. Nonetheless some of them will have overcome their scruples, taking the picture on the linen to be a special sign; a sign whose importance they were probably not able to appreciate, but which was to be revealed to them one day. If their Lord and Master Jesus Christ had left the remembrance of his Passion in this way, impressed on white cloth, there had to be good reason. Perhaps, one of them may have thought, this seal of his presence in an earthly body might one day become the key to a deeper understanding of his true nature. How could they have comprehended the full spectrum of the personality of Jesus? After all they had hardly been a year at his side and must have learned so many new and baffling teachings. They were stricken with uncertainty. The cloth from the rock tomb was in a way the only tangible bequest of Jesus; a legacy which had to be respected, and above all preserved.

The followers of Jesus suspected that his departure meant that the end of time was imminent. It was in their hands that the fulfilment of the covenant now lay. For as long as Jesus was staying among them, he was not very interested in mission on a large scale, indeed he practically forbade it. He wished only to renew Judaism: 'Go not into the way of the Gentiles, and into any city of the Samaritans enter ye not: But go rather to the lost sheep of the house of Israel.'[32]

One has to remember the stressful situation the followers of Jesus found themselves in. On the one hand they were inspired by a strong motivation to give out their new teaching to the whole world as they had been instructed to; a motivation which is a normal feature of the psychology of the chosen ones of a Messianic community. On the other they had to contend with the inner battles which necessarily arose from the disparity between the promise and the reality they confronted. We cannot think of the activity of the followers of Jesus as an automatic affair, a matter of course. For many disciples, especially for those who were not counted among the inner circle, it was probably not at all clear how they were to view the Messiah. They were a colourful bunch of hopefuls in a time of numerous interweaving creeds and political forces. Some came from groups of political extremists, seeing in Jesus the liberator from the House of David; others came from valiant sects inspired by expectations of an imminent change in the world. And over all of them hung the constant fear of being exposed to a mob of persecutors and mockers, which continually fed their doubts as to whether the beliefs they had chosen were the right ones. Even the mutual support they found among themselves sufficed for these souls – so fiery and yet despairing, hungry for action and yet timid, keen on mission and yet reactionary – to make them feel confirmed in their faith, and to renew it in unflagging Messianic fervour.[33]

In such a situation it is easy to see how efforts would be made to bring the precious linen cloth to safety. One recalls the meeting with Abgar's envoy in Jerusalem and the interest of his ruler in the miraculous cures of Jesus. The choice fell on a man of firm faith, Thaddaeus. He would have had no objections to taking this 'unclean' burial cloth with him. On his mission to the pagans he was to bring it to Edessa and see that it was well looked after – no mean task. In Edessa Thaddaeus would have thought about how he could entrust a shroud to the Toparch without causing him deep offence. Perhaps this state of affairs was not as problematic as it would have seemed to a Jew. For thousands of years the Mesopotamians had been at home with their dead, as it were: they were interred under floor tiles and in the wall cavities of their homes. Still it would have seemed objectionable to Thaddaeus to just hand over the Shroud. Then there was the problem that he would hardly be able to win Abgar for Christianity for very long, used as the latter was to believing in war gods and demons, if he just laid this evidence of a 'naked, injured, dead god' at his feet. Thaddaeus most probably discussed the matter with his friend Aggai. Aggai knew the moral sensitivities of the Edessans, as well as the King's character. He was, judging from his reputation, evidently a creative man, and he soon hit upon a most brilliant idea to solve the problem: the Shroud had to be made partially unrecognizable, without causing damage to it in any way. He had it folded three times, so that first only the image of the front view, then only the head and thorax, and after the third fold only the head was visible. Then he set about constructing a worthy casing for the linen thus folded, following his hereditary craft.

We recall that Aggai was referred to as the maker of the royal headdress or crown, and crafter of golden chains. From the old Syrian texts we learn that this activity called for skill in the goldsmith's art as well as familiarity with fine fabrics, especially silks. The headgear of the kings and the high priests of Bel and Nebu were complex, usually tall, conical or cylindrical affairs. They were made from silk and muslin shawls, as precious turbans in the east still are, interwoven with golden, net-like patterns and figures. One can gain a good idea of the superb artistic quality of such headgear by looking at the statues of Parthian rulers, such as those of the kings Sanatruq and Uthal in the museums of Baghdad and Mosul. The crown of Princess Washfari is particularly impressive. It is adorned with many chains of medallions, and combined with a neck veil, and bears an image of a deity in a small, shell-shaped recess at the centre. Aggai must have applied all his skill and tried to make the visage of Christ on the folded cloth appear as precious and as impressive as he possibly could. This is another reason why Thaddaeus had to wait a while before he could submit the picture to Abgar: work of such quality could not be hurried.

Perhaps it was necessary at this stage to sew on the side-strips referred to, to shift the picture to the centre of the frame. Because the cloth was folded, it did not matter that the side-strips were not exactly the same length as the main cloth. It seems that the picture was covered with a fine golden netting, such as we know from the robes on the royal statues of Sanatruq and Uthal. How else could one have stretched the fabric on a frame without using a large glass plate, and without damaging it? A circle was left free in the middle, where the face of Jesus was. If one looks carefully at the picture on the Turin cloth, one sees that an area under the face is left clear, before coloration is found again at the level of the chest. If the face is enclosed in a circle, it appears strangely bodiless, not even a neck region is to be seen. Anyone seeing the Shroud folded in the net frame like this, would have at once thought it was a simple image of a face. Nothing suggested there was more of the picture than the round section left exposed, hidden behind the protective cover.

The transformation of the Shroud into the Mandylion was perfect; and with its elegant simplicity Aggai's work achieved an extraordinary artistic effect. He had expressed something of the transfigured Jesus, when 'his face shone like the sun' (Matt. 17:2). For when Thaddaeus presented the Mandylion, raised above his head in a gesture of reverence, to the king, the splendour which shone from the picture overwhelmed Abgar with blessed awe.

This reconstruction would be little more than a romantic artifice were it not for the fact that we have the revealing reference that first made it possible. In the sixth century text called the *Acta Thaddei* there is a description of how they thought the image had come to be formed on the cloth. It says that Jesus, desiring to wash himself, was offered a towel; and when he dried his face with it, his likeness was left on the cloth. The reference would have no further interest were it not for the fact that the word used for the 'towel' was the unusual coinage, quite unknown elsewhere, *tetradiplon*.[34] *Tetradiplon* means 'four-double' in the sense of a 'four layered' folded object; the triple folding produces four times two layers! As Bulst and Pfeiffer point out, the same thing could have been expressed quite simply by the word *oktaploun* ('eightfold', 'eight-folded'). 'The elaborate formulation can only be understood if both the "four" and the "double" mean something.' The meaning is that the Shroud was folded in the manner described, so that four double layers resulted. Modern scientific techniques have shown that the Turin cloth was in fact folded in the early days.[35]

There is, however, one very interesting point still to be cleared up: how could any author of the sixth century – at about the time when the Mandylion was rediscovered – speak of a *tetradiplon*, if really only the face was visible in its ornamental frame? One can rule out the possibility that he knew of the full contents of the casing; because then the complete picture would almost certainly have been taken out and displayed, and the whole cloth would have been known to us from then on. We have to see the term *tetradiplon* as an invaluable hint about the way the cloth brought to Edessa was mounted; and this especially because it was applied without the cloth having been taken out. Let us try to cast a little light on this enigma.

After the Edessa Portrait was discovered, many copies were made. These were circulated in the whole region of Asia Minor and copied yet again, so that the Edessan Mandylion came to be represented in numerous churches and monasteries. Unfortunately hardly any early copies have come down to us; few survived the time of the iconoclasts in the eighth and ninth centuries. When the Mandylion arrived at Constantinople it was still in its original state, 'mounted on a panel decorated with gold', as the sermon says. It was again copied many times, and the copies became a popular adornment for church niches. Inspiring depictions in frescoes, illuminated manuscripts and icons have come down to us from this period. The copyists were very careful to reproduce the original as exactly as possible. This basic principle of Byzantine sacred art allows us to infer the original from the copies.

The commonest form of representation shows the bodiless face of Christ, ringed by a circle. On most of the pictures the neck is missing, as on the Shroud. Outside the circle one repeatedly finds a net structure of criss-cross lines with repeating decorations in the interstices. Of special interest are the fringes which are to be seen on most of the Mandylion copies. These fringes are often shown at the side edges, and sometimes on the upper and lower borders. The fringes end in thickened sections, and are clearly meant to represent nails (see Plates 37–39).[36] One of the oldest copies of this type (1077) is found on a fresco in the Shakli Kilise in Cappadocia, although unfortunately it is not very well preserved.

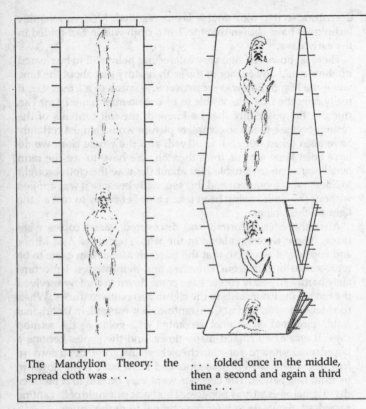

The Mandylion Theory: the . . . folded once in the middle,
spread cloth was . . .   then a second and again a third
                                time . . .

*Fig. 2. Folded in four (eight layers), the cloth of over 4 m was reduced to a
manageable size, shifting the face to the central area. The new 'Mandylion' was
mounted on a panel and enclosed in a frame with a kind of netting.*

Thus, without running into any special difficulties, we can
suggest the following picture of how the Mandylion was framed.
The Shroud was folded into four double layers. Aggai took the
greatest care to avoid damaging the cloth in any way. He probably supported the long linen with a lining of fine silk material on
the inner surface, so that he could tauten it better and at the same
time prevent it being damaged at the fold areas. Under the uppermost layer, and perhaps in various layers below it too, he drew a
network of strong but fine threads. These appeared as a short

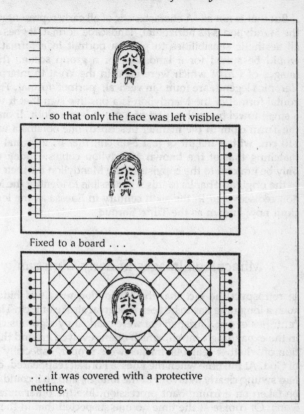

. . . so that only the face was left visible.

Fixed to a board . . .

. . . it was covered with a protective
netting.

fringe at two, or possibly at all four, sides. They were fixed with
golden decorative nails on a wooden panel. Over this came the
precious net-like covering. If there was a frame, then it would
only have been over the wooden panel, not on the Mandylion,
otherwise the fringe with the nails would not have been visible.
In this way an observant onlooker, allowed to examine the Mandylion, could see when looking from the side at one of the fringe
edges that it must be a large cloth folded several times. Only thus
can the otherwise inexplicable epithet *tetradiplon* have originated.

But that is not all. A characteristic of all early representations of the Mandylion is its horizontal, 'landscape' format. It goes against all aesthetic sensibilities to paint a portrait in a format which would be suited for a landscape or a group scene. Thus the images of Christ which were used in the West to interpret the Veronica legend, are found in vertical, 'portrait' format. The horizontal format of the Mandylion is a positive sign that it was not a small towel but rather part of a much larger cloth. If one folds the Turin cloth in the manner described, one obtains a width of 110 cm, with a height of just 54.5 cm; that is, a format closely matching that of the known Mandylion copies. Today we can only be grateful to the copyists of the Mandylion for their fidelity to the original. Thanks to this it is possible to identify the Mandylion rediscovered in the sixth century in Edessa as the length of cloth now known as the Turin Shroud.

Miraculous Images in Early Christianity

In retrospect the fact that the Mandylion remained hidden for such a long time has to be seen as a great stroke of luck. The early centuries of our Christian era were marked by vigorous conflicts in the expanding Church, which often revolved around the question of whether religious images were proper, especially images of God. At the time when the Edessa Portrait reappeared, opinion had swung clearly in favour of the images, and so it could at once be taken on a triumphant procession, like the other miraculous icons. Of course at the time no one suspected that in the eighth century a vigorous counter-movement was to develop, known as the Iconoclasm and that the Jesus portrait would again be in danger of being destroyed.

Following its discovery, the Edessa Portrait exerted an important influence on the received idea of what Jesus looked like. This point is tremendously important when we come to consider the question of whether the image on the Turin cloth really did exemplify the form of Jesus in a decisive way for all later times. We will deal with this point in what follows. One cannot stress too strongly the importance of this question in the field of Christological studies. Hence I will briefly go over the roots of the image question in the history of ideas, and especially the evaluation of 'God-made' or 'Heaven-sent' images.

When Thaddaeus handed Abgar the divine portrait, in one sense the recipient was not overly surprised. Miraculous images were not unheard of or totally unknown; they formed part of the oldest mythological traditions. The God-sent picture was one among a continuous series of tangible messages from heaven which have accompanied humanity since the first stirrings of religious sentiment. From the dawn of history the human individual has begun to ascribe a place for the celestial powers true to the name: the mysterious beings which influence all the phenomena of nature were felt to live somewhere over the horizon. The eagle, which dares to venture farthest on the winds, was taken by the early tribes as a messenger of the gods. The celestials sent down signs of their benevolence and wrath from above: sun, rain, storms, snow, lightning and thunder. On the firmament of night they penned their history in trails of stardust. Whatever man experienced of the gods came from above – from beyond the dome of blue where the view merges with the infinite.

The gods, who had sent signs from ages past, continued to reveal their presence in this way as the consciousness of humanity followed its evolutionary course. But the meanings of their messages were constantly interpreted anew. We now know that the enigmatic stones falling from the skies to the earth – the meteorites – have been invested with an aura of the sacred from earliest times. They were thought to be tossed straight from the dwelling-place of the gods to the earth. The Australian aborigines still believe that the vault of the heavens is made of crystal stone – stones of light. If fragments of this break off and fall to earth, they become heavy and dark. But they still keep their celestial brilliance occultly present. Thus in the last pre-Christian millennium meteoric iron was thought by Iron Age peoples to be imbued with a sacred power. The 'celestial metal' was a sign from the Beyond, an 'image of transcendence' as the historian of religions Eliade puts it.

Since the flowering of classical antiquity coincides with the Iron Age, it is not surprising that the idea of a transcendent divine image in the form of meteorites has persisted as a topos for many centuries. When the Romans came to Pessinus to collect the image of the great mother goddess worshipped there, they were given a stone which was said to have fallen from the sky. Appian, the second-century Roman historian and imperial procurator in Egypt, attributes a meteoric origin to this stone. The only idol that Islam has retained from the time of the old Arabian paganism is likewise a meteoric stone, revered to this day in the Kaaba in Mecca.

In classical antiquity these beliefs were continued with the so-called *diipetei* – images sent from the gods to Earth, whose sacred power remained undiminished and so gave them a special protective function. The newly developing Christianity had to take a stand towards these ideas, because the Heaven-sent images of gods continued to play an important role in the popular folk traditions. They seemed to conflict with the divine order not to make any image of that which is in Heaven. The young Church actually had a tough battle.

On the one hand there were the folk beliefs, pressing for a graphic representation of the Divinity to make it a living presence; on the other hand the Mosaic law had to be respected. A way had to be found between the two extremes – a way which could be theologically justified. Were it not for the embodiment of God as Christ, the decision would doubtless have come out against graphic forms for good. But could one hold that Jesus was not to be portrayed simply as he was in his human form? The Christian protagonists of images always came back to the fact that it was precisely the act of God becoming man which made possible his representation in an image.

In the early days of Christianity those in favour of images were already lined up against those who were not. Up until the fifth century we find no clear position with regard to the provision of religious images. Many different opinions, often contradictory, governed the views about images of Christ. On the one hand the importance of his bodily image came to be played down, under the influence of certain sects (especially Gnostic ones); on the other hand it is precisely among the Gnostics that we find the earliest images of Christ – in the first half of the second century Church leaders were already warning that the Gnostic 'heretics' were worshipping images. Hippolytos, for example, accused the Sethians of dogmatically appropriating for themselves a heathen painting in Phyla. Irenäus accused the Carpocratians of possessing painted and metal images of Christ, to which they offered worship as in the Greek schools of philosophy. On the other hand the pagans accused the Christians of having no temples, altars or statues. The soul of the faithful person, the apologists countered, was the real holy temple, altar and image of God.

Nevertheless Gnosticism was basically opposed to images, for images pertained to the material world, which in Gnostic thought was subject to the opponent of the good God of the spiritual world. So images of the body could have no religious value for the Gnostics; they would only add strength to the dominion of dark powers. Any worship focused on the corporeal would hinder true gnosis ('knowledge'), and thus the liberation from the human vale of tears. For the Gnostic to worship God in an image was tantamount to blasphemy; for did they not search, as the apocryphal Gospel of Thomas says, 'for the treasure which passeth not and which lies where no greedy moths can enter and no worm gnaw at it' (log. 76) – that is, only in the realm of the Spirit?

The early Christian Gnosticism was subject to a transformation when it was used as the basis for a renewal of the Platonic philosophy, known today as Neoplatonism, first by Plotinus (around 205–70). From this time on the image worshippers received philosophical and theological support. Plotinus' lines of thought are of special significance for the theology of the image. Plotinus presents 'The One' (God, 'The Good') as the source of all being. This One scatters itself, by radiating out into the indeterminate darkness of matter. The world spirit, the world soul, and all life, proceeded from that by emanations. The process of coming forth is a graded descent. First the spirit radiates from the One like the warmth and light from the sun. The Platonic ideas exist in that. As the intermediary between the world of ideas and the world of senses it creates the soul. Plotinus conceived the corporeal world and matter as reflections of the radiations of the One in the non-being. The soul, as the intermediary, receives the ideas from the spirit and maintains the images of the physical world here according to the archetypal images there. This radiation is in a way made psychologically known for the human individual as the longing for the divine origin which flowers in the human soul – the spiritual urge. Here Plotinus is indebted to the Gnostics. His view that the One can be attained in the ecstatic vision goes back to Plato. In this way the person is freed from the self-deception of 'individual' existence and finds his original primal nature, his real self, his inner homeland.

Neoplatonism improved on the Gnostic concept of opposites. Where for the Gnostics the soul was subject to the constant struggle between two rulers – one of the spirit and one of the world – the new thought, by its philosophical refinement, promised relief. Neoplatonism denied any absolute evil and so avoided the insurmountable dualism. Evil was seen simply as graded degrees of distance from God. In this philosophical system gnosis becomes a stepping on the path up steps of mystical knowlege as instructed in the teaching – back to the primal unity, to God. According to the Neoplatonic view the material world is arranged as a 'golden chain', which reaches from the topmost being and from the one which is beyond even existence, down to the last shimmer of being in matter, joining plane with plane in their essence. Ascending the chain the beings climb back to the summit of all being.

If Christianity was marked in the early days mostly by the confrontation with Gnostic thought, it was later moulded by the dynamic tension with Neoplatonism. As the intellectuals turned more and more from the Gnosis and towards Neoplatonism, so the views about the permissibility of religious works of art changed. It is a result of this process of evolution in the history of ideas that the hostility to images was gradually replaced by their free worship.

The Neoplatonist could recognize in a skilful image the embodied form of an inner vision and thus the transparency of the material world to the luminosity of spirit. The picture was for him or her a reminder of the primal image which manifested in the corporeal plane following the graded descent. And the Neoplatonic teaching of emanations was perfectly suited to properly placing the 'heaven-sent' images, the *acheiropoieta*. Already in the third century Plotinus and Porphyry (234–304) had devoted some writings of their own specifically to the images of deities. Porphyry's disciple Iamblichus (around 250–330) distinguished between artifically produced images and those that fall from Heaven. He claimed that the Divinity could reside even in artifically created images; that was for him the sole distinguishing criterion between such images and ordinary, profane ones.

When the Emperor Julian (361–63) was found encouraging Neoplatonism more than the newly developing state Church of Christianity, for which he was named Apostata ('the deserter') by the Christians, a relapse to paganism was feared. In reality, in the course of his reign of just three years the discussion of Neoplatonic views and ideas proved fruitful for Christianity. In subsequent years they gained more and more in importance among the teachers of the Church.

There is, however, a second historical line which is of importance for later image worship. While the Neoplatonic views are mostly of a theoretical nature and fundamental to the development of the theology of the icon (image), the second line of tradition grew out of the emotional folk beliefs, from the worship of relics, which in turn drew on the tendency to acknowledge the dimension of the magical.

We have identified touch as the key element in the formation of legends about the *acheiropoieton* of Edessa and the face-towel of Veronica; it is also at the basis of the early beginnings of relic worship. It preserves some remnant of the old heathen beliefs, going back to the animistic view of the world. The magical worldview of this level of consciousness rests on two fundamental principles which guided the religious and moral sentiments and also provided explanations for diseases and accidents. The first we would describe as the law of similarity, whereby like gives rise to like. The consciousness mingles similarity and identity and so projects a complex pattern of magical relationships. The second law, linked with this one, we will call contagiousness. Here adjacency or proximity is mingled with identity. Objects which were once in contact together are viewed as remaining connected for ever.

It is this turn of consciousness which allows us to understand the old magical customs, such as for example the sorcery of puppets, where the 'victim' became identical with a figurine; or the conception that in a part of a person, such as a lock of hair, the whole person, including the person's psychological nature, was present. And it is precisely this fact which is behind the origins of the belief in relics. If even today one still sees believers touching or kissing the shrines of relics, it is a genuine expression of the active magical consciousness that is still active – especially in the archetypal, deeper emotional levels. To this subliminal mode of thought a fragment of the person revered counts for as much as the whole person. And this holds as much for the 'false' relic as for the 'genuine' one. The former is no different from the genuine article if it has been touched to it just once. Thus countless relic fragments could come to be scattered widely, relics which had only obtained their status by being brought into contact with the (alleged) original object (otherwise they were just profane objects similar in some way). What seems quite ridiculous when looked at in the cold light of reason, is here a matter of course: the thing which 'catches the contagion' of the aura of the sacred is genuine, and so effective in a numinous way. Infection by the sacred was envisaged as a contiguous series of touches: from the saint, who of course was himself in touch with God, through his bones or his possessions on to a humble stroking of the fingertips over the reliquary, or even over a statue of the saint, which is deemed to be favoured by 'inwardly touching' the being of the one portrayed.

The taste for such relic worship was great among the common people, and it was the real problem that the opponents of images had to deal with. Relics were excepted from the items of prohibited worship. In this way the cult was able to develop rapidly among the people, desiring tangible objects to worship. The starting point was the worship of the Cross, which became established very early on as *the* symbolic image for Christianity. Cross worship received a special boost from the symbolic identification of the instrument of Christ's Passion with the *labarum*, the victor standard of Constantine. On coins in the third decade of the fourth century we find for the first time the standard in the form of a cross, as an image known throughout the Empire, images which one could say were to pass through everyone's hands. Soon after this we hear mention in the pilgrims' reports of the worship of the column of the scourging of Christ and the 'burial cloth'.

One of the earliest hymns in praise of the relics has come down to us from Gregory of Nyssa (334–94), who describes in almost ecstatic passages the joy of those having the good fortune to touch the relics. The martyr's virtue, Gregory says, survives in the complete body. Could not a complete image of the martyr preserve it too, perhaps in a more perfect way than just a little piece of him? André Grabar, one of the leading experts on the history of Byzantine art, has shown how the cult of relics was indeed gradually dominated and replaced by the cult of images.[37] Soon the attitude of the faithful towards icons could not be distinguished from their attitude to relics. Both forms are direct descendants of the magical world-view. In the fifth century there arose the custom of adorning the reliquaries with iconographic forms; the image of the saint revered was permanently linked to his or her relic. The icon was not yet sacred in its own right, but with such worship and the magical setting in which the religious images were seen, the cult of the images started gaining in strength right from the time of its inception.[38]

Towards the end of the fourth century, at the time of the great Cappadocian Fathers, we find the cult of the Cross and the relics in full bloom. So it is not surprising that pictorial representation was already an issue. They dealt with it along with their criticism of Neoplatonism. Gregory of Nazianzus (329–90) and Basil (330–79), still viewed the soul as 'a part of the Divinity'; while Gregory of Nyssa described it as a creature which is destined to become permeated by God through the action of Grace. With the radiance of God's Grace pouring into it, it becomes like a mirror, which takes the light into itself without losing its identity in the light. Gregory of Nyssa understood Christanity in a fundamentally Neoplatonic way. As far as images were concerned, the Cappadocian Fathers took a pragmatic approach. They were considered to be helpful didactic instruments for the uneducated masses. The first to go beyond their educational value was Gregory of Nyssa. For him religious images were able to assist in the mystical ascent to intimacy and communion. Absorption in the one represented not only stimulated the religious education of the beholder and his emotions, the image could actually become a medium through which the faithful may attain to the Divinity.

It seems that Gregory, the father of mysticism, was speaking in terms of Neoplatonic thought given an inward, spiritual turn. And indeed towards the end of the fifth century the writings of Pseudo-Dionysius were to take up the idea of the image as a channel of communication with God, and it assumes an important place in his mystical Neoplatonic teaching.

The image as an aid and guide leading from the visible to the invisible – this now became the central argument of the protagonists. It was not difficult to go on to speculate further on this basis: the Neoplatonic idea of the hierarchical structure of the worlds, which now allowed a graded reascent of the soul to God through the means of the image, could be applied in a reverse form as a theory of the Presence of God made immanent in the image. By a gradual descent God becomes imaged and reflected in forms of the inferior spheres, finally in the objects of this physical plane. As such these objects can be named icons ('images').

Thoughts such as these were sometimes taken to such extremes that systems were derived which were no longer in harmony with the Scriptures, fully surrendering to the animistic, magical worldview. Some iconolaters (image worshippers) even toyed with the idea that an image was the actual residence of the person portrayed.

Augustine (354–430) made the first reference to Christians in the act of revering images. He mentioned among those who had introduced superstitious practices into the Church those who were worshipping the images and the tomb of Christ. And in about 440 we learn from Theodoret of images of St Simeon Stylites which were placed at the entrances of Roman workshops, with an apotropaic function.

Despite the urgent need for a theological solution to the image question, after the fourth century a further two hundred years had to pass before systematic efforts were made to develop a theory of images.

Developments in the Image of Christ

The decisive turning-point which marked the transition from the largely image-hostile early centuries to a positive evaluation of the images of Christ, had already taken place under Constantine the Great (306–37). The sentence from Psalm 45:2, 'Thou art fairer than the children of men: grace is poured into thy lips: therefore God hath blessed thee for ever', provided the leitmotif for the contemplation of Christ. Here the adoration of the image of Christ has its origins.

But the portrayals of Jesus from the time of Constantine show how unsure the traditions about his appearance still were. The artists seemed to be groping in the dark, and often drew from images of pagan deities when presenting Jesus' features. They also copied the way philosophers were portrayed in the Greek world. Even the Emperor's portraits came to serve as a model for the early icons. This was only to be expected because the Emperor's portraits, identified with the person portrayed, were the object of a quasi-religious cult. The *imago clipeata* – the round shield-like portrait of the Emperor on the legions' standard – was even carried along during processions on certain occasions.

In the case of the icon of Peter in the monastery of St Catherine (sixth–seventh centuries), one can clearly recognize the picture's origins among the Emperor portraits. Above the central motif three medallions are to be seen, with Christ in the middle, Mary on the right and John on the left. This form of composition corresponds exactly to the secular icons of the ruling houses: John replaces the consul, Christ the Emperor and Mary the Empress.

To follow the developments in the image of Christ from its early beginnings to the final form is a most satisfying task for the art historian. With the exception of a portrait of Jesus from the middle of the third century in Dura Europos, Syria, we find most of the oldest surviving pictures of Jesus – from the late third and early fourth centuries – in the catacombs of Rome and Naples.

We find a great variety of Jesus portraits up until the sixth century. Then we encounter a remarkable and decisive change, when the style of Jesus' face was laid down for all later times. This event is strikingly apparent to anyone who flicks through the illustrated books on early Christian art. In the early period we always see Jesus as a clean-shaven youth, often following the type of the Good Shepherd – the commonest form of portrait in the Roman catacombs. Numerous sculptures have similarly preserved this style. The facial features were treated in diverse ways. The hair is now short, now long again and cap-like; on some pictures it is parted in the middle. In these early pictures one can clearly see how the pagan iconography was assimilated for Christian use. The philosopher became Christ, an apostle or a prophet. Scenes of the apotheosis were transformed to become depictions of the Ascension. And the Good Shepherd had his origins in the pastoral style of the period.

In the history of art we find that the early Christian sarcophagi provide an especially fruitful field for images of Christ. Besides the Good Shepherd, there is the type of the teacher or philosopher, and then that of the world judge. And here we also find an increasing number of scenes from the Gospel accounts. Jesus is almost always portrayed as young and clean-shaven. On an ivory cabinet kept in the Museo Civico in Brescia, a relief of Jesus is to be seen which portrays him with rounded boyish features, a cap-like fringe across the forehead. Very similiar to this is the figure on an ivory table showing the scene of the Ascension, in the Bavarian National Museum in Munich (*c.* 400 – see Plate 40).

Besides the unbearded type, isolated examples of bearded Christ images are found, mostly in the post-Constantine period, such as in the catacombs of Peter and Marcellinus or the famous portrait of the Commodilla catacomb. In the art of the late fifth and early sixth centuries, showing Byzantine influence, still no uniform Jesus type is to be found. In Sant'Apollinare Nuovo, Ravenna, Jesus is portrayed standing before Pilate with a long, bearded countenance (c. 500–26); while the beardless Jesus of the upper mosaic frieze in the nave of the same church, where he is shown in the act of blessing the loaves and fishes, appears somehow feminine with his copious long hair beside his short-haired disciples. This portrayal, with the strange melancholy look, reminds one of the Majestas-Domini picture of Hosios David (also beardless) in Thessaloniki (before 500). The enthroned Christ of Santa Pudenziana in Rome, on the other hand (c. 400) shows us an older Jesus, gazing into endless space.

With Emperor Justinian I, whose reign lasted thirty-eight years (527–65), we enter an epoch when there was an immense upsurge of image worship. And at this time we notice a striking change in the style of the Christ portrait; a change which was to introduce into art the 'true countenance' of Jesus for all coming times. The expansion of the cult of images continued until the time of the Iconoclasm (726–843), and after emerging victorious from this it was again taken up with undiminished fervour. In this period it becomes more and more common to find pilgrims in the Holy Land writing about images, where before we heard no mention of them. We have already heard from Antoninus of Placentia (c. 570) about the Christ image of Memphis 'not made by human hands'. He also says he worshipped a picture of Jesus in Pilate's praetorium which was supposed to have been painted during his lifetime. The ground was prepared for the triumphant advance of the Christ image. It was allowed to stand as an equal of the relics and was valued as an aid to help the soul soar in the divine skies. Indeed, it even surpassed the relics, for the way the image evoked the presence of God by its perfect portrayal of his Incarnation, was unexcelled. It is during Justinian's reign that we observe the reappearance of the Edessa Portrait and its many miraculous and artistic copies, such as the *acheiropoieton* of Camuliana.

After the appearance of the *acheiropoieta* and their public exhibitions, the faithful no longer feared to let their image worship, long pursued in secret, come out in public. We hear plenty about it in the late sixth and seventh centuries. Everywhere the sagas and legends tell of the numerous miraculous images that were appearing; besides the *acheiropoieta* there was Luke's image of the Madonna, icons which shed blood, those which healed the sick, and even those which brought the dead back to life. The icon as cult image had won through against all the opposition.

Without question the most highly revered image of the period was the *acheiropoieton*, by which one could almost say God himself had settled the image affair. Indeed the 'God-made' images were absorbed into the superstructure of the theological teachings in this very sense. Their epithet *acheiropoieton* itself emphasizes their unimpeachable status. The word has only been found in Christian literature. It seems to have first been used for everything which is not made by human hand, such as nature itself. Closer study, however, shows the term to be taken directly from Neoplatonic philosophy. According to this view, all earthly things have their true archetypes in Heaven. Because they are formed purely by the spirit of God, they are called *acheiropoieta*. It was mainly the Alexandrian church fathers who followed this up with the assertion that God had created and also artistically formed everything. Later Methodius (788–847) even compared God to an artist and the world to a statue whose beauty is admired by men.[39] An image is only an *acheiropoieton* if it originates miraculously. There is another reason why this term is noteworthy. The use of the term was intended to lift the miraculous Christ images above all possible taint of idolatry, by presenting them as 'not belonging to the realm of art'.

In this period the miraculous images of Christ sometimes assumed peculiar forms. It was said that the hands, chest and face of Christ were visible on the pillar of the scourging in Jerusalem, corresponding to the way he had been tied to it. Dobschütz suggests that one imagine the imprints of Christ as depressions in the stone, for according to one account by our most informative pilgrim Antoninus, the faithful used to make wax pressings, which they wore around their necks as amulets against diseases. Dobschütz errs here by translating a Latin word too freely without any corroboration.[40] In fact it was probably a case of paints applied to the pillar by some inventive person to exploit the demand of the faithful for miraculous signs. Due to the ravages of time and the repeated superstitious stroking of the image on the pillar, it became more and more faded. Forty years before Antoninus the pilgrim Theodosius had still been able to see the hands, chest and face of Christ on the pillar in the house of Caiaphas, while Antoninus of Placentia could only make out hands and chest. Later it seems that only the hand-prints remained visible.

Acheiropoieta are particularly well suited to providing direct and lasting mementoes of the incarnate God. For they themselves originated by an act of reproduction which echoes the miracle of the Incarnation on a lower level. In fact the origin of the Camuliana image was described as a kind of new incarnation, and Camuliana itself celebrated as the 'new Bethlehem'.[41]

When the Mandylion surfaced in Edessa there were a number of strong Church communities in the town. The Chalcedonian-Greek Church, with close connections to Constantinople, confronted the Monophysite and Nestorian branches. Nestorianism was based on the teaching of the patriarch Nestorius (381–*c.* 451), who claimed that the divine and human natures were separate in Christ. This teaching was condemned at the third Ecumenical Council at Ephesus. Under the influence of the patriarch Cyril of Alexandria, who opposed Nestorius, Monophysitism developed as an opposing theological system. The Monophysites taught that there were not two natures, the divine and the human, joined in Christ, but only the one undivided nature (mono-physite) of God made flesh. Monophysitism also came into disrepute and was stamped as a heresy at the Fourth Ecumenical Council at Chalcedon (451).

Interestingly, there are strongly Monophysitic Syrian sources which concern the Edessa Portrait. These are the chronicles of two Monophysite patriarchs, Michael the Great and Abulfaradj bar 'Ebrajâ. They hardly mention the Greek community of Edessa, so we can assume that the Mandylion was at that time in the possession of the Monophysites. This is surprising, because they rejected religious images, especially those of Christ, holding that a portrait can only ever show the visible form of *one* kind of nature, not the indivisible whole they taught. The Mandylion was probably originally in the keeping of the Chalcedonian-Greek community of the imperial Church. Eulalius, the person who was said to have discovered it by a vision, is revealed by his name to be a Greek. Nonetheless the value of the image of Christ 'not made by human hands' was so great, especially because it was sent to the town by Jesus himself, that all the Edessan churches probably wanted to have it, regardless of their stance towards the image question. Of course they could not all have it. So we find that the sermon speaks of three miraculous images of Christ in Edessa. We have to assume that two of the churches had copies and one the original.

However, after Edessa was taken by the Arabs in 639, it appears that the genuine Edessa Portrait did actually come into the possession of the Monophysites. The wealthy noble Athanasius, from the Gumäens family which had always been Monophysite, who enjoyed the favour of the Caliph as tutor of Prince Abdul-Aziz, had numerous churches built. In one of these he had a portrait of Christ installed which he had obtained from the Arabs for an enormous sum. To be on the safe side he hid the Mandylion between two stones in the crypt, to protect it from his brother believers, who continued to take a hostile stance to the Greeks' cult of images. The peculiar term 'Mandylion' was most probably coined at the time of Arab rule in Edessa. It appears to be a euphonic adaptation of the Arab word *mandil*, which refers to a veil, towel or handkerchief. The Arab term in turn derives from the Latin *mantele*, towel. A *mantele*, in colloquial Latin a *mantellum*, could mean a cloak or coat. Thus it is quite possible that the manner of fixing the Mandylion on the wooden panel which we have described earlier was known to them – that it was actually quite a large cloth, and they chose this term for this reason.

It is interesting to note that the Mandylion appears on miniatures of the thirteenth century as a long cloth. In a Paris manuscript the tale of Abgar is accompanied by twenty-four miniatures, including one which shows the discovery of the Mandylion beside the gateway in Edessa. On the illustration the cloth is drawn out from the niche in a way which suggests that it is quite large (see Plate 31).[42]

A miniature from the chronicle of John Scylitzes, which is preserved in the National Library at Madrid, depicts the arrival of the Edessan Mandylion in Constantinople. Here too one cannot avoid the impression that Constantine VII Porphyrogennetus was given the Mandylion in the form of a long, folded cloth (see Plate 41).

After the appearance of the Edessan *acheiropoieton* of Christ, the discussion of images took on a completely new quality. The portrait was repeatedly referred to for support in the debate. Not only did the news of the holy image spread with great rapidity, it is also quite apparent that the image itself did, too. *En face* depictions of Christ as the 'true countenance' of the Edessa Portrait are to be found everywhere in the sixth century: on ampullae in Monza, on bracelets, buckles, decorative discs and pendants not only in the Christian lands of the Mediterranean, but also in Gaul, in the Rhineland and in southern Germany.[43]

The Original Image of Christ in Edessa

In the sixth century all the unbearded, rounded or feminine Jesus types disappeared suddenly as did the elements of Roman or Hellenic style. What remained was the Jesus portrait with large eyes, long face, distinctive eyebrows, a striking long nose, upper lips and chin beard (often parted in two), and long wavy hair with a parting in the middle; in brief, the face familiar to us from the Turin cloth.

This was the period when the image worshippers were in the clear. But the theologians of the image would not agree to just any picture said to represent Jesus. If the presence really was to be invoked in the material image, they had to see that the icons sanctioned by the authorities came as close as possible to the true appearance of the Lord. And they could not rely on reports of Jesus' contemporaries about his facial features and figure – there were none.

In the midst of this debate the Edessa Portrait made its entrance. Here was a picture bearing the features which the Lord himself had imprinted on the linen! The authorities in icon theology first had to establish whether a miraculous image of Jesus of this nature did in fact exist. That would not only mean that Jesus was portrayable, but also that he himself had produced the image and so given his approval for it. To keep the cult of images on the right track, it was important that the original was adhered to as far as possible. What was more natural than to take the details of anatomy and physiognomy direct from the Mandylion? The numerous copies which were cropping up everywhere soon spread the features of the 'true countenance', and it must have been evident to every artist that he had to follow the model of the picture on the 'face cloth' when designing a portrait of Jesus. In fact, the fascinating hypothesis which we are considering holds that the image on the Turin cloth, known as the Mandylion of Edessa, was the key to the most crucial change in the iconographic representation of Christ – the prototype of the 'true picture of Jesus'.

Individual artists were probably commissioned to copy the Mandylion, keeping true to the original, and specially requested to try and do justice to it. We have an example of such a copy from as early as the sixth century, which is indeed remarkable. It is a portrait of Jesus in a medallion without a halo – also absent on the Shroud figure – which matches the image of the cloth down to its details. The half-length portrait is found on a silver vase from Emesa (near Edessa) which is now kept in the Louvre in Paris (see Plate 32). On the vase, a number of apostles are also pictured on the medallion. One very telling fact is the way the artist shows all the apostles in side view with bowed heads; only the Christ figure is strictly frontal, and treated in a different way stylistically from the other figures. One has the impression that the artist painted the apostles vividly from his imagination, but for the portrait of Jesus he had to follow a model which restricted his artistic freedom. This model was most probably based on the Mandylion.

Another picture which strikes me as most interesting in this connection is a silver paten from Riha in Syria (565–78), on which Christ is seen at the Last Supper, portrayed twice (see Plate 33). Again the two portraits of Christ appear rather stiff and formal, in their similarity to the Shroud picture, while the features of the apostles' faces are lively, vivid, sometimes even grimace-like.

In the monastery of St Catherine in Sinai there is one of the most beautiful sixth-century icons of Christ. It is without equal in its technical perfection and artistic expressiveness. Looking at the face, one feels that the painter tried to bring to life the shadowy image of the Shroud, true to the original (see Plate 42).

In the 1930s Paul Vignon turned his attention to the role played by the Shroud image in the history of art, and one day he discovered a peculiar geometrical figure between the eyebrows on a portrayal of Christ in the Roman catacomb of Pontianus. It was a U-shaped mark. Vignon was very surprised, because the line served no purpose and did not seem to have anything to do with the rest of the painting. He was more excited when he realized that he had seen this mark at the same place on the Shroud face! It is not clear how it got there. It most probably does not belong to the actual features of the 'Man of the Shroud'. In any case the researcher had opened up a new field of study. He had already noticed that the portraits of Christ from the sixth century onwards were remarkably similar to the Shroud face. But now he had a new piece of evidence, worthy of further pursuit. Had an artist, authorized for this sort of work, been given the order to copy the Shroud image so exactly that he even included irregularities, folds, accidental and mechanical alterations on the surface? And were his copies then distributed widely, to serve as 'true likenesses of Jesus' as the standard model for religious iconography? The idea was at least not too far-fetched. Vignon did not yet know about the transformation of the cloth into the Mandylion and the special repute of authenticity it enjoyed because of this, as *acheiropoieton*. He worked on the assumption that the Shroud was well known at that time. Of course in its folded form it would have had the same authority, owing to its preservation of the 'true likeness' of the Lord.[44]

Vignon reasoned that if the mysterious copyist did in fact proceed with such meticulous attention to detail, so that he even reproduced lines and marks whose significance he did not understand, then one should examine the face on the Shroud for all its conspicuous and not-so-conspicuous characteristics, and find whether these recur in the new image of Christ of the Justinian period. Vignon, and after him Edward Wuenschel, identified no less than twenty special features which a hypothetical Byzantine artist could have copied for his 'true likeness' of Jesus.[45] Wilson accepts only fifteen of these, because the Shroud image is so faint that several can no longer be identified with certainty. These are as follows:

1. A horizontal stripe on the forehead
2. The U-form or three-sided 'square' on the forehead
3. A V-shape at the bridge of the nose
4. A second V-shape inside feature number 2
5. A raised right eyebrow
6. An accentuated left cheek
7. An accentuated right cheek
8. An enlarged left nostril
9. An accentuated line between nose and upper lip

10. A heavy line under the lower lip
11. A hairless area between lip and beard
12. The fork to the beard
13. A horizontal stripe across the throat
14. Heavily accentuated, owlish eyes
15. Two loose strands of hair falling from the apex of the forehead[46]

Correspondences with a number of these specific attributes are already found on the few surviving icons of the sixth and seventh centuries, for example on the icon of Christ at St Catherine's monastery, on the Emesa vase, on a seventh-century icon of the martyrs Sergius and Bacchus, and finally on coins – for at the end

Fig. 3. At least fifteen different, unmistakable features can be identified on the face on the cloth, which are also found on the portraits of Jesus made by Byzantine artists.

of the seventh century Justinian II (685–95 and 705–11) introduced a revolutionary innovation. He had his coins struck with the portrait of Christ, with the inscription *Rex Regnatium*, 'king of kings', and this early image also shows many of the distinguishing marks worked out by Vignon and Wuenschel (see Plates 45 and 46).

With the face of Christ appearing on coins, the cult of images was now not only permitted, but even in a sense arranged politically by the state. From this time on the picture was carried to the remotest corners of the empire on the coins. After the Iconoclasm, the emperors incorporated the portrait of Christ on the *solidus* (gold coin), and so confirmed the right to image worship. On the coins of, for example, Michael III (842–67), Basileius I (867–86), and Constantine VII Porphyrogennetus (913–59), many details of the portrait in Vignon's catalogue of features can again be found.

In recent years Alan Whanger has invented a method to show the correspondences with the image on the cloth in a striking manner. He uses two slide projectors, one displaying the face of the man of the Turin cloth, the other precisely superimposing over this a picture for comparison – such as one from a Byzantine coin. By using a polarizing filter, a rapid or gradual transition from one picture to the other can be made, so that the precise positioning of features can be demonstrated in a direct visual manner (see Plates 43 and 44).

If one looks at the Byzantine images of Christ, or those showing Byzantine influence, in the centuries after the discovery of the Edessa Portrait, one is struck by the correspondences, particularly the peculiar geometrical marks on the forehead, the locks of hair or the asymmetrical nose. For example on the Christ Pantocrator in the church cupola in the monastery of Daphni near Athens (end of the eleventh century), no less than thirteen of the features can be identified, especially the V-form on the bridge of the nose, the open square at the top with a further V-form inside it, the streak across the forehead, the accentuated eyes and the raised eyebrow, and the asymmetrical face. Comparable pictures are the Christ enthroned in the south gallery, and one above the royal door, which probably derive from the ninth or tenth century, in the Hagia Sophia (see Plate 34); the Christ in the church of Sant' Angelo in Formis, Italy; the image of Christ in the apse of the cathedral of Cefalù, Sicily (1148), and the one in the cathedral of Monreale, also in Sicily (*c.* 1180); the famous *acheiropoieton* icon of

Novgorod (*c.* 1200, see Plate 48), or the holy countenance of Laon, (twelfth century, see Plate 49).

Have such comparative studies really proved the dependence of the image of Christ in its final standard form on the original of the Shroud? The sindonological literature treats this approach as one of the most fruitful. Much energy is applied to establishing the precise changes during the development of the image of Christ, to uncover its roots; and above all to research in detail the peculiar features and their development in the artistic reproductions. Although there are diverging views about the origin of some of the special features in the portraits of Jesus, most sindonologists agree that the developments of the Christ figure offer a basic proof for the existence and knowledge of the Shroud in the sixth century. It is worth looking more closely at this conclusion, because so much value is placed on it. Elucidation of this aspect of the problem could be extremely important from the theological standpoint. It might provide decisive new facts showing the significance of the cloth relic in the course of the history of religions, and in Christology.

Let us take the strands of hair for example (No. 15 on our list of features). In their extensive studies, Bulst and Pfeiffer came to the conclusion that the imprint on the Shroud did indeed exert a lasting influence on the Jesus portrait. They considered that the two or three strands of hair (especially noticeable on the Christ of Cefalù) 'derive ultimately from the blood mark at this place' (see Plate 35). Another author sees the strands of hair as independent of the blood mark (in the shape of an elongated E), describing them as short strands of hair in Λ-form, which are actually visible; and because they are crossed by a weave line they can appear to be two or three strands.[47]

What are we to make of all this? Are strands of hair really visible on the cloth image, or did an earlier copyist make the blood mark, 'not recognized as such' as Bulst and Pfeiffer suggest, into a lock of hair? This is a decisive point when assessing how far the copies were faithful to the original. We have to presume the copyists did have orders to render the face of the Shroud as true to the original as possible, for it was the true countenance of Jesus. Only on this basis can one speak of correspondences, especially when it comes to inconspicuous details. The artist must have had the chance to examine the Edessa

Portrait at leisure. Of course he would not have been allowed to borrow it because it was so sacred. He was most probably allowed to examine the Mandylion where it was kept in the Hagia Sophia of Edessa, with the shrine opened. The ambient lighting here was by no means optimal. According to all that we know about this church (which is no longer standing), it was built expressly for the purpose of enshrining the Mandylion. It was a large cathedral, liberally decorated inside with ornamental mosaics. The Mandylion was kept at the east end to the right of the apse which was illuminated by three windows. It was located in a sanctuary with its shrine. The windows of the church were not very large, so the light coming in would have evoked a mystical twilight. It was not much use for the artist to be able to come specially close to the original, since everyone who has seen the Shroud from close up agrees that there is little to be seen. The delicate image disappears if one tries to get too close to study the details. Let us suppose anyway that the copyist was at least able to observe the face of Jesus on the cloth for longer and more attentively than anyone before him, while keeping the picture of the Turin cloth in our mind's eye. Are not the blood marks the most noticeable elements? It is unthinkable that the copier did not recognize the clear blood trace on the forehead for what it is, as Bulst and Pfeiffer would have us believe.

It is true that the members of the Turin investigating committee found that with the lighting even slightly reduced it is hard to make out any difference in colouration between the body image and the blood marks; but the sources of the eighth to the tenth centuries speak of the 'blood-sweat' of Jesus, visible on the Edessa Portrait, so evidently a careful observer could clearly see that blood was included in the cloth picture. But even if the copyist had erred and taken the blood mark for a lock of hair, the short strands leading from the top of the head of the Christ portraits would be impermissible and inexplicable extras. The picture ought rather to show a long, conspicuous lock on the left of the forehead, running to the eyebrow, but I have not come across a single image of Jesus of this kind. If we now imagine a meticulously observant copyist, who did see two or three short streaks on the top of the head which looked to him like strands of hair, then it is impossible to see how he could overlook the much more noticeable blood mark. Yet it is never incorporated in the Christ portraits, not even in those which explicitly represent the Mandylion itself.

We find ourselves in a difficult dilemma. The most likely solution is that an exact copy was commissioned, but what I would like to term 'theologically edited'. I have already mentioned that the Mandylion was first in the possession of the Greek congregation of Edessa, and that the Greek conception of Christ centred on the victorious, radiant Pantocrator, the all-sovereign. The idea of Pantocrator goes back to a prophetic saying of the Old Testament, which Jesus uses in the Sermon on the Mount (Matt. 5:34 f), and which is cited by the first Christian martyr, Stephen the servant of the poor, in his defence before the high council (Acts 7:49): 'Heaven is my throne, and earth is my footstool ... saith the Lord' (Isa. 66:1). The ideal of the Pantocrator has to be understood in the context of the Greek world of ideas. It is anchored in the idea of the radiant, triumphant God, which was already a source of inspiration for religious feeling in pre-Christian times. Of course, it would have been a psychological blunder to portray the Christ who stood 'guarding in front of his town', as a person suffering at the hands of his persecutors. To whom could a helpless tortured person offer protection? The protection of such a God had to be made plausible for the simple populace. Hence we can assume the artist omitted the marks of the Passion from his otherwise faithful copy. Only this can explain why none of the blood marks, including those near the hair, were pictured; but they were not 'wrongly interpreted' either.

But our problems do not end here. On the photographs which convey a fairly accurate impression of how the Shroud colourations actually appear to the unaided eye of the viewer, some of the features of Vignon and Wuenschel (which we recall were already reduced in number by omitting some of the more far-fetched ones) cannot be made out however hard one looks. It is true that on black and white negatives developed with particularly good contrast, on which the structure of the linen weave is clearly displayed, one can easily see geometrical shapes on the forehead and other features. This does not help us further, however, because an artist at the end of the ancient era did not have the blessings of the latest technology to fall back on. It would be fairer to concentrate solely on marks which are recognizable on the original, such as the V-form on the base of the nose.

Moreover, it seems to me that the detection of concealed marks on photographs of the Turin Shroud developed by special techniques has since become a regular obsession in the case of certain sindonologists: claims are made of the discovery of a band tied around the forehead with a phylactery over the base of the nose containing letters, of coins of Pilate on the eyelids, of Hebraic letters which had been placed on the forehead, of imprints of flower petals strewn over the whole of the cloth, even of an amulet which Jesus wore on his chest.[48] I cannot avoid the feeling that desperate people are at work here, who view the cloth like some sort of enormous Rorschach ink splotch, into which they can project whatever they like. The more photographic fine analysis contributes to our understanding of the cloth, the more barren the wrong tracks it leads some researchers on, as they constantly try to trace new micro-forms. Put in terms of information theory the matter is simple: the more unclear a picture is, the more it tends to lead to chance differences of light and dark tones being grouped as forms, and information being drawn from them which they do not contain at all. In order to contribute a responsible piece of research in this field, one has to ensure that one is ruthlessly aware of such tendencies. Only thus can one avoid the danger of finding that everything which one carries around as preconceived hypotheses comes to be confirmed in the end.

Such caution is especially needed in the field of the iconography of Christ. To take one example, how are we to fit in the pictures of saints, angels, even of lay persons, who are similarly shown with the two or three strands of hair?[49] And what is to be made of faces of saints and others who bear the same peculiar geometrical shape on the forehead as the unique Jesus portrait?[50] The arguments of the sindonologists are pretty weak in this regard. Wilson supposes that they were given to the saints as a special sign of their sanctity. This reasoning seems counter-productive to me. Was it not to bring out the uniqueness of Jesus that the precise copies of the Edessa Portrait were made? These obscure markings themselves support this view. To transfer them to other people would then be contrary to all logic. Here the supporters twist and turn to prevent an argument which has been taken too far from collapsing, an argument which would far better serve the Shroud researchers if it were offered with a dose of restraint, honesty and scientific exactitude.

For the 'feature hunters' have committed an unforgiveable methodological error, which considerably impairs the scientific validity of their discoveries. If one wishes to compare pictures which are similar in appearance, it is not enough to name certain elements and note their presence on various pictures of the same content, or possibly to list them and derive statistics from them. This is all the more true when the same features occur in pictures of a *different* content – that is, those which do not show Christ. The closeness of the match can only be seen if the *differences* which are found are listed as well. This the sindonologists studiously forgot to do – or covered up.

The portraits which were reproduced for example by Bulst and Pfeiffer, and by Wilson, to support their theses, show almost without exception long, wavy hair which clings to the head as if it was tied at the neck. Furthermore, in the overwhelming majority of cases the ears are visible, only half covered by hair. The enthroned Christ in the narthex of the Hagia Sophia has lines on the cheeks which look like long furrows; that of Sant'Angelo in Formis has pronounced marks under the eyes and on the cheeks, which are a common iconographic attribute in the region of southern Italy. These are just a few of the conspicuous departures from the face on the Turin cloth: here the hair falls straight on the shoulders, and the earlobes cannot be made out, nor the folds or round cheek patches.[51] A copyist true to his subject, as we always have to assume he would be, would surely not have committed such blunders as these. When does one allow later 'copiers of the copies' artistic licence, and when are the elements part of the primary original? Only if the latter are also found on the Shroud? That would be poor research indeed!

One has to do the opposite, to judge how good the match with the Shroud is by looking at portraits which display a high degree of similarity even though they do not represent Jesus. There are some quite astonishing examples here, such as the ceramic icon of St Theodore (ninth or tenth century) at Preslav in Bulgaria; the apostle Paul on a manuscript of the homilies of St John Chrysostom (end of the ninth century) in the National Library at Athens; and John the Baptist on the mosaic in the church of Hosius-Luke in Central Greece (*c.* 1000).

To keep the favoured hypothesis afloat, our valiant 'primary copyist' is supposed to have been a poor observer and behaved quite stupidly to boot. While Bulst and Pfeiffer accuse him of seeing the blood mark on the forehead as just some thin strands of hair, Wilson defends him by saying that he saw open eyes because they really look like that on the cloth.[52]

The fact remains that the high art of the early icon paintings, the frescoes and mosaic works, show that we are dealing with artists who had a much deeper understanding of the graphic religious portrait than certain modern critics would allow. There is nothing to suggest that the Mandylion copyist was a poor representative of his profession; on the contrary, in view of the unique importance of his commission, he was presumably the best and most theologically educated one to be found. He would know from the Abgar story that Jesus had pressed his face in the cloth; he would have realized that Jesus instinctively closed his eyes when he did so, as anyone would have done. So it would have been clear to him that the man on the cloth had his eyes closed. The fact that he still painted him with a vivid gaze is due to the status which the picture of Christ held. A portrait of the Lord with closed eyes was unthinkable. The clear gaze is an inherent feature of the triumphant Christ as the model of divine power and spiritual authority, and in no way impairs the copy's fidelity to the original. The artist had not added anything that was not permissible.

The analysis of the artistic portrayal of Christ remains a difficult subject. Yet I find it is one of the most exciting fields of inquiry concerning the Turin cloth. The correspondences of the 'new' Jesus figure from the sixth century with the 'Man of the Shroud' are remarkable. Because of the great complexity of all the related fields of study, I have turned a critical eye on the various forms of approach. I consider it essential to proceed with the utmost caution in this central field of research, to make sure that the highly promising lines of study do not lose credibility because of fanatical, unscientific 'feature hunters'.

The portraits of Jesus from the middle of the sixth century which originated in the immediate vicinity of Edessa are the most promising for intensive studies of copies of the cloth – for example the vase of Emesa or the silver paten from Riha. They were made in the years following the discovery of the portrait, and in such geographical proximity that they could very well be direct copies of the original.

Regarding comparisons of a more general nature, I think that it is proper and proportionate to our material if we keep to the basic constants, or fixed attributes, of the Shroud face. It is beyond doubt that the Jesus pictures of the post-Justinian period are remarkably similar to the face on the cloth, with occasional distinctive features supporting this similarity, but in view of the simultaneous presence of clear differences this cannot be conclusive proof.

The unusually long nose, for example, is indeed a striking characteristic. Everyone who sees the Shroud for the first time immediately notices it. It is in a sense the distinguishing physiognomic feature *par excellence*. On the post-Justinian Jesus portraits it appears correspondingly long and narrow, often unusually so. The prominent nose served the Byzantine iconographers as a measure for building up the facial proportions for Jesus: the head was framed from two circles, one and two nose-lengths in radius. The halo was often constructed as a third circle with a radius of three nose-lengths. This construction came to be used for picturing all holy people, and the markedly long nose was widely taken up. The centre of the composition was also the centre of the circles: the base of the nose between the eyes. This is thought to be the reason why the base of the nose was emphasized in a special manner in Byzantine art (with points, circles, V-shapes, triangles etc.). This manner of construction, with the emphasis on the base of the nose, was justified because the point was understood to be the centre of the head, the seat of wisdom.

The picture of the cloth in Edessa laid down the basic features of the Jesus portrait for all time. With this as a basis, the theology of the portraits and icons were able to develop freely. The 'true image' had been found and declared to be correct and permissible. Now all they had to do was see that only 'true' images were allowed in sacred art. The decisive contribution to this was made at the Second Trullanian Synod in Constantinople in 691–2. This produced the famous Canon 82, which led to the active promotion of images. It is true that the canon actually dealt with images showing John the Baptist pointing to the Lamb, but the judgement which is formulated in it was taken in a much wider sense. It prohibited any further portrayal of Christ as 'Lamb of God, who taketh away the sins of the world' (Isa. 53:7–8,12; John 1:29; Rev. 5,6:12–13), and declared, 'Therefore in order that that

which is perfect be shown in form and colour for the contemplation of all, the Christ our God who takes away the sins of the
world shall in future be represented on the images by his human
form instead of the old symbolic form of the lamb.'

While assessing the consequences of the synodal decrees for
the image question, however, there is another canon which we
have to take into account, which has not become so famous. In
Canon 100 we find the words 'We decree that henceforth no more
pictures are to be painted, be they on panels or presented in some
other form, which deceive the view in any way and corrupt the
mind . . .' The pictures allowed were those which were 'true to
nature', and yet 'do not corrupt the mind'. This is an important
requirement, because the theology of icons in the Orthodox tradition leads to the view that the person should be portrayed in the
icon in a form that is natural but not merely earthly. The person
represented was seen to transcend the natural bodily form required by Canon 82 of the Second Trullanum, thanks to the
supernal, glorified existence which the picture rendered.

Nowhere is the enthusiasm for images more clearly visible at
this time than in the three discourses given in their defence by
St John of Damascus (675–749). He started his reflections by
looking at the two divine natures: on the one side the unmanifest
triune God, who is invisible, unlimited and without form; on the
other side the God manifested, incarnated in Jesus Christ. He
then distinguished between five types of images, pertaining partly
to the invisible and partly to the visible: first, the natural image in the
Divinity, that is that of the Son in relation to the Father; secondly,
the archetypal images of all things, as they exist in God; thirdly,
the bodily forms of the invisible and discarnate entities, that is
God and the angels described in the Bible, which make them
tangible for human beings; fourthly, the archetypes in the Old
Testament as early forms of what was to come (such as the brazen
serpent as the symbol of the crucified one); and fifthly, the images
which preserve the memory of an event. Art, John of Damascus
held, derives directly from the latter type of picture.

John of Damascus defended the icons of Christ by relating them
to the way he assumed human form. He understood the act and
form of incarnation as 'art', portraying not the invisible Godhead
but his visible human form. He argued that since the invisible was
made visible by the incarnation as man, it was right to paint him

on wooden panels and offer the form for contemplation, a form of the One who had chosen to assume a visible form. The Incarnation of the Logos was the reason for the images. The portrayed body of Christ became the means to attain the invisible One. As long as God remained incorporeal and formless, he was simply unportrayable; but after he had become visible in the flesh and had dwelt amongst the people, one should portray that which God has made visible of himself. Never was this need more truly satisfied than in the Edessa portrait and its copies.

The Mandylion Comes to Constantinople

In the eighth century, after the images had triumphed, the flood of miraculous icons of Christ flowed westwards. Patriarch Germanus, to save a miraculous image of Christ from the iconoclasts under Leo III the Isaurian (717–41), entrusted it to this westward current, which carried it to Rome to Pope Gregory II (715–31). In 752, when Pope Stephen II, then under threat from Aistulf, left barefoot with ash-smeared head for the church of Our Lady ad Praesepem, he had precious relics taken along. Among these was 'the most holy picture of the Lord, our God and Saviour, Jesus Christ, which is called *acheiropoieta*', which the Pope carried himself. It is still kept as an icon of the Saviour in the Sancta Sanctorum Chapel of the Lateran Basilica, Rome, in a precious shrine donated by Pope Nicholas II (1277–80).[53]

A number of teachers of the Church felt that there was something strange about the way the cult of images was flourishing. They feared the spiritual values of Christianity might be swamped by the heathen cult traditions, and the religion would be taken over by them. The iconoclasts were probably overestimating the effect of images, but to stem the feared development, in 726 Emperor Leo III banned the worship of images in the whole Eastern Roman Empire. Constantine V (741–75) further encouraged the Iconoclasm with theological arguments and political measures, and in 754 he called together a council at Constantinople at which the image opponents tried to make the painters out to be swindlers greedy for money. They were, they said, attempting to portray that which was simply unportrayable. And to portray the saints with lifeless colours while in reality they were shining in their supernal radiance, was nothing but a despicable imitation of heathen customs. It was contrary to the hope of resurrection. Images of Christ were said to conflict with the teaching of the incarnation and to lend support either to Nestorianism or to Monophytism.

The destruction of images followed. Everywhere the zealots destroyed religious icons wherever they could lay their hands on them. In the space of a few years an irreplaceable treasure-store of works of art was reduced to ruins. Soon the Iconoclasm spread to Byzantine Italy. Fortunately Leo III's domination did not reach as far as Sinai, so the excellent examples of earlier icon art in St Catherine's monastery were able to survive unscathed. In 787 an end of sorts was made to the Iconoclasm thanks to the efforts of the Empress Irene at the Seventh Ecumenical Council at Nicaea. But really the conflict continued. Even after it had met its dogmatic and liturgical end in 842 with the introduction of the Feast of Orthodoxy, the waves of the battle were not yet calmed. The synods of the late ninth century were still condemning the iconoclasts.

Perhaps it was the Mandylion's special good fortune that it had already had to be hidden for a lengthy period in Edessa, because of the image-hostile attitude in the Monophysite camp. And it was also advisable to keep the cloth away from the Arabs, because of the extremely hostile attitude to images taken by the new faith of Islam, which would have meant more danger for it. In any event the relic was able to survive even the Iconoclasm.

The preservation of images for Christianity was mainly due to the way the image idea of the pre-iconoclastic period (deriving from Neoplatonism) was replaced by the Aristotelian idea: the image was no longer seen to derive its importance because it allowed a mystical participation in the nature of the one portrayed, but because it was a sign, a sort of script in fact. John of Damascus, who compared the tradition of the image with that of writing, had anticipated this development, but his Neoplatonic approach slipped more and more into the background and the Aristotelian view finally came to determine theological thought on images in the Byzantine Empire.

A hint of the development leading to a positive evaluation of images of Christ has come to us from the year 829, when the Mandylion was summoned as a fundamental argument in favour of images: the patriarchs of Antioch, Alexandria and Jerusalem wrote to Emperor Theophilus that Constantine had caused Christ to be painted according to the precise description of the facial features on the Abgar picture.[54]

In Edessa the Mandylion was revered most highly. At first it was, as we have shown, kept in the Hagia Sophia erected specially for it, then it came into the possession of the Monophysite nobles. It certainly seems to have encouraged the mood in favour of images. This in turn led to more people examining it more closely. We encounter more and more descriptions which speak of the tender, almost colourless character of the image which is a feature of the Turin cloth, and which mention a bloody sweat. Patriarch Germanus of Constantinople referred to it as a 'face towel' (*soudarion*). In a reworking of saints' legends by Alexius in about 800, there is mention of the '*bloodied image* of the Lord', which was kept in Edessa.[55] A few decades later in the synodal letter of the orientals to Emperor Theophilus (829–42), along with the 'face towel' there was mention of the 'divine sweat' washed off with it, which was said to have caused the picture. A hundred years after this the author of the festive sermon spoke of a 'dampness without colouring or the painter's art', and said that the 'blood-sweat' of Jesus at Gethsemane could be seen on the Mandylion. The incomparable value of the cloth was recognized throughout the Empire. And so, after the blow against Iconoclasm had been delivered, efforts were undertaken to bring the Edessa Portrait to Constantinople.

It was Emperor Romanus Lacapenus (920–44) who had the Mandylion brought from Edessa to the imperial capital. The end of the conflict about images lay in the distant past, as in 942 the Feast of Orthodoxy saw its centenary celebrations. The Emperor's enemies had learned to fear the valiant Byzantine soldiers after many battles. His people would certainly have been overjoyed to see the protective image of Christ also bearing witness to his power in Constantinople. In any case, it was not acceptable that such a precious and widely famous relic, whose existence had decisively influenced the theological resolution of the image question, was still left in a distant town which to everyone's horror was still controlled by the Arabs. So in 942 the Emperor sent his most capable man to go and fetch the image of Christ.

In October the Byzantine general Curcuas descended on Mesopotamia and Armenia, took Arzen, Dara and Maiphercat and, after a hard battle, Nisbis and so the whole of Mesopotamia. In 332 AH (4 September 943 – 23 August 944) Curcuas, at the height of his fame, led the Byzantine host at the siege of Edessa. In the course of this siege, he was said to have forced the town to surrender the picture. He is said to have offered to renounce the taking of Edessa, to release all Muslim prisoners, and to pay 12,000 silver crowns if the highly sacred relic was handed over to him.

The historians are not agreed abut the facts behind the surrender of the Mandylion. It seems that the Edessans were under pressure to act. Curcuas had the town in his grasp, and it is difficult to see why he did not just smash everything to pieces, take the picture and leave (he had had enough practice at this sort of thing from countless sieges of towns before this one). The reports of the chroniclers suggest that the proposal to surrender the sacred article came from the Edessans, when they saw no way of avoiding certain defeat. But in such a situation it is unlikely that the Emir could have been able to demand liberty for the town, the release of the prisoners and even the payment of a large sum.

What probably happened was this. The General faced a special test of his diplomatic skills. Romanus Lacapenus had ordered him to force the surrender of the Mandylion *without* razing the town to dust and ashes. It was imperative that Edessa be kept intact, because the sacred protection which it enjoyed owing to the letter of Christ and his portrait was not to be tested under any circumstances. What would people think of this sacred *palladium*, if it could be violently wrested from the bleeding hands of those whom it was meant to protect? Would it not have lost its charisma if it came to Constantinople like this, and would voices not have been raised decrying it as a forgery, a swindle, if the promise of Jesus were not fulfilled? Curcuas intended to apply just enough pressure on the town so that they finally had to agree to the Emperor's demands, but it seems he wanted to make the decision easier for them by offering to leave the town undamaged.

Nonetheless the surrender of the Edessa Portrait was no simple matter. The political situation did not allow a rapid conclusion to the operation. The Mandylion was still in the possession of one of the Church communities of the town. The Emir could not just snatch it away from the congregation, and besides, in such questions, which were of a primarily religious nature, the permission of Caliph Al-Muttaki was needed. A period of difficult and tough negotiations began, arranged before the Caliph with the summoning of *kadis* (jurists) and *fakihs* (theologians). At first they were reluctant to give the picture up, seeing that as a sort of humiliation. But finally the diplomatic tug-of-war for the prisoners won the upper hand, and the Emir was directed to hand over the Mandylion. Then a new set of problems arose. The Christian communities and citizens of the town did not want to lose the precious relic at any cost. Then the Byzantines invited Archbishop Abramius of Samosata, who was greatly admired in Edessa, to come. He was to see that the clergy did not cause any difficulties, and also to take care that Curcuas was given the genuine picture. This precaution proved to be a necessary one, because after it had become clear that the transaction could no longer be prevented, an attempt was made to substitute a copy. Abramius finally had all three of the pictures in Edessa handed over to him, and then applied his knowledge to decide which one was the original. The tradition tells of a miraculous test in which the true Edessa Portrait revealed itself.

In 944 the matter was finally settled. The Byzantines released 200 captives, counted out the pieces of silver, decreed freedom from aggression of every kind by the Greek armies for the area of Edessa, Haran, Sarug and Samosata, and made their way back with the relic they had forcibly obtained. Once again waves of hatred and calumny were stirred up. The citizens of the town felt they had been deceived and tried to prevent the removal of the relic by an uprising literally at the last minute, but to no avail. In the company of Archbishop Abramius, the Chalcedonian bishop of Edessa, with his archpriests, several Christian notables from the town and an envoy of the Emir, the ship bearing the image of Christ moved off along the Euphrates. There were reports of numerous miracles taking place on the long journey to Constantinople, in a sense confirming that it was the genuine picture, and also fitting for a suitable passage to the capital. The Imperial Chamberlain, Patrikius Theophanes, came to meet the procession on the bridge over the river Sangarius, which had been built under Justinian.

The entry into Constantinople took the form of a triumphant reception, choreographed in grand style, with a fine sense for dramatic detail. On the evening of the sacred feast day of the Assumption of the Virgin Mary, 15 August 944, the Mandylion arrived at the famous church of Our Lady at Blachernae, where the entire court, with the exception of Romanus because of his illness, was able to admire the blessed relic. The two sons of the Emperor expressed their disappointment at the picture: they could hardly make out anything on it. Finally the relic was placed in the imperial chapel of the Pharos. The next day a delegation of high ecclesiastical and secular dignitaries circled the whole town with the sacred relic on the imperial galley. Everywhere the crowd exulted at the procession, the faithful casting themselves to the ground before the image. The procession was continued on foot from the west to the walls and the Golden Gate. Then the *palladium* was taken to the middle of the town, where it was put on display on the throne of mercy in the inner sanctuary of the Hagia Sophia. Finally the *Rex Regnatium*, in the symbolic form of his presence in the Mandylion, was placed on the throne of the worldly ruler in the Blachernae Palace and crowned, until the time came for it to take up its final place in the Pharos chapel.

At the end of the great festive action, on the evening of 16 August 944, Archdeacon Gregory, leader of the large congregation of Constantinople, gave a commemorative sermon before the 'enthroned' Edessa Portrait in the Boucoleon Palace, providing us with a document of inestimable value for our thesis. The Italian scholar Prof Gino Zaninotto discovered the original text of the sermon in a manuscript of the period and published the most important parts.[56] It is interesting to note that the author was an expert in questions both of history and of art. Gregory first related the story of the Mandylion and its journey, and declared that the image on the cloth can be traced back to the sweating of blood at Gethsemane. Then he asked those present to view the features of the countenance *as if in a mirror*, and *not applied with the ordinary paints of the artist's craft*. In the art of the icon, Gregory said, the splendour was achieved by using the most diverse colours; and he listed them showing how they were used to paint the individual parts of a portrait. On the cloth, however, 'the splendour *was derived solely from the drops of sweat at the agony in the garden, which emerged from the countenance, which is the source of life, flowing down like drops of blood and imprinting with divine fingers.*' And then he continued his talk with a statement which at once casts a completely new light on the cloth and which can truly be termed sensational: 'These are truly the beauties which the colour of the imprint of Christ has brought forth, which were finally improved [coloured] by *the drops of blood flowing out from his own side* . . . I say it is these [blood and water] which have been imprinted on the cloth.' Again a second time he emphasized the side wound, and so provided us with what is probably the crucial key – the proof of the identity of the Mandylion and the Turin Shroud. It could not be a face towel from Gethsemane if the wound of the lance thrust was visible. It would have to have originated at the time immediately following the crucifixion.

Zaninotto suggests that when the Mandylion was checked in Edessa and compared with the two copies, the picture was taken out of the frame and on closer inspection the side wound was seen on one edge. Possibly the cloth was folded in such a way that when the frame was removed the chest could be seen up to the side wound. But why do we hear nothing of the side wound in the famous 'Narratio', the festive sermon at the court of Constantine VII Porphyrogennetus?

Gregory was probably relieved of his office, as was usual in such cases, when the Emperor Romanus was removed from power by his sons in December 944 and deported to the island of Prote. The authorities who had been involved in getting the image of Christ out of Edessa now found themselves in an embarrassing situation. The protection-bestowing image had been brought to Constantinople at great cost, and now it turned out that it was a burial shroud, not the picture praised down the centuries. That was most upsetting. When Constantine VII sent Romanus' two sons into exile in January 945, and at last stood alone as the legitimate Emperor at the head of the state, his court wished to preserve the continuity of the tradition back to the Abgar episode. This is evident from the festive sermon given in the same year and from the famous icon of the monastery of St Catherine at Sinai, which shows Abgar with the Mandylion: Abgar bears the features of Porphyrogennetus (see Plate 30). It *had* to be the Mandylion.

A Secret is Revealed

For many decades the Mandylion remained in its place of honour in the Pharos chapel. Next to it was displayed the stone with the miraculous imprint, the Keramion, which had been transferred to Constantinople by Nicephorus II Phocas (963–9) in 965. We are told of occasional processions in which the Mandylion was carried. Nobody seemed to remember anything of the observation by Archdeacon Gregory. Then the secret of the Mandylion must have come to light at some time during the eleventh century. How it happened is not known. Perhaps Aggai's old frame, which had after all withstood a long millennium, was worn and needed to be restored or replaced by a modern mounting. Then, as this was being done, the whole cloth was exposed.

The earliest written reference to this is found at the opening of the twelfth century. In a sermon which was given by Pope Stephen II in 769 at the Lateran synod, we find a section inserted at around this time, which is of great interest. It says,

> For the same intermediary between God and humanity [Christ] himself, in order to satisfy the king [Abgar] in every way, stretched out *his whole body* on a cloth white as snow, whereupon the glorious image of the countenance of our Lord and *the length of his whole body* was so divinely pictured, that it suffices to allow all those who were not able to see the Lord bodily in the flesh, to see the transfiguration visible on the cloth.[57]

In the Church history by Ordericus Vitalis (*c.* 1141), it is said that Jesus had a precious cloth sent to Abgar 'on which the image of the Saviour appears portrayed in a miraculous manner; which allows the viewer to see *the bodily form and proportions of the Lord*.'[58] Gervasius of Tilbury, in his work *Otia Imperialia* ('Imperial Leisure Hours') which he composed between 1209 and 1214 for Emperor Otto IV, recounted the version where Jesus imprints his whole body on a cloth and has it presented to Abgar.[59] Interestingly Gervasius saw a connection betwen the imprint of the Edessa Portrait showing the complete body of Christ, and that on a cloth Jesus was placed in while being taken from the cross, which was also said to have preserved his features. Gervasius linked the shroud image to the legend that it was Nicodemus who started the tradition of the model crucifix in art: Nicodemus fashioned the crucifix in wood showing the features of the Christ image miraculously preserved in the cloth he was placed in when being taken from the cross. It is difficult to say with certainty whether an *acheiropoieton* is being invented here to emphasize how true to the original the artistic copy was, or whether the shroud with the image was known in Gervasius' day in certain circles.

In any case, on the basis of these statements we can follow a line of tradition between the eleventh and thirteenth centuries which documents the transformation from Edessa Portrait to Shroud. Thus at the start of this period the cloth must have been revealed in its full length.

Further support for this is provided by the tradition of Christian art. The oldest representations of the events from the deposition to the burial only show the scene of Jesus being placed in the tomb, usually with him wrapped like a mummy leaving just the head free. In a ninth-century psalter of the monastery of the Pantocrator on Mt. Athos, there is a miniature showing Joseph and Nicodemus carrying Jesus into the tomb. Jesus is carried as if in a sack, only his classical bearded face visible.[60] The famous Chloudoff Psalter from the end of the ninth century in the Historical Museum in Moscow shows the same scene with Jesus wrapped up like a mummy.[61]

At about this time the Passion story was expanded to include an iconographic novelty: after Jesus was taken down from the cross, before the burial, he was placed on the ground and the women mourned for him, while Joseph of Arimathea and Nicodemus were busy with the burial preparations. Later the figure of the Virgin was added. Although the placing in the tomb is described in all the Gospels, this scene of the lamentation has its origin in the apocryphal Gospel of Nicodemus, especially in the later recension B which contains the 'Lamentation of the Virgin'. The lamentation theme was introduced as an intermission during the burial. A typical example is the famous codex of the Homilies of Gregory, written and illustrated for Basil I in Constantinople shortly after 880.

But not until the eleventh century was the lamentation scene portrayed in a manner which immediately brings to mind the Shroud picture: Jesus lies on a flat piece of linen, usually quite a lot longer than his body, in a rather stiff posture, hands crossed over his loins. This form of portrayal is completely new and at this period is found, with the special posture of Christ, in two further artistic forms: on liturgical cloths (*epitaphios* and *antiminsion*), and as a half portrait showing him with the marks of the Passion emerging from a coffin-like tomb.[62] The latter form of portrayal, a reminder of the agony, became the widespread figure of the man of suffering in the Western view of Christ, under the influence of the contemplative mysticism of the Middle Ages. In the East, where the suffering Christ was less favoured, it played only a subordinate role.

An interesting lamentation scene is found in the church of St Panteleimon in Nerezi, Serbia. It was done in 1164 and shows Jesus on a cloth with a diamond-shaped pattern such as we know from the Mandylion pictures (see Plate 50); this may be an attempt to reproduce the herringbone pattern of the Turin cloth, or perhaps we may infer a direct connection to the Mandylion, taking up the pattern on it without being aware of its earlier significance as decorative surround. Comparable portrayals can be found for example in the church of Our Lady at Studenica, Serbia (1235); or as a miniature in a Gospel lectionary of the eleventh or twelfth century in the Biblioteca Vaticana, where Christ is seen flat on the shroud, which appears to be made up of several layers, with a net pattern.

We have to take into account the Byzantines' limited understanding of the suffering of Christ when analysing the artistic treatment of the lamentation scenes and the *epitaphios* picture. For even with all the correspondences with the figure on the Shroud, the numerous wounds indicating the agony are often missing. The suffering of Christ is mostly reduced to a contorted facial expression, while the body – quite unlike the image on the Shroud – appears as if completely unharmed. Often even the nail wounds are found as small hints or totally absent, and on many *epitaphios* cloths one looks in vain for the side wound.

Why, one may ask, do these depictions of Christ only appear at such a late stage – had it not already been decreed in 692 at the Trullanian Synod, in its famous Canon 82, that Christ was not to be shown as a lamb but pictured in his natural proportions, true to his bodily appearance? The sacrificial bread used in the celebration of the Eucharist had always been described as a lamb (*amnos*) even in the early centuries, and this symbolism was retained in the liturgical texts even after the Trullanian ban.

The icons of the lifeless body of Christ finally came to be embroidered on the liturgical cloths following the model of the Shroud. But no images of this kind are known to us from the period immediately after the Trullanum, although Basilius Grolimund suggests in a very interesting essay that 'the Shroud of the Lord then (that is at the time of Trullanum) preserved in Byzantium and now in Turin . . . probably exerted an influence on the iconography.' My inquiries showed that he relied on testimonies which were not historically attested to, wrongly identifying the alleged shroud of Christ in Constantinople – which we know already existed in the fourth century – with the Turin cloth.[63] And he was also unable to give any information about depictions of Christ on *epitaphios* or related liturgical cloths dated before the eleventh century. The oldest surviving depiction of the lifeless body of Christ as Lamb of God is found on the Stroganov icon in the Hermitage in St Petersburg. Its enamel pictures date from the eleventh and twelfth centuries. Below the central Crucifixion icon, Christ is pictured on the Shroud, with the archangels Michael and Gabriel to the right and left. One notices that Christ is not shown in the usual way with the loincloth, but his nakedness is covered with a square cloth (*velum*), like the one used for wrapping the liturgical offerings.

Portrayals of the lifeless body of Christ similar to that on the Stroganov icon are found adorning the apse of the abbey church of St Maria Agyptiaca in Messenia, Peloponnese (end of the twelfth century); in the prothesis in the church of St Nicholas at Melnic, southern Bulgaria (thirteenth century); or on the *epitaphios* of Milutin Ures (*c.* 1300) in the Museum of the Serbian Orthodox Church in Belgrade.

There is a picture of Christ fully unclothed in a Budapest prayer book which is dated as early as 1192, and is known as the Pray manuscript (see Plate 52). It is interesting on two accounts, if we take the Turin cloth as its model. The miniature, which unfortunately shows little artistic skill, is divided into two scenes. At the top one sees the naked Jesus being anointed by Nicodemus; he lies on a cloth. Below, the scene of the women before the empty tomb is shown; an angel points to a smaller cloth. The open tomb is shown in a way which allows various interpretations – hence the limited artistic skill of the miniaturist. The upper portion, which is probably meant to show the covering drawn back, is drawn with a pattern of steps and crosses, the lower one just with crosses. This structure of ornament is most unusual for the depiction of a tomb, even for a sarcophagus. Dubarle has therefore proposed that the two sections are to be viewed as the unfolded Shroud. The geometrical patterns would be an attempt to reproduce the conspicuous herringbone pattern of the Turin Shroud. His hypothesis is specially interesting because he points out small circles which appear on both sides of the 'shroud', quite abruptly and without significance for the composition or as decoration.[64] These correspond both in position (almost exactly) and in proportions to the four sets of four burn holes on the Turin cloth, which must therefore have been formed long before the fire of 1532![65]

One explanation for the absence of comparable pictures from the period immediately after the Synod of Trullo might be the violence of the Iconoclasm. But then we would expect to find pictures of the body of Christ in the form described after the restoration of images in the mid-ninth century. Yet as we have seen we have to wait a further 200 years after this. The new iconographic themes and peculiarities, the references to a full body impression of Christ on the Abgar cloth, the stylistic and liturgical connections between Mandylion, Shroud, *epitaphios* and *velum* – all these elements make it very clear that the secret of the Edessa Portrait was first definitively made known in the eleventh century.

Understandably enough this was not broadcast to the whole world. If this was the picture of the story published in the festive sermon, it would mean that some deception, or at least error, had taken place right at the beginning, going back to the closest friends of Jesus. It was a baffling theological problem, which could hardly be made comprehensible for the simple populace. Up to then they had believed that Edessa possessed a protection-bestowing, miraculous portrait of Jesus, which the great Emperor Romanus Lacapenus had had brought to the capital with massive military outlay, so that there it could display its qualities as an excellent *palladium*. Now suddenly the highly revered *palladium* was shown to be a shroud, on which the injured body of Christ can be seen! We recall that the Greeks never liked to show Jesus as a picture of suffering. Their image of Jesus was that of the Pantocrator, the Ruler of the Cosmos. Only such a strong God could offer protective power. And although one sees streams of blood on the face of the Shroud, thanks to the frontal viewpoint with the large, apparently open, eyes and the relaxed features giving no hint of suffering, it after all remains a picture of strength, authority and all-penetrating insight – in short the face of a true Pantocrator. But the unfolded linen reveals quite a different form: the victorious God of the Mandylion was actually like a corpse. The Pantocrator no longer looked with knowing gaze upon the creatures of the world, his eyes were firmly shut.

The theologians had a problem. One could not undermine the thousand-year-old, sacred story of the Mandylion in this way and remove the Byzantines' imperial *palladium*. And yet the precious cloth which wrapped the body of Jesus had to be preserved. The solution would probably be to put a copy in place of the genuine Mandylion next to the Keramion in the Pharos chapel. Few had ever seen the original. During processions it was led through the streets enclosed in a shrine, and even those who were fortunate enough to get a glimpse of the cloth would not have been able to see much. Thus it was not difficult to present a copy as the genuine Mandylion from then on. After touching it to the cloth, this picture made by human hands could, by the peculiar logic of relic multiplication, be counted as 'genuine' and worthy of reverence.

What then happened to the Shroud is difficult to say. On the one hand they already had 'shrouds' of Christ anyway; on the other they did not want to keep the sensational find a secret. Gradually the dignitaries of Church and State, and selected artist monks, would have been allowed to come for viewings. Whether these always took place in the Pharos chapel, we are not told.

In time news of the precious relic reached the West. In the year 1095 the Byzantine Emperor Alexius I Comnenus wrote a letter to his friend Robert, Duke of Flemings, and to all princes of the realm, complaining that the Empire was under constant threat from the Turks. He would prefer it if instead of the heathens, Western Christian armies took the capital Constantinople, especially because the most important relics were kept there, among them 'the linen which was found in the tomb after the Resurrection'.[66] Such a strange request on the part of a ruler, inviting the conquest of his own capital city, has to be viewed with distrust. Most modern researchers consider the letter to be a forgery, made in the West perhaps shortly before the First Crusade (1096), to make propaganda suggesting Constantinople as a possible target of conquest. In fact Alexius did approach Pope Urban I and the Western nobles for aid. But it was unthinkable that a Crusader army would take Constantinople – such an important town of Christendom. In any case, the forged letter confirms that the presence of the Shroud in Constantinople was known at the end of the eleventh century. A hundred years later the taking of Byzantium by a Crusader army was to become a terrible reality.

The Portrait of Christ and the Fourth Crusade

It was 1199. Innocent III had just assumed the supreme office of the Church, and he was already driven by a strong urge to settle the conflict between Empire and Papacy once and for all in favour of the religious power. The imperial throne had lain vacant since the demise of Henry VI in September 1197. In Germany the Hohenstaufen and Welfen families were contesting the Emperor's crown, in England Richard's brother John and his nephew Arthur were competing for the throne, and the French King Philip was actively involved in the English conflicts. All around them the crowned and yet uncrowned heads were busied in forcing their way against rivals and challengers.

Pope Innocent must have thought it a lucky turn of fate when just at this time Frankish knights gathered around Count Tibald of Champagne, convinced of the need for a Fourth Crusade. He at once saw his chance and backed Tibald's idea of a new Crusade with great enthusiasm. Very soon an impressive number of noblemen from Flanders to the Rhineland were ready to ride under the cross with their knights. When Tibald died unexpectedly in 1202, Boniface of Monferat was chosen to lead the Crusader movement.

The leadership of Boniface was to cause the whole undertaking to get out of hand, and finally end in the disastrous results which have rightly given the Fourth Crusade a notorious place in history. Boniface strengthened an old friendship with Philip of Swabia, who hoped soon to become Emperor of the Holy Roman Empire. He spent the winter months of 1201 with him. Philip was married to Irene Angelina, the daughter of the Byzantine Emperor Isaac Angelus. During a palace revolution in 1195, his father-in-law was overthrown, and was blinded and thrown into prison together with his son Alexius. But Alexius managed to flee. In winter 1201 he fought his way to his sister at the court of Philip. There Philip and Alexius discussed a fateful plan with their guest Boniface: the planned Crusade could simply make a small detour to Constantinople, and with the help of the Crusaders the rightful ruler would regain his throne.

For a hardened politician like Boniface this was indeed a tempting proposal. Not for nothing was Byzantium considered one of the most important trading partners of the Italian port towns. Its wealth enjoyed a fabulous repute. Boniface thought a whole range of advantages could be gained by such an action. The power-hungry were never at a loss when it came to grasping opportunities for themselves.

When deciding whose ships should be used on the Fourth Crusade, Innocent favoured Venice. Enrico Dandolo, the Doge of Venice, said he was prepared to get ready a fleet and provisions for the Crusaders at a price of 85,000 Cologne silver marks. Dandolo was an out and out merchant, a classic example of the diplomatically skilled Venetian, who wished to expand the economic empire of the republic through clever tactics and cool calculated decisions. He is the third great figure of the Fourth Crusade and without doubt one of the most extraordinary men of his time. When he presented his offer to the Crusaders Dandolo was at the advanced age of ninety-four, and was actually blind. He had lost the use of his eyes during a fight in Constantinople thirty years before. Despite his age and serious disability, this dynamo of energy and zeal did not hesitate for a moment to take to the bridge of a seafaring galley and lead the Frankish knights against the East – and this at a time when every long sea journey was a daring risk even for young and robust natures.

The Crusader army had been perched together on the small island of San Niccolo di Lido since early summer 1202, but they were unable to raise the money demanded by Dandolo. Through the mediation of Boniface a courier from Philip of Swabia arrived with a message from Alexius. If the Crusaders snatched Constantinople from the usurping ruler and restored Alexius to power, he would take over all the debts and also finance the remaining journey for the conquest of Egypt. Enrico Dandolo was enthusiastic about the proposal. He would be paid well, and in addition he could significantly expand his trading privileges in the Byzantine Empire.

Innocent faced a dilemma. Could he allow a Crusade to be so twisted as to turn against Christians in the East? Alexius was of no consequence to him. But behind all these considerations an old dream of the Roman Church inspired the zealous Pope's fantasy: the reunion of the Churches. Perhaps the devious Crusade would mean the end of the Schism, and he, Innocent, would become the great unifier of a fragmented Christendom. The support offered for the campaign to Egypt with funds, provisions and 10,000 Byzantine warriors was excuse enough for him to give his agreement to the plan.

In July 1203 the Crusader army stood before the walls of Constantinople, and an attempt was made to take the city by force; for the Frankish soldiers were not received with open arms as Alexius had promised. When the usurper on the throne could see no way out, he fled with his favourite daughter, a sackful of jewels under his arm. In their dire straits the nobles of Constantinople resorted to a final act of cunning. They had the blinded Isaac taken from the dungeon and declared him Emperor once again. After brief negotiations they accepted his son, Alexius IV, as co-regent, and the Crusaders settled without storming the city.

Everything seemed to have turned out well once more, and the army of knights finally had time to recover from their exertions. They took up quarters opposite the city near the tower of Galata. In that summer of 1203 the city at the gateway to the Orient, thronging with the people of many lands, saw numerous Franks wandering amazed through its streets. They came from areas that were backward in comparison: rough forests and simple villages. For the first time they saw a splendour and opulence of treasures which exceeded their wildest dreams. Geoffroy de Villehardouin, one of the leaders of the Crusade and chronicler of the events, wrote:

> In fact many soldiers from the army wandered through Constantinople in amazement, and among the opulent palaces and high churches, of which there were many, and the great treasures, greater than in any other city. One does not even have to mention the relics, because there were as many in the city at this time as those in the whole of the rest of the world put together.

Robert de Clari (1170–1216), a follower of Count Pierre de Amiens, was also passing through at this time. He was a poor but intelligent and pious man. In Constantinople he saw the shrines and relics which Villehardouin was unwilling to detail because of their great quantity. We have him to thank for the informative observation of the Shroud on which 'the figure of our Lord' was to be seen, to which we have already referred.

Obviously to satisfy the curiosity of the Western visitors, the authorities had even opened the gates of the Pharos chapel in the Boucoleon Palace. Prior to this visits to the chapel were the privilege of a small circle of individuals. From these visitors we have descriptions of the Passion relics kept there; and they pose quite a few problems for the historian.

They talk of a *sudarium* (face-towel), of *fasciae* (wrappings), of a *syndon* (linen) and a *linteum* (sheet, canvas), and it is not always clear whether a large shroud, a cloth piece or even the 'towel' that is the alleged Edessa Portrait, is meant. In 1150 an English pilgrim told of a *sudarium* and a 'golden vessel, which contains the *mantele* [towel]', which Jesus had pressed to his face and which had preserved his image. In 1157 the Icelandic pilgrim Nicholas Soemundarson listed in his detailed inventory of palace relics, '*fasciae* with *sudarium* and blood of Christ'. Fourteen years later we learn from Archbishop William of Tyre that he had seen the *syndon* of Christ in the royal treasury chamber. An anonymous inventory of 1190 lists 'parts of the linen in which the crucified body of Christ was wrapped' and also a *syndon* and the 'towel' with the image of Jesus which the Lord had sent to Abgar. In 1200 Antoninus of Novgorod saw a *linteum*, and a second *linteum* with the face of Christ.[67]

When the soldier Clari was allowed to enter the Pharos temple, he could not get over his amazement. The sacred chapel of the Boucoleon Palace was of such an immeasurable opulence, he said, that no object normally made of iron was not of weighty silver or gold. No pillars stood there that were not of marble or porphyry. Among the numerous relics of the chapel, Clari focused on a selection which shows what the immense value of this treasure chamber of Christian history must have been: two fragments of the true cross, the lance, the 'two [sic] nails which were driven through the middle of his hands and through the middle of his feet', the blood of Christ in a crystal container, his tunic, the crown of thorns, the head of John the Baptist. In the centre of the chapel two golden vessels hung from heavy chains of silver. One of these obviously contained the copy of the Edessan Mandylion. In the other container was the Keramion, the stone with the miraculous imprint. Clari gave a distorted version of this legend. Its origins in the Abgar narrative were, it is true, unmistakable; but Abgar and Edessa were no longer involved. Instead the cloth with the image of Jesus was traced back to an apparition of the Lord which appeared to a pious Byzantine citizen. While the man was renovating the roof of his house, Jesus came to him, asked for a cloth, pressed his face into it and gave it back. The form of Jesus vanished, but his countenance remained preserved on the cloth in a miraculous fashion. The man kept the precious towel under a stone until the time of Vespers, and thus the image was transferred onto the stone too.

Clari's observation is very informative. The picture in the golden show-case in a prominent position, right next to the Keramion, was doubtless meant to represent the Mandylion. It seems that only visitors well versed in ecclesiastical history knew of the link with Abgar. The story that was being told about the miraculous portrait, and which Clari circulated, departs from the original tradition. After the secret of the Edessa Portrait was discovered, the patriarchs would have decided gradually to play down the importance of the Mandylion. They came to learn that there had never been a Mandylion like the one praised in the festive sermon. The story was allowed to be forgotten, and the one still known of in Constantinople, when Robert de Clari stood admiringly before the Edessa Portrait, shows just how unimportant it had become in the meantime. For a long time there had been no more mention of the term 'Mandylion'.

At some stage, however, the real Shroud must have been brought to the Blachernae church, because it was there that Clari saw it. Many researchers dealing with the time the cloth was kept in the Blachernae church run up against a problem: why was this important relic found in the Blachernae church and not in the chapel of the imperial palace with the other major relics of the Passion, where one would have expected it to be?

The Boucoleon Palace was an extensive complex in the most ancient core of the city, to the south-west of the former Acropolis, in a way a town within the town. This was by far the best-protected place. The Blachernae church on the other hand belongs to the palace estate of the same name at the extreme northern edge of the city, some 5 km away from Boucoleon. The Blachernae Palace was adjacent to the town wall, which had been completed by

Emperor Manuel I just a few decades before the Fourth Crusade. The church itself, which was, like the Pharos chapel, consecrated to the Virgin Mary, adjoins the north-eastern end of the wall on the coast overlooking the Golden Horn. This location was certainly very exposed and most unsuitable for a secure place of safe-keeping. How did the cloth come to be here? Was Clari perhaps mistaken? It is quite possible that soon after the discovery the decision was made to keep the Mandylion copy at a separate location away from the Shroud. Naturally the 'new' Mandylion had to remain in the imperial chapel at Pharos, its traditional place. The Blachernae church provided a convenient alternative for keeping the Shroud, especially because it belonged to an important palatial estate offering security and protection. The site was also a good choice from the theological and liturgical stand-point, for the Blachernae church already housed the robe of Mary. But we can no longer say exactly when the cloth was moved.

To find satisfactory answers to the questions arising in this matter, we first have to cast an eye over the events that followed the enthronement of Alexius IV as co-regent.

It very soon became clear that Alexius was not in a position to raise the promised cash. At first he attempted to win time by making extravagant gifts to the Venetians and the Crusader leaders. He attracted the wrath of the Eastern Church by trying to get them to acknowledge the sovereignty of Rome, and he even had Church silver melted down to allow him to make the first pay-ments. The situation in the city grew tenser by the day. The Byzantines with their refined manners were becoming tired of the rough, drunken mob of uncouth soldiers, who were constantly causing fear and terror in the surrounding villages. Once again the cunning Dandalo immediately grasped the situation: if his demands could not be met, much more was to be gained by the restless army moving in. He made more and more extortionate demands, so as to drive the desperate Alexius quickly into a corner. In February 1204 Alexius conceded defeat, but at the same time the seething pot of Constantinople boiled over. In the up-rising the mob almost succeeded in lynching a delegation of Crusaders. Instead the citizens took and killed Alexius. Alexius Murtzuphlos succeeded him on the throne as Alexius V, the city gates were bolted shut, and the friendly political helpers from the West suddenly become the besiegers.

Dandolo seemed close to achieving something he would never have dared imagine as he departed from his harbour at home. The collapse of the government of Alexius IV put an end to any possibility of securing the Crusaders' onward passage diplomatically, so Constantinople had to be coerced by force. A Latin emperor in Byzantium, and what is more one who had been brought to the throne with active Venetian support, would provide the best trading concessions and the gain of important naval bases for the republic. The Crusader leaders had their eyes on the conquest of new lands in the vast realms to the east.

After one failed attack, the knights, who had sworn to drive out only Muslims from the sacred sites, took Constantinople on 13 April 1204. Murtzuphlos fled, while the Crusader leaders settled in the Boucoleon Palace that very night. But the conquerors made an unpardonable error of diplomacy: to satisfy the soldiers, they gave them the run of the town for three days of plundering (see Plate 47).

The terrible scenes which ensued, and the horrible destruction caused by the mob of raging vandals, have found their place among the darkest annals of world history. The plundering of the city tore a rift in relations with the Western world for a long time thereafter, while the new Latin Empire in Byzantium, completely misreading the situation, believed they had almost ended the Schism.

The Byzantine historian Niketas Choniates (*c.* 1150–1215) gave an eye-witness account of the terrible ravages of the plunderers, how they forced their way with horses and oxen into the palaces and churches, looting the sacred vessels and anything of value, how they smashed chairs and prayer benches, and even ripped precious ornaments from their supports and doorways. Niketas himself fled from one friend to another during this time; but nowhere was he safe from the fury of the horde. Finally he had to abandon everything to the plunderers and run from his beloved city. There seemed to be no limits to the terror. Harmless citizens were indiscriminately struck down, the 'Christian' conquerors violated nuns in the convents, and in the Hagia Sophia they put a whore on the throne of the patriarchs. Niketas' cry of torment, the plea of a disillusioned and broken man, echoes down to our times: 'Even the Saracens would have been more merciful!'

Only the estates of the Boucoleon and Blachernae palaces

1. The baroque high altar in the royal chapel of Turin cathedral. Behind the grating set in the frame that is visible in the centre of the picture is the shrine in which the cloth lies.

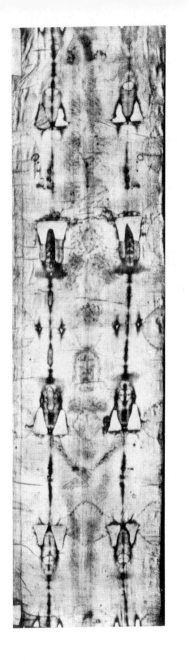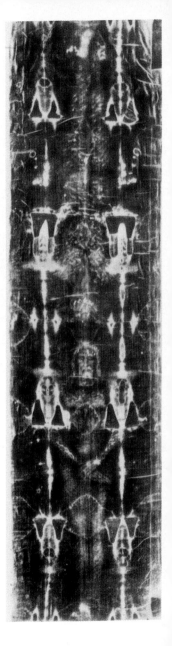

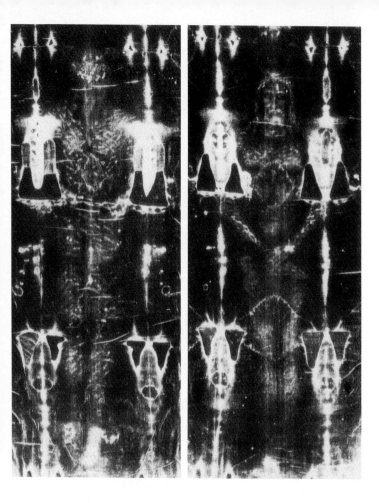

2. *(Opposite left)* The cloth in its full length of 4.36 m (width 1.10 m), as it appears to the naked eye.

3. *(Opposite right)* The complete cloth in reverse as a photographic negative. It is the negative which first shows up all the details clearly.

4. *(Above)* In the negative many astonishing details on the front and rear sides of the body come to light.

5. It is the negative which shows the face radiating grace and dignity.

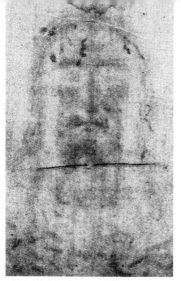

6. To the unaided eye the portrait has a mask-like appearance.

7. The structure of the weave is what is called a herringbone pattern, which at the time of Jesus was found only in the region of Syria.

8. The body was laid in the cloth in this way, as shown on this painting from the sixteenth century.

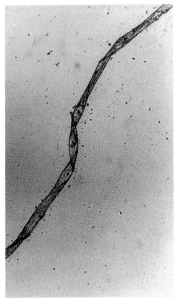 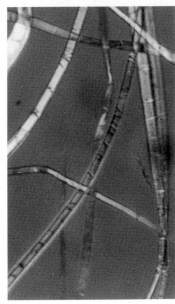

9. *(Above left)* These twisted cotton fibres were found in the fabric of the cloth. (Enlarged)

10. *(Above right)* These flax fibres from the Turin cloth have a structure like bamboo. (Enlarged)

11. *(Opposite top)* The sample which was taken in 1973 for the Belgian textile expert Prof Raes was some 4cm long and 1cm wide (front and rear surface).

12. *(Opposite centre)* This postage-stamp-sized piece of fabric was received by the radiocarbon laboratory in Oxford for dating.

13. *(Opposite below)* A portion of the sample which was dated in Tucson, Arizona.

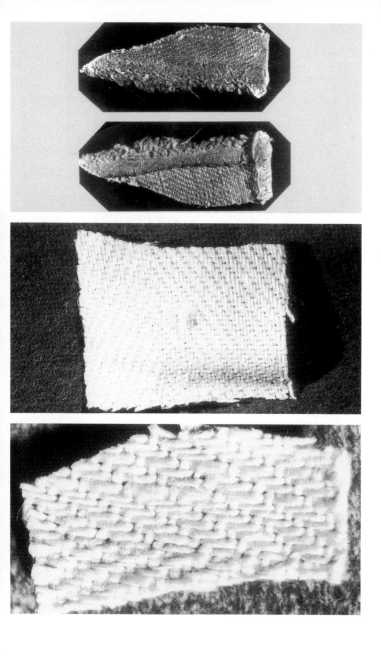

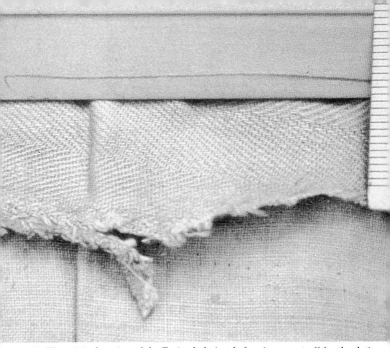

14. The original section of the Turin cloth, just before it was cut off for the dating test. This photograph serves as a comparison for the portions which the laboratories received.

15. Prof Raes during his lecture at the 1989 Shroud symposium in Paris.

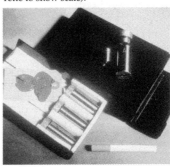

16. The containers which were given, sealed, to the three laboratories (cigarette to show scale).

17. After the secret distribution Dr Tite brings the samples from the sacristy.

18. Prof Wölfli in his laboratory in Zurich. Before him are the containers with the various samples.

19. Hall, Tite and Hedges (from left to right) at the official announcement of the dating results at a press conference in London in October 1988.

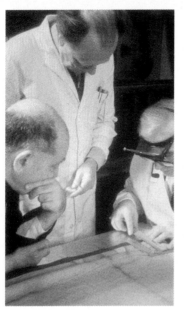

20. *(Above left)* Under the watchful eye of Cardinal Ballestrero (left) and Prof Testore (standing), Giovanni Riggi cuts the original strip from the Turin cloth.

21. *(Above right)* Prof Hall beside the accelerator of the test apparatus in his institute in Oxford.

22. *(Opposite top left)* Pollen of *Epimedium pubigerum* from the region of Constantinople.

23. *(Opposite top right)* Pollen of the plant *Sudea aegyptiaca*, which grows in the salt deserts by the Dead Sea.

24. *(Opposite below)* Only five of these threads from the rear surface of the cope of St Louis of Anjou were actually used for the mysterious blind specimen No 4.

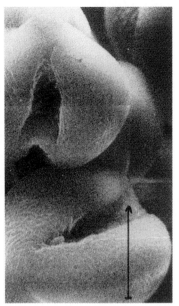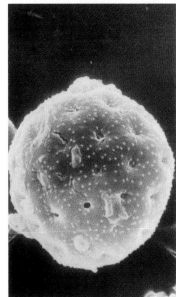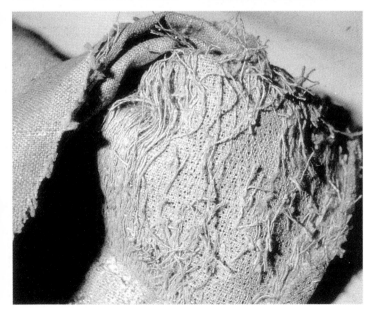

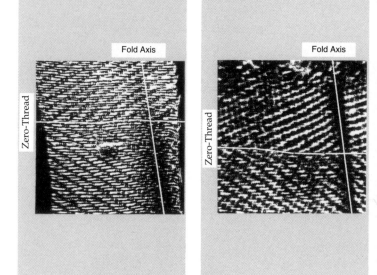

25.*(Above left)* The Oxford sample 01 digitized by computer.

26. *(Above right)* The original strip of the Turin cloth was digitized and given co-ordinates, so that it could be compared precisely with the Oxford sample.

27. *(Opposite top)* By superimposition the threads of Plates 25 and 26 are matched up. The diagonal weave lines do not run from the same points on the cut edge: a further proof that the two samples are not identical.

28. *(Opposite below)* Unlike Plate 27 the diagonal weave lines are matched up here. Now one sees that the horizontal threads no longer line up together. The fabric samples of both pieces are clearly distinguishable by the different closeness of weave and the differing thread thicknesses.

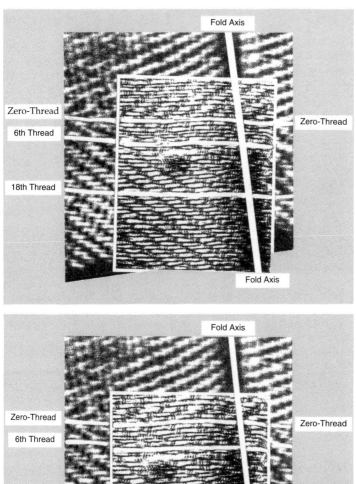

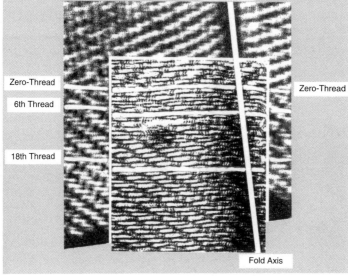

29. *(Above left)* On this miniature from the fourteenth century Thaddeus, 'the messenger of Jesus', brings the cloth to give to King Abgar of Edessa. 30. *(Above right)* King Abgar with the cloth which Jesus had sent to him (icon, tenth century).

31. *(Below)* After being lost for a long period, the Mandylion was rediscovered in Edessa (miniature, thirteenth century).

32. *(Above)* One of the first 'authentic' Jesus portraits similar to the cloth is found on this silver vase from the sixth century.

33. *(Below)* In this picture of the Apostles' Communion from the sixth century the depiction of Jesus is readily seen to be similar to the portrait on the cloth.

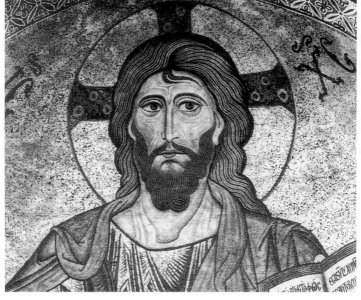

36. Mandylion in the Armenian church of St Bartholomew at Genoa (fourteenth century).

34. *(Opposite top)* This 'Christ enthroned' (mosaic in the Hagia Sophia, ninth or tenth century) also matches the face on the cloth right down to details.

35. *(Opposite below)* Mosaic portrait of Jesus in the apse of the cathedral of Cefalù (twelfth century).

37. *(Top)* Copy of the Mandylion in Gradac, Serbia (twelfth century). The proportions correspond to the folded cloth. 38. *(Centre)* Copy of the Mandylion at Spas Neriditsa near Novgorod (twelfth century). 39. *(Below)* Copy of the Mandylion from the Studenica monastery, Serbia (thirteenth century).

40. Jesus during the Ascension as an unbearded youth following the Greek ideal (ivory c. 400).

41. The Edessa Portrait was brought to Constantinople in 944 (miniature, fourteenth century).

42. Encaustic (painted with wax colours) icon from the monastery of St Catherine, Sinai, bearing the proportions of the Turin cloth (sixth century).

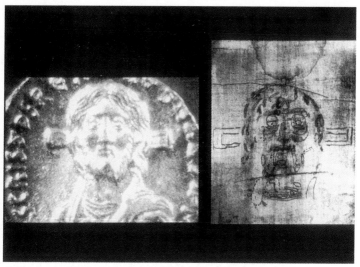

43. The face on this Byzantine coin (solidus, 692) matches the portrait on the cloth in a remarkable manner.

44. The icon of Christ (Plate 42) compared with the cloth image, showing correspondences.

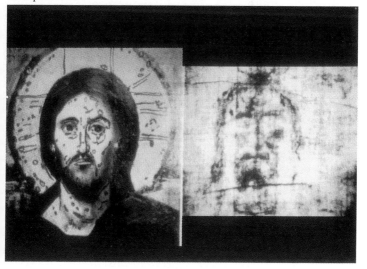

45. *(Opposite top)* Portrait of Christ on a gold coin (solidus, Justinian II, seventh century).

46. *(Opposite below)* Christ portrait on a Byzantine solidus of 945, shortly after the cloth was brought to Constantinople.

47. *(Above)* The army of the Fourth Crusade attacking Christian Constantinople (miniature, fourteenth century).

48. The famous icon 'not made by human hand' of Novgorod (c. 1200).

49. The Holy Countenance of Laon, France (twelfth century).

50. The Lamentation of Christ on a fresco of 1164 in a church in Nerezi near Skopje, Macedonia. The position of the body and the rhombic pattern on the cloth suggest the model on the Turin cloth.

51. This fourteenth century *epitaphion* from Thessaloniki shows the body and the pattern of the weave as in the Turin cloth.

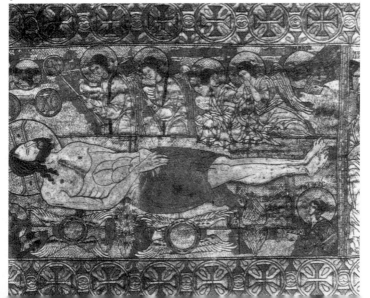

53. This panel painting from Templecombe, England (date uncertain) was found in a settlement of Temple Knights. It may have been the cover of a chest in which a copy of the 'idol' of the Templars was kept.

52. *(Opposite)* This depiction from the Budapest prayer book (Codex Pray) of 1192 shows the conspicuous type of weave of the Turin cloth in a schematic form, and shows most clearly the four burn holes arranged in an L-shape in precisely the same formation as on the original.

54. The last Grand Masters of the Templar Order, Jaques de Molay and Geoffroy de Charnay were burnt at the stake in Paris in 1307 (miniature, fourteenth century).

55. Knight of the Templar Order in armour (copperplate engraving, eighteenth century).

56. Knight of the Templar Order in civil costume (copperplate engraving, eighteenth century).

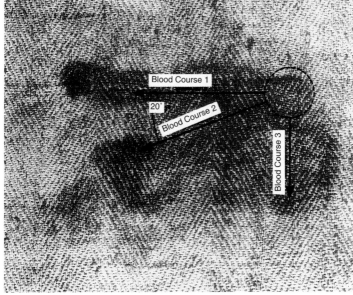

57. The courses of blood from the nail wounds on the wrist prove that blood continued to flow after the body had been placed in the cloth.

58. This pilgrim's medallion from Lirey (1357, enlarged) is the first depiction of the Shroud in its full length. Note the plait-formed blood flow under the back.

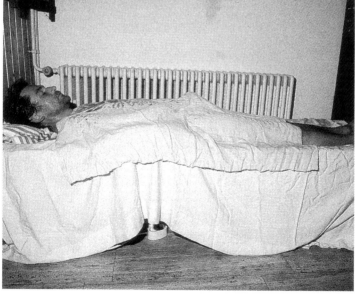

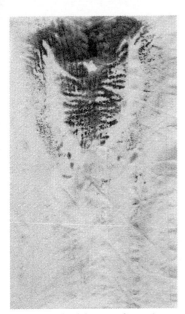

61. The result of the second experiment was still unsatisfactory

62. At the third attempt an image was formed which did reproduce the contours clearly, even though they do appear somewhat distorted in width.

59. *(Opposite above)* Holger Kersten grinding the aloe and myrrh for the experiment to study how the image was formed.

60. *(Opposite below)* Holger Kersten coated with the tincture beneath the cloth made of untreated, hand-worked linen fabric.

63. The two-part Arizona sample *(front)*, immediately after being removed from the foil *(middle)* and the steel receptacle *(behind)*.

64. In 1983 Pope John Paul II made a special journey to Portugal to persuade ex-king Umberto II in his exile to bequeath the Turin Shroud to the Vatican. Shortly thereafter the former king of Italy died.

escaped the plunderers' hands, because they were occupied by the commanders immediately after the attack. On 16 May 1204 Count Baldwin IX of Flanders and Hennegau was crowned the Latin Emperor of Byzantium, Baldwin I.

The Shroud Disappears

All trace of the Shroud was lost in this time of hectic change, and it was only to surface again after 150 years, in a provincial church in France. Robert de Clari, remarked, 'Nobody knows, neither Greek nor Frank, what became of the cloth after the town was taken.'

It seems that Clari was so interested in the relic that after the conquest of Constantinople he went looking for it, but without success. According to all that we know about shroud relics in Constantinople before the conquest of 1204, they were kept in the chapel at Pharos. We have a list of the Passion relics kept there in 1201, prepared by Nicholas Mesarites, Curator for Church Treasures in the Great Palace.[68] He mentioned the burial *sindones* of Christ. It was of linen, a cheap and easily obtainable material. It was still fragrant with myrrh and had remained preserved from decay because it was said to have wrapped 'the mysterious, naked dead body after the Passion'. It is difficult to say whether Mesarites is referring to the shroud which Clari claimed he saw two years later in the Blachernae church. I have already emphasized that there were probably a number of shroud relics, all laying claim to authenticity. Wilson points out that the choice of the words 'after the Passion' rather than 'in the tomb' could mean that it was not the actual burial cloth, but the cloth used to assist in taking Jesus down from the cross. Perhaps the reference to the 'naked body' can be taken as showing a knowledge of the image on the cloth. There is another term which Mesarites used which is of interest here. Describing the body which lay in the cloth, he used the expression *aperilepton*, which can have the meanings 'undefined', 'unlimited', 'indescribable' or 'mysterious'. If we decide against a symbolic interpretation, the passage may, as Scavone shows,[69] refer to the picture known to us which is 'undefined' because it is strangely lacking in clear outlines. Mesarites described the Passion relics as if they were talismans or charms, serving as a protection when an unruly mob rose up during a palace revolution. And he spoke of the great holiness of the chapel, saying Christ rose again here, and the *sindon* was the clear proof of it: in a way a new Resurrection had taken place here, because the times of the Passion and burial were brought to life by the relics.

Also located here were the Keramion and the Mandylion copy in the caskets on the silver chains which Clari described. Mesarites himself mentioned the miraculous portrait of Jesus on the *cheiromaktron* (towel) and the stone. It is significant that he no longer used the term Mandylion, and described the picture on the towel as formed 'by a certain art of drawing, not made by hand'.[70] The reference to the 'art of drawing' appears to me to be a clear indication that the observer could see that it was an artistic work, that is to say the portrait was of quite a different kind from the image on the Shroud. After all the secret of the Mandylion had been revealed by this time, and the old Edessan picture was only kept as a 'genuine' copy.

The well-known researcher of the Turin Shroud, Werner Bulst, suggests that Mesarites was still referring to the true Mandylion/ Shroud, and Clari had just seen an *epitaphios* cloth with the painted or embroidered image of the body of Jesus in the Blachernae church, such as 'had been used in many Eastern churches for the service on Good Friday, at least since about 1300'.[71] The true Shroud with the image was, he maintains, still kept in folded form as the Mandylion in the Pharos chapel. Recently Bulst has even suggested that the chapel itself was named after the most important of the relics kept in it: in Homer the word *pharos* is used in the sense of 'shroud'.[72] Constantine would have had the chapel built to house the folded shroud next to the *labarum*. Then, at the time of the pagan counter-attack during the reign of Julian Apostata the picture was brought to safety in Edessa. When it was recovered it was again taken to the Pharos chapel, now as the Mandylion. The relic, he holds, only disappeared from Constantinople in 1247, when the last Latin Emperor, Baldwin II, pressed by an acute shortage of funds, made over a range of important sacred articles to King Louis IX, the Saint. These included a *sancta toella tabule inserta* ('holy towel mounted in a panel'). For Bulst there is no doubt that this was actually the Mandylion/Shroud, sent to Louis from the treasures of the Pharos chapel.

On closer study this theory is seen to rest on very weak foundations. Firstly Bulst errs in the assumption that Constantine built the Boucoleon Palace and the Pharos chapel. The chapel was only built centuries later, under Constantine V Kopronymos (741–75); it was built on the terrace opposite the lighthouse called the Pharos. Evidently the chapel was named after the famous lighthouse.[73] Furthermore, an image-bearing cloth could not have played any role at the time of construction. The Shroud itself was situated in Edessa; and it would have been unthinkable for Constantine V, known to be a radical iconoclast, to erect a chapel to house a divine image.

To say that Robert de Clari had merely seen an *epitaphios* cloth in the Blachernae church is another very bold assertion on the part of Bulst. People have, it is true, tended to portray Clari as over-pious and credulous, but in fact he has to be seen as a reliable observer. Numerous events which he described as happening during the Fourth Crusade do agree very well with what Villehardouin describes. He gave us an exact description of the sacred treasures of the Pharos chapel – which, one should add, Bulst himself relies on – and it is not clear why he should have made such a crude blunder just when describing the cloth in the Blachernae church. Clari was quite capable of distinguishing between painted, embroidered and other types of cloths. He must have seen numerous relics, and not just briefly – he held them in his own hands. According to the tradition, Clari brought a great number of relics with him from Constantinople to his home town of Corbie in Picardy. Specially noted was a cruciform crystal reliquary, which, one should add, contained a fragment of the *'sudarium* of our Lord' and came from the Pharos chapel. No less than 54 relics are mentioned in an inventory of the contents of the *sanctuarium* which Robert de Clari brought back with him from Constantinople.[74] There was a 'Holy Countenance' among them. This was almost certainly a copy of the Mandylion. The similarity of this to other portraits of its kind such as the Edessa Portrait in the Matilda chapel of the Vatican, or the picture in the Armenian church in Genoa, is remarkable.[75] A person with such an intimate first-hand knowledge of the relics has to be considered trustworthy in this field. Clari's statement that it was the Shroud, on which the figure of Jesus was clearly visible, which he saw in the Blachernae church, and the additional comment that neither

Franks nor Greeks knew where it went to, should not be dismissed too lightly. He obviously made inquiries among Greeks and Franks as to its whereabouts. One can assume that Clari had resolved to bring this important relic back home with him if at all possible.

A further weakness in Bulst's argument is the way he insists that the Shroud remained in the form of the Edessan Mandylion up to the time of its transfer to Paris. But he himself says that a knowledge of the complete figure on a folded cloth had been arrived at much earlier, and had decisively influenced the iconography of the lamentation and deposition scenes, as well as depictions of the 'man of suffering', in the West. As I have said, it is unthinkable that after the discovery of the complete cloth it was folded up to form a portrait. That not only goes against all logic, it would have meant the Byzantine Church was robbing itself of its most important relic.

Bulst attempts to support his thesis by citing the obituary speech which Nicholas Mesarites gave for his brother in 1207. In the course of this the former Curator of the Pharos chapel repeatedly mentioned the Passion relics, and the portrait of Christ, which Bulst takes to be the original Mandylion; then the Shroud/Mandylion was still present in Constantinople in 1207. But since the assumption of power by Baldwin all the ecclesiastical positions had been transferred to Latins, and Mesarites had had to give up the office of Curator. As the historian Daniel Scavone impressively shows, Mesarites made use of his own statements from 1201 for the eulogy, with almost the same wording for the rhetoric.[76] It can provide no proof that any of the relics mentioned were still in the Pharos chapel in 1207.

The difficulties in identifying the shroud in the Blachernae church in 1203, and its subsequent disappearance, have spawned a number of hypotheses, some of them highly speculative. One of these is that of Noel Currer-Briggs. It is given here next to the thesis of Bulst, because they are both constantly referred to in the literature. Currer-Briggs starts from the assumption – and here he follows Ian Wilson – that the Mandylion, again taken as the genuine folded shroud, was used as a *palladium* of the Empire during the siege by the Crusader army. It was meant to ward off the Latin aggressors from Constantinople, just as it had once kept the Persians from Edessa. Currer-Briggs supposes that the

Mandylion was taken from time to time from the Pharos chapel and brought to the Blachernae church at the city wall, where it was to prove its worth as a *palladium*. When the city was taken in April 1204, however, it was not found in the Blachernae church, because this was plundered; it must have been in the Pharos chapel. The widow Empress Margaret (who had married the Crusader Boniface of Monferat after the death of her husband Emperor Isaac II), took the cloth for herself. After the wedding the couple took the precious relic along with them, first to Thessaloniki. Then the cloth had an adventurous journey, stopping in Klis and Trogir, in what is now Yugoslavia, until it was sold to the Templars by King Bela IV of Hungary in 1242 because of a financial emergency. Strangely enough the cloth was mounted as the Mandylion in a frame which was also supposed to contain the Keramion. The latter was said to have come into the possession of the Cathars of Languedoc, leading to the idea of the Grail as a stone – the *lapis èxilis*.

To subject each of Currer-Briggs' proposals to a thorough criticism would take us too far afield; and many of them do not warrant the effort because they are based on incorrect historical assumptions. We will just look at the essential elements connected with the Shroud. The idea that the Mandylion was still serving the function it had as a *palladium* in Edessa, at the beginning of the thirteenth century, seems to me to be quite untenable for various reasons. First the Mandylion must have lost a large part of its usefulness as a protection-bestowing object the moment Edessa was taken. The protection guaranteed by Jesus in his letter to Abgar related explicitly to Edessa itself; and what value could a *palladium* still have if it was not even able to protect itself? After all it was taken away from Edessa by force. It is fair to assume that Romanus Lacapenus was no longer much concerned about in the protective function of the Edessa Portrait; he was much more interested in the special reverence which the holy object received everywhere. And he was probably also keen to see that this important relic was not left in a provincial capital, certainly not in one which was controlled by the Arabs.

There is nothing to suggest that the Mandylion still served as a *palladium* in Constantinople. Quite the contrary. During the brief rule of Emperor Alexius V Murtzuphlos from February to April 1204, he made a surprise attack against the Crusaders. The usurper took 4000 men to pursue Henry, the brother of Baldwin of Flanders, after he had set off with a small force towards Philae. In this attack Murtzuphlos had 'the icon with him, a picture of the Virgin, which the rulers took along whenever they entered an affray', according to Clari, and 'in which the Greeks had great faith'.[77] Murtzuphlos was conquered and lost the icon, which was set entirely in gold and studded with splendid gems. It was entrusted to the bishop of Troyes (and later passed on to the Cistercian abbey at Cîteaux). Shortly thereafter it was festively carried on a ship around Constantinople, to show the inhabitants that it was in the attackers' possession. The Greeks, seeing a bad omen in this, became nervous and opposed the usurper Murtzuphlos.

This episode clearly shows that a very different image, an icon of the Mother of God with a valuable mounting, had assumed the role of *palladium*. The Crusaders had at once recognized this and 'reversed' the power of the *palladium* by the maritime procession with the icon around the walls of the city. The Mandylion no longer played any role in such matters. It is, moreover, quite inexplicable why the Mandylion should be opened up every time, as Currer-Briggs suggests, to get it into the Blachernae church as an unfolded shroud. That makes no sense at all. Clari's account clearly indicates that the cloth in the Blachernae church served a special liturgical function, which suggests an established institution and not a hectic swapping here and there. Clari spoke of the cloth being displayed every Friday, with it so arranged that the *figure* of Jesus was clearly visible. This Friday ceremony can only mean a theological context, not a political one, and clearly shows that its use was to aid the recollection of Christ's Passion.

Currer-Briggs tries to track the subsequent journey of the Mandylion/Shroud by finding either a Church of the Holy *Acheiropoieton* or one in which the Mandylion or a 'suspicious' lamentation scene is pictured, at every stopping place. He gives particular importance to the first stop in Thessaloniki, even though by doing so he commits a major error. He assumes that the term *acheiropoieton* is always used in connection with pictures of the Shroud portrait, and does not take the trouble to study the consecration of a Church of the Holy *Acheiropoieton* in more depth. The term itself is neutral, as we have seen, and certainly was not used only for the Edessa Portrait. And churches to which this epithet is applied were always connected with the Virgin Mary, of whom numerous images 'not made by human hands' are known in the tradition. In recent research this very example of the *Acheiropoieton* Church of Thessaloniki has been taken to illustrate this fact.[78] And finally, were we to draw our conclusions from frescoes and mosaics in churches, we could easily outline a journey for the Mandylion/Shroud through the whole region of Asia Minor, the Balkans and Italy. But there is not the least historical evidence that the Edessa Portrait or the Shroud had been brought to any of the places mentioned by Currer-Briggs, and we hear not a word about the remarkable textile from any of the alleged owners of the cloth until it came into the possession of the Templars. Of course Currer-Briggs also owes an explanation for the motive in his far-fetched, quite misleading hypothesis, which has Margaret taking the relic for herself.

In such attempts to try and explain the mysterious disappearance of the cloth and the impenetrable silence which hung over its history, we can see an inadmissible combination of tenuous hints taken against the backdrop of a precarious political situation. All influential people in the thirteenth century suddenly come under suspicion. According to these arguments anyone could have desired the Shroud, some perhaps only wanted to get hold of the old imperial *palladium*. According to Willi K. Müller, André de Joinville gained possession of it in 1203 and brought it to Akkra, then between 1229 and 1245 it made its way to Germany. Again he bases his hypothesis on artistic works in churches, this time in the Frankish region. Bulst, who uses Müller as a reference, brings in the Hohenstaufen dynasty, who he says wanted to own the *palladium*. There are endless lists of interested parties, numerous options, so much historical science fiction.

Ian Wilson does more justice to the historical sources. He finds it logical to recognize that at the time of the siege of Constantinople the Shroud was not the same object as the Mandylion, and the latter survived only as a copy. But who acquired the Shroud, and how, remains a mystery for him. Whoever it may have been, they must have finally made it over to the Order of the Templars.

Wilson supports this thesis with the following arguments. Since the period of 'submergence' extends to over a century, one has to infer a continuity of ownership. Consequently it was more likely to have been a group rather than an individual. The group must have been in close contact with the Crusaders, and must have been very wealthy to avoid the temptation of selling the relic. The owners must have been in a position to guarantee secrecy and security, they must have had a motive to act in this manner, and they must have been Christians. Finally they must have had a historical link to Geoffroy de Charny, the French knight who has gone down in history as the first acknowledged owner of the Shroud. 'Who, therefore, had such a high opinion of themselves that they considered Christ's most precious relic their exclusive right?' The answer which Wilson gives to his own question is: the Templars. This hypothesis is quite impressive and not at all far-fetched. The central element, which brings the face on the Shroud to the fore, is the famous, mysterious cult of a bearded head, which the Templars were said to have worshipped as an idol in their secret meetings. I will later come to analyse in detail the possibility that the Templar idol was taken directly from the Shroud image, and that the Order was probably the owner of the Shroud in the thirteenth century. But first one has to deal with the question of how the cloth could have come into their possession. Wilson and all those who have followed him in the search for answers, are unable to find any. They console themselves by referring to the aura of mystery surrounding the Templars –. they would have had their methods.

The Templars' Manoeuvre

Such a reply is unsatisfactory, although it is very likely that the Templars did play some role in the drama of the cloth. If they had really been interested in the cloth, they would have tried everything they could to secure possession of it. They were certainly well informed about it in Constantinople. They were among the privileged ones who were allowed entry to the hidden shrines. Everard de Barre, Grand Master of the Templars, had the opportunity to see the Passion relics in Constantinople during the Second Crusade in 1147, while in the entourage of Louis VII and his consort Eleanor of Aquitaine.

The Templars had been at the front line in the Crusades and the battles against the Muslims since the Order's founding in 1119.

But during the Fourth Crusade they were not among the knights at Constantinople; they had vowed never to fight against Christians, and their restraint was impressive. But as soon as the city was taken, they were back in the picture.

The Pope's legates to Constantinople had in their retinue a number of great churchmen and knights. There were also a number of Templars on the ships which departed from Akkon for Constantinople in 1204. If the Templars wanted to get the Shroud, they would have had to act quickly.

We can assume that reliable men from their ranks, who were to carry out the coup, were sent into the city immediately after it was taken, or had already been slipped in with the Crusader army as 'secret agents'. But the mission was not easy to accomplish. Despite the great confusion which reigned during the days of plundering, there were two districts which remained free from the ravages. One was the Boucoleon Palace, of which the Marquis Boniface of Monferat took possession; and, contrary to what was often previously supposed, the Blachernae Palace with its church was also spared from the plundering.[79] It was secured by Henry of Flanders, the brother of the later Emperor Baldwin, immediately after the Crusader army burst through, not far from it. Villehardouin describes the events in these words:

> Just as that palace [the Boucoleon] was given to the Marquis Boniface, the one at Blachernae was given to Henry, the brother of Count Baldwin, together with the lives of those in it; here they found another great treasure, no less rich than that of the Boucoleon.

None of the relics could simply be looted by the plundering hordes. Instead they were carefully distributed among the clerical and secular leaders. Conrad, Bishop of Halberstadt, who had especially good relations with Boniface, gradually acquired so many relics from the Pharos chapel that he was later asked to return some of them. Hence we can assume that the Shroud was removed from its traditional site with the permission of the Flemish count. But why do we have no report about this?

One of the Templars who followed the developments in Constantinople rather like secret agents, was Brother Baroche, Magister of the Order in Lombardy.[80] When Baldwin chose a messenger to communicate the news of his selection and crowning with a circular to the Pope and the Christian nobles, the Templar

Baroche was appointed. It is remarkable that a relatively un-known Templar was chosen for such a special task, which after all meant no less than to announce the promise to reunite the divided Church. There were enough renowned warriors who had contributed to the daring undertaking from the start and who had fought at Baldwin's side at the conquest of the city. They would gladly have accepted the honour of going to Rome as emissaries of the Latin Emperor. Yet Baldwin settled on an unknown – but a Templar. Practically nothing is known about Brother Baroche. With the exception of this commission it seems that he never served in any important role, diplomatic or otherwise.

How the task came to be given to Baroche remains a mystery, but if the Templars did want to get hold of the cloth they now had an excellent opportunity. It would have been impossible for them to obtain such a precious and unique relic as this on the 'open relic market'. Immense sums were paid even for insignificant fragments of Passion relics. And the Holy See would probably have made its claim, if this Order, whose influence was already so great, was seen to acquire the cloth with the image of Jesus.

Baldwin did not send his emissary on the journey empty-handed. He filled his ship with costly tapestries, gems, gold and relics. Now the Templars had their chance. They had managed to position their man in the coveted post, now they had to get the cloth from the Blachernae church. Baroche had to convince Emperor Baldwin how important it was to bring the most im-portant relic of the Byzantine Empire to Rome, the centre of Christendom, to make a gift of it to the Pope. In this way the Emperor would testify to his devotion and win the favour of the Holy See. Moving the sacred object to Rome would symbolically affirm the city's role: Jesus himself would make his triumphant entry into the Eternal City in the form of his bodily imprint on the cloth!

Baldwin was won over. Brother Baroche soon departed for Rome on a Venetian vessel. He bore with him a missive from the Emperor and valuable gifts; among the latter, well guarded, was the Shroud of Jesus. He would certainly have instructed Baldwin to keep quiet about the precious cargo. It would be better to depart into the Sea of Marmara without attracting attention; the times were unsafe, and many dangers might yet have to be faced on the long journey. Moreover, it was difficult to judge how the clergy and the Crusaders were going to react to Baldwin's moving the most precious relic out of the country without their consent, not to speak of a possible disturbance among the Greeks. It would be best to proceed with all caution, to maintain the political peace at home.

The journey by ship from Constantinople to Rome could be made in a few weeks. But if the conditions were unfavourable this period could easily stretch to months. One can no longer determine exactly when Brother Baroche headed out to sea, but after about a week the small delegation would have reached the island of Andros, where there were copious bubbling springs for them to fill the water vessels for the remaining journey. Then their course led along the coast, past the three southward-facing promontories of the Peloponnese, which was then known as Morea. Shortly before the ship passed the last western tip of land before the harbour of Modon, to steer into the Ionian Sea, what they had feared happened: a small fleet was seen heading towards Brother Baroche's vessel, obviously with the intention of capturing it.

Sea journeys in those days were fraught with danger. Particularly in the eastern Mediterranean, on the important trade routes, there was frequent feuding between the major maritime powers of Venice, Genoa and Pisa. In times of war the aim was to overcome the enemy's merchant vessels by squadrons of nimble ships. But even in more peaceful times important trading ships or whole merchant flotillas had to be protected by ships of war. There was a lot to lose with a large trading vessel and it made a good catch for skilful pirates. None too fine a line was drawn between the guarding of one's own fleet and piracy. Often individual ships were allowed to go off pirating on their own, while the main part of the fleet sailed back to port. The business of piracy did not carry any ignoble connotations, and often citizens would take part in feuds and battles using their own vessels under official supervision. Bishop Conrad of Halberstadt, for example, narrowly escaped an attack by pirates with his two ships filled with sacred articles from Constantinople.[81]

Baldwin's envoy had no such luck. Off Modon he found himself facing no less than six Genoese galleys, each sporting about 140 oars,[82] which would not let his ship escape. The Genoese annals for 1204 mention this successful attack: they looted large sums of money and many relics of saints and splendid crosses, brought them to Genoa and distributed the sacred items among the churches of the town.[83]

Should we therefore assume that the precious cloth ended up with some rogue in Genoa, and that the Templars, so close to their goal, were deprived of it? Far from it. It is more likely that the surprise raid off Modon was part of the Templars' plan: the cloth could disappear without them being accused. Let us look at this hypothesis more closely.

Baroche, who had succeeded in convincing Baldwin to send the cloth to the Pope, could have instructed other Templar agents to make a deal with the Genoese: on a certain date they were to ambush a poorly guarded ship off Modon. They were to leave unharmed the ship, the envoy, and a plain relic which was merely a valueless long cloth, and in return they could keep the precious treasure which was on its way to Rome. It would be good, for appearances' sake, to set off with an overwhelmingly larger force; then there would not be any resistance worth mentioning. This would avoid too much bloodshed without making the ship's crew suspicious.

Another possibility is that the cloth was removed from the ship during a stopover, and the ship then sailed on to the pre-arranged attack. In this case one could even do without the collaboration between Templars and Genoese, which might have had unforeseen consequences. The Templar agents could have spread rumours about the ship heavily laden with gold and silver, while making it clear that it was on a diplomatic mission for the highest authorities and it would therefore be advisable to leave ship and crew unharmed. Perhaps Baroche dropped anchor just off Modon in Kalamata and brought the cloth to the Templar settlement at Fuste nearby. When his ship was later ambushed, the relic was no longer on board.

Whatever the circumstances, it is striking that the pirates left the ship and crew unharmed, for Brother Baroche arrived at Rome in 1204 and handed Baldwin's letter to Pope Innocent. This is indeed unusual. Captured ships were normally taken to Genoa, where they were integrated in the local fleet. Where the ships were too badly damaged, or were difficult to bring back for some other reason, they were burned. Why should these Ligurians, notorious for their ruthlessness, depart from their normal procedure in this particular case? Simply because this was how they had planned the attack.

Innocent, who heard of the raid from Baroche, threatened the guilty with excommunication and the city of Genoa with severance from the Church, if the stolen articles were not returned to the Apostolic See and the Templars. The Pope's letter dated 4 November 1204, which deals with this, is very informative.[84] It lists the objects which Baldwin had wanted to present as gifts. These included a jewel, a ring, an embroidered altar cover and 1000 pieces of silver for the Holy See. The Templars were to receive two icons, a relic of the true Cross with numerous gems, two golden crosses, almost 200 topazes, emeralds and rubies, a crystal ampoule, two silver goblets, a gilded casket, two relic chests, a silver box and fifty pieces of silver. Compared with the treasures meant for the Templars, the gift for Innocent seems quite modest!

One is struck by the fact that all the relics listed were meant for the Templars. But this does not mean that the Pope was only to receive gold and jewellery. The absence of any relics for Rome in this list speaks for itself. Innocent was meant to receive the most important of all Passion relics, beside which every other relic would pale. Baldwin had obviously decided against sending him other relics besides the cloth, probably thinking to enhance the dramatic effect.

It is understandable that the Shroud does not appear in the list of stolen articles. Baroche had not made any announcement about it. Perhaps he had discussed the possibility of an ambush with Baldwin and agreed to keep quiet about the cloth in such a contingency. It would certainly be better this way. One just has to imagine the embarrassment which knowledge of this piece of freight could have caused: the Latin Emperor wanted to take the Shroud secretly from the Blachernae church and send it to Rome as a gift to pacify the Pope, only to have the precious relic snatched from his envoys by a mob of ruthless pirates. What an unspeakable profanation, Jesus himself in the form of his presence in the sacred cloth, as loot in the hands of drunken pirates! What a setback for the Emperor! To make such a desecration known would be quite unthinkable. For the Templars, this meant that they could be sure that Baldwin himself would not reveal anything about the secret operation. Besides, he would have had little time to do so. Some months after the raid became known, on 15 April 1205, Baldwin was captured by the Bulgarians after a battle and died in prison shortly afterwards.

Thus the Shroud came to disappear from Constantinople and slipped unnoticed into the possession of the wealthiest and most powerful Order of the high Middle Ages.

The Power and Secrets of the Order of the Knights Templar

The Templars are still considered one of the most controversial communities of the Middle Ages. Countless stories, legends and rumours have been woven around the Order of the Poor Knights of Christ. Even today the Order, which for 200 years influenced the course of world politics, has lost nothing of its fascination. Despite all the rational analysis, in the esoterically oriented annals of history the Templars figure as the true guardians of the Holy Grail, the preservers of a spiritual tradition and a hidden knowledge, which was later passed on to the circles of secret societies such as the Renaissance Hermetics, the Rosicrucians and the Freemasons. It is not necessary to discuss the role of the Templars in the esoteric literature; the references are too widely ramified, truth and fiction too inextricably tangled. One can however gain some idea of how current the 'Templar problem' still is, if one considers how Umberto Eco's novel (*The Foucalt Pendulum*), which is based partly on the occult history of the Templars and their continued activity down through the centuries, became a bestseller.

This means that when analysing the role played by the Order in the history of the Turin cloth, it is particularly important to see that one is not led astray by current preconceptions, and that the journey one traces out can be supported by the documents.

We still have to deal with the question of the motive: why the Templars wanted to have the cloth. This only becomes clear when one sees the full extent of the relic's significance. The critical clue pointing to the Templars as owners of the cloth is their mysterious idol cult, which was followed in the utmost secrecy. They were said to have worshipped a bearded head, revering him as saviour. Was the idol of the Templars the Jesus of the Shroud, or a copy of him, and where did the Templars take the Shroud when they were suppressed? To get any closer to answering these difficult questions, we first have to cast some light on the Order and the historical circumstances which led to its formation and dissolution.

The foundation of the Order of the Poor Knights of Christ can be traced back to Hugh of Payens. He brought it into being in 1119 with eight like-minded people, while he was a Crusader under Baldwin II, King of Jerusalem. The small group of knights took the three classical vows of poverty, chastity and obedience. In addition to these there was a fourth vow: to fight against the infidels. Later the protection of pilgrims was added, and became their primary task. Baldwin II granted them a part of his palace at the old Temple of Solomon, and for this reason they became known as the Temple Knights, or Templars.

An effective propaganda weapon, in form of support from the charismatic Bernard of Clairvaux (1091–1153) secured for the Templars a rapid ascent which is without parallel in history. Hugh of Payens was able to win the eloquent churchman to his cause, and with his help the Rule of the Order was declared at the Synod of Troyes in 1128. Stephen, the Patriarch of Jerusalem, supplemented the Rule in 1130. Then with the appearance of Bernard's work, *De Laude Novae Militiae ad Milites Templi* ('In Praise of the New Knighthood'), the breakthrough was made and the Temple, as it was called, was assured of a strong intake.

In the ensuing period the Order skilfully expanded its sphere of influence and its possessions. Assets and privileges were heaped on the Templars by both the Church and the ruling families. Pope Innocent II granted them extraordinary, almost unbelievable, privileges. The Templars were subject to the Pope alone. They were exempted from paying tithes, and were moreover allowed to collect the tithes on their land for themselves. They were also allowed to keep the entire booty from their battles, which often ran to considerable sums. In a very short time the Order became so rich that it was in a position to finance wars and crusades, and not infrequently it was their word which tipped the scales of politics. The region of the Templars' influence expanded from France, their country of origin, to take in Germany, England, Spain, Portugal, Italy, the Balkans and of course Palestine. Members of the Order often had the final say when it came to important decisions, and their wealth influenced the results of political contests. Even at the end of 1306, less than a year before the blow that destroyed the Order, the Templars were playing an active role in the royal finance system. On 6 November of that year Philip IV the Fair, King of France (1285–1314), directed the Templars to pay the wages of the soldiers who had served in Flanders.[85]

Philip was one of the most imposing figures of his day. Dominating and warlike, he was constantly short of funds. He confiscated the assets of the Lombardy merchants, and he even taxed the clergy, which made him an arch-enemy of Pope Boniface VIII. Then he plundered the Jews and hounded them from France in July 1306. But the funds were still not enough. A devaluation of the currency followed, and finally the idea of going after the almost inexhaustible riches of the Templars. First he demanded that the 40,000 livres which his father Philip III the Cunning had made over to the Order in a testament, be paid back. The Treasurer in Paris paid up, without informing the Grand Master Jacques de Molay. Molay punished this infringement of the Rule by expelling him from the Brotherhood. Pope Clement V refused the King's request to have the guilty man readmitted to the Order. From this day on the Templars were in the King's line of fire; dependence on the wealthy Order was humiliating for such a proud and power-hungry ruler, and it might even have become a danger to him in the long run. The only way for him to be free of the society, which was operating so successfully on an international scale, was by liquidating it.

On 14 September 1307 Philip the Fair ordered a massive wave of arrests against the Order. In a swooping action under cover of darkness, troops loyal to him appeared in the houses and castles of the Templars. Taken totally by surprise, the brethren were unable to put up any defence.[86]

To justify the surprise attack, as recorded in the arrest warrant bearing the title *Rex Jubet Templarios Comprehendi*, Philip formulated the charges which many Templars were later to confess to under torture: that in their initiation rites the novices had to tread the Cross underfoot or spit on it; that they were kissed on mouth, navel and buttocks by the brothers; that the brothers were led to homosexual relations; that they omitted the words of the Consecration at Mass; and so on. The accusations revolved around cult actions in which the Templars were said to show reverence to a cat or a mysterious man's head. This figure was their saviour, who 'made all trees blossom and the harvest ripen'. Philip managed to present the cult rituals of the Templars in a way which made them look unlawful.

Philip had been unsure of the Church's support for a long time. Pope Boniface VIII was at odds with him over the priority of religious over secular power. On the death of Boniface, the Church suffered a noticeable decline in influence. In 1305 Clement V came to occupy the See of St Peter, with the support of Philip. He was the first Avignonian Pope, and although he was well aware that Philip really just wanted to appropriate the wealth of the Order, he was in no position to oppose him. Philip, in his turn, knew that the brothers of the Order could only be sentenced by a Church tribunal; only the clergy were allowed to pass judgement in matters of heresy.

Jacques de Molay, the Grand Master of the Order, had for this reason thought he was quite safe from injust sentencing. The Pope had assured him that he would hold an inquiry into the accusations brought against the Templars, and clear up everything in a way which would satisfy the King. But the strike against the heart of the Order in France happened overnight. On 12 October, just a day before his arrest, Molay was one of the coffin-bearers at the funeral of Catherine, Philip's sister-in-law.

In contrast to the suddenness of the attack in Paris the Templars in other countries had time to take measures against possible arrest. In Aragon they reinforced their castles, and exchanged goods for gold which could more easily be concealed. Ships were also chartered for escape. In the surrounding countries, where Templars were also interrogated, there was nowhere such sweeping action against them as in France. When the Order was finally dissolved, numerous former members were scattered across Europe still at liberty. This fact has encouraged fantasies about Templars in hiding, continuing their line to this day.

One very important aspect of the accusations is the way they attempted to make the Templars out to be like the Cathars. They were accused more or less openly of following certain customs and rites for which, a century before, that sect had been decimated in bloody crusades. It was known that the Cathars looked down on the Cross; for them it was a symbol of being bound to things earthly. The divine body of Jesus could not be crucified, but Satan tried to kill that which he thought was the material body. This devilish operation could never be the object of reverence. To accuse the Templars of dishonouring the Cross and treading it underfoot was one of the worst charges, and probably the one with the most effect. Philip wanted to speed up the clergy's decision. What could be better calculated to drive even the most well-meaning Church examiner to white-hot rage, than the sight of brothers of the Order confessing to have spat on the most sacred symbol of Christianity?

But the dishonouring of the cross had also awakened another association, one which was much worse and which would certainly have horrified everyone. The Franciscan Fidenzio of Padua had reported from the Holy Land in the late thirteenth century, that Christian boys taken prisoner by the Muslims were forced to spit on the Cross and on pictures of Jesus. Instead of the Templars having established Christianity at the holy sites during their long stay in the Holy Land, they were accused of being infiltrated by Islam there. The secrecy of the Order helped to allow the wildest rumours to flourish. Islam, so the charge ran, was rife among the ranks of the Templars. Satan had set up camp within a bastion of Christianity. There was the implied danger that the Saracens who had been eradicated in the Near East would rise again in France as Poor Knights of Christ of the Temple of Jerusalem.

Here the chivalrous ideal of the early Templars was being turned against them. They did of course fight the Muslims, but they also showed a generous tolerance, which must have seemed extremely suspicious to the narrow-minded. They gave the envoy of the Emir of Damascus a mosque which had already been converted to a church, as a place of worship. A Frank, horrified at the sight of a non-believer at the consecrated place, maltreated him, whereupon the Templars drove out their countryman and apologized to the envoy. Such events were presented in the prosecution in a way which hinted at a subliminal sympathy for the Muslims.

The other charges complete this picture of frightful Islamic-Catharic devils, so that in the astonished faces of those who had just recently been highly honoured knights, they saw despicable scoundrels. The accusation of homosexuality also contributed to this view.

It is difficult to decide which of the charges brought against the Templars were rightly confessed to. Evidently Philip and his advisors had thought much about the catalogue of charges and formulated them in a way calculated to evoke the most vigorous reaction by the ecclesiastical authorities. The accusations were certainly not entirely fictitious. However we do not have any reliable records from the members themselves to give us a balanced view of life in the Order. Our information is drawn mainly from the prosecution documents, and these have to be used with great caution. Torture had often forced many mouths to confess to whatever the inquisitors wanted.[87]

We have only these court documents to go on in tracing the details of Templar idolatry. We will try and reconstruct the idol of the Templars from these statements as best we can. What we are looking for is a connection between the cloth taken from Constantinople by a clever manoeuvre and the mysterious man's head before which the Templars apparently prostrated themselves on the ground in a kind of Byzantine submissiveness. Were the idols copies of the face on the Shroud?

The Mysterious Idol of the Templars

Among the charges listed by Philip one finds an interesting passage claiming that the brothers wore cords which had been touched to their idol: '. . . and these cords touched or encircled an idol which had the form of a man's head with a large beard. They kissed his head and worshipped him in their provincial capitals. But not all the brothers know of it, apart from the grand master and the senior members.'[88] The idea that the Templars carried with them cords which had previously been laid on the idol bears a remarkable resemblance to the similar custom of the early pilgrims in Palestine at the pillar of Christ's scourging, as recounted by Antoninus of Placentia. The sick hoped for a cure by wearing cords which had been placed round the pillar. Gregory of Tours (538/9–94) tells how pilgrims brought back cords which they had placed around the pillar of the scourging. One can assume that a similar custom was still known in the Holy Land at the time of the Templars, and practised at the few remaining shrines. And the practice of using cords to measure the length of Christ's tomb has survived to this day in folk religious customs. Taking the Templars' custom against this background, two things emerge. First, the Order obviously practised a cult of a relic which, following the classical pattern, was thought to be made effective by touch. And secondly, one can assume that the various Templar idols derived from a single 'prototype' and were in a sense 'authentic substitute copies'. Only in this way was there a guarantee that the winding or measuring with the cord actually brought about a connection with the original, which put every brother directly under the protection of the Templar saviour.

If we take the statements of the brothers about the worship of the idol individually, then despite the basic similarities there are differences which also become apparent. It is almost always a bearded man's head, but it is described in different ways. Sometimes it seems to have been a statue, sometimes a panel painting; some claimed to have seen large figures, others said that the master of the initiation had taken the idol from a pocket in his robe at the time it was needed. John of Turno, the Treasurer of the Paris temple, just speaks of a 'bearded man's head'. For brother Bartholomew Bochier the idol wore a cap and a long grey beard of wood, metal or bones.[89] Sometimes the descriptions of the Templar idol assume grotesque forms. Once there is mention of 'a small image of a lion, probably of gold, with the likeness of a woman'.[90] Abraham Bzovius, who continued the Church history of Cardinal Baronius, said that the head had a pale, 'almost human' face and black frizzy hair. They kept this frightful statue in a chamber under the ground. It was variously referred to as *figura Baffometi* or 'Baphomet'. Perhaps this capricious name-giving was meant to provide a link to 'Mahumet' (Mohammed) – a further indication that the Templar heresy was seen as an inadmissible syncretic mixture of creeds.[91] These statements clearly show that there were many, readily distinguishable copies of the head, which were kept in the various chapters (see Plate 53).

Wilson puts forward the view that the Templars had hidden the Shroud in Paris. He attempts to support his hypothesis by showing that the idol kept in Paris bore conspicuous similarities to the image on the cloth and that consequently they were the same. Wilson refers to the *Chronicles of St Denis* by Guillaume Paradin to support this view. This says that the idol consisted of an old skin embalmed like polished cloth.[92] 'To anyone who has seen the Shroud,' Wilson adds, 'this is not an altogether impossible description. Even today the cloth is characterised by a surprising surface sheen.'[93] He also presents the statement of the Servite Etienne de Troyes, who says he saw a 'mysterious object', 'a human head without any silver or gold, very pale and discoloured with a grizzled beard like a Templar's'. These observations do indeed seem astonishing. But it would be premature to rush to the hasty conclusion that the Templars had kept the cloth from Constantinople in their Paris temple and displayed the head portion on special occasions. Wilson suggests this to lend weight to his favourite hypothesis, but he is guilty of adapting the quotations to fit his theory, or of inadmissibly abridging them. This is very unfortunate, because in doing so he casts doubt on his own ideas which are of great interest in themselves.

For the *Chronicles of St Denis* go on to say that in the depths of the eye sockets of the idol shone two jewels, bright as the sky. Of course this changes the picture entirely. The author is obviously not describing a cloth with a faint image on it, but a solid figure inlaid with jewels. The statement of Etienne de Troyes has been tampered with in a similar way. Wilson has reproduced it in a completely distorted form. Etienne de Troyes gives us a comprehensive description of the idol ritual. In Poitiers in 1308 he declared before the cardinals and the Pope, that the Templars had held an annual chapter on 24 June which continued over a period of three days. He himself took part in it a year after his admission in Paris. While Wilson's 'mysterious, pale and discoloured object with grizzled beard' at once brings to mind the cloth, the complete statement of the brother in fact provides a fairly exact description of quite a different object. During the first watch of the night a priest brought in a head. Before him walked two brothers with two large wax candles on silver candlesticks. The priest placed the head on two cushions, covered with a silk cloth, on the altar. This head seemed to him to be of flesh, with dog hairs, and without gold or silver ornamentation, but from the neck region to over the shoulders it was completely strewn with gold and precious jewels. The head had a bluish colour and spots. It had a beard of black and white hairs, similar to the beard worn by some Templars. Then the visitor, Hugues de Pairaud, stood up and spoke to the congregation: 'We must worship him and render homage to him, for he helps us and does not abandon us.' And they all walked to the front with great reverence, paid homage to the head and worshipped him. Brother Etienne de Troyes says he learned that it was actually the head of the first Grand Master of the Order, Hugh of Payens.[94]

There can be no doubt about the form and appearance of the head as here described. Wilson seems to be leading off on the wrong track. The historian Malcom Barber supposes that the head referred to could really have been a relic of Hugh of Payens, containing his skull.[95] Whatever the true facts about the head, this and other specific statements led to instructions being given to Guillame Pidoyé, the royal administrator and curator of the Templar possessions, to search for heads of wood or metal in the Paris Temple. Obviously Pidoyé did not wish to disappoint his employers, or else he had been told that he simply had to come up with a *corpus delicti*. After all, they had to have something concrete in order to proceed against the brothers.

It was weeks before Pidoyé and his two colleagues Guillaume de Bisorcio and Rayner Bordono finally did come up with a head relic. We can assume that they found nothing suspicious in the temple in Paris and just used the first piece of 'evidence' they could lay their hands on. The Paris temple was in the Velleneuve du Temple, opposite the King's palace. It was certainly a massive building and there were probably plenty of good hiding places inside, but one has to ask why the Templars would hide the head so well.

The object procured by Pidoyé was a large 'gilded silver bust in the form of a woman's head, containing the bones of a single skull, wrapped in a white linen cloth and sewn up with a red cloth over it. A certain document was sewn up inside it, on which was written capud LVIII.'[96] Several people claimed it was the head of one of the 11,000 virgins.[97] Evidently Pidoyé had procured a relic from some church, quite precious but by no means out of the ordinary, labelled with the inventory number 'head No 58'. There was certainly nothing unusual in that. Such relics of heads were much liked at that period and followed the artistic taste of the times.[98] Good examples include the head of Mary Magdalene mounted in silver in the crypt of the basilica of Maximin mentioned earlier, the relic of St Eustachius, a German work of the early thirteenth century, which is now kept in the British Museum, and various works produced by Godefroid de Huy, such as the bust relic of Pope Alexander (1145) in the Musées Royaux d'Art et d'Histoire in Brussels, or the famous Cappenberg Barbarossa head, which has served as a relic since 1156.

When the find was presented to the Templar Guillaume d'Arreblay, preceptor of Soissy and former royal paymaster, he could only shake his head. This was not the idol. The head which was worshipped in the chapters had two faces he said, it was bearded and moreover of a terrifying appearance. The idol was often shown on feast days and he would certainly have recognized it if he saw it.[99]

Such confident statements lend weight to the idea that a head idol did in fact exist, playing a role in the Templars' secret cult. But they also make it clear that the brethren, although arrested in a surprise attack, had taken good precautions. The King's henchmen were unable to find an authentic Templar idol anywhere. Pidoyé's 'head No 58' was an embarrassing side issue which could not conceal the total lack of factual evidence. When a full search was made for compromising material, there was hardly anything to be found of the Templars' fabulous riches. Either the leading personalities knew of the imminent arrest and had taken everything of value to safety, or they had always practised a policy of concealing their wealth. But where had the gold and coins and the many idols got to?

The inventories of the Templars' branches, which were drawn up after the arrest, are sobering documents: anyone expecting to find gold and coins, treasures, relics or weapons, was in for a disappointment. Let us take a look at a typical inventory of the 'treasures' of a Templar estate. The only place where items worth noting are found is in the commander's room: three silver mugs, two large and one small; a small cup of onyx with silver base; two onyx cups with silver bases in poor condition and three wooden cups. No money was found, because the commander had used it to pay his debts.[100] Nothing was found apart from cups. Was this all that the mysterious brotherhood had to offer? Did the commander of this Maison de Baugie do nothing but drink constantly from different cups?

As King Philip remarked in the text of his accusation, it was to be expected that the less important brothers would not be able to make any useful statements about the idol, because only those belonging to the inner circle were initiated. Indeed the statements of the simpler members of the Order, who could neither read nor write and did not understand the Latin words used in the ceremonies, show that they had just attended the mysterious, often terrifying, dramas without knowing anything about the theatrically presented 'lead actor'.

Thus it is interesting to hear the statements of higher-ranking members of the Order on this point, to get a clearer idea of the whole affair. Raol de Gisy, the Preceptor for Champagne, claimed that he has seen the idol in seven chapters, under Hugues de Pairaud and others. It was 'the frightful figure of some demon which one called *maufé* in France. Every time he saw it he was filled with such horror that he could hardly look at it, trembling with fear.'[101] Another Preceptor, John of Anisiaco, was seated too far away when the idol was shown to be able to make out anything. Besides, it was nearly midnight and the chamber was lit only by a candle.[102]

One person was terrified, so he did not look at all; another claimed to have seen nothing because, although he was a leader of the Order, he sat in the back row; and they all said, like the lesser brethren, that they knew nothing at all about what the idol actually was. That is quite remarkable. Strangely enough this even applied to the statements of Hugues de Pairaud. Pairaud was the second man in the Order after Molay, but the most powerful. During his forty-four-year career as a Templar he had admitted numerous brothers into the Order in various chapters in France. If anyone knew about the inner affairs and teachings of the Temple Knights, he was the man. Pairaud himself had displayed the idol during the initiation rites with great proficiency. One would expect from him a description of the image that was a little more specific.

Actually his statement may be quite important in connection with the hypothesis that the Templars had worshipped the Christ of the Shroud. Let us then hear it, as it was recorded in the court documents during his interrogation on 9 November 1307.

> When asked about the head mentioned above, he stated under oath that he had seen, held and touched such a thing in a chapter at Montpellier, and that he himself and other brothers present had worshipped it . . . To the question where it was kept, he said that he had returned it to Brother Peter Alemaudin, the Preceptor at Montpellier, but he did not know whether the King's men would find it. He stated that the head in question had four feet, two at the side of the face and two at the back.[103]

No one knew any details, no one possessed an idol. All the Templars questioned spoke about the strange head as if they themselves were never aware of what or whom they were actually worshipping. Did they then never ask themselves what idol it was that they had to worship in this way? Even in the case of such a high leader as Hugues de Pairaud, who had displayed the idol himself, the poor description of the head at Montpellier sounds rather like a circus performance whose meaning he had never been able to grasp.

It is likely that the lower ranks of the Templars really were not initiated into the true secret of the idol. Perhaps most of them had only seen copies of the genuine article. But if the highest initiates knew the secret, they skilfully kept their knowledge to themselves. One can of course ask why they mentioned the idol at all. After all, they must have wanted to conceal its true identity. Would it not have been better just to deny that such an idol had ever existed? The initiated Templars obviously proceeded in a very clever way. They knew that many of the simpler brethren would talk of their encounter with the idol, and even say that the initiates had introduced it to them. In one way this could be useful: it was a guarantee that the descriptions of the head would all turn out very different and the prototype would never be discovered. If the most senior members of the Order had said the mysterious object did not exist, they would only have aroused the suspicions of the inquisitors, who of course had long known that the thing must have existed. The initiates made no denial. Butthey spoke of the idol in a cursory manner, just as 'uninformed' as the others, as if they had been watching the exotic fetish of a remote tribe. This was all to make the idol a relatively 'uninteresting' matter, and so protect the original from a large-scale search operation. Hugues de Pairaud acted his role very well, for example when it came to the significance of all the actions during the chapter meetings. He mimicked an ignorant brother, as if he were a novice just doing his honest duty: he had only done it all because it was the custom according to the Statutes of the Order. [104] That is the sum of the statements in the defence of the supreme Templar of France.

Could the examiners believe it? It is a great puzzle why the inquisitors, who were otherwise quite happy to grapple with sophisticated niceties, did not go any deeper into the question of idol worship. The lower ranks had little to offer the inquiry, that much had become clear. But it was impossible for people like Hugues de Pairaud and the Preceptors not to have known what the idol was. They themselves obviously kept copies of it. Why do we have to make do with these nebulous reports? Why did they not keep digging in this case until they were able to describe exactly the form the heresy took and denounce it? Was it Satan the Templars worshipped, or Mohammed, or someone else?

The answer can only be that the inquisitors saw no benefit in letting details about the idol reach the public. If everything stayed a mystery, it meant that there were plenty of opportunities to fill the gaps with suitable theories. But that also means that they were well aware that a definite solution to the enigma of the idol could cause their entire argument to collapse like a house of cards. Thus we can assume that they knew the Templars worshipped the idol of the head of Jesus, even if it was in a very mysterious way; but it was a Jesus who was kept quite separate from the death on the Cross which was so important for institutional Christianity.

Amid all the confusion about the head, it was almost irrelevant whether what the initiates were saying about the idol was true or fictitious. It almost seems as if Hugues was making fools of the inquisitors with his apparently grotesque statement that the head had four feet, two at the front and two at the back. Are we to take this as meaning a pedestal, or do we really have to imagine a head with four feet? And yet it is possible that Pairaud was not lying at all in this account. Perhaps it is the clearest indication that the Templars really did have the Shroud. If they did, copies and statues would have been made of the head. But it is conceivable that on special occasions the original itself was brought out. Possibly they had put up a board the size of a man and draped the cloth over it, so that walking round it one could see the front and rear side of a man standing upright. Thus two feet would appear at the front, 'on the side of the face' as Pairaud put it, and two at the back. Many of the brethren tell us that the idol had two faces, or was 'doubled'. Was this a reference to the twofold image on the cloth?

Of course if the Templars really were worshipping the Christ of the Shroud, one has then to ask why such a great secret was made of it, why they did not just frankly admit it. There was nothing in this that the papal commission could have found objectionable, and the brethren would have had a chance of saving their lives. We can only explain the silence of the brothers and the mystification of the Templar rituals by assuming that they did indeed worship Jesus, but that it was an image of Jesus completely different than that of orthodoxy. Their refusal to say more prevented the inquisitors from determining the form of the heresy more precisely. That such a heresy existed was shown even by the omission of the words of consecration of the bread and wine in the ritual of the Mass.

The Templars probably did have a living esoteric Christian belief related to the Cathar tradition. But their beliefs were certainly not identical to those of the Cathars. While the latter totally rejected the use of weapons, combat was prescribed in the Statutes of the Templar Order, although admittedly with the proviso that they should never raise their swords against fellow Christians – hence the Templars' absence at the conquest of Constantinople and their reluctance to defend themselves when they were arrested by Philip's men. It is quite conceivable that in their radical rejection of the Cross the Templars were close to the Cathars' contempt for the world, and that the Jesus of the Shroud figured as a special symbol for them in this regard. The contemplation of the 'true face' of the Lord may have taken a central place in Templar mysticism, according to the words of Paul, 'But we all, with open face beholding as in a glass the glory of the Lord, are changed into the same image from glory to glory, even as by the Spirit of the Lord.' (2 Cor. 3.18.) The figure on the cloth does not convey the impression of a corpse, just as the portrait on the Mandylion appears to the viewer as very much alive. The Jesus of the cloth showed them that the contemptible Cross could do nothing to him, because his true nature could not be killed.

One might even hold that Bernard of Clairvaux, the patron of the early Templars, had fired them with the desire to possess the Shroud. The Templars in Jerusalem already had a close symbolic relationship with the tomb of Christ and viewed themselves as *Advocati Sancti Sepulchri*, 'Advocates of the Holy Sepulchre'. In the contemplative mysticism of Bernard, reflection on the suffering and death of Jesus Christ was recommended as the supreme occupation for the pious people of his day – and what better method of meditating on the Passion of the Lord for the first servants of the Holy Sepulchre, than looking at the Shroud?

The question of the relationship between the cloth and the idol could be more easily solved if we had precise information about the origins of the idol cult and possible changes as time passed. It would be especially helpful to find a definite lead about a special meeting of the leading members of the Order shortly after 1204, when the cloth may have been exhibited. But the Poor Knights of Christ, true to their reputation, maintained a silence on this. We know nothing of any major event after the arrival of Brother Baroche, nor do we know anything about the origins and development of the idol cult. We are left with our speculations, like everyone else.

On 18 March 1314 the cardinals called an extraordinary session in Paris. In the presence of the Archbishop of Sens, Philippe de Marigny, and many prelates and doctors of theology and canon law, the leaders of the Order were brought before the court: Jacques de Molay, Hugues de Pairaud, Geoffroy de Gonneville, Preceptor of Aquitaine, and Geoffroy de Charnay, Preceptor of Normandy. All of them were sentenced to life imprisonment. Surprisingly no protest was heard from Hugues de Pairaud, who was certainly an ambivalent leader figure. Geoffroy de Gonneville similarly acquiesced in the judge's decree. But the ingenuous Molay and Geoffroy de Charnay, concerning whom we have hardly any historical material, surpassed themselves at their hour of extremity. The monk who took up the chronicle where Guillaume de Nangis left off, said of this event:

> But lo, just when the cardinals thought they had put an end to the affair, quite suddenly and unexpectedly two of them, namely the Grand Master and the Master of Normandy, defended themselves vigorously against the Cardinal who had given the sermon, and against the Archbishop of Sens, reverting to a denial of their confessions and everything they had confessed to.[105]

Pairaud and Gonneville were locked up, but the king wanted to do away with the relapsed Molay and Charnay quickly. Obviously he was taking no chances. He had had enough of the to and fro of confessions and retractions – the clergy might finally give way. Besides, putting an end to the two most important leaders by burning at the stake would probably be the best deterrent. At about the hour of Vespers of the same day, therefore, Molay and Charnay were taken without much fuss to the Ile des Javiaux, a small island on the Seine, where they were delivered up to the flames. This island was under the jurisdiction of the monks of Saint-Germain-des-Prés and not the King. Everything happened very quickly, and later Philip had to apologize to the monks and assure them that the execution did not affect their rights on the island in any way. Philip was thus able to avoid a popular uprising (see Plate 54).

Who was this Geoffroy de Charnay, whose fame as a Knight Templar seems solely due to his ending up on the pyre with Molay? He certainly belonged to the leading committee of the Order, but he seems to have kept a low profile. Perhaps this was the person who had been given the task of securing the safety of the Shroud, a person with very reliable family connections outside the Order. For, a few decades later the Shroud was to enter the stage of official recorded history in the ownership of a man of this very name.

The Shroud Resurfaces

In the Musée de Cluny in Paris one can see a fragment of a pilgrim's memento which was recovered from the Seine near the Pont du Change. It provides us with the oldest surviving picture of the complete Turin cloth showing front and rear images (see Plate 58). The amulet commemorates the exposition in the collegiate church of Lirey in 1357. In the upper part one can recognize the stoles of two clerics who are holding the cloth, below in the middle one sees the open tomb within a circle. At the left is the coat of arms of Geoffroy de Charny (three small shields on a red background), to the right the coat of arms of his second wife, Jeanne de Vergy. Charny and his wife were the first documented owners of the cloth, and they were the ones who made it so popular by sensational public expositions. These allow us to track its movements distinctly from here on. It was this policy of theirs which also provoked the disapproval of the Bishop of Troyes, Pierre d'Arcis, as described in the first part of the book.

What interests us most here is the possible relationship

between Geoffroy de Charny, owner of the cloth, and Geoffroy de Charnay, the Templar. If the Templars did take steps to get the cloth to safety, they would have entrusted it to a person who was not personally involved in the Order and yet had some connection with it. Perhaps the cloth came into the possession of a relative of a leading member of the Order. Had the Preceptor of Normandy, Geoffroy de Charnay, entrusted it to a member of his family, with whom it resurfaced several decades afterwards? The slightly different spelling of the two names is not important. In those days there were no regular rules of spelling and we find many different forms for the names of both persons in the documents of the period. I am merely keeping to the most common orthography.

About Charnay the Templar we know precious little. Born in Anjou in 1248, he entered the Order of Knights Templar at 18, and lived for a while in Cyprus. Apparently there were no direct descendants. The case of the 'second' Charny is quite different. Wilson claims that his origins were shrouded in obscurity, but he was actually one of France's most brilliant generals under Philip VI. Reconstructing a useful genealogy was no easy task. But countless hours of meticulous searchings in archives, contemporary documents and libraries did finally bear fruit.[106]

Ponce de Mon-Saint-Jean, Seigneur de Charny, Samaise, Noidan and Thorey-sous-Charny, was the third son of Hugues I de Mont-Saint-Jean and Elisabeth de Vergy. In the early decades of the thirteenth century he was granted Charny, situated in the département of Côte-d'Or, and a portion of Chastel-Sansoy, and so became the founder of the Charny lineage. From his marriage with Sybille de Noyers was born Hugues de Charny, Seigneur de Pierrefitte, Montbutois, Arcy, Châtel-Censoir and Lugy, the grandfather of Geoffroy. The son of Hugues de Charny and Mabile de Savoisy was Jean de Charny. He married Marguerite de Joinville, the daughter of Jean de Joinville, the biographer of Louis IX the Saint. His last mention in the documents was 1318; in 1323 he was no longer alive. Jean de Charny had four children, Isabeau, Dreux, Jean and Geoffroy. Dreux must have been the eldest son, because he inherited Charny and passed it on to his daughter Guillemette. Geoffroy received the possessions from the dowry of his mother, the estates and the small settlement of Lirey in *départment* of Aube. Later he also became Seigneur de Savoisy and Monfort, and his first marriage was to Jeanne de Toucy, daughter of Guy I, Sire de Bazarne, Pierre-Perthuis and Vault-de-Lugny. In a second marriage he was wedded to Jeanne de Vergy, daughter of Guillaume de Vergy, Seigneur de Mirabeau. From his marriage with Jeanne de Vergy two children were born, Charlotte and Geoffroy II.

In all this we find no relationship to Geoffroy the Templar. However we should say that the genealogy is anything but complete. A lot of work would be required before any light could be thrown on the family tree of the Templar Geoffroy de Charnay; it is altogether a more difficult undertaking than the search for the family tree of the other Charny, who was a famous knight. The absence of a direct proveable relationship may be just due to the paucity of well-researched contemporary documents, resulting in the fragmentary state of our knowledge about medieval family ties. Perhaps a patient scholar will manage to trace the missing link at some future date.

Geoffroy's whole life was spent in encampments, garrisons and tournaments, building a reputation as the ideal knight. In 1337 he took part in the wars in Languedoc and the Guyenne. From 9 March 1339 to 1 October 1340 he fought at the Flemish border. In 1341 he accompanied Raoul d'Eu, Duke of Brienne, to England. In 1345 he was in the retinue of the Dauphin Humbert II of Vienne for the pointless Crusade against Smyrna (now Izmir). In the summer of 1346 he was knighted during the siege of Aiguillon and shortly afterwards made general of Saint-Omer. On the night of New Year's Eve 1349, he was taken prisoner by the English outside Calais. King John II the Good (1350–64) bought his freedom two years later for the enormous sum of 12,000 gold écus, and made him his ambassador to Picardie, Flanders and Artois.[107] Shortly after this he promoted him to become bearer of the sacred standard of St Denis. In 1355 the King sent him to Normandy on a secret mission and, following the battle of Breteuil in July 1356, gave him two houses in Paris. Geoffroy had little time to enjoy them; On 19 September 1356, during the battle at Poitiers against the English, he threw himself before his King to protect him, and fell, the sacred standard of France in his hands. The King had him buried in a tomb of honour in the Eglise des Celestins in Paris.

This was the man who possessed the precious relic. But we find no mention of it by him throughout his entire life. There is nothing to suggest that he had received it at a certain time. The first historical document emerged in 1389, more than thirty years after his death, when Pierre d'Arcis sent his 'memorandum' to Pope Clemens VII and referred to the exhibition of the cloth during Geoffroy's lifetime in his church in Lirey.[108] Geoffroy II claimed that his father had received the cloth as a 'generous gift'. The granddaughter of Geoffroy and the last Charny, Marguerite, insisted on her right to ownership of the relic during a court action in 1443 in Dôle, by stating that her grandfather had received the cloth *par feu*, 'granted to him in fee'. [109] To conclude from this that Geoffroy was given the cloth by the King himself, as Bulst and Pfeiffer do, is most precarious. No contemporary document records such a bequest; the well-preserved papers in the archives provide us with no such reference. Besides it seems impossible that a monarch, should he ever have possessed this most precious of all relics – for which there is not the slightest evidence – would have given it away to a subordinate. The authors base their view on a document from 1247, by which the Latin Emperor of Constantinople bequeathed the 'holy cloth mounted on a panel' to Louis the Saint. This can only have been a copy of the Mandylion, certainly not the Shroud. Together with this letter the Emperor sent 'pieces of the shroud of the Lord'.[110] These were obviously either relic fragments of a cloth which was also considered to be a shroud and was still kept in the Pharos chapel, as we saw earlier, or possibly actually fragments of the Turin cloth, because original pieces may have been removed from the side and from one end, without showing anything of the image on them.

Marguerite also claimed that Geoffroy had 'conquered' the cloth. This statement has led many researchers to suppose that the enterprising Geoffroy really brought the cloth back as loot from a campaign, perhaps even from Smyrna. About this, again, nothing is known. The conflicting statements of his descendants merely seem to show that they themselves did not know where the cloth came from, and were just trying to prove their lawful ownership of it.

There is a legend that during his imprisonment in England Geoffroy made a vow that he would build a church in Lirey if he was released unharmed. He was said to have attributed his 'miraculous' rescue to this vow. But actually he was involved in this project years before his arrest. In 1343 he approached Philip VI for an annual donation to help him to found a small church. He even secured the legacy of an aunt for the project, but not much money seems to have been collected. In 1349 he announced to Pope Clement VI the completion of the collegiate Church of Our Blessed Virgin Mary of the Annunciation in Lirey. John the Good granted the canons of the church an annual stipend of 120 livres.

Strangely, the documents for the foundation of the church give the date for the start of construction work as 20 February 1353, and its completion as 10 June that same year. At this time Geoffroy was trying to gain a higher status for his church, now consecrated to both the Holy Trinity and the Virgin of the Annunciation, with Pope Clement's successor, Innocent VI. King John increased the stipend to 180 livres.

What is the meaning of these conflicting documents? It is hardly likely that Geoffroy would announce the construction of a house of prayer to Clement in 1349, if he had not actually built one. What seems to have happened is that he resolved in the meantime to enlarge the original small building, to increase its importance. Dorothy Crispino, who has explored the history of the cloth owned by the Charnys in a number of works, suggests that this change of plan may indicate that Geoffroy came into possession of the cloth between 1349 and 1353, and wished to build a more worthy abode for it.[111]

But this theory too has a weak basis. Even the 'second', allegedly larger, church was ready in a few months. It was just a simple wooden construction, of which today only a cornerstone remains. We find no reference to the Shroud in the documents of the foundation, although they record many donations of relics. If Geoffroy had wished to carry out the extension work because of the cloth, a message to the Pope would have sufficed. But the linen was never mentioned. At the end of May 1356 Bishop Henri de Poitiers delivered a eulogy about the church. But again there is no mention of a shroud, and he would hardly have forgotten to draw notice to this important relic. His successor Pierre d'Arcis claimed in his alleged letter to the Anti-Pope that Henri de Poitiers had denounced the monstrous deception with the cloth in Lirey, but at least at the time of the foundation of the church, there can have been no question of this having happened.

Four months later Geoffroy fell in battle. It is highly unlikely that the cloth was first exhibited in Lirey in the short time between the Bishop's sermon and Geoffroy's death, because it was not mentioned at Geoffroy's requiem mass, nor in an inventory of 1357. The facts seem rather to suggest that during his imprisonment Geoffroy thought of enlarging his church building, which had by then been started or perhaps even finished, should he ever again tread the soil of his homeland. The cloth probably played no role in his deliberations.

A cult of the cloth must have existed, however. Proof of this is provided by the medallion and by the objections raised by Bishop Pierre d'Arcis.[112] A solution to the riddle may be provided by the pilgrim's medallion itself, which bears both the coat of arms of Geoffroy and that of his second wife, Jeanne de Vergy: this might mean that the exposition only took place after Geoffroy's death, and was arranged by his wife. This is a legitimate hypothesis, when one considers that no contemporary statements by Geoffroy de Charny about the cloth in his possession are to be found. Why should he keep silent about his possession of the cloth throughout his lifetime?

For Wilson the matter is closely related to the relic's Templar background. Even if it is not possible to prove an actual relationship between the Templar Charnay and Geoffroy de Charny, Seigneur de Lirey, Savoisy and Montfort, there still remains the possibility, and the likelihood, that it was passed down in this way.[113] Naturally Geoffroy could not reveal anything about the relic. He had been entrusted it on his honour, truly as a 'generous gift', according to the words later put into his mouth. But it was unthinkable to disclose where the cloth came from. The brutal suppression of the Templars in France was certainly still fresh in people's memory. Could the standard-bearer of France allow himself to be connected with the strange Order? He may even have known that the accusation of heresy and idolatry against the members of the Order was based on this very image on the cloth. Pierre d'Arcis, who wanted to prevent the exhibition of the cloth under Geoffroy II at all costs, may have known something of this background; he apologized to the Pope that due to ill health he was not able to speak to him in person, because in writing he could only 'inadequately express the serious nature of the scandal, the shame which was caused to the Church ... and the danger for souls'.[114] Did the true nature of the scandal which he was reluctant to put on paper, lie in the fact that Christian pilgrims were now praying before the very 'idol' of the Templars, and that this 'idol', the Shroud of the Lord, had lain for over 100 years in the hands of a heretical brotherhood?

The accusations d'Arcis made, saying that the cloth was a forgery, were meant to make the Pope ban its exposition. Evidently the charge was not very well founded, however, because the Pope's opinions and decisions about it are unclear, contradictory even;[115] this suggests that the Pope was unable to form any clear picture of how things stood. Another puzzling thing is the total absence of documents relating to the defence against the accusations. Were they suppressed, or did the accused have no need to clear their names of the charge of forgery, since everyone could see for themselves that the cloth was no painting? Finally, one should not forget that the charge met with no success. Instead, the Church was to try repeatedly to gain possession of the extraordinary relic in the coming decades and centuries. It only succeeded in this after the death of ex-King Umberto II on 18 March 1983: he had bequeathed it to the Holy See in his will after Pope John Paul II had visited him in his Portuguese exile a short while before and asked him for it (see Plate 63).

There can be no doubt that Geoffroy de Charny was fond of the chivalrous ideal of the Templar Order. In a long poem, which shows him as an effusive and poor writer, he described, besides the many dangers which await the knight in the Holy Land, the ideal of knighthood. His memories of the operation with the Dauphin Humbert II of Vienne in Smyrna seem rather blurred. He sketched the dangers of the raging sea, the pirates, the Turks and the Christians. But he did declare that nothing could make him deviate from the ideal of the pure knight. A noble Grail knighthood lived on in his fantasy, ever ready to risk all for God, honour and country. 'There are in this world two particularly noble callings,' Geoffroy wrote, 'religion and chivalry.'[116] In January 1352, in an attempt to unite these two, as the gentlemen of the Temple had once done, he founded the Order of the Star, or the Order of Our Lady of the Noble Lineage, together with like-minded colleagues. The King authorized this religious-cum-military order after the model of the Round Table.[117] It did not last long; by the Battle of Poitiers in 1356 it was all history. But this short episode shows that Geoffroy de Charny wanted to continue the ideal of the Templars in some way. Perhaps he had vowed to keep up the Templar spirit at the time when he was given the relic.

The cloth was probably slipped to safety long before the Preceptor of Normandy suffered the flames at the side of his Grand Master, certainly by the time of their arrest in September 1307. It was probably taken away when the leaders began to feel threatened by the hostility towards the Order. We do not know how old Geoffroy, the later standard-bearer, was at this time. It may be that he was not born until the beginning of the fourteenth century, but it is more likely that he was already a young man by then.[118] That could mean that Geoffroy did not obtain the cloth directly from the hand of a Templar, but was 'second in line' to receive it.

It may be that we are reading too much into Geoffroy de Charny, the man who certainly possessed the Shroud, but who never mentioned the relic in a single recorded utterance throughout his life, despite his notably pious and chivalrous character. Did he perhaps not know what the object he was given for safekeeping was? Did he dutifully store the closed chest in a safe place and never open it all his life? Then after his death his second wife could have become curious and looked at the mysterious heirloom, so that the astonishing contents came to light. When Geoffroy died, Jeanne de Vergy was still a young lady and, it appears, in financial need. She would quickly have realized that if the cloth were displayed it would bring a plentiful stream of visiting pilgrims and an excellent source of income. Not knowing where the treasure had originally come from, she might have said that her husband had received it in fee or as booty on one of his expeditions. The canons in Lirey would have been delighted about the relic; they would have envisaged a favourable reaction when the cloth was displayed. So it came to be shown publicly in France for the first time, in the church of Geoffroy de Charny, who had, however, by this time died.

Excursus: A Historical Puzzle

In the course of my research into Geoffroy de Charny, I came across some facts which I ought to mention for the sake of completeness. The path I have described for the cloth, from Constantinople via the Templars to Geoffroy, seems to me to be the most plausible one. There are many circumstances to support it. But as in all things where final certainty is wanting, there are alternatives. I will briefly outline one of these, with all due reservations, and leave it to future researchers to uncover more of the facts.

There are two documents which suggest that the cloth was present in Athens, at least for a short time, after its mysterious disappearance from Constantinople. After the taking of the city, a series of meetings took place between the leading Greek clergy and Papal delegates. Nicholas of Otranto, Abbot of the Casole Monastery in southern Italy, was present as interpreter at these discussions.

During such a discussion in 1207, he said that the Franks had entered the city like thieves and found valuable relics in the royal palace, including the *fascia* (wrapping), 'which we later saw with our own eyes'.[119] This *fascia* is often translated as 'shroud', especially because it is included in the list of Passion relics. The word is Nicholas of Otranto's Latin translation of the Greek *sparganon*. Apart from the fact that there is no mention of any image on the cloth, *sparganon* really means 'nappy'. Presumably this particular term was used to describe a small piece of cloth connected with the Passion which was worn somehow like a 'nappy'. This can only have been the loincloth, which was an essential component of the iconography of the crucifixion. If we still insist it was a shroud, it could have been one which was already in the city before the arrival of the Mandylion, and which was still counted as such. In 1206 Nicholas accompanied the papal legate Benedict of St Susanna to Thessaloniki and Athens. Scavone presumes that it was there that he saw the cloth 'with his own eyes'.[120]

For there is another contemporary document which suggests that the Shroud was brought to Athens after the taking of Constantinople. In a letter to Pope Innocent II dated 1 August 1205, Theodore Angelos, the nephew of Isaac II Angelos, who was deported following the Fourth Crusade, complained about the raid on his city and its plunder by the conquerors. He said they had 'taken away the most sacred of all relics, the cloth in which our Lord Jesus Christ was wrapped after his death and before his Resurrection. We know that the holy objects were kept by the thieves in Venice, France and other places, and the sacred cloth in Athens.'[121]

Some scholars doubt the authenticity of this letter, particularly because it all too obviously supports a hypothesis which has long been known, but which is erroneous. This is the so-called Besançon hypothesis. A manuscript of the eighteenth century, which is kept in the library of Besançon with the inventory number 826, notes the donation of a 'holy shroud' to the bishop of the town, Amedeus de Tramelai, by Ponce de la Roche in 1208. Ponce was the father of Othon de la Roche, one of the best-known knights of the Fourth Crusade, who became the ruling noble of Athens. Othon, it was said, had sent the shroud to his father. The cloth stayed in Besançon until it disappeared without a trace in a fire in 1349.

This simple and plausible-looking story does, however, have its snags. The first mention of a shroud in Besançon itself was only in 1532. It was the copy of the front view of the Turin cloth. Besançon never laid claim to having the genuine cloth, although it was displayed not far away in Lirey shortly after the alleged disappearance, and the later argument between Margaret of Charny and the canons of Lirey was actually settled in the court of Besançon. The supposed donation by Ponce de la Roche has not been verified. The Besançon manuscript refers to three documents which no longer exist even in copy. A bull of 1208 speaks merely of a Ponce de Lyon, Treasurer of the Latin Emperor Henry I, who had brought 'certain relics' with him from Constantinople which he was to donate to the Archbishop of Lyons. In 1902 the Benedictine Dom François Chamard simply changed Ponce de Lyon to Ponce de la Roche and started the theory and its confusion. The papers of the Archbishop Amedeus de Tramelai in the Paris National Archive make no mention whatever of a shroud, nor is Ponce de la Roche named.[122]

Let us suppose for the sake of argument that the Shroud was brought to Athens. It would probably have been Othon de la Roche who brought it. Othon had left for the West with Boniface of Monferat and Geoffroy de Villehardouin, to take the lands the Emperor had given them in fee. While Geoffroy de Villehardouin, spurred on by Boniface, won the principality of Achaia, (Morea), Othon became the Lord of Athens. If Othon really did send a shroud to his father, it was unlikely to have been the genuine cloth. Whatever the cloth was that was in Besançon in the thirteenth century – if there was one there at all – it was not the Turin Shroud. The genuine Shroud would have remained hidden in Athens or in a castle in one of the regions governed by Othon. Othon returned to his homeland before 1229, leaving the Greek lands to his nephew Guy I, from whom his son Guy II (1287–1308) inherited them after his death.[123]

In 1305 Guy II married Mahaut de Hainaut, heiress to the principality of Achaia. Mahaut was the sole offspring from the marriage of Isabelle de Villehardouin, heiress of Achaia, and Florence de Hainaut from the family of the Latin Emperor of Constantinople. Mahaut de Hainaut, the last direct descendant of the Villehardouin line, was born in 1293. When she married Guy II she was just twelve years old and brought the large estates of the Villehardouins on the Peloponnese as dowry for the wedding. Three years later Guy II died, and young Mahaut became heir to the most extensive estates in Morea.

After facing increasing unrest in Achaia, Philip the Fair, already involved in his action against the Templars, decided to arrange some marriages to consolidate the Latin powers in Morea. He married the fifteen-year-old Prince Louis of Burgundy to Mahaut de Hainaut. Towards the end of 1315 the couple set out for their distant estates; in their train were a large number of Burgundy nobles. In Venice Louis sent his wife ahead with some of his retinue, while he stayed on to sign his will. Jean de Charny, the father of Geoffroy, later the standard-bearer of the king, also added his signature to the will. In April 1316 Prince Louis reached Morea accompanied by members of the Charny family.[124] Just four months later the prince died. Mahaut was left in Morea, still in the throes of a crisis, a widow for the second time. But Louis had previously made sure that the important characters in his retinue would be granted lands. Thus Dreux de Charny, 'the brother of Geoffroy de Charny' as the Aragon chronicle of the times notes,[125] received a number of estates spread throughout the whole region, and in addition to these, by marriage, the regions of Vostitsa and Nivelet.

One can no longer say exactly what areas were included here, especially as the region of Nivelet can not be precisely located. In any case one thing is sure: by the first marriage with Guy II de la Roche, Mahaut de Hainaut inherited the estates of de la Roche.

If the cloth was still somewhere in these estates, it was certainly not in Athens; the city was no longer under Frankish control at this time. The Catalan Company, which had fought against the Turks since the start of the fourteenth century as commissioned by the Byzantines, began to make Asia Minor and Greece insecure by increasingly wild plundering. In 1311 the Catalans defeated the Franks in Athens and routed Duke Gauthier of Brienne. The dukedom of Athens became a Catalan principality.[126]

It is quite conceivable that Mahaut and Prince Louis granted land to Dreux de Charny which was previously owned by de la Roche. Perhaps it was there, in a church in some Frankish fortress, of which there were many, that he stumbled on the treasure of Othon de la Roche – the Shroud. To secure the safety of this fortunate find, he sent the cloth to his homeland, to his younger brother Geoffroy.

One has to admit that this variant, based solely on genealogical studies, sounds improbable. But in a case as delicate as this, so deeply hidden in the shadows of history, one is allowed to follow up clues whose worth is not immediately apparent.

The 'Official' Story

The remaining history of the cloth is very well documented and can be quickly told. For a while it remained in the possession of the Charny family. In July 1418 it was moved to the fortress of Montfort, then to Saint-Hippolyte-sur-Doubs, for protection against marauding bands of robbers. In 1443 the patrons of Lirey made a claim for it. Margaret, the last Charny, was granted custody by the court in Besançon and retained it. In 1452 she publicly exhibited it in a castle in Germolles. She then searched for a family to whom she could pass on her valued possession, for want of suitable heirs. She decided in favour of Louis, the Duke of Savoy. In gratitude for 'valuable services', as he put it, the duke gave her Varambon Castle in Geneva and the income from the estate of Miribel near Lyons. After Margaret's death in 1460, Louis of Savoy paid the canons of Lirey 50 gold francs in lieu of the cloth. From then until 1983 the relic remained in the possession of the Savoy family.

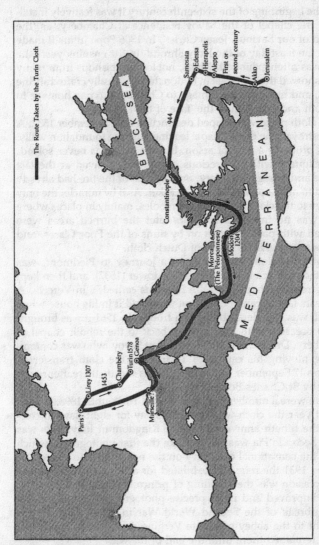

Fig. 4. *The most important locations and dates in the 2,000 years history of the Shroud*

At the beginning of the sixteenth century it was festively installed in the chapel of the Savoy residence at Chambéry, as 'the
Shroud of our Saviour, Jesus Christ'. In 1506 Pope Julius II made
4 May the feast day of the Holy Shroud. In the ensuing years the
cloth was often exhibited. Kings, nobles and bishops from many
lands showed their interest in it, donated artistically crafted shrine
pieces, and made the pilgrimage to Chambéry to pay homage to
the cloth and pray before the 'face of the Lord'.

The cloth narrowly escaped destruction on 4 December 1532. A
fire destroyed the castle chapel leaving only the foundation walls.
It was probably a case of arson, but the case was never solved.
The reliquary with its precious contents was saved at the last
minute and brought to safety. But the heat of the fire had already
started to melt a part of the silver casket. As if by miracle, the only
damage to the cloth was a few burn holes, mainly in places where
there was no image. Two years later the burned areas were
repaired with patches sewn on by nuns of the Poor Clares, and
the linen was given a lining of Dutch cloth.

Finally the cloth was taken on a journey to Piedmont, was
exhibited in Nizza from the Bellanda tower (1537), and then kept
in the treasure chamber of the Eusebius cathedral in Vercelli. A
few years later a canon of the cathedral hid it in his house when
Vercelli was plundered by French troops. In 1561 it was brought
in a procession with much pomp back to the rebuilt chapel of
Chambéry. Duke Emmanuel Philibert of Savoy, who was contem-
plating moving his capital to Turin, had the cloth transferred
there on 17 September 1578, where it was shortly thereafter rever-
enced by St Charles Borromeus.

There were a number of expositions in Turin until 1898. In May
of that year the cloth was put on display for eight days to celebrate the fiftieth anniversary of the Kingdom of Italy. This was
when Secondo Pia was able to take the first photograph, which
led to the sensational discovery on the negative plate. From 2 to
23 May 1931 the relic was exhibited for a full twenty-two days.
The occasion was the wedding of prince Umberto of Piedmont.
New, improved and more precise photographs were taken. At
the outbreak of the Second World War in 1939 the cloth was
brought to the abbey of Monte Vergine, in Avellino, for safety,
and it remained there until the end of the war.

In June 1969 the first scientific commission was allowed to

examine the cloth under the supervision of Cardinal Pellegrino. On 1 October 1972 an unknown person climbed over the roof of the ducal palace, forced an entry into the chapel and attempted to set fire to the cloth. An asbestos layer on the inside of the altar shrine saved it from destruction. In November 1973 the first threads and samples from the debris on the surface were removed for scientific examination, and in October 1988 scientists, having no idea of the long history of the Shroud, declared that it was a medieval forgery.

Part Three

THE SECRETS OF GOLGOTHA

Elmar R. Gruber

Two Burials in St John's Gospel

Our investigation of the thrilling history of the extraordinary linen cloth has taken us on a long journey. We have told of its repeated concealment and rediscovery and of its passage through the Near East to Constantinople and finally France. We have described the scientific studies which have shown the cloth to be authentic. They have clearly confirmed the origin, age and historical route of the textile. Opposing this is merely the radiocarbon dating, which has been fully exploited by the media. And this has turned out to have been manipulated. It is not the cloth that is a fraud, but the age test by the C-14 technique.

In this section and the one following we will reveal the motives which have led to the manipulation, and show the nature of the deception and its execution. Until now none of the authors who are similarly convinced of the deception have been able to offer a plausible motive for the affair. This is due to the general misinterpretation of the significance of the image on the cloth. It is commonly considered by sindonologists to be the 'miraculous' sign of the Resurrection of the Lord made visible. But the behaviour of the Church authorities has shown that they themselves promoted the questionable dating experiment in a way which opened the door to fraudulent manipulation. The Vatican called off its own supervisory bodies, reduced the number of laboratories, and before the age test was out the curator of the relic, Cardinal Ballestrero, made it quite clear that he did not believe it was authentic. It would be against all logic for the Church to rob itself of this unique piece of evidence to support the doctrine of the Resurrection; the Resurrection which Paul set at the centre of the Christian Faith with the words, 'And if Christ be not risen, then is our preaching vain, and your faith is also vain.' (1 Cor. 15:14). The solution to this puzzle lies concealed in the enigmatic image on the cloth itself. It emerges when one looks at the Crucifixion and burial of Jesus independent of Christian myth and Christian theology, bringing to light the true facts of the case.

Therefore let us go back to that dramatic hour on Good Friday, when Jesus was nailed to the cross and the same day hurriedly put in the tomb. The story of the Crucifixion has been passed down to us in the Synoptic Gospels, the Gospel of John and several apocryphal texts. If one makes the effort to read the Gospel texts in parallel, one notices a whole series of differences besides the points of agreement, which make it difficult to form a clear and consistent picture of the events. There are marked discrepancies even in the date of the Crucifixion: according to Matthew, Mark and Luke it took place on the day after the Passover; according to John on the day before it.

In general the Gospel of John shows the greatest independence with relation to the other three. This is why the Gospels of Matthew, Mark and Luke are also termed the Synoptic Gospels — synoptic means taken together. One can compare the many points of agreement of the texts placed side by side, a fact which suggests that they derive from the same single source. John does not fit into this comparison. Although the text of John was completed towards the end of the first century in Ephesus, and is the last of the Gospels, it is considered to be the most authentic of the four narratives. It includes episodes which do not occur in the other canonical texts, such as the wedding at Cana, the talk with Nicodemus and the resurrection of Lazarus. The detailed and historically correct knowledge of geographical features (especially those of Jerusalem before the uprising of 66), leads us to conclude that 'John' himself, or the informant behind this name, was present at these places at the time of Jesus. The striking mystical and Gnostic tone of the account and the immediate proximity to Jesus suggest that John is the best witness not only for the events, but also for the teaching of his master.[1]

Thus when it comes to the Crucifixion and burial of Jesus we should look mainly at John's narration, which in this matter too is the most reliable. Reading the text, one immediately has the feeling that one is listening to an eyewitness account. While the Synoptics merely state that Jesus received a burial according to the Jewish custom, John tries to present it in the context of the discovery of the burial clothes on Easter morning, as witnessed by him or told to him at first hand. The Italian professor of literature Gino Zaninotto demonstrates this in an excellent piece of philological analysis, although he then draws the bold conclusion that John was a witness to the Ascension. Such a conclusion is obviously taking things too far.

The first precondition for an unencumbered study of these Bible passages is to approach them in a 'natural' way, avoiding as far as possible the theological interpretation. Let us then turn to the text of John as a record which describes a historical event. There is one story in the middle of the Gospel of John which can in a way be taken as the crux of the whole text. It is the account of the resurrection of Lazarus (John 11:1–45). The episode is not found in any of the other canonical Gospels. It appears that it was included in an original form of Mark's Gospel, but was later removed, evidently at the behest of Bishop Clement of Alexandria.[2] The Lazarus story is of great interest for our study, because while telling it John provides a precise description of the burial customs of his time. Although the narrative is ambiguous on many points and has constantly given rise to different interpretations, it does assert that Lazarus was dead. He is described as being bound hand and foot in grave clothes, for which the Greek word *keiriai* is used. Here we already encounter the first problem in translation: how are we to take 'bound hand and foot'? The Jews are not known to have bound the limbs of the dead, except perhaps for transporting the corpse to the grave.[3] The expression *keiriai* denotes long bands of linen, which would be wrapped round the whole body. Hence we should not take this passage to mean that Lazarus was only tied at the wrists and ankles, but rather that his whole body was wrapped in linen bands up to the hands and the feet. If his feet had been tightly tied, it would be hard to see how he could have come out from the grave by himself at Jesus' command (John 11:44). One can add that Nonnos, the important Greek epic poet of the late classical period, used the same expression in his paraphrase of the Gospel of John, to say that Lazarus has been 'wrapped in linen bands from head to foot'.

Interestingly, John uses quite a different term to describe the cloths in which Jesus was wrapped in the tomb, *othonia*; and this without any relation to specific body parts. But *othonia* are definitely not bands; the term simply refers to cloths. We will return to this point later.

Lazarus' head was 'bound about' (*peridedemenos*) with a so-called *sudarium*. This may suggest a chin band, which was actually used to bind the head of a corpse to prevent the lower jaw from falling down. John uses different words to describing the burial of Jesus. His head was not bound about with a *sudarium*, but rather 'covered' (*entetyligmenon*) by it. Indeed, he says quite clearly that the cloth was 'placed on or over the head' (*epi tes kephales*), probably to exclude other readings, especially binding. In the sindonological literature, for example that of Barbet, Bulst and Pfeiffer or Currer-Briggs, one constantly finds the idea that a chin band can be seen in the image on the Shroud.[4] In fact no trace of any such band is to be seen. It would at least have pressed the hairs to the sides and the beard distinctly to the head. The 'chin band' is one of those odd phantoms which were introduced into the image because of some favoured hypothesis.

By using these quite distinct forms of expression, it seems that the author of the Gospel of John intended to distinguish between the burial of Lazarus and that of Jesus; he uses different words for events which only *appeared* to be similar. In this way he probably wished to make it clear to the attentive reader that these were two fundamentally different events. The raising of Lazarus from the dead was described in a way which showed that it was an event taking place after the burial of a dead body. In the case of Jesus, however, everything suggests that it was not an ordinary burial.

In the Lord's Tomb

Let us then continue our study of these differences. Lazarus came forth, it is said, without any help (*exelthen*). He ascended from the grave and was then released from his linen wrappings, so that he could move freely. The typical Jewish tomb consisted of a chamber cut into the rock, in which oven-like cavities (*kôk*, plural *kôkim*) about 50 cm wide, 80 cm high and 200 cm deep were cut. the bodies were inserted lengthwise into these.[5] We have to infer from the narrative that the burial of Lazarus was in fact a final interment.

The burial of Jesus, however, is described to us in quite a different way. He was not pushed into a tomb cavity, but instead placed on a bench. On the morning of the 'Resurrection' Mary Magdalene sees the angels, as they are called, 'the one at the head, and the other at the feet, where the body of Jesus had lain'. (John 20:12). This proves that Jesus had certainly not been pushed into a *kôk*, because in that case no one could have sat at the head end.

At this point one might think that Jesus could have been buried in what is called an arcosol tomb. This form of tomb architecture is characterized by a vault cut into the side wall of the burial chamber above a rock bench or a sarcophagus-shaped trough. In this case it would be quite possible for the angels to sit at both ends of the tomb. However, the archaeological evidence does not support this idea. Arcosol tombs were only developed in the early Byzantine period, that is about 200 years after Jesus' burial. Prior to this there was a short period when late Roman shaft tombs were in use, but the most widespread and typical tomb structure of Jesus' time was the *kôkim* tomb, and quite evidently the tomb in which Jesus was placed was also such a construction.

The *kôkim* tomb was reached through an entrance below ground level, which was often closed with a rolling stone. It consisted of a large inner chamber, in the sides of which a number of *kôkim* were usually cut, each to take one body. At the centre of the inner chamber there was a square hollow, which served as a drainage area. At the side of the pit, at the same level as the entrances to the tomb holes, the body was laid out for washing and oiling. Lamps were placed in niches. Jewish law did not allow burials at night, but in these cave-like structures illumination was also required during the day.[6]

John tells us that the 'favourite disciple' ran to the grave (20:5) and 'stooping down, and looking in' saw the linen clothes. Mary Magdalene 'stooped down, and looked into the sepulchre' (20:11), and saw the two 'angels' at the place where Jesus had lain. These statements allow us to draw two conclusions. One is that the reconstruction of Christ's grave by Brother Hughes Vincent which is often reproduced, is certainly incorrect. This suggests that Jesus lay in an arcosol tomb in a rear tomb chamber which is reached by passing through one in front. It would be impossible to see the place where Jesus lay by stooping in front of the entrance. The second point is that these statements support our assumption that the burial of Jesus had not been completed. If he had already been lying in a *kôk*, the place would again not be visible from the tomb entrance. The light passing through the very low doorway only reaches the middle of the tomb chamber. Only here could the body of Jesus have been lying. It would have been on the ledge around the central pit of the tomb chamber, certainly not inside one of the tomb holes.

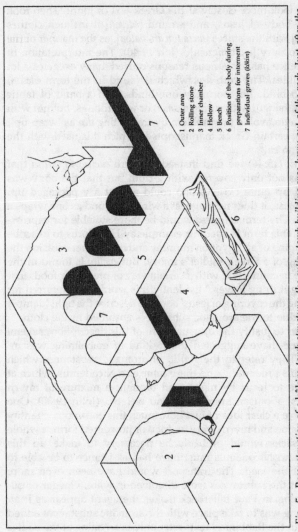

Fig. 5. *Reconstruction of a kôkim tomb structure: the entire tomb building was hewn out of the rock. Just after the entrance is a depression, at the side of which the dead were washed, embalmed and wrapped on a bench. Then the corpse was pushed head first into one of the chambers, which were sometimes sealed with a slab. (Adapted from Nitowski/ Claycombe)*

1 Outer area
2 Rolling stone
3 Inner chamber
4 Hollow
5 Bench
6 Position of the body during preparations for interment
7 Individual graves (kôkim)

Let us look more closely at the Greek text of John: 'Then took they the body of Jesus, and wound [*edesan*] it in linen clothes [*othoniois*] with the spices [*meta ton aromaton*], as the manner of the Jews is to bury [*entaphiazein*].' (Joh 19:40). The interpretation of this sentence has for various reasons caused many exegetes a lot of difficulties. The verb *deo*, which is found in the form *edesan*, means to bind. But normally one binds with a band of fabric (*spargana, keiriai*), with cords (*desmoi*) or with thongs, but not with cloths. Savio avoids the problem by translating *deo* as 'wrap up', following certain Greek manuscripts in which it is used with the preposition *en*.[7]

In Mark (15:46) we find instead the verb *eneileo* to stress that Jesus was not only covered with a cloth but that the body was wrapped up quite closely, one could almost say packaged up. Nevertheless, it does not suggest a winding round as one wraps a mummy. The term *kateilisso* would be more suitable for expressing that. This term is used for example by Herodotus to describe the wrapping of an Egyptian mummy and on another occasion the bandaging of a Greek soldier's injury. But *eneileo* is found in the literature in connection with a certain way of preparing food, first wrapping it in fig leaves.[8] Evidently this word was preferred for describing the covering of Jesus' body, to describe the tight (damp?) packing due to the aromatic substances absorbed in the cloth.

In order to justify the unusual form of this description, several interpreters have suggested that a kind of embalming was intended. They refer to the 100 lb of aromatic substances which Nicodemus procured: 'And there came also Nicodemus, which at first came to Jesus by night, and brought a mixture of myrrh and aloes, about an hundred pound weight.' (John 19:30). One has to have a clear idea of just how much this enormous quantity is. If the aloe and myrrh were in dried or powdered form, a whole row of sacks would probably be necessary to make up this weight, and Nicodemus must have had assistance to be able to transport the load. The transport would have been even more difficult if the substances were dissolved in wine, vinegar or oil. The theologian Paul Billerbeck makes the event appear as if an embalming was to take place with the aromatic substances added to oil.[9] But the Rabbinical texts refer only to an oiling of the bodies of the departed. The addition of spices is nowhere mentioned, let alone in these quantities, and was never part of Jewish custom;

nor was embalming.[10] Moreover it would be pointless to perform the embalming in the way described. One would have had to remove the entrails to stop the decomposition gases from bursting the body; an incision which would be extremely repulsive to the Jews, and the substances applied would not have served this purpose on their own. Consequently many Bible experts find this passage in St John's Gospel confusing and pointless. One of them, the exegete Haenchen, can only conclude, 'The writer of this verse did not know the Jewish burial rites, nor was he well informed concerning embalming.' But let us pause a moment to consider the matter. We have already seen that John intentionally drew a clear distinction between the burial of Lazarus and that of Jesus, and it is most likely that he chose his words after careful thought, to reveal to those who can read between the lines an event which is not apparent to a superficial understanding of the text. The differences between the Lazarus episode and the burial of Jesus had already made one thing clear to the attentive reader: there was one completed burial and one that was unfinished. But why would the loyal devotees have given their beloved master a half-finished burial, after being in such a hurry to get him into the nearby tomb? That makes no sense at all.

The interpreters have a lot of difficulty with this strange 'burial' of Jesus. They often try to avoid it by saying that Jesus' burial was unusual because the Sabbath was approaching as the sun went down on Good Friday, and no burials were allowed to be performed on the Sabbath. Therefore haste was needed. The burial of Jesus is then seen as an incomplete, hurried operation which just served to satisfy the customs. But this idea makes little sense for a number of reasons.

For one thing the view that no complete burial could be undertaken on the Sabbath is not correct. The Rabbinical texts do not state this unequivocally. One rule says that a complete burial is allowed on the Sabbath, and another is the corpse should first be covered with sand to preserve it until the Sabbath is over, when the burial can be completed.[11] Moreover Joseph of Arimathea and Nicodemus had already taken a stand which overruled all the customs, so it is hardly likely that they would care much about keeping the Jewish customs when it came to actions of such extreme importance.

Although there did not have to be a shortened, hastily performed

burial merely to comply with the customs, everything suggests
that the followers did act very quickly, and at the same time most
efficiently, after a long preparation. So what really happened in
the tomb building? Let us read the crucial sentence again in the
light of what we have said: 'Then took they the body of Jesus, and
wound it in linen clothes with the spices, as the manner of the
Jews is to bury.' The spices were aloe and myrrh, this much we
know. Myrrh was used as an ingredient for embalming by the
Egyptians, but not for the burial rites of the Jews. Instead the
Jewish custom prescribed that the body of the departed be
washed and oiled, the hair cut and tidied, the corpse dressed
again and the face covered with a cloth. The washing of the body
was of such crucial importance that it had to be carried out even if
it was the Sabbath.[12] Yet there is no mention of any of this, not
even the oiling. Instead it is said that on Easter Sunday the
women came to the tomb to oil the body. Joseph and Nicodemus
were occupied in activities which simply had nothing to do with
the Jewish burial rites. John says that they buried Jesus in the way
customary for the Jews, and then goes on to describe a burial
which openly contravenes the custom!

Why would he do this? Did he really not know the burial rites?
Of course he knew them, because he described a standard burial
in the Lazarus story. Here too, as in the comparison with the
raising of Lazarus, we have to see what John really wanted to say
behind the apparent contradictions. So what happened in that
rock-hewn tomb, if it was not a burial?

The Mysterious 'Aromatic Substances'

The most striking element in what happened in the tomb building
was the procuring of the large quantity of herbs. What was the
significance of these herbs, which had no role in a burial? Contrary to the view of some authors that the aloe mentioned by John
is *Aloe perryi*,[13] one has to assume that the species used was *Aloe
vera*.[14] *Aloe vera* is a plant native to south-western Arabia and on
the island Socotra (for which reason it is occasionally called *Aloe
soccotrina*), where it appears together with over a dozen other
types of aloe. In south-western Arabia it grew not far from the

classical trade routes which led from southern Arabia to the Mediterranean. Being a fleshy, juicy plant it could quite easily survive the long caravan and sea trade routes without drying out. It is well known that a brisk trade in plants took place from southwestern Arabia to Palestine and the adjoining areas. Aloe was used in medicine and for incense as far back as the second and third millennia BC. The sticky gel from the plant was used in antiquity, especially for healing wounds, inflammations of the skin and burns. The gel was obtained by scraping the thin cells of the leaf pulp from the harder outer layers. The yellow exudate which dripped from the cut ends dried off to leave a waxy mass; this finally reached the old medicinal herb markets as bitter aloe, a compound rich in phenols, especially aloin.[15]

The second type of spice which Nicodemus applied was myrrh, a gum resin from shrubs of the genus *Commiphora*, which belongs to the Burseraceae. Its aromatic fragrance played an important part in old Indian and Oriental rituals. The sacred anointing oil of the Israelites also contained myrrh as a herbal perfume of the 'noblest kind' (Exod. 30:23). Old Egyptian records describe how myrrh came from the legendary land Punt, which was probably located on the coast of what is now Somalia. Hippocrates praised its disinfectant power. It was used for healing wounds from very early times. In the Middle Ages myrrh was considered to be one of the most important treatments against epidemics and infectious diseases.

Both substances, aloe and myrrh, were commonly used for the treatment of large injured areas, because they could easily be made into ointments and tinctures. Some researchers claim that the Jews often mixed myrrh with labdanum, the resin of the cistus rockrose.[16] This was used especially for plasters and bandages.[17] Clearly one has to see such mixtures as the most specific means for the rapid and effective healing of wounds, combined with the greatest possible efficacy against danger of infection, at the time of Jesus. There can therefore be no doubt that Nicodemus procured an astonishing quantity of highly specific medicinal herbs with the sole purpose of treating the wounds on the body of Jesus. These spices could have served no other purpose.

There gradually dawns the conviction that John's secret style of writing was intended to reveal a tremendous event to the attentive reader, while concealing it from the eyes of the ignorant: Jesus

was not meant to be buried, because he had not died on the cross!
The author of the text, or his informant, who was a witness at the
'tomb' of Jesus and well informed by Joseph of Arimathea and
Nicodemus, wrote in a way which would show anyone who
knew how to read between the lines what really happened
during and immediately after the Crucifixion. Thus he makes it
clear to us that the show of a burial according to Jewish custom
was presented, while in reality they set about 'bringing Jesus
back to life', in the privacy of the tomb building, under the
direction of Joseph and Nicodemus. And they did not try to do
this by imitating his miracles, but by applying the art of medical
healing.

Jesus and the Essenes

In order to form a proper assessment of these events and the
subsequent narrative, one must first point out that Jesus was
close to the sect of the Essenes, indeed it is likely that he belonged
to a branch of the sect. The Essenes formed a kind of monastic
community of strict observance, but they also had members who
lived 'in the world', like a third order. Their ideal was inner self-
perfection. Essene communities existed in the Diaspora before the
destruction of Jerusalem, and as late as the seventh century were
still exerting an influence on the newly developing Islam through
the Jewish-Christian Ebionites.[18]

The roots of the Essenes go back to Zadok, the first high priest
at the time of the foundation of the Temple by Solomon. The
members of the priesthood were allowed to call themselves the
'sons of Zadok'. In the course of time a section of the sons of
Zadok broke away because they considered the priesthood corrupt
and compromising. The dissidents were called *bene sadok*. In modern terminology they are called Zadokites or, as the Greeks called
them, Essenes. This term derives from the Aramaic *assaya*, which
means doctor or healer. Many of the monastic followers, who
devoted themselves to their ascetic practices of prayer and
penance with great zeal, developed astonishing abilities. These
gifted monks, called therapeuts, seem to have attracted special
attention with their public healings.[19] The Essenes are not

mentioned anywhere in the New Testament, although their numbers were at least as great as the Sadducees and Pharisees (Joseph estimates there were about 4000 of them). This would suggest an element of intentional secrecy regarding the influence of the sect on the teaching and work of Jesus.

The Essenes had various communities in Palestine, with the main centre at Qumran on the shores of the Dead Sea. The sensational discovery of numerous scrolls in a cave at Qumran in 1947 made it possible to gain glimpses into a community which practised in a way a 'Christianity before Christ'. As is well known, the translation of the material was systematically boycotted, and only very recently almost all the Qumran texts have appeared in print. Similarities between the teachings of Jesus and those of the Essenes are obvious. This astonishing resemblance is shown in the same theological themes and the same religious institutions. As long ago as 1831 the Stuttgart town vicar and repetitor at the Tübingen Seminary, August Freidrich Gfrörer, although he did not yet know of the Qumran texts, wrote: 'The Christian Church developed from the Essene community, whose ideas it continued and without whose regulations its organization would be inexplicable.'

Qumran lies directly within the orbit of Jesus' early activity. His first public appearance occurred in this region. It is a striking fact that the place where Jesus received the ritual baptismal bath in the Jordan at the hands of John, was only 5 km from the monastic settlement of Qumran. There is of course a reason for this. John the Baptist was a *schaliach*, an apostle of the sect of Qumran. An independent tradition had developed in John's circle, a sort of third order of Qumran.[20] John led a community of Essene moderates.[21] After his baptism one should similarly count Jesus as a member of one of these communities, and refer to him as a Nazarene. This later led to the falsely translated and irrational description of him as 'Jesus of Nazareth', a place which was not even in existence at the time of Jesus. Later a sign was said to have been fixed to the Cross, giving the charge against him as membership of this sect: *Jesus, Nazarenus, Rex Iudaeorum* – 'Jesus, Nazarene, King of the Jews'.

Immersion in water, as a purifying baptismal bath, was a rite of special importance to the Essenes. Among the many preachers John was doubtless one of the most successful of his day, and his influence was felt out in the Diaspora. He probably had a much larger circle of followers than Jesus. In the meeting of Jesus with the Baptist, at the beginning of his public activity, his close connection to the Essenes can clearly be seen. John was in a sense his spiritual director, and Jesus a disciple. Other elements of the story – that Jesus should really have been baptizing John, and that after the baptism of Jesus the divine voice sounded – have to be relativized by John's questions in Herod's dungeon, when he asked if Jesus was the awaited Messiah or if another was still to come. This question seems completely irrational in view of the events at the baptism, but perhaps part of the baptism story was appended later. But it is very likely that Jesus was taken as the Messianic pretender after the arrest of the Baptist. People even occasionally thought he might be the reincarnation of John. Jesus emancipated himself from John only after the latter's arrest, when he emerged from the shadow of his teacher and went his own way (Matt. 4:12; Mark 1:14; Luke 4:14f). A further point suggesting a dependence on the tradition of John and so of the Essene way is the fact that Jesus was at first loyal to the ideal of his 'master' and entered the desert alone, like John.

The recluses of Qumran refer in their writings to the area where they live as 'the desert'. This was where John lived, possibly in the Qumran caves; here Jesus withdrew for forty days and experienced the temptations by the devil (Luke 4:1–13). In Mark's Gospel it is said that Jesus 'was with the wild beasts; and the angels ministered unto him'. (Mark 1:13). The 'angels' or messengers of God were probably Essene monks, who supervised the 'novitiate' of Jesus in a cave outside Qumran.

From the writings of Flavius Josephus we learn the following about the monastically organized part of the sect:

> They rejected riches, and what is admirable about them is the communality of possessions, so that one finds none among them who owns more than any other. For there is the rule that anyone entering the sect has to sacrifice his possessions for the whole, and so one never observes extreme poverty or superfluous wealth, but they all like brothers make use of the total assets of the pooled goods of the individual members of the Order. They view oil as dirt, and if one of them has ointment applied against his will, he washes off his body. For they consider having a rough skin as honourable as their habit of constantly going around in white robes.[22]

This form of living with communal possessions was also taught by Jesus. And he too asked his followers to leave house and family and join the wandering monks without property. The life of the Essenes was described by Pliny the Elder in his *Natural History* as follows: 'A solitary and most remarkable people in the whole world, without any women, who have renounced human love and live by the palm trees without money'.[23] Young Jewish men were duty-bound to marry. The single state was frowned upon. But Jesus personally renounced family ties on his own spiritual path (Luke 14:26; Matt. 10:37). He even spoke radically and in a revolutionary way against the traditional family cohesion (Matt. 10:35-6). This alien attitude can be explained if one remembers that Jesus was rooted in the spiritual tradition widespread in the East, of perfect renunciation of all earthly fetters and the dissolution of the earthly desires. 'The foxes have holes, and the birds of the air have nests; but the Son of Man hath not where to lay his head.' (Matt. 8:20). And to the man who wished to follow him but first wanted to bid farewell to his family, Jesus countered: 'No man, having put his hand to the plough, and looking back, is fit for the kingdom of God.' (Luke 9:62). Jesus set an example for his followers of the life of the wandering preacher free of possessions. In the apocryphal Gospel of Thomas the call is potently put: 'Jesus said: be ye wanderers.' (log 42.)

We cannot present all the correspondences between the teachings of the Essenes and those of Jesus here. They are so clear on many points that it was this which probably led to the persistent obstruction of the translation of the Qumran scrolls. The Essenes wished to form the 'New Covenant' with God, which Martin Luther later translated as 'New Testament'. They called themselves the 'New Covenant'. Jesus was described as the founder of it only much later. This 'New Covenant' was said to last from the day of the taking of the One Teacher until the Messiah of Aaron and Israel arose. At the end of one Qumran scroll the strict regulation of the seating arrangement at the festive eschatological meal is described; later the apostles argued about this at the Last Supper (Luke 22:24). In the hymns of thanks it is said that the Essenes announced to the poor the joyous message (*evangelium*) out of the fullness of God's compassion, and that they wished to be the messengers of good news.

Despite the plentiful parallels between Jesus and the Essenes, it is the differences one has to make especially clear. The emergence and teaching of Jesus is to be understood as a revival movement on the basis of Essenism. He worked to clear away hardened and encrusted customs and habits. His attitude stands out from that of others because of his tremendous tolerance. Above all he shows how a freer relation to the Torah and the law is possible. According to Jewish law the violater of the Sabbath who fails to heed the warnings must die. The Damascus text of Qumran forbids the killing of the Sabbath violater, and Jesus expands this view: 'For the Son of Man is Lord even of the Sabbath day.' (Matt. 12:8).

The difference is particularly marked in relation to the love of one's enemies. The Essenes hated their enemies. The people of Qumran were proud of their separation from the world. They fostered an elitist attitude. Jesus on the other hand, by reaching out and contacting the sinners, tried to bring light to those who seemed lost, and stressed that he was specially 'sent to the lost sheep of the house of Israel'. He explicitly opposed religious intolerance and claims to membership of an institution with exclusive rights to bless.

Another decisive point is that Jesus reinforced his mission by his miraculous cures rather than wise utterances alone. Here he does not stand in the line of tradition of the prophets,[24] but in that of the Essene therapeuts, who were of course not only healers but also teachers, scholars and sometimes prophets. Jesus distanced himself from the Order by his innovations, but certainly continued to have very a close relationship with other Essenes.

Flavius Josephus' comment that the Essenes were recognizable because of their white clothes seems to be an important point. As early as the eighteenth century, philosophers of the Enlightenment considered the Crucifixion and Resurrection to be just a clever drama put on by Essene monks. The youth who spoke to the women at the empty tomb is shown by his white clothes to be a member of the Essenes. Following the same line of thought over a century ago the idea arose that Jesus may have been the son of an Essene, whom Mary had approached in an ecstatic state. The child was then given to the Order, something which Josephus reports was a usual practice for Essenes.

On Dying on the Cross

Reading the passages in the text in this unbiased way, the events which took place in the rock tomb, not far from the site of execution, are seen as an attempt by members of an Essene community to treat the seriously wounded Jesus with medicinal herbs. The meaning of the verb *eneileo* used by Mark now becomes clear. We have seen that it was used in connection with the cooking of foodstuffs wrapped in leaves. To treat Jesus the therapeuts evidently used a sweat-promoting packing formed with the help of an excessive quantity of herbs, similar in a way to the cooking method. One has to see John's *edesan othoniois* ('and wound it in linen clothes') against this background, to get to the true meaning. What was meant was not binding round in the sense of wrapping up, but the way a heavy plaster covered or went round the whole body. Dioscorides, the Cilician doctor of the first century, also used both the verbs *deo* and *eneileo* to denote wrapping in linen clothes.[25]

There was evidently no intention to bury Jesus. Instead he was to be brought to a safe place where he could be healed in peace. What better place for this man than the tomb of a person believed dead. Naturally we also hear nothing of the washing of the corpse which was so important in Jewish burials. Joseph did not wash Jesus, because he was not dead. Medically speaking, such a washing was definitely not to be recommended. The act of washing would only have caused the many wounds covered in clotted blood to start bleeding again. Joseph and Nicodemus would have applied the curative herbal solution to the body with the utmost care, to make sure that this did not happen.

When such bold conclusions as these are offered, the question presents itself whether a person can survive a crucifixion at all. The death on the cross was thought by the Romans to be the most demeaning and frightful form of execution. Cicero called it the 'most horrible and repulsive capital punishment'. Only in exceptional cases, were Roman citizens ever sentenced to this punishment, and only those from the lowest social strata. But in the lands occupied by the Romans crucifixion was a favoured deterrent, to keep the rebellious peoples obedient. Palestine had long been notorious as a place of nationalist unrest. From the time of the Maccabees in 167 BC until Bar Kochba in 134 AD, there were some sixty-two rebellions, wars and uprisings against the pagan yoke, first that of the Greeks and then that of the Romans. Sixty-one of these disturbances started from Galilee, the home area of Jesus. It is therefore hardly surprising that crucifixions were almost a routine affair there.

Crucifixion was alien to the Jews. Their methods of capital punishment were stoning, burning, decapitation and strangling. According to the Mosaic Law it was, however, permissible to hang up a criminal who had already been executed 'on wood', as an additional punishment and humiliation: 'for he that is hanged is accursed of God' (Deut. 21:23). And hence a crucified person was under no circumstances to defile the Sabbath, which starts in the evening of the preceding day, the day of preparation.

The Romans made sure that they did not wilfully offend the religious sentiments of the Jews, to avoid even greater unrest. If the official Roman death sentence *ibis in crucem* – 'you shall ascend the cross' – was passed, care was taken to see that the execution was completed before the Sabbath. The greatest haste was therefore called for in the case of Jesus' Crucifixion, because it took place on the day of preparation. It had to be over before the onset of evening. But that was not easy to arrange, because the special feature of crucifixion was its protracted, agonizing torture. It was done in a way which meant the agony usually extended over a period of days, until the person finally expired.

There could be considerable variety in the form of the cross and the way the victim was fixed to it. If the body weight hung solely from the wrists, death would ensue within five or six hours, as a result of gradual suffocation rather than as a result of something such as loss of blood. In this extreme posture the breathing is so severely hindered that the body can no longer be supplied with enough oxygen. After a relatively short time unconsciousness would result and then the forward-drooping head would further reduce the breath intake.[26] To prevent such a 'quick' death, a small wooden cross-piece called the *suppedaneum* was often fixed to the vertical post of the cross, for the delinquent to prop himself up as long as his strength allowed. This cross-piece should not be imagined as an oblique board, as it is shown in Byzantine Crucifixion scenes. The *suppedaneum* was a smaller, horizontal cross-beam, which the victim could actually stand on. It is not without reason that the oldest depictions, such as on the so-called mock crucifix of Palatin, show the crucified person standing.

Crucifixions were carried out either by binding with thongs or by nailing the hands and feet. The victim could then delay his death by his own effort, by supporting himself on the point of attachment, the nail or foot beam, and pushing the body upwards. Occasionally a piece of wood to sit on (*sedile*) was also fixed behind the abdomen, which presumably alleviated the pain somewhat, but prolonged the agony even more. As Nero's personal philosopher Seneca wrote in a letter, 'The life of the person thus sentenced trickled away drop by drop.'

The Gospels report that Jesus was nailed on the cross at the sixth hour (noon) and gave up his spirit at the ninth hour (about 3 pm). Towards evening he was taken for dead and was removed from the cross. This unexpectedly rapid death puzzled Pilate himself, who was obviously extremely surprised and asked the leading centurion if everything was in order (Mark 15:44). As far as this astonishment is concerned, little has changed to this day. Many studies, especially by medical people, have been carried out to try and explain the phenomenon of the all too rapid 'death' of Jesus, and the authors have their difficulties. The course which is usually adopted is to blame the mistreatment of Jesus before the crucifixion; it had so severely undermined his general condition that he succumbed to the torture of crucifixion after just a short time. But this explanation is fairly weak.

For one thing, unlike the strict group of monastic Essenes, Jesus was no frail ascetic,[27] but a relatively tall, strong and robust man in his prime (according to the cloth about 1.82 m (6 ft) tall, and 79 kg (12½ stone) in weight). After the night of torment he talked to the court in a very clever way, obviously in full possession of his mental powers, and this would not have been possible in a state of exhaustion. Then, he was relieved of the burden of carrying the cross-beam of the Cross (*patibulum*), by Simon of Cyrene, for a good part of the stretch of about 550 to 650 metres from Pilate's *praetorium* to the site of execution. Many interpreters have taken this as a proof that Jesus was extremely weakened and no longer able to bear the weight of the beam. This too has to be queried.

As far as the whiplashes are concerned, Jesus was not treated any differently from others. Everyone who was sentenced to death on the cross had first to endure such abuses. By Hebraic law thirty-nine lashes could be given; a third of these on the chest or front side, the remainder on the back. The priest carried out this punishment in the synagogue with a three-thonged whip of calfskin. Of course we are not told whether they kept to the correct number in the case of Jesus.

In the Gospel of Peter it says, when Jesus is being nailed on the cross: 'But he kept silent, as if he felt no pain.' It is probable that during his training Jesus had become practised in the art of mastering pain by meditation, in a similar way to the Indian yogis. Exercises which lead to this result are known from numerous religious sects throughout the East; they have been scientifically investigated and well documented.

In most cases the arms of the sentenced person were first fixed to the *patibulum*, which he then had to carry on his shoulders to the place of execution. The weight of this beam varied between about 18 and 30 kg. Hence considerable strength was needed to be able to transport this heavy load. From the Gospel accounts it is seen that Jesus was only nailed to the cross at the site of execution. He was laid naked on the ground, where his wrists were nailed to the *patibulum*. Then he was raised together with the cross-beam on to the upright post (*stipes*) of the Cross.

Is it not odd that the death throes of others lasted so much longer than those of Jesus, considering his well-trained and strong constitution? In the autobiography of Flavius Josephus, through whose writing we learn much about the customs and events in Palestine at the time of Jesus, we even find an informative passage which tells of a crucified man who recovered after being taken from the cross:

> I was sent by Titus Caesar with Ceralius and a thousand riders to a certain town by the name of Thecoa, to find out whether a camp could be set up at this place. On my return I saw many prisoners who had been crucified, and recognized three of them as my former companions. I was inwardly very sad about this and went with tears in my eyes to Titus and told him about them. He at once gave the order that they should be taken down and given the best treatment so they could get better. However two of them died while being attended to by the doctor; the third recovered.[28]

It is difficult to understand why Jesus departed the body so early and that 'with a loud cry', an exit that is quite mysterious and puzzling to all the doctors. A closer study, however, shows that this too is an important indication that Jesus was taken unconscious from the cross.

The way the two people crucified next to him died is graphically described in St John's Gospel:

> The Jews therefore, because it was the preparation, that the bodies should not remain upon the cross on the sabbath day (for that sabbath day was an high day), besought Pilate that their legs might be broken, and that they might be taken away. Then came the soldier, and brake the legs of the first, and of the other which was crucified with him. (John 19:31–2).

So the two criminals crucified with Jesus, who had certainly been as much abused beforehand as he was, were still alive. Their legs were broken so that they could not straighten themselves up on their own any more, and so they painfully suffocated within a few hours.

'But when they came to Jesus, and saw that he was dead already, they brake not his legs' (John 19:33). This is very strange and inexplicable behaviour on the part of the Roman soldiers. Why did these hardened men not break Jesus' legs too, to ensure death? The theological interpretation, that the word of the prophet in Exod. 12:46 had to be fulfilled ('. . . neither shall ye break a bone thereof'), is not very helpful. One should instead ask what the soldiers were thinking to make them exempt Jesus from this terrible treatment. It is beyond question that they had their doubts about his being dead, and viewed his unconsciousness with scepticism. Otherwise they could also have spared him the lance thrust in the side. Would one not have expected them to break the legs of all the crucified men, to be sure that they were all dead? Up to this point we hear how Jesus was treated with even more than the usual contempt, with blows to the face, the mock sceptre and the crown of thorns on his head. Why this sudden change of mood, this 'privileged' and rather merciful treatment?

The Gospels do not provide us with any consistent answer. The only point they agree on is that Jesus died at the ninth hour with a loud cry, while those crucified next to him obviously continued their agony. According to John (19:33–5) one of the soldiers drove his lance into Jesus' thorax, and some blood and water flowed out. Luke and Matthew are no help to us on this point, because neither of them mentions this event. Mark, however (15:44–5), gives us an interesting clue. Pilate, surprised that Jesus was already dead, summoned the centurion, who confirmed the death, and Pilate then released the body of Jesus. The centurion is the same one who, moved by the events during the crucifixion, praised Jesus as the true Son of God (Mark 15:39; Mark 27:54; Luke 23:47). Who was this centurion?

In the apocryphal *Acta Pilata* he is called Longinus and presented as the captain who supervised the Crucifixion. According to a tradition testified to by Gregory of Nyssa, Longinus was said to have later become a bishop in his Cappadocian homeland. This change of heart may mean that he had some connection with Jesus and his followers before the Crucifixion, or was even a secret follower of Jesus. This would make many of the problems about the events during the Crucifixion understandable. Joseph of Arimathea, Nicodemus and the centurion Longinus were among the secret followers of Jesus. Since they held influential positions, they were informed well enough in advance about what the revolutionary exposure of Jesus was leading to. Joseph was highly respected as a member of the Sanhedrin. Since the second century BC this had been the high council of the supreme Jewish authorities for all affairs of state, judicature and religion. It consisted of seventy members under the chairmanship of the high priest. Nicodemus, who was initiated by Jesus under cover of night (John 3:1–22), was also a Jewish councillor. Thanks to their positions Joseph and Nicodemus had surely been kept well informed about the time and place of the execution and were thus able to plan the rescue of their master. We hear an echo of the advance information given to Nicodemus in a highly revered hagiographical legend of the Middle Ages. It tells how Nicodemus, in a letter sent to Mary Magdalene, warned Jesus about the attack by the Jews, when he was in Ephraim (John 11:53f).[29]

Joseph and Nicodemus knew that the Crucifixion itself could not be avoided. But if they could manage to take Jesus down from the cross early enough, and everything was well planned, it would be possible to keep him alive, and he would probably be able to continue his mission unobserved. It was crucially important to the whole operation that the apostles were not involved. They had gone into hiding for fear of persecution. Nothing would be done against the respected councillors Joseph and Nicodemus or the Roman centurion. So for a limited period there was a chance that the daring operation could be carried out successfully.

The Side Wound and the Miracle Drink

Let us return to the stabbing with the lance. A detailed analysis shows that the term used in the Greek original for the thrust of the soldier, *nyssein*, means a light scratch, puncture or stab to the skin, not a thrust with full force, let alone a deep penetration. In the Vulgate (the generally recognized Latin translation of the Bible) one already finds the incorrect translation *aperire*, which means 'to open'. But actually this is not the meaning at all. The procedure served as a kind of 'official confirmation' of death: if the body did not show any reaction to a light stabbing, it could be assumed that the person was dead. Probably the centurion mentioned in the Gospels had performed this test himself. It was not meant to be a death thrust at all; Jesus was considered to be dead already and for this reason he had already been spared having his legs broken. One might add that an experienced soldier would hardly have made a fatal thrust to the side; it would have been frontally into the heart.

The exegetes find it difficult to explain the emergence of the blood and water. Some can only see this occurrence as a miracle, since the circulation stops at death; for others it is the symbolic interpretation of the elements blood and water which comes to the fore. Scientific explanations have also been attempted, where the water is seen as blood serum which forms when blood decomposes. But such decomposition starts at the earliest six hours after death takes place.

We should not, however, set aside this passage in the Gospel of John as of no significance, because we have to assume that the eyewitness (the source of the text) wanted to place special emphasis on the blood and water. For the sentence following this observation in the text runs: 'And he that saw it bare record, and his record is true; and he knoweth that he saith true, that ye might believe.' (19:35) This is crucial and fits nicely into the picture we have drawn of John's style of writing: a depiction as it were on two levels, with a superficial way of reading for the masses and with the refined references, which we keep discovering strewn throughout the text, for those who know how to read between the lines. The special emphasis so clearly given to the testimony about the blood and water which flowed from the side of Jesus, was really meant to show that Jesus was still alive.

Even if many centuries were to pass before the discovery of the circulation system, it was a known fact at the time of Jesus that corpses do not bleed, and blood serum is not seen on the wounds of a body which has just died. Even Origen (185–254), who did actually believe Jesus was dead at the time when the blood and water came out from the wounds, pointed out that corpses do not bleed. Before the middle of the last century little thought was given to the causes of Jesus' death. In 1847 W. Stroud published for the first time a theory about his passing. But even he, the first scientist to dare to deal with the problem, came up against great difficulties. At first he suggested total exhaustion as the cause of death, but he had to discard this hypothesis because of its improbability, and went on to postulate that he died of a broken heart (from a sort of despair). Forty years after Stroud, Sir James Risdon Bennett concluded that Jesus may have died 'from a heart broken by mental agony', compounded by the lance stab. Later authors expressed the far-fetched notion that Jesus may have succumbed to an acute expansion of the stomach due to shock. Others were even prepared to explain the light fluid which came out with the blood after the lance wound was inflicted, by simply shifting the stabbing forwards and down into the abdomen, so that urine came out when the bladder was damaged. But the text of John leaves no doubt that the minor perforation was done in the side of the thorax.

Recently three Californian authors claim to have reconstructed the precise medical train of events for Jesus' Passion and death – the pathologist William P. Edwards, the anatomist Floyd E. Hosmer and the Methodist pastor J. Gabel Wesley. The problem of how to explain Jesus' cry just before his death is side-stepped by making it out to be a kind of harbinger of some disastrous event having lethal consequences. The death was, they said, traceable to a number of factors, such as severe exhaustion, so-called hypovolemic shock, acute cardiac insufficiency and, as the immediate cause of death, a thrombosis or fibrillation. Capping it all, an illustration for the article shows in addition to all this the hypothetical lance thrust through the chest – 'an event which almost certainly did not take place'.[30] The scenario depicted, beginning with the results of the whipping, is a terrible one. Just reading the article is almost enough to make one's heart stop in horror. But what they present in such sober and impressive medical language is nothing but a string of suppositions, which are neither true to the Biblical accounts, nor able to stand up to the fact that all the other crucifixion victims treated in the same way as Jesus continued to hang for days on their instruments of torture until they finally suffocated.

It appears that the expression 'blood and water' is a traditional idiom from the ornate Arabian language, intended to emphasize a certain happening. Today we can say someone 'sweats blood' – the German equivalent is 'to sweat blood and water', '*Blut und Wasser schwitzen*' – if he works hard or is very anxious, without meaning that blood actually comes from the pores. The same expression, applied when observing a wound, could simply mean that a lot of blood is visible. The eyewitness was doubtless surprised to see so much blood pouring out from a supposedly dead body through a minor scratch wound, and aptly expressed his surprise. Evidently Jesus was only apparently dead. The way the copious emission of blood is emphasized by confirming that it was a true observation, was meant to point to this very fact.

Everything had been carefully prepared by Joseph and his helpers up until the lance thrust. But the man from Arimathea had begun making the necessary preparations much earlier than this. The first thing he had done was to purchase a garden in the immediate vicinity of the Crucifixion site.[31] With wise foresight he decided to have a new tomb cut from the rock on the estate, somewhere the supposedly dead body could be quickly brought for safety. It was essential to have an unused tomb ready: to place Jesus in a tomb in which others were already buried would have given rise to legal objections, because people who had been executed would normally be thought to dishonour the bodies of the faithful which had already been placed in the tomb. There would be no objection to a 'burial' in an empty tomb, particularly since, as Josephus reports, political criminals who were executed by the Romans – and Jesus was such a person – could be allowed an honourable burial which would be denied to an ordinary criminal.[32] Naturally Joseph of Arimathea could not say that he was busy preparing a tomb for Jesus. Therefore we read in the Gospels that Joseph brought the body of Jesus to his own new family grave. Let us consider this a moment. Why on earth should Joseph, who came from Arimathea near the Samarian border, build his family tomb in Jerusalem of all places?[33] He certainly had no intention of moving and settling there. We read in the Pilate texts that after the burial the Jews came to visit him in his home town of Arimathea, to which he had returned. In compliance with the tradition Joseph would certainly have had his family tomb in his home town. The official line in the text saying that it was Joseph's own tomb building, was meant for the uninitiated, who would not think twice about it. Actually the new tomb construction in the garden near Golgotha was not meant for the dead, neither Joseph and his family nor anyone else. It was intended solely to serve as an alibi, to avoid having to move the seriously wounded Jesus very far, should they succeed in getting him off the Cross soon enough. The persecutors of Jesus would then be satisfied, thinking him dead in the grave.

The fact that the Crucifixion took place on the day of preparation was advantageous in a way, because it meant that they could greatly speed up the 'burial' without arousing suspicion. Of course they had to make sure that Jesus really did appear to have died. This too they could not just leave to chance.

In the Gospels a certain event is reported as happening just before the alleged death of Jesus. 'Now there was set a vessel full of vinegar: and they filled a sponge with vinegar, and put it upon hyssop [a plant used for ritual sprinkling], and put it to his mouth. When Jesus therefore had received the vinegar, he said, It is finished: and he bowed his head, and gave up the ghost.' (John 19:29–30).

How did it happen that Jesus seemed to die immediately after he had taken the bitter drink? Was it really vinegar which he was given? It was fully in line with Jewish custom to offer a person sentenced to death wine spiced with myrrh or incense, to alleviate the pain by the slight narcotic effect. In the Talmud there is a passage which says: 'The one departing to be put to death was given a piece of incense in a cup of wine, to help him fall asleep.' (Sanh. 43a). But there is no mention of a spiced wine. All the evangelists agree that it was a brew with a very bitter taste. In Latin vinegar is called *acetum*, from *acidus*, 'bitter'. The Roman soldiers did not merely tolerate the drink, one of them even helped Jesus to take it (Matt. 27:48; Mark 15:36; Luke 23:36; John 19:29).

Let us look more closely at this statement. The sponge was offered to Jesus on a hyssop stem. Hyssop is a plant with a weak stem and hardly suitable for holding up a wet sponge. Even a bundle of hyssop would not have the rigidity required to make it possible, although one does not have to assume the Cross was very high – there were crosses on which the sentenced person was fixed with the feet just above the ground. In such a case the sponge would not have to be lifted up very high to be offered. But perhaps the instrument used to offer Jesus the 'vinegar' was confused by a simple error: *hyssos* ('short spear') was taken as *hyssopos* ('hyssop'). It is a soldier who offers Jesus the sponge, as the Synoptic authors relate. Hence it is likely that this confusion did actually occur. Therefore it is not unreasonable to suppose that the centurion Longinus raised the sponge to the lips of Jesus on his spear.[34]

One notices how the vinegar drink was introduced into John's narrative as if it had been brought to the Crucifixion for this very purpose. It was a part of the preparations which Joseph, Nicodemus and the centurion had made in order to carry out their plan. One can only speculate as to what the bitter fluid consisted of. In those days there was a wide assortment of pain relieving and intoxicating substances, and the healing arts of the period were excellent at making mixtures which had unusual effects. Perhaps the drink was made of a bitter wine to which a measured portion of opium had been added. The exceptional anaesthetic and narcotic effect of opium was well known to the Jews even in pre-Christian times. Opium is the milky juice of the scratched, unripe seed-heads of a certain poppy plant (*Papaver somniferum*). This type of poppy was widespread in Palestine. Hence one may surmise that Jesus was given opium dissolved in some fluid while on the cross.

The narcotic effect of opium is so strong that it can lead to a state of stupor in which the person is completely without external sensation. The main active ingredient is morphine, which has a sedative, narcotic and breath-inhibiting effect. The alkaloid papaverine has a pronounced cramp-relaxing effect. Combined with the many other effective components, and by the admixture of various additional substances, opium solutions can be well adjusted for a particular purpose. Hence the effect of this drug was in many ways ideal for Joseph and his friends: not only was Jesus given the best of pain-killers, the dose was designed to make him lose consciousness in a short time and so be able to hang on the cross 'as if dead'. The appearance of a sudden death was enhanced by the fact that opium strongly lowers the heart rate, calms the breathing to an extraordinary degree, and makes the body completely limp. And yet, administered in the correct dosage, as was known to the experienced Essene therapeuts, it involved no danger to the heart; on the contrary it strengthened it.

If Jesus was actually close to suffocation – which almost all the medical opinions assume was the cause of death – the loud cry before he 'died', which the three Synoptic evangelists expressly mention, would be quite impossible. A suffocating person could hardly manage a whisper. But Jesus cried out. And in John we read, 'When Jesus therefore had received the vinegar, he said, It is finished: and he bowed his head, and gave up the ghost.' (19:30). Jesus was able to say these words after he had taken the drink and felt the narcotic effect increasing. He was able to say them because he was not close to death but to a deep, induced state of rest.

The Open Rock Tomb

The moment Jesus was seen to hang unconscious from the cross, Joseph made haste to secure the release of the body as soon as possible. He exerted his full influence on Pilate to achieve the fastest possible release. One exegete even suggests that the wealthy Joseph paid a high sum in bribery, to speed things up.[35] That is quite conceivable. Joseph was pressed for time, and any means would have seem justified to him when it came to shortening the slow bureaucratic process. The other crucified men had their legs broken, but in Jesus' case the centurion just checked with his 'lance stab' that he was dead. Pilate released the 'corpse', and at once Joseph and Nicodemus took Jesus from the Cross and brought him to the nearby rock tomb.

In the seclusion of the tomb chamber, preparations for the

healing of Jesus were underway on the middle bench. The opium drink helped him to sleep deeply beyond pain, and the medical packing using the enormous amount of herbs was intended to make the wounds heal faster. Joseph and Nicodemus knew they could not leave Jesus in the tomb for long. The Jews were extremely suspicious and feared that his followers might steal the body to pretend there had been a miraculous resurrection. According to Matthew (27:62–6), they asked Pilate for someone to guard the tomb. The Sabbath would prevent them from forming a watch at the sepulchre themselves. It was gradually growing more difficult to get Jesus out unobserved. One can no longer say whether a Roman watch really was assigned to the tomb – only Matthew reports it. It does seem, however, as if it was introduced into his text to add dramatic effect to the angelic apparition. The Jews' desire to set a guard on a corpse must have seemed most peculiar to the Romans, and it is very unlikely that they would have complied with such a request.

During the Sabbath, then, the helpers had time to take care of Jesus, but as soon as he came round they had to move him quickly elsewhere, to avoid further problems from the Jewish authorities.

When the women came to the tomb with the oils for anointing on the first day of the week, they found the stone rolled aside and the tomb empty. Let us hear what the Gospel accounts say. Luke (24:1–5) writes:

> Now upon the first day of the week, very early in the morning, they came unto the sepulchre, bringing the spices which they had prepared, and certain others with them. And they found the stone rolled away from the sepulchre. And they entered in, and found not the body of the Lord Jesus. And it came to pass, as they were much perplexed thereabout, behold, two men stood by them in shining garments: And as they were afraid, and bowed down their faces to the earth, they said unto them, Why seek ye the living among the dead?

Mark (16:4–6) relates:

> And when they looked, they saw that the stone was rolled away, for it was very great. And entering into the sepulchre, they saw a young man sitting on the right side, clothed in a long white garment; and they were affrighted. And he saith unto them, Be not affrighted: Ye seek Jesus of Nazareth, which was crucified: he is risen: he is not here: behold the place where they laid him.

After the so-called Resurrection Jesus was said to be constantly entering through locked doors and surprising his followers (John 20:19–26). Why then, one has to ask, was the massive stone rolled aside from the tomb, from the very place where this miraculous 'Resurrection' was said to have happened? It would surely have been a more astonishing miracle if it had been necessary to push the stone aside to let in the ladies with the oils for anointing, and only then find that Jesus had vanished from the sealed chamber. The open tomb shows us that someone had had to act quickly and move Jesus out. Evidently friends were still at the tomb – the men with the shining garments of Luke, the young man with the white garment of Mark. The shining white robe suggests that they were Essenes. Probably Jesus had been led out just a short while before. Since the feast day of the Passover always coincided with the full moon, it was easy to travel in the bright night. Perhaps the Essenes who stayed behind were going to collect certain items and seal the tomb. The shocked ladies received clear replies to their questions by the Essenes: Jesus had risen again and therefore was no longer here. He had indeed risen, that is from his deep coma. The Luke text is even clearer: 'Why seek ye the living among the dead?' Does that not compel us to assume that Jesus was alive, that it had been possible to save him? Is this not the clear message we get from these Gospel passages?

John, who does not report the episode with the women at the sepulchre, relates in detail an event which it seems must have taken place before the women arrived (John 20:1–18): Mary Magdalene came to the tomb early in the morning, when it was still dark, and saw the stone rolled away. Shocked, she ran to Peter and John and lamented that someone had taken the Lord out of the sepulchre. When the pair arrived at the tomb and peered in, they saw only the linen clothes, with no trace of Jesus anywhere. Mary Magdalene, who stood weeping before the tomb, asked the gardener if he had carried the body away. When he addressed her by name, she realized it was Jesus.

It is remarkable that Mary Magdalene took Jesus for the gardener. Is this the gloriously resurrected one, a figure unrecognized by his closest companion? Probably they had just led Jesus out of the tomb when Mary Magdalene appeared. So as not to attract attention, they had dressed him in simple garments such as a gardener might wear. The weakened Jesus might even have been given a garden implement as a makeshift walking stick to lean on, which led to the confusion. Moreover, a gardener's skin would be burned to a darker brown by constant work out of doors. Jesus' face would have been swollen by his injuries, and the aloe-myrrh solution would leave a characteristic brown colouration. This was why Mary Magdalene could not recognize her master in the early twilight, not because he showed himself in a 'transfigured' body as one 'resurrected'.

Mary Magdalene then evidently fell to her knees before Jesus and wanted to touch his feet, like the ladies in Matthew's account (28:9). But Jesus stopped her with the words, 'Touch me not!' (John 20–17). This could be a clear indication that his still wounded and painful body needed to be treated with care and could not bear much touching.

We have an interesting confirmation of this thesis in the apocryphal Gospel of Peter. This says that the guard at the tomb saw three men emerge 'and two of them supported the other one'! Does some gloriously resurrected person need support at all? Certainly not, but an injured person, who needs to be brought to safety, and who has just come round from a coma, does.

After these events the scanty remaining passages about Jesus in the Gospels become less reliable, because they are mingled with the myth of the 'Resurrection' and the theological interpretation which takes the man Jesus as the resurrected Christ. Many of the passages are accordingly ambiguous. One thing can however be safely said: Jesus met his disciples again for a while, perhaps in Jerusalem itself, but mainly in Galilee.

The period in which the events after the disappearance from the tomb take place is described in such a muddled manner that no precise conclusions can be drawn. The three days which were said to have passed between Crucifixion and reappearance, denote a mystical number which played a role in the older Resurrection myths. Jesus may well have been looked after for a longer period, until he gradually came to show himself to his followers. In any case the meetings seem always to have been of short duration and secret. It is obvious that he could not show himself publicly, otherwise he would have been arrested again at once. It seems that at first his appearance was affected by his injuries, and his face was probably swollen for a while, so that even his colleagues had difficulty in recognizing him immediately.

When assessing the apparitions of Jesus, we have always to bear in mind that they were only recorded in compliance with the theology of Resurrection which was developed. The entire twenty-first chapter of the Gospel of John, which contains the appearance of Jesus by the Sea of Tiberias, has been added by a different author. This text seems to derive from the presbyter John, who is identified with the favourite disciple on account of their similar names.[36]

At first the disciples had withdrawn and gone back to their earlier callings. Simon Peter, Thomas, Nathaniel of Cana and the Zebedee sons went back to fishing (John 21:2). Only when Jesus told them he would meet them himself in Galilee, were they fired with fresh enthusiasm (Matt. 28:10). His encounters with his old companions are presented as 'apparitions', because Jesus is said to have entered into their midst through locked doors, and yet his corporeality is clearly emphasized. The disciples were baffled, because most of them were probably not told about the rescue operation by Joseph and Nicodemus, who did not belong to their circle. The last thing the Gospels report about Jesus, shortly before his departure from Palestine,[37] is his continued attempt to make it clear to the disciples that he had survived the Crucifixion and had recovered. But at first they considered him to be a spirit:

> And he said unto them, Why are ye troubled? and why do thoughts arise in your hearts? Behold my hands and my feet, that it is I myself: handle me, and see; for a spirit hath not flesh and bones, as you see me have. And when he had thus spoken, he showed them his hands and his feet. And while they yet believed not for joy, and wondered, he said unto them, Have ye here any meat? And they gave him a piece of a broiled fish, and of a honeycomb. And he took it, and did eat before them. (Luke 24:38–43)

Jesus was keen to demonstrate to his followers that his body was quite earthly in nature, just as it was before. He stressed his bodily presence by allowing them to touch him, and by eating food, and clearly told them he was not just a spirit. To prove that his body had also not been transformed, he showed the marks of his wounds and even asked the doubting Thomas to touch his side wound with his hand. Later he revealed himself to the eleven, as they were sitting at the table, and criticized their disbelief and the hardness of their hearts because they did not believe those who had seen him after his rising again (Mark 16:14). This presence of Jesus did not depend on a confusion, a deception or hallucinations, his body was not transfigured, it was no ghostly astral body – this is the message of his instructions to his disciples.

The Linen Clothes in the Sepulchre

We have now thrown some light on the true events of the Crucifixion and burial, purely by looking at the written testimonies as they are, without viewing them from a theological standpoint. Everything joins to form a harmonious picture. There is the compelling inference that the alleged burial of Jesus was not one at all, because he did not die on the Cross. We have seen how his suffering was counteracted by the narcotic drink, how he was taken down after a short time and moved to the protection of a tomb building where he was given treatment, and how he was later led out of the hiding place in the morning twilight, supported by his friends, and taken to safety elsewhere. We should now turn again to the details of the Gospel reports, to see if they can tell us anything about the cloth used to cover Jesus in the tomb hiding place.

In the text we encounter two terms used to refer to the cloth: *sindon* and *othonion*. Besides these we also find the noun *soudarion* used in the same general context.

The Synoptic Gospels use the word *sindon*. This noun is used to render the Hebrew term *sadîn*, which we find in the Old Testament, bearing the meaning 'robe' in Judg. 14:12–13 and in 1 Macc. 10:64, and 'dress' or 'cloth' in Prov. 31:24. In the Talmud it is also used to denote a simple 'burial robe' (J. Ketubôt 12:3, J. Terumôt 8:10). In Mark's Gospel (14:51) *sindon* is used for a cloth wrapped around (*peribeblemenos*) the body. One can assume that the original Hebrew text of the Gospel of Mark had the term *sadîn* and so carried the connotations of both robe and cloth. In Greek texts *sindon* signifies a precious cloth, used to make robes and sheets of linen. In Latin the term *sindon* can mean either a large cloth or a large cloak.

So we see that *sindon* can be used for cloths of quite different sizes, which can be used for many different purposes. It is impossible to decide the form of the object referred to on the basis of this term alone. It can only be settled by looking at the use the cloth was put to. In any case we can rule out a long linen band, such as that used to wrap a mummy. We have seen from the comparison with the burial of Lazarus that only the term *keiriai* would be used for such a band. On closer analysis, one has to conclude that *sindon* refers to linen in its most general form. It is the generic term for the finished strip of linen cloth, from which various cloths, cloaks, sheets or towels could be manufactured.

In John we find the term *othonia* in the sense of 'cloths'. Luke (24:12) had Peter see 'linen clothes' when he looked into the empty tomb, by using the term *othonia* in the plural. Shortly before this he described the deposition from the Cross with the help of a 'linen', using the term *sindon* in the singular (Luke 23,53). The term *othonia* is suggested by this passage to mean 'cloths made from *sindon*'. The use of this term shows us one thing quite clearly: the evangelists specified that this cloth, in which Jesus was to be wrapped, was not a long linen band. The general term 'cloths' or 'linen' suggests rather that one or more larger cloths were brought to the tomb hiding place.

On our search for more exact clues about the nature of the cloths, we turn again to the Gospel of John. The discovery of the cloths on the first day of the week (Sunday) by Peter and John, was intentionally described in a way which brings out the eyewitness viewpoint: 'So they ran both together: and the other disciple did outrun Peter, and came first to the sepulchre. And he stooping down, and looking in, saw the linen clothes lying; yet went he not in. Then cometh Simon Peter following him, and went into the sepulchre, and seeth the linen clothes lie. And the napkin, that was about his head, not lying with the linen clothes, but wrapped together in a place by itself.' (John 20:4–7). The author uses the historic present tense for the observations of John and Peter, to relive the eyewitness account authentically. Zaninotto even goes so far as to translate the Greek *blepei keimena ta othonia* ('he sees the cloths lying') in his interpretation as, 'he sees the cloths spread themselves out'. He does this to show that John looked in the inner chamber of the tomb just at the moment when the cloths were sinking down because the resurrected one had somehow 'vanished' from within them. This was he says, a sign of John's belief in the Resurrection.[38] This is a highly speculative line of reasoning and quite obviously more of an unfounded act of interpretation than an accurate translation.

The *sudarium* is without doubt the most important of the cloths left behind in the tomb. The unexpected mention of it in John is most interesting. Normally *sudarium* is translated as 'towel' or 'napkin'. Some exegetes have thought it might be a chin band. But why should a chin band be emphasized in this way? Such an article would have to be considered quite secondary in the overall sequence of the burial procedure. But in John's text the *sudarium* is pointed out in such a striking manner that one has to assume the author wished to make some special point. The sentence which directly follows the mention of the *sudarium* provides the answer: 'Then went in also that other disciple, which came first to the sepulchre, and he saw, and believed.' (John 20:8).

The *sudarium* lay to one side, and the sight of it gave faith to the favourite disciple. But why do John and Peter describe it as set apart and folded up? One might think it was a piece of cloth which was not used for the work in the tomb at all, and was therefore left lying quite clean and untouched, away from the other cloths that were spread out there. One has to interpret the passage as meaning 'the *sudarium* which was meant to be placed over his head'. But it had not come to this, because no burial took place. The linen cloth whose only function was for the burial, was left unused; it was left where it lay, still untouched, folded up, still there the next day – is this what John was trying to tell us? Opposing this is the statement that it was the *sudarium* which had been 'about his head'. Naturally one has to ask how the author of the Gospel of John could be certain that the cloth had been on Jesus' head. It is not said exactly how Jesus had been laid out for resting, and probably the author of the Gospel did not know much about it either. After all this task was carried out not by apostles but by the outsiders Joseph and Nicodemus. Perhaps the evangelist simply assumed that it must have lain 'about his head'.

All these proposals are made difficult to believe by the marked emphasis on the *sudarium*, and the fact that the favourite disciple suddenly 'believed' on seeing it. Considering all we have learned so far about the secret purpose of the text of John, there can be no doubt that the attentive reader was meant to notice something about the *sudarium* immediately. If the *sudarium* really had been

on Jesus' head, the state it was found in when the empty tomb
was discovered would suggest that there had not been any grave-
robbing, nor a resurrection – in both cases the effort taken to
carefully fold up this one cloth on its own would be quite incomprehensible. Who could have done this and above all, why?

Regarding the faith the favourite disciple gained from seeing
the *sudarium*, the usual explanation is that he gained faith in the
Resurrection of the Lord when he saw the cloths left in the tomb.
This is also suggested later on in the Gospel text. But in the
narrative context there is another aspect which seems more decisive. We recall how Mary Magdalene had run, shocked, to the
disciples after she had seen the open tomb. She feared that someone had taken the body of Jesus. Peter and John anxiously ran off
to see what was going on. They found the tomb chamber open.
Inside they could only see the cloths and, placed apart from them,
tidily folded up, the *sudarium*. Were they just relieved because
this was a clear sign that the body had not been stolen? Robbers
would hardly have taken the trouble to unwrap the body from its
clothes when they took it. Therefore the sight of the empty tomb
with the cloths could be a clear sign that Jesus had not been
'snatched'. Was this then what the favourite disciple believed
when he saw the various cloths in the dim light of the tomb –
simply that Jesus had not been 'stolen'?

To answer this question, we have to see the *sudarium*, which
was introduced so unexpectedly, in the context of what we have
learned so far. According to Zaninotto an *othonion*, that is a cloth,
which is placed on the head, is called a *soudarion*. It gains this
meaning, he says, in the same way as a cloth placed around the
shoulders is called a shawl, around the head a veil, around the
hips a dress, and over a table a tablecloth.[39] The *soudarion* has
nothing to do with the function of a chin band. The word was
merely introduced to make clear that it was a cloth which lay over
the head. This meaning can be seen even when we look at the
origins of the term. It probably derives from *soudara*, an Old
Testament term (Ruth 3:15) which denotes neither a towel nor a
chin band but a linen cloth which was placed over the head, and
which might occasionally cover the whole body down to the feet.[40]
According to Ghiberti, *soudarion* could derive from the Aramaic
sôdara, which has various meanings and refers to piece of fabric
small or large.[41] Lavergne supposes that in the time of Jesus the

term had assumed the meaning which it also had in Latin, namely a cloth used to wipe away perspiration.[42] Of course these various uses of the word do not allow us to reconstruct the object it referred to. But its use in the period does suggest that it always had some link with perspiration. One example of this would be the cloths which Paul held over the sick for healing (Acts 19:12).

The Latins themselves had never used the term *sudarium* in the context of burial rites. For some, this fact makes the analysis of John's text more difficult. Zaninotto, who pulls out all the stops in his philological analysis to show that *sudarium* was used to mean a large cloth in which Jesus was covered, comes up against the connotation of 'towel for perspiration'. He remarks that such a cloth would have no sense in a burial, since there would be no perspiration to dry off. Also it is unlikely that the evangelist had borrowed the term from the Latin, because he always used the Latin expressions purely in their technical sense, such as *praetorium*, *flagellum* ('whip') or *linteum* ('linen cloth').

One person's hurdle can be another's springboard. We have come to know the author of John's text as the unknown person who wanted to communicate the mysterious events of the Crucifixion and burial of Jesus in a hidden way. Hence John intentionally played on the special meaning of the cloth as a perspiration towel, which comes through in the Latin; he had indeed used the term in its technical sense as usual. The length of linen which was placed around the body of Jesus was a towel of a special kind. Not only did it absorb his perspiration but it was with its herbs itself part of a therapeutic packing which was most probably sweatinducing. Then what function did the other cloths in the tomb serve? It was important for Joseph and Nicodemus to give the wounded Jesus a comfortable place to lie on. They could have strewn some hay, but that might have attracted suspicion – what was straw doing in a grave? So they decided to procure a large quantity of inexpensive cloths which were suitable for a burial. Using these they formed a soft layer to lay Jesus on in the long healing cloth coated with the herbal mixture. When Jesus was taken out of the tomb early in the morning, the first thing to do was to remove the healing cloth. It was folded and laid to one side, while the other cloths, which had served as kind of mattress, were left crumpled up where they lay. Therefore the statement about 'the *sudarium* which had lain on his head' is correct, and it was only natural that they wanted to take care of the long strip of cloth. Fine linen was extremely expensive. Good linen fabrics were comparable in value to gold, silver and silk, being used for sacred functions in the temple, and prescribed for the robes of the priests. Since it could not be obtained in the usual marketplace, one has to assume that Joseph had specially commissioned the linen cloth with the costly herringbone weave. Of course they did not want to leave this very expensive fabric in the tomb chamber with the plain underlay fabrics.

The description of the 'shroud' of Jesus as an unworked strip of fabric matches the Turin cloth exactly. Interestingly the size of the Turin cloth matches precisely the unit of measurement which was used in Palestine at the time of Jesus, the philetaric cubit. This means the cloth which Joseph ordered was of a standard size. The philetaric cubit was about 53 cm. If one starts with the assumption that the cloth has stretched a little in the course of the centuries, the size is exactly 2 cubits wide by 8 cubits long.[43]

Resurrected or Arisen?

The philological analysis of John's text, taken in relation to the Synoptic Gospels, allows us to propose the following reconstruction of events. On the ledge by the central pit in the tomb chamber, a number of *othonia* (cloths) made of an undyed (*kathara*) piece of linen (*sindon*), were laid out. Over these cloths another strip of linen (*soudarion*) was spread out. A solution of the healing herbs aloe and myrrh was applied to the naked body of the unconscious Jesus, and the body was placed on the length of linen. The cloth was lifted and folded over to cover the body. In this way the whole body was covered (*entylisso*) and the function of a *sudarium* achieved. The quantity of the aromatic substances in the cloth (some 33 kg) made the gigantic wound plaster so heavy that it had a real pressure-packing (*eneileo*) effect on the body.

If we now read again the whole passage in John's Gospel describing the events at the discovery of the empty tomb (John 20:1–18), keeping in mind the reconstruction we have managed to make so far, the full meaning becomes clear. First Mary Magdalene ran to Simon Peter and the favourite disciple and excitedly told them that someone had taken the body of Jesus away from the tomb. She definitely did not say that the body was stolen in any way. Her statement was neutral regarding the manner in which Jesus had disappeared from the tomb. We are not even told why Mary Magdalene went to the tomb early in the morning when it was still dark. It is not said that she wanted to anoint the corpse, as was the case with the women of the Synoptic Gospels. When talking to Peter and John, she simply said, 'They have taken away the Lord out of the sepulchre . . .' It is as if the people she was talking to knew who 'they' referred to.

Even from this first sentence we can form a picture of events. In the night, after the curative packing had been seen to, Joseph and Nicodemus visited some of the followers of Jesus. They approached Mary Magdalene, Simon Peter and John, who could be regarded as intimate companions. They briefly explained to the three what role they themselves were playing, and the fact that they were trying to save Jesus from death with the aid of Essene friends. Jesus would have to be taken as soon as possible from the unsafe hiding place, and brought to safety, away from the alert eyes of the Jerusalem priesthood. They did not want to say any more for fear of putting their plan in jeopardy. After all it was possible that one of the disciples would be arrested and, if tortured, betray their plans.

Mary Magdalene, totally stunned by what she was hearing, was unable to contain herself any longer. She made off for the tomb, to see for herself the truth of Joseph's words. There she found the stone rolled away from the entrance, ran immediately to the two others and told them that it had happened. As Joseph had said, 'they' – his helpers – had removed Jesus from the tomb. And she was quick to add, 'and we know not where they have laid him'. If she had been talking about a grave robbery, this additional remark would have made no sense at all. When a robbery happens one obviously does not expect to know where the stolen goods have been taken. She was evidently referring to the Essenes who, after waiting as long as they could while still under cover of night, had taken the first steps to get Jesus away.

Now it was the turn of the two disciples to be utterly amazed, and they broke into a run. The youthful John was faster and reached the entrance first, from where he cautiously peered inside. But Peter went right on into the tomb chamber and looked around. He noticed a crumpled heap of cloths and, separate from them, neatly folded, the healing cloth which Joseph had mentioned. Only now did John also dare to enter the building, and, as the report says, 'he saw, and believed'.

As we have seen, this most interesting passage is usually taken as the starting point for the creed of the Resurrection. This seeing and believing, which assume an important place in Johannine theology, is commonly interpreted as an action which somehow makes the reality of the Resurrection of Jesus directly apparent to the eye. Of course it is said that only the favourite disciple 'saw and believed', while Peter just 'saw'. The next verse provides the solution: 'For as yet they knew not the scripture, that he must rise again from the dead.'

One can argue that at the time when the Gospel of John was composed, the creed of the Resurrection, as formulated by Paul (especially in the fifteenth chapter of his first letter to the Corinthians), was generally accepted by the early Christians. Thus it was natural that the author of the Gospel, who obtained his facts from an eyewitness, was concerned about presenting the events in a theologically correct way. Therefore he went on to forgive Peter for not believing after seeing what he did, because after all he did not yet know the Bible passage where the Resurrection was foretold. But we have to remember that in John we always find a two-tiered approach, so he is not really talking about the death and Resurrection, but about the rescue of Jesus. So let us briefly have a look at the scriptural passage that the disciples did not know about.

It is not easy to identify. Most exegetes agree that according to Acts 2:25–8, it has to be Psalm 16:8–11. In this passage we find:

I have set the Lord always before me: because he is at my right hand, I shall not to be moved.

Therefore my heart is glad, and my glory rejoiceth: my flesh also shall rest in hope.

For thou wilt not leave my soul in hell; neither wilt thou suffer thine Holy One to see corruption.

Thou wilt shew me the path of life: in thy presence is fullness of joy; at thy right hand there are pleasures for evermore.

Is this the promised Resurrection, as exegesis shows us? Try as one will, one cannot find any mention of it here. Quite the contrary: the precondition for resurrection, as Paul stresses, is death. One can only say that a person is resurrected if he has died. It is on this basis that the Christian says in the Creed, Jesus died and then 'rose from the dead'. But the Psalm speaks rather of saving from death. Peter misinterprets it when he refers to it in explaining the secret of the Pentecost as the promise of resurrection (Acts 2:25–8). Perhaps this has something to do with his not believing when he saw the linen cloths in the tomb, because he remained loyal to the mythical tradition of the Resurrection. For, taking the facts as they are, the 'seeing and believing' of the favourite disciple can only be understood as his believing what Joseph of Arimathea had told them. The favourite disciple saw that no one was buried in the grave, and the various cloths confirmed for him the statement that Jesus must still be alive. He therefore believed not in the Resurrection but in the rescue of Jesus. That is the key to this Bible passage.

It is possible that the Resurrection tradition in the Bible comes from a source which knew about the efforts to heal Jesus. During my studies in this area I did not think that finding support for this idea would be easy, but the interesting works of the philologist and theologist Father Günther Schwarz, which I came across more or less by accident, have opened up an exciting new view of the matter. For the terms 'rise' and 'coming back to life' which we find in the translations of the Bible, originally derive, as Dr Schwarz shows, from an Aramaic verb which means 'resuscitate'![44] He explains:

> The lexical evidence is conclusive: not 'resurrection' but *'resuscitation'* is the only meaning possible for both these Aramaic words, one of which Jesus would have used. I am referring to the synonymous words *achajuta* and *techijjuta*. Both nouns are derived from the verb *chaja*, 'life', and consequently mean – I repeat – *resuscitation* and nothing else.[45]

This discovery is quite sensational and at once gives a meaning to the texts which is in perfect agreement with our analysis so far. Even the Greek does not suggest the translations of the Aramaic original concept which are given in the Christian usage: *anhistemi* means to 'awaken' (transitive), and to 'get up', 'come forth', 'present oneself' (intransitive); *anastasis* means 'rising up'. Only by the later Christian interpretation is *anhistemi* made to mean 'raise from the dead' (transitive) and 'resurrect' (intransitive), and *anastasis* 'resurrection'.[46]

Let us again consider the passages in Mark and Luke, where the women at the tomb were told about the disappearance of Jesus by the men clad in white, in the light of what we have learned. Mark (16:6) wrote, 'And he saith unto them, Be not affrighted: Ye seek Jesus of Nazareth, which was crucified: he is risen, he is not here: behold the place where they laid him.' This is comparable to Matthew 28:6, although there the actual events are given a fairytale setting with theatrical angel magic, an earthquake and petrified tomb guards. The terse remark of the white-robed men in Luke (24:5) asking why they seek a living person among the dead, is as clear as can be. Jesus lived, he was rescued, he had no business in a tomb any more, the living belong among the living. He had gone ahead to Galilee, where his followers could see him. We have already shown how Jesus had great difficulty in convincing the disciples of his presence in the flesh. The reason for this is twofold. First, the majority of the disciples had not been told about the resuscitation attempt, and so were convinced that they were looking at a dead person or a spirit. And secondly the first Christian theologians started to take over at the supposed death by crucifixion of Jesus: according to the official dogma the story of the human individual Jesus ended there, and in its place came the story of Christ – the mythically glorified Reality.

Transmission of the Secret Knowledge

We are now in a position to see quite easily why the cloth was removed from the sepulchre. Ordinary burial clothes were very simple, inexpensive fabrics. The Turin cloth was no ordinary shroud, it was certainly very dear and so was probably meant to be cleaned for reuse. When the spices, which stuck loosely to the fabric, were washed off, the 'miraculous' image, which could not be washed out, came to light.

Because it was a healing cloth, for the initiates it was always a proof of the secret that Jesus had survived the Crucifixion. What has recently become an obvious fact for many well-known bestseller authors, was preserved in this manner down through the centuries by initiates, who wished to preserve the one piece of evidence, and protect it from the clutches of the enthusiasts who wanted to impose on Jesus an institutional role as the Christ.

The questions which we have been dealing with in this historical section are now answered. It was not difficult for the Essenes to remove the sweat cloth from the tomb because for them it was not a ritually impure object. The same holds for the messenger Thaddaeus and the artisan Aggai. Both these early keepers of the cloth knew of Jesus' rescue. Seen in this way the actions of Thaddaeus and Aggai are understandable. With them the line of tradition of those who knew the facts came to an end, or at least that was how it looked outwardly.

Thus the cloth which Thaddaeus brought to Edessa was no burial shroud, although the image on it made it look like one. And probably only a few of Jesus' followers knew that their master had not died. The knowledge of the successful healing was secretly handed down by the Essenes. This tradition survived under the protection of certain sects in the Middle East and it must also have reached the sect of the Cathars, which spread in the Balkans and the Near East before becoming established in France in medieval times.

Who were these Cathars, and are they really comparable to the Templars, as is often assumed? Does the Templar Order perhaps represent a continuation of Cathar ideas? The sect's ancestry can be traced back to the third and fourth centuries. Cathar communities arose in Italy, France, the Iberian peninsula and even in the East, a development which took place against the background of the terrible persecution of Christians in 249 and 250 under Decius. After the death of the Emperor in 251, a dispute ensued among the Roman congregations. One strict group refused to accept those who had denied their faith during the persecution, and made the Presbyter Novatian counter-Pope against Cornelius, who was supported by Cyprian. They argued that the Church did not have a 'power of attorney' to forgive sins. They called themselves Cathars, the pure ones, and developed theological ideas which represented an extraordinary danger for the orthodoxy: they contested the power and authority of priests to forgive sins, which gave them a hold over the people. One has to realize what this meant for a Church in the formative stages: the Cathars threatened its foundations, rejected intermediaries of Jesus on

Earth and relied totally on the power of the Holy Spirit, which works from the inmost being of each individual.

The Cathars disappeared as an organized sect in Europe quite suddenly in the first half of the fifth century. But in the East the Novatian Cathars continued, supported by the apocalyptic sect of the Montanists. In those turbulent times, when Augustine could count twenty-eight heresies, and Gnosticism and Manichaeism were fully developed as churches, the Cathars went underground. Five hundred years later they re-emerged in the half-pagan Bulgaria and Bosnia, where they called themselves Bogumiles. Some scholars contest that these medieval Cathars had anything in common with the Cathars of Novatian except their name. 'But names and ideas, forms of belief and doctrines which have once been symbols are not simply taken up unless there are deeper spiritual links, and the old sources nourish the new life.'[47] In the eleventh century Cathar teaching penetrated to Italy, and in around 1150 to southern France, where the most important centre developed in the town of Albi. The Cathars were also called Albigensians after the name of this town. Streams of people poured in to swell their ranks, because the Cathar preachers – the *bonhommes* – lived what they preached were the spiritual ideals of their Church, whereas the orthodox medieval Church was mainly interested in extending its power and influence.

St Bernard of Clairvaux, the great patron of the Templars, laid the foundation stone for a development which was to characterize a dark age in European history. For this strangely contradictory mystic, the renewal of the inner Church allowed only one choice for those of other beliefs: convert or be destroyed. With this motto he introduced the age of the Crusades led in the name of the Almighty, and the destructive war against the Cathars which was to go down in the annals of history as the Crusade against the Albigensians.

The Cathars opposed the secular power of the Church just as the Novatians in the time of Constantine I had done. Their bishops lived solely for the faith, without possessions, without pomp, without sinecures and lands. The Cathars preached self-salvation after the example of Jesus, and dispensed with sacraments and saint cults just as they rejected the idea of the crucified Jesus. Following the Gnostic line of thought they rejected matter as evil; also the Old Testament, the book of the creator of matter, and so of evil. They said that the opposition of good and evil went back to the deepest roots of life, to the Deity itself. They rejected war as anti-Christian, and lived according to the view of the faithful set down in the first letter of John, where it is said, 'Love not the world, neither the things that are in the world. If any man love the world, the love of the Father is not in him.' (1 John 2:15).

Interestingly, the Cathars believed in 'resuscitation' in the form of reincarnation. They taught metempsychosis emphatically, among other highly non-orthodox Christian doctrines, even extending it to include animals. Souls could only find release from this wandering transmigration if they came to dwell in the body of a Catharically 'perfect one' or 'good Christian'. It appears that this teaching influenced the oldest cabbalistic convention in the south of France in the twelfth century, from where it penetrated into the esoteric currents of later times. The soul has to wander until the mystically illumined one (Cabbala) or pure one (Cathar) has fulfilled the true destiny of human life. This corresponds in a way to the Buddhist idea of rebirth with liberation of the soul in the body of a Buddha or Bodhisattva, and clearly shows its oriental origins. Even the teacher of Jesus, John the Baptist, understood the resurrection of the dead in the context of rebirth.[48]

The rejection of sacraments and all mediated actions and functions, and the negative attitude to the Cross, all show quite clearly the influence of Gnostic oriental sects. It seems that this discounting of the Cross was a sort of declaration of war against the false 'Christianity', which had stylized the Crucifixion death as its central symbol. In these sects they tried to propagate a teaching of Jesus which the developing Church was now regarding as heretical, following the word of the Lord, when he reminded the people of Psalm 82:6. '. . . Is it not written in your law, I said, ye are gods?' (John 10:34). If the Spirit is present within, no intermediaries are necessary. The person thus awakened to the Spirit can say with Jesus, 'I and my Father are one.' (John 10:30). Jesus himself was not considered to be an intermediary for them, he was a human being who had been granted extraordinarily deep intuitions – an awakened one. The Cross had neither killed him nor led to his Resurrection. It was therefore abhorrent as a symbol of the false belief of mythical vicarious atonement.

At the eleventh ecumenical council in the Lateran in 1179, Pope Alexander III pronounced the anathema on the Cathars and everyone who followed their teachings and defended them. All the faithful were called upon zealously to oppose this 'pest', and even take up arms against them. Whoever killed a Cathar was given an indulgence worth two years' penance and the protection of the Church as a Crusader.

Twenty years later, in the final year before the opening of the thirteenth century, at the time when the idea of the ominous Fourth Crusade was being born in Champagne, Pope Innocent III issued his terrible heresy decree. But the warnings of the Church leaders against the heretics did not have the desired effect. Wherever the Cathar preachers made their appearance, they were found to be superior to the puffed-up churchmen. The afflicted people, who were repelled by the pomp and power of the hated Church which was oppressing them, ran to the Cathars in their droves. Finally the Pope let loose his loyal 'Christians' against the Cathars. In July 1209 an army of knights and ruffians stormed the town of Bézier under the command of the Cistercian Abbot Arnauld-Alméric. The inhabitants were brutally and indiscriminately cut down, regardless of whether they were men or women, children or the elderly, Albigensian or Catholic. The Cathars refused to use weapons, even in the face of certain destruction, allowing themselves to be struck down without fighting. The Abbot proudly informed the Pope of their success with 'about 20,000' people slaughtered, for whom he had said the 'Te Deum'. Maybe the last 'pure ones', as they voluntarily gave themselves up to the besiegers outside their fortress of Montségur on 12 March 1244 and walked to their death at the stake on the Champ des Crémats, the 'field of the burned', found consolation in the words of their favourite letter of St John: 'Marvel not, my brethren, if the world hate you.' (1 John 3:13).

The courageous 'pure ones', on their eternal search for supernatural solace, have in the course of the centuries gathered a patina of mystery, rather as the Templars have. They were said to be initiates of knowledge, guardians of the Holy Grail, just like the Templars. This esteem is not without cause. The Holy Grail, so the tradition goes, was the vessel in which Joseph of Arimathea collected the blood of Jesus. It was probably part of the legend that Joseph stood under the Cross and caught the precious blood in a cup. In fact he had more important things to do, hurrying to sort out the release of the crucified man. And yet

Joseph had indeed collected and preserved the blood of Jesus – *in the healing cloth!*

It would take us too far afield to discuss the Grail story in depth here – it would fill another book.[49] This much one can say: the idea of the Grail as a bowl, cup or dish is by no means the only theme. The origin of the word remains wreathed in obscurity, despite all the etymological studies. Perhaps the derivation from the Provençal *Sangraal* (*San Gral*, Holy Grail) is the correct one. Originally this meant *sang real*, 'the true blood'. Hence it means the true blood of Jesus. In what could the true blood of Jesus have been caught, if not the Turin cloth? If the Cathars and later the Templars are seen as the guardians of the Holy Grail, it seems that this reflects the fact, of which only a fragmentary knowledge had filtered through to the public, that they were the keepers of the secret tradition of the rescue of Jesus.

The Templars, unlike the contemplative Cathars, were men of action, and were not satisfied with being just the preservers of a secret tradition. They wanted to possess the 'holy blood' themselves, to ensure that the priceless cloth would not be left in the hands of the ignorant.

During the ritual of admission to the Order, reference was made to the immortality of God and so to the intactness of the Son of God. John of Cassanhas, Templar Preceptor of Noggarda, tells how the leader of an admission ritual declares, 'Believe thou in God, who has not died and will never die.' Then Psalm 133 was read, '*Ecce quam bonum et quam jucundum.*'[50] The Psalm is a pilgrimage eulogy of David:

> Behold, how good and how pleasant it is for brethren to dwell together in unity!
>
> It is like the precious ointment upon the head, that ran down upon the beard, even Aaron's beard: that went down to the skirts of his garments;
>
> As the dew of Hermon, and as the dew that descended upon the mountains of Zion: for there the Lord commanded the blessing, even life for evermore.

It contains a reference to the mission of the Temple Knights in Palestine; there awaited them there the blessing and eternal life, the heavenly anointing. Perhaps the Templars felt they were the new, true disciples in the Holy Land, and they therefore always travelled in pairs, just as Jesus had once sent the seventy ahead in groups of two. They were champions of the Holy Sepulchre, spiritual guards, who watched and honoured the site of their Saviour's rescue. In Templar mysticism the ideas of the rescue of Jesus from death by crucifixion were mingled with the ideas of eternal life. It is only natural that the warlike Templars wanted to gain possession of the cloth, the most important relic from that tomb which had never held a corpse. It may be that in their contemplation the Templars drew courage and strength from the idols of the cloth and its copies to risk their own transient bodies in battle, well knowing that their being was indestructible. The Templars, who trod the Cross underfoot, broke with the wrong symbolism. Like the Cathars they revered the man Jesus, whose special insight into the nature of the world was for them an example worth following. The continuity of this tradition was connected with the cloth. As heralds of this knowledge they saw themselves as legitimate keepers of the cloth.

The Templars were therefore not able to admit to the papal commission that they simply revered the Jesus of the Shroud in their chapters. For their image of Jesus was heretical and wicked. The death by crucifixion had no place in it. In reality the death by crucifixion, raised to the level of a dogma, had falsified the teaching of Jesus. The early Church was forced to introduce a completely different turn, because it was simply unthinkable that the Son of God could die. Therefore Paul put the idea of the intact Resurrection at the centre of the Faith. The Faith would be pointless if Christ had not been resurrected (1 Cor. 15:14). Hence Durwell can describe the Resurrection as the 'mystery of salvation' *par excellence*, because for Paul and the whole early catechesis it was the basic object of the faith. Without the Resurrection, Paul made quite clear, there could be no release from sins. Paul was only able to conceive of the death of the Son of God as an important act of the most far-reaching consequences. Otherwise it would have been irrational, inconceivable. 'Christ died for our sins,' he says unequivocally in the first letter to the Corinthians, the official form of the Easter message. In this way he makes this, *his own personal idea*, into the actual foundation of the Christian Faith, on which everything is built up.[51]

It is interesting that Paul nowhere presents the empty grave as proof of the Resurrection. The exegetes claim that he could have made good use of the account of the empty grave, but 'he knew nothing about it or did not consider it to be attested to reliably. For him the apparitions were not connected with it.'[52] Hence Bultmann supposes that it was a legend that arose only later, which Paul still did not know of. That is most unlikely, because the tradition of the apparition stories is clearly older than that of the Resurrection and grave stories. The reports of the empty grave, however, are also found in uncanonised early writings. Such information was moreover unuseable for Paul since the empty grave was open. He would have had to reply to those who rightly viewed this circumstance as suspicious. An open grave suggests that someone pushed aside the stone and took Jesus from the grave. Such arguments are difficult to refute. The open grave is simply unuseable for the Resurrection teaching. Therefore Paul confined himself to the apparitions of Jesus in his reasoning in support of the Resurrection. He listed them all, up to the final apparition which was granted to himself, the 'miscarriage' as he calls himself.

Since the rescue operation was not allowed to become generally known, the Crucifixion and 'death' of Jesus had to be interpreted differently. For this very old pagan ideas were dug up: the death was made into the death of atonement – God offered his beloved Son for the sinful humanity. However an immortal God has to rise again. The old rebirth ideas, which are found everywhere in the New Testament, were well known, but they were not suitable for a Christ. They were too generally widespread – every prophet could be a reincarnation. As the Son of God Jesus was exceptional, unique. He could not re-embody himself in another person. Therefore he had to be physically resurrected. To guarantee his uniqueness was the key to the Resurrection theology. Of course by making Christ a kind of deputy in this way, they made possible the 'great hope' of the Christians, which forms the attraction of Christianity to this day: through his vicarious offering Christ allowed the people (or to be more precise, only Christians) to share in his bodily immortality on the day of judgement, and this without any personal effort at all.

Part Four

FRAUD OF THE CENTURY

Holger Kersten

Jesus: the 'Man of the Shroud'

We have been able to identify this simple, precious sheet of cloth as a shroud from the Bible references. The special attention paid to it by John suggests that there must have been something important about it. Otherwise why make such a great fuss about a burial cloth which was unembroidered and moreover ritually impure, 'repelling'? Obviously it had something to do with the discovery of the image, the physical legacy of Jesus, who was able to be saved from death.

Let us recapitulate the major arguments in support of the age of the cloth. One often hears the objection made that the cloth is in a surprisingly good state of preservation. And yet an unexpected discovery awaits anyone who makes the effort to examine ancient fabrics in museums. There are numerous linen items in existence which are much older than 2000 years and are preserved even better than the Turin cloth. In the collections of the Egyptian National Museum in Cairo, the Turin Egyptian Museum and also the Egyptian departments of the museums in London, Paris, Berlin or Hildesheim one can find fabrics in an excellent state of preservation, some of which are 3500 or even 5000 years old.

The Shroud is made in what is called a 3:1 twill weave, resulting in a herringbone pattern. At the time of Jesus this was an extremely rare kind of weave, requiring a complicated technique and for this reason alone it must have been costly. In the first century this type of weave was only to be found in the Roman province of Syria, the neighbouring province to Palestine. The twill weave has been known in the West only since the fourteenth century.

The cotton fibres which Prof Raes found on the cloth come from the very kind which was cultivated in Syria at the time of Jesus. At that time cotton had yet to be grown in Europe. It is quite evident that the linen was woven on a Syrian loom on which cotton had previously been worked. It would certainly have been difficult to obtain such fabrics in the bazaars of Palestine, especially because the kind of material and the weave made it one of the most costly textiles, but Joseph of Arimathea could easily have decided on the type of weave, material and size for the special purpose he had in mind, and given the order to a Syrian dealer. And we should note that the cloth corresponds in size to a unit of measurement current in Palestine at the time of Jesus.

Chance contamination of the cloth, with cotton fibres for example, allows us to make a kind of 'fingerprint' of the relic. Nowhere is this clearer than in the pollen studies. They provide an inestimable aid to determining the age and origin of the cloth. The pollen grains have convincingly recorded the early stopping places: Syria, Jerusalem, Edessa, Constantinople.

An additional argument for the authenticity of the cloth is provided by the remnants of herbs mentioned in John's text which have been found on it. The criminologist and pollen researcher Max Frei was even able to find epidermal cells from *Aloe soccotrina*.[1] Baima Bollone and his colleagues have shown the presence of aloe and myrrh by chemical analysis; Sam Pellicori showed it by spectrographic techniques.

The hypothesis of a medieval forgery has been shown to be utterly absurd. There is not the least indication that the Turin cloth is the product of an ingenious painter. No artist would have used such a soft linen material for a picture. The material would have had to be stretched on a frame or over a board to provide the necessary tautness before it could be painted on. No colour pigments can be found on it. If paints had been applied they would have penetrated deep into the fabric. Such a surface work affecting only a few fibres of each thread could not be achieved even by using the finest available brushes. The high temperatures during the fire in Chambéry and the effects of the water poured on it to put it out would have caused strong chemical changes to a painted picture. This too did not happen. The iconography of the image is quite inexplicable. The picture is without precedent in the history of art, in form, composition, content and style. Not a single example of a negative image can be found in the whole history of art before the invention of photography. The frontal and dorsal image is a unique and most original type of representation, which similarly has no comparable instances. Pictures in the Middle Ages and in the Renaissance, primarily religious, were of a didactic nature. This is quite lacking in the Jesus portrait of the Shroud. Jesus bears no symbolic decorations, no halo. The picture shows not a Christ but an ordinary person.

Why should an artist have created such a delicate work, which is no longer even visible when viewed close up? That contradicts the basic principle of a work of art, which aims by its form of depiction to bring out the view of things presented by nature more strongly. The Jesus figure of the Middle Ages is strongly influenced by the Byzantine form of painting, and was only later emancipated to show a more naturalistic form. The anatomical features and realistic proportions of the human body were only introduced much later in art. But the 'Man of the Shroud' is anatomically exact and with true-to-life dimensions.

Regarding the content of the picture, the naked figure of Christ was never portrayed in the whole of Christian iconography. To show it would have been tantamount to blasphemy. We have mentioned the only known exceptions, and they follow the example of the Shroud. What medieval artist could have suspected that the crown of thorns was really a cap, as the wounds on the head show, and not a ring as the artistic tradition prescribed? No artist would have positioned the scars on the hands at the right place, they were always on the palms. Only on the Turin cloth do they appear on the wrists – medically the only spot possible. The side wound is shown reversed on the picture. This again is a detail which an artist in those days would hardly have thought of. Then there is the rust-red fluid flowing from the larger wounds which testify to the lashes, and which correspond precisely to the dumbbell-shaped thong weights. It is in fact blood, human blood, as science has now conclusively established. To paraphrase a remark by Schopenhauer, whoever still considers the Turin cloth to be the product of a clever fourteenth-century forger, should be called ignorant rather than unbelieving. The wealth of evidence has made one thing quite clear: a man lay in this cloth, a man, who was mistreated and crucified, a man who corresponds in so many details to just one person – Jesus, the man from Galilee. The Jesuit priest Herbert Thurston wrote in 1903: 'As to the identity of the body whose image is seen on the Shroud, no question is possible. The five wounds, the cruel flagellation, the punctures encircling the head, can still be clearly distinguished . . . In no other person since the world began could these details be verified.'

The Image of a Living Person

After all that we have described there can be no doubt: the Turin cloth is the cloth in which Jesus was placed for healing after being taken from the Cross. If this is so and Jesus really was still alive when he was placed in the tomb, we should be able to find evidence of the fact on the Turin cloth.

Joseph Blinzler used the peculiar position of the body as an argument *against* the genuineness of the Turin cloth: '[It is] difficult to understand that when burying the Saviour the disciples would have placed the hands in such an unsuitable and impractical position as we see on the Turin image.'[2] Quite apart from the fact that there is no mention of the presence of the disciples in the tomb room, the posture corresponds exactly to the position of skeletons which have been excavated in the cemetery of the Essene monks' settlement at Qumran by the Dead Sea. Were any stranger by chance to look into the tomb, the posture of Jesus would suggest that he was being kept ready for a burial.

It is true that the sindonologists have had the greatest difficulty explaining the burial of Jesus with the cloth. In Palestine the dead were not covered lengthways in a cloth in this manner, but wrapped up like Lazarus.

Father Rinaldi, the assiduous American Shroud researcher, claims that rigor mortis can be clearly seen on the Turin sheet. That is nonsense. On the contrary, the 'Man of the Shroud' gives the impression of lying there in a relaxed state; there are no signs of stiffening at all. The inquiries made by the British author Hoare with the experts of the East Midlands Forensic Laboratory were part of a long line of discussions about whether the image shows a corpse or a living person. The decisive point which made the scientists decide in favour of a living person was the even distribution of the markings. In the case of a corpse there are usually different temperatures in different regions of the body. The even distribution of the markings – however it was produced – indicates a functioning circulatory system. In any case one would expect stronger impressions on the buttocks and shoulder blades, because the blood in a dead body would sink to the lowest points by gravity. The scientists concluded: 'Taking into account all the facts, by the criteria of the twentieth century the body which lay in the linen was still alive.'[3]

The onset of rigor mortis is part of a process that has still not been fully explained. We have devoted many hours to studying the specialist literature, and questioned a number of experts. No clearcut statement could be obtained. Only one thing was agreed on, namely that rigor mortis does happen. According to the latest finds of thanatology (the science of dying), the peculiar stiffening of the musculature after death (rigor mortis) can be observed after just thirty minutes, and becomes complete after 3–6 hours depending on the temperature of the environment. By the so-called Nysten principle, it most often begins at the masticatory muscles, then it appears on the other muscles of the face, then on the neck and trunk and the arms, finally on the legs. This course of spreading (known as the descendent type) is found mainly in the case of athletically built people. The ascendant type, with the events running in the opposite sequence, is often encountered where the person was asthenic.

However the medical experts are not agreed about this. Another view is that it begins at the extremities, at the fingertips, toes, tips of the nose and lips, and continues towards the middle of the body, then returns back to the extremities.

Rigor mortis is caused by complex biochemical processes: the main event is the lowering of the ATP (adenosine triphosphate) level after cessation of the heart's activity. The entire skeletal musculature stiffens in the posture assumed by the dying person. After 36–90 hours the rigor mortis disappears again spontaneously. The more healthy the person was, the longer the rigor mortis lasts. The stiffening is shorter in the case of the elderly and those weakened by long illnesses.

It has been noticed that animals dying from poisoning may enter a cataleptic sort of rigor mortis in a matter of a few seconds: shortly after the final breath the animal can be completely stiff. In the case of humans a very early onset of rigor mortis is observed in the case of acute brain diseases, poisonings and those dying from convulsions.

After Jesus had fallen unconscious hanging on the cross, his body sank down from the erect posture, so that his legs folded sharply at the knees, because his whole weight was taken by the nails in his wrists. His head tipped forward, and his chin lay on his chest. His body would have to have stiffened in this posture in the three or four hours during which he hung like that on the

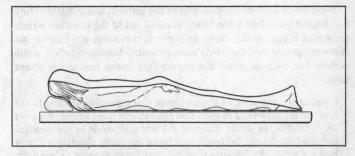

Fig. 6. The body lay stretched out quite flat on an even underlay, slightly cushioned (with cloths). There was a kind of pillow under the head which can be traced down to the shoulders.

cross. But if one looks closely at the impressions of the back of the body on the cloth, one sees at once that not only the back and the head, but also the thighs and the shanks of the 'corpse' were lying perfectly flat on the freshly laid-out cloth.

The theologian Karl Herbst has intensively studied the question of whether the image of the Turin linen shows a dead or living person. He was previously a Catholic priest. In his critical book, *Der wirkliche Jesus* (The Real Jesus), published in 1988 he investigated the historical Jesus and this led him to me some time ago. In the course of his research he also made an in-depth study of the Turin cloth. The results of the radiocarbon dating seemed suspect to him, because they contradicted all the facts which had hitherto been discovered. Herbst undertook to search for the 'error' in this 'conclusive' test and so came to meet Prof Wölfli in Zurich. The latter referred him to me. Our renewed contact led to a very fruitful exchange of ideas. We owe a great debt of gratitude to him for placing his correspondence and further scientific material at our disposal for our studies.

When Karl Herbst approached the Director of the Institute for Court Medicine at the University of Düsseldorf, Prof W. Bonte MD, asking whether one could say from any indications on the shroud whether rigor mortis had already set in, he received the definite reply: 'I would like to clearly deny this. The posture visible on the shroud could in my opinion also be assumed by a living person, that is to say a person who only appears to be dead.'[4]

Now let us look at the position of the arms in this context. They too would have had a tendency to push out to the position which they had taken on the cross. In reply to this some sindonologists have supposed that the arms were probably bound together at the wrists. Let us hear what the expert Prof Bonte has to say about this.

> I cannot see the point of the argument that a possible binding in the forearm region would suggest that rigor mortis must already have set in. A binding or rather fixing of the arms or hands in the position recorded on the shroud could only make any sense if the rigor mortis had *not* yet set in, because it would only be an attempt to bring the hands into a position which would then be frozen in place, so to speak, when the rigor mortis finally occurred. If on the other hand rigor mortis had already set in and the hands were not folded over each other in the desired position, it could not be achieved simply by binding them together. One would first have to break the rigor mortis by a considerable exertion of force. But then after doing that no binding would be needed anyway. In other words, they have not convincingly demonstrated that the forearms were actually bound together, although one cannot definitely rule out this possibility. Even if a binding did take place, it does not prove the presence of rigor mortis. Such a find would rather indicate that rigor mortis was not present.

Regarding the binding, it only takes a proper look at the part of the cloth concerned to show the absurdity of this idea. A cord would have interrupted the continuity of the picture, and of course also the bleeding of the hand wounds. But we see an uninterrupted image. That applies to the head as well as the hands, where certain researchers imagined they could see a chin band. Moreover, to tie the hands together one would have to cross them over at the wrists and tie them there. In fact the left palm lies on the back of the right hand – a most unsuitable posture for binding. In this case the cords would have had to cover the greater part of both hands, but the hands are clearly visible.

Bulst and Pfeiffer, after first establishing that the shroud picture cannot possibly be the work of an artist, open their arguments in favour of a corpse being involved with a baffling remark: 'Never in the history of art has rigor mortis been so perfectly portrayed as here.' It seems strange that the authors draw on the history of art, after having just rejected any artistic origin for the image; but stranger still is the firm conviction that rigor mortis can be read off the picture. As it is not clearly established when exactly the rigor mortis relaxes again, it might just possibly be the picture of a corpse *after* the relaxation of rigor mortis; that would be a hypothesis worth discussing. But to see rigor mortis in the appearance of the image must be seen as an attempt to force through a preconceived argument. In fact to the unbiased observer the 'Man of the Shroud' looks remarkably relaxed. There is nothing bent, skewed, distorted, crooked or stiff about him at all. He looks like a peacefully resting person.

What Bulst and Pfeiffer noticed above all was the 'conspicuously expanded chest cavity fixed in the position of extreme inhalation, the withdrawn epigastrium [upper stomach] and the protruding hypogastrium [lower stomach]'.[5] These would be typical features of the corpse of a person who has died suspended by the arms, but apart from the fact that the withdrawn upper stomach contrasting with the protruding lower stomach cannot, try as one might, be made out, the whole statement is a surprising leap of interpretation. The researchers could only see the 'expansion', 'protrusion' and 'withdrawal' by looking at the coloration on the cloth. As we have said, these are independent of the position of the linen above the body. If the cloth sinks low enough, for example on the lower stomach, and rests there, a more intense image results at this place. This does not mean that the 'Man of the Shroud' had an extended lower stomach, but merely that the contact between cloth and skin was closer at this point than at others. The cloth in fact follows the contours of the body. The fact that the chest does actually appear expanded is a result of the posture of the body. Anyone can test this by lying on a flat surface. In this position the chest automatically expands, and the chest area protrudes. There can certainly be no question of 'fixation in a position of extreme inhalation'.

Monsignor Giulio Ricci, a member of the Roman Centre for Sindonology, solves this problem in his own way by assuming that the cloth was tied tightly round the stiffened and bent corpse with cords. But this explanation appears nonsensical, just as absurd as his quaintly adventurous reconstruction of the Passion with specific details which he has supposedly 'seen' on the Turin cloth. It is impossible that the material lay tightly wrapped round the body. In this case we would have a completely distorted image, and also the sides of the body would have been included in the impression. One can do a simple test with body paints and for example paint over one's thigh, then take an imprint with a sheet of paper or a soft cloth by placing it over the painted area. The result is a grotesquely broadened thigh, quite unlike the anatomically correct image of the Turin cloth. Also, if the cloth had been tightly bound to the body it would have caused numerous small creases in the material. The picture would then again have been 'fragmented' by the pattern of creases.

Revealing Blood Marks

There is even more evidence, apart from the absence of rigor mortis: the testimony of the blood marks which are visible on the linen.

We can be grateful that Joseph of Arimathea and his helpers did not wash the body of Jesus for medical reasons, because this allowed the traces of coagulated blood to be imprinted on the cloth. Two different types of bleeding can be clearly distinguished. Firstly there is the dried blood which came from the whipping, the crowning with thorns, the side wound and from the nails fixing the body to the Cross. Secondly there is the fresh blood which flowed when Jesus was already lying horizontally in the cloth. The fabric quickly became saturated with the resinous aloe, and was thoroughly impregnated with it. This meant that most of the blood was not absorbed into the cloth, but just spread out over the surface. This would explain the surprising fact, observed by modern researchers, that most of the blood marks cannot be seen on the reverse side even though the material is quite thin. The careful treatment with the herbal solution also had the effect of resoftening the coagulated areas of blood, so that they too were transferred on to the cloth.

In the specialist literature it is often suggested that the separation of the blood marks into a central area and surrounding serum border can be taken as evidence that it was corpse blood. Here one can simply state the fact that corpse blood in the first phase following death is practically indistinguishable from the blood of a living person. In fact corpse blood used to be used on a large scale for transfusion purposes.[6]

The blood coming freshly on to the linen formed serum borders, as the solid components of the blood left lumpy aggregates in a watery serum. This process can easily be demonstrated with a drop of blood on a glass plate. The blood corpuscles are surrounded by the serum fluid like a halo. The blood marks which had first dried on the body and were just softened by the contact with the saturated cloth have quite a different appearance. These blood marks show no serum borders, as we see most clearly on the photographs under ultraviolet light, with wood light, transmitted light and by electronic processing. Here the fibrin has caused a thick wall to form at the edges of the marks.

Now we turn to the blood marks on the head. The sharp points of the mass of thorns which was pressed mockingly onto Jesus' head have left stab wounds, small but penetrating, in the thin skin of the head. As long as the 'crown of thorns' was on the head, the thorns sealed the tiny 1–2 mm diameter wounds quite well. The little blood which could flow out past the thorns coagulated at once and became encrusted in the hairs, as we observe in the case of all the smaller wounds. But in the skull region at the back of the head the cloth image clearly shows many larger blood streams running in all directions. This blood obviously trickled on to the cloth when the body was laid on the linen only after the thorns had been removed shortly before. The blood vessels in the thin skin of the head are very small, and are supplied with blood by the circulatory system. When the heart stops, the blood is withdrawn a little from the capillary vessels under the skin surface. The capillaries are emptied of blood, making the skin colour 'pale as a corpse', and there is no way any more blood can leave such small wounds, because intravascular blood clotting immediately sets in. In fact the emptying of the blood from the skin capillaries starts even when the heart flags during the death throes.

Looking at the portrait of Jesus on the linen, one notices the large blood mark on the forehead in the form of a reversed 3. Such an unusual shape can only be formed if the head is slightly raised from the horizontal (most probably a kind of pillow was placed under the back of the head). Then the slowly flowing blood runs down to a fold or wrinkle in the forehead, spreads a little, and as fresh blood comes out it flows further to the second fold in the

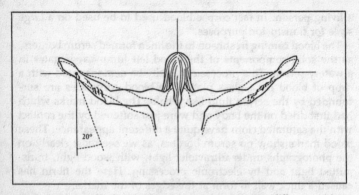

Fig. 7. While sagging down and straightening up again, two different positions of the body on the cross occur. The different angles can be calculated from the blood traces on the hands and arms.

forehead. This forehead wound, also caused by the crown of thorns, is located on the uppermost point of the entire body. Even if it is possible for blood to flow from large wounds on a corpse in certain conditions, it would not be possible in any circumstances at the high forehead. Such bleeding is only possible if the circulatory system is active.

Almost as high as the forehead are the hands, placed one over the other. Here one sees particularly well how fresh blood came on to the cloth in addition to the blood that had already dried. Three blood courses can be clearly distinguished on the wrists, running in different directions. Simple angle measurements provide clear indications about the way these originated. The left hand lies over the right and covers its wound, so the calculations only involve the visible wound on the left hand. When the nail was driven through, some of the blood ran into the groove between the tensed muscles along the forearm, and it finally dropped vertically downward, following gravity. These small, vertical streamlets all run nearly parallel. From their direction we can work out the angle of the arms to the crossbeam of the cross: it was about 20°. This also allows us to determine the free distance between the erect and sagging postures of the crucified person.

There is still one fact which remains obscure: why is a third blood mark visible on the image not mentioned by any of the well-known sindonologists? Although this 'third mark' is clearly visible, it was simply 'hushed up'. It is quite easy to see why this happened: the shape and direction of the third blood channel proves that it could only have been formed after the nails were removed from the wounds. This made the nail wounds start bleeding again, with the blood spreading out across the hand lying flat. It can also clearly be seen that the borders of Trace No 3 are much less sharply outlined than those of for example Trace No. 1. This allows us to conclude that Traces 1 and 2 had already dried and were 'softened' again by the aloe in the cloth, while the fresh blood of Trace 3 shows serum fringes. Such serum fringes are only formed by the activity of fibrin present in fresh blood, and they only appear if the blood collects on a shallow sloped surface and cannot flow away freely. As long as Jesus was hanging on the cross, the blood could flow from the wounds and hence the coagulated blood without any serum borders, and with clearly defined contour edges (see Plate 57).

On the cloth the right arm appears a little longer than the left. Such minor distortions on the front view image show that the linen did not lie like a board on the body. This fact also made it possible for the side wound to leave a clear imprint. On the frontal view one can see, right next to one of the patches on the burn areas, clearly outlined streamlets of blood which derive from the cut in the side, and which had coagulated on the Cross.

If we place the front and back views on the Turin cloth side by side and compare them, we can make a most interesting observation. At the level of the side wound we see a conspicuous blood trace running transversely across the back. It has a quite different appearance from the blood on the front. Blood outlines and serum surrounds can clearly be distinguished, a sure sign that this too was blood which flowed when the body was lying in the cloth. By the laws of physics this blood – and there is a considerable quantity of it – can only have flowed on to the cloth when the body was already lying in the horizontal position. Otherwise one would find a blood streamlet running in the direction of the lower abdomen. This blood trace certainly comes from the side wound. As Jesus lay in the healing cloth on his bed of stone cushioned with cloths, the side incision was bleeding again because of the movement.

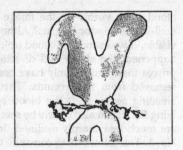

Fig. 8. Blood has collected in the cavity between the back and the buttocks. This shows clearly that the blood must have flowed only after the body was laid horizontally.

Naturally this blood rivulet did not run towards the loins but (by gravity) sideways under the right arm, gathering across the back. At this place the image of the back is especially faint, almost absent, except for the blood marks. This means there was a small gap here between cloth and skin. Naturally when lying flat a hollow back is formed. The spine alone seems to have been closer to the cloth, because it is visible along its length in the image. At this point the blood track is at its narrowest; here it has as it were sought out a narrow path and then spread out again on the more open left side. Unfortunately there are patched areas at the level of the two upper arms, right next to the side wound, so we cannot locate the precise starting point of the secondary bleeding from the side down to the back and on to the cloth. The amount of blood which flowed out in this manner must have presented quite a sight for someone looking at the undamaged cloth.

On the pilgrim's medallion commemorating the first exhibitions of the cloth in Lirey in the fourteenth century, the artist has brought out the transverse blood mark in an very distinct manner, like a twisted plait (see Plate 58). One notices that the blood mark is not only found within the body image, it extends left and right far from the body. The extended trace is clearly shown on the pilgrim's memento, and a good part of it is still visible today on the rear image of the Turin cloth. This proves that the blood must have flowed while the body lay in the cloth, and the mark cannot be a kind of 'imprint' like the traces of coagulated blood on the skin.

Let us hear what the experts have to say about this. If one raises the arms in the Crucifixion posture, then the side wound shifts

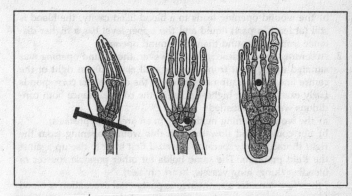

Fig. 9. The nails through hand and foot do not damage any bones or major blood vessels. Without anaesthetics these injuries would certainly have been very painful, but in no way fatal.

upwards a fair distance. The scientists of the East Midlands Forensic Laboratory consider it to be most unlikely that a stab at the site of the side wound could have touched the heart. They see no life-threatening danger even if the point penetrated. The lance would only have pierced the pleura, causing 'blood and water' to flow out, a watery fluid which had collected between the lungs and the thorax during the violent treatment.[7]

Concerning the problem of the side wound, Karl Herbst asked Prof Bonte whether blood could flow from an open wound between the fifth and sixth ribs about 10 cm right of centre, from a corpse lying flat on its back, without applying mechanical pressure from outside. The wound, the theologian explained, was first inflicted with the body in the erect position and then later the person was laid in the supine position. Herbst says: 'In my letter I intentionally avoided mentioning that the matter of Golgotha and the Shroud' was involved, since he was to remain completely free in his assessment, both from subconscious pro or contra tendencies and also from the fears of possible consequences.' Bonte replied:

1. Blood can flow spontaneously from the wound of a corpse only if:
   a) the wound opening is located in the area of so-called hypostasis, that is in the area of livor mortis; or

    b) the wound opening leads to a blood-filled cavity, the blood is still (at least in part) liquid and the upper level has a higher distance from the ground than the wound opening.

2. According to your description, however, the wound opening was situated in the right front thoracic wall about 10 cm right of the centre line. With a supine position of the corpse this corresponds fairly exactly to the highest point of the corpse. Hence both conditions were not satisfied:
    a) the wound opening neither lay in an area of hypostasis;
    b) nor could blood flow through this wound opening from the right thoracic cavity, because it would first have to rise up against the fluid pressure. The same holds for other possible sources of bleeding (lung, lung vessels, heart cavities).

3. I therefore consider a spontaneous postmortal evacuation of blood from a wound aperture in such a location to be out of the question.

4. On the other hand an outflowing of blood in the quantity you described, together with the direction of flow, would be in agreement with the supposition that the person concerned was at this time still alive. It is not uncommon to find, in forensic medical practice, that blood flows from a wound opening in precisely the location described here and in the direction of flow you have described, from a victim still living, lying on the back. This is especially true if larger arterial vessels are opened and if the blood pressure provides the necessary *vis a tergo* [push] for the rising of the blood column against the hydrostatic pressure.'[8]

This reply from an expert who was unaware of the delicate subject on which he was preparing his expert opinion, is remarkable in many ways. It shows that an unbiased analysis of the facts leads to quite different results from those that people who want to use the Shroud to prove the death of Jesus would have us believe. Afterwards, when Karl Herbst informed Prof Bonte of the real object of the expert opinion, and told him about some of his colleagues' arguments, his response was clear:

I do not wish to repeat my earlier reasoning. In my view everything suggests that the circulation had not yet stopped. Of course I concur with Prof Bollone, that an emission of blood from a stab wound in the chest can ensue during the transport of a corpse in a sort of passive way. But then one would have to ask whether the shroud was wrapped around the body at the beginning of the transport. And if this were the case, no 'static' traces and imprint patterns would have been formed, which always allow a direct topographic alignment with a supine body. I would rather have expected numerous traces from brushing contact, arranged in a more random and irregularly scattered manner. To my mind the pattern which is actually found suggests that the person concerned was wrapped in the cloth only at the entombment, and this most probably by first laying the body flat on the cloth and then placing the other half of the cloth over the body. *I cannot see how a passive emission of larger quantities of blood could happen during this operation of laying out the body.*

Severe bleeding can also be seen on the nail wounds of the feet. On the rear image one can clearly see how the blood from the wound runs down to the heels, collects there and, because fresh blood is constantly flowing out, then has to run out on to the cloth to the right. The 17 cm blood trace is interrupted, because the blood trickles over a fold in the cloth, before flowing further to the right. The last part of this blood mark can be found right at the other end of the cloth sheet, where one end of the sheet lay over the other, so that the fresh blood trace formed on both places. Here again the fact holds: blood can never flow like this from a corpse which has been dead for several hours. The heart and circulatory functions were still intact, though the breathing was greatly reduced.

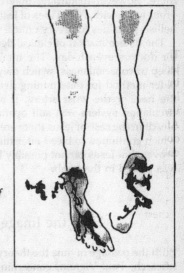

Fig. 10. The bleeding in the region of the feet shows the flow of fresh blood very clearly. The movements that occurred while laying out the body caused the open wounds to start bleeding again, and the blood spread out in all directions.

The impression of the streamlets 'in positive' leaves no doubt that this blood reached the cloth only after the entombment. The blood trace too is so clear that the artist of the pilgrim's medallion specially emphasized it.

It is also interesting to look at the right arm at the level of the elbow. Along the whole forearm there is the clear imprint of a blood trace, evidently one of those which coagulated before the entombment. At the end it jumps over the elbow and forms a blood mark on the cloth a few centimetres away from the arm. This blood track too can only have been formed while the body was actually lying in the cloth.

All these points of evidence have already been published in the many technical publications about the Turin Shroud. We have merely drawn new conclusions from the results of over eighty years of research, conclusions which are in harmony with the analysis of Bible references. Naturally we are aware that these results may appear provocative to many people. But the individual elements and the pieces of circumstantial evidence which have led to their formulation combine to build a long chain of logical proof which only allows this one conclusion. The facts are there, however disturbing they may be in the minds of those brought up with a fixed idea of Jesus, who tremble before 'eternal' hellish penalties for every critical inquiry about the dogma.

The determination of clinical death is not without its problems for doctors even today. The intake of drugs can bring about a deep unconsciousness, which may lead to faulty diagnoses. One older method for determining death was to make a small cut in the heel or the wrist artery. If arterial blood spurted out, the circulation system was still operating – corpses simply do not bleed! In the case of Jesus there are a total of twenty-eight wounds which continued to bleed after his removal from the Cross. This proves that Jesus cannot possibly have been dead when his body was placed in the tomb.

How the Image was Formed

With the passage of time the theory of the great pioneer of Shroud research, Paul Vignon, concerning the formation of the image, came under fire from all sides as the critics' objections increased. One important argument against it was the precondition of body warmth and sweat secretion. Corpses do not sweat or have fever. Vignon's vaporographic theory just could not be right. What should not be, could not be. Now we know that Jesus was not dead when he was laid out in the tomb chamber. The traumatic fever and the warm coverings meant that an increased perspiration was to be expected. This means that we can reinstate Vignon's theory and examine it further.

One objection to the idea that an evaporation process formed the image was the fact that the flax fibres of the cloth are oxidized and discoloured only at their surface. In the case of an image formed by a vapour bearing the chemical components of body oils, sweat, aloe and myrrh, the scientists would expect to find the picture permeating through all the fibres, including the edges, and not only on the surface. But this is not inevitable in such a process. The individual threads are flattened together because of the tightness of the weave. Because this makes them lie closely one over the other, only a surface oxidation is to be expected, even in the case of a vaporographic process. Moreover, there is always the possibility that the picture has changed in the course of the centuries. Considering such factors as these, it is necessary to view all the experiments which attempt to imitate the formation process with caution.

Looking at the photographs of the Turin Shroud, one may gain the impression that the image on the cloth is quite well defined, a quite sharply outlined picture of light and dark tones. But when actually viewed with the naked eye, the picture on the ivory-coloured cloth seems like a shadow lightly breathed on to the cloth, which is only visible at all at a second look (see Plate 2). If one goes closer to the cloth to see the picture better, one cannot see the image. The optimum viewing distance is about 2–5 m.

No satisfactory explanation of the origin of the picture has been found to this day. A considerable number of imaginative hypotheses have been thought up over the years, but most of them have to be viewed as highly speculative. The indefatigable sindonologists are still setting up experiments with heated metal reliefs or models. Of course these quaint experiments do not come anywhere near to the actual conditions and can only produce unsatisfactory results. Only a few researchers have carried out experiments under realistic conditions, one of whom is the forensic doctor Romanese, whose texts involving imprints of faces coated with aloetic mixtures have been mentioned in Part I. The results of his attempts, however, are grotesquely distorted, mask-like faces, rather off-putting and not at all like the Shroud image.

At Easter 1986 the American archaeologist Eugenia Nitowski and a team of colleagues tried to obtain images on a cloth draped over a dummy. The dummy, which lay for twenty-seven hours in a tomb cave in Jerusalem, was filled with hot water and coated with a solution of aloe. The setting for the experiment was very good, but the plastic dummy was a totally unsuitable test object. None of the various biochemical processes that can occur in a living body could take place on it. Nitowski had the dummy filled with hot water because she assumed that the body heat made a significant contribution to the formation of the image. But she favours a most roundabout explanation: she speaks of an obscure 'post-mortem fever', which is supposed to occur sometimes in corpses. The phenomenon is reported in the older technical literature, by Billroth for example; it is extremely rare and connected only with certain kinds of death (such as tetanus).[9] A cooling of the corpse is the usual physical symptom accompanying death. In most cases the temperature starts falling even during the death throes, and continues to fall after death until it matches the ambient temperature. Besides this, there is the drying out which starts immediately after death: the replacement of new fluid passed to the skin which happens in the living body ceases, and the surface layer where evaporation takes place quickly dries out.

The scientific results of Nitowski's tests were very modest. As if by way of compensation, she came to adopt the Christian faith. Today, known by the name Sister Damian of the Cross, she is a nun of the Carmelite Order at Salt Lake City.

An interesting discovery was made by the American researchers Jackson and Jumper, the pair who obtained the three-dimensional picture of the 'Man of the Shroud' by using a computer. They were able to demolish all the theories which viewed the image as the result of a kind of light radiation. The radiation theory was for a long time the favourite of the sindonologists who believed in a miraculous origin. They tried with all the means at their disposal to make the analysis of the Shroud prove Christ's Resurrection.

At the moment of the Resurrection, they claimed, Jesus had 'disappeared' from under the sheet covering him: in other words, dematerialized. During this process an unknown light energy was released, which imprinted the image of the Lord on the white cloth for posterity. But light spreads out from the source in rays travelling in all directions. The projection of the light and dark areas on the cloth is always vertically above the corresponding body part. Just as with an imprint formed by direct contact, radiation of light would lead to a distorted picture. Whatever it was that produced the picture must have obeyed the law of gravity. Jackson himself drew some very strange conclusions from the rejection of the light theory. At the international symposium in Paris in 1989 he declared that he could only explain the formation of the image by a miracle. According to him the picture must have arisen when the cloth suddenly 'fell through' the body! The body of the 'Man of the Shroud' was transformed into an immaterial state. The cloth sank down through the virtual body to the other half of the sheet serving as an underlay. The image was formed by the high energy released in the process. So one miracle was substituted for another. The cloth became evidence of the Resurrection, which was seen as a mysterious process of dematerialization.

Faced with this unsatisfactory state of affairs, we decided to do our own experiments. We obtained aloe (*Aloe capensis conc.* with an anhydrous aloin content of 22.9 per cent) and myrrh (*Myrrhae* grains with a 33.3 per cent insoluble component).

We took about 80 g of each of the coarse-grained, crystalline substances and ground them separately to a fine powder with pestle and mortar (see Plate 59). We then mixed the powders together and stirred them into a strong white wine. We let this mixture stand overnight. The following day we found that a fraction of the solid components had settled on the bottom of the glass, but most had dissolved in the liquid and formed a thick brown emulsion.

First we wanted to coat the cloth or the body with the mixture and test whether the rising chemical components of the perspiration would cause surface oxidation process on the flax fibres. Because I happened to be an ideal match in size and body weight for the 'Man of the Shroud' (which could be quite accurately determined from the Shroud image data stored on computer), I had to be the one to volunteer as test subject. For the first run of the experiment we brushed our tincture on to a linen cloth. This gave the fabric a strong brown colour (The aloin present in the aloe at up to 25 per cent has light-sensitive properties and darkens in light and air.) Our reasoning, following on from Vignon's and Pellicori's experiments with perspiration and body oils, turned on the chemical reaction of these components with the herbs absorbed in the fabric. Prior to the actual test I spent three consecutive sessions of about twenty minutes in a sauna, to subject my body to intense heat. The idea behind this was to stimulate the traumatic fever of the 'Man of the Shroud' with the copious secretion of sweat. After the third session in the sauna I lay down on a level surface in the same posture as the 'Man of the Shroud', and Elmar Gruber covered me with a prepared cloth of hand-spun, hand-woven, naturally bleached linen (see Plate 60). To keep things simple we decided to cover my body with the cloth only from the chest to the thighs. I had to endure forty-five sweating minutes of this. It turned out that the sheet became somewhat stiff, so that it did not cling to the body but sloped downwards from the protruding parts on which it lay.

When we removed the cloth, no conspicuous markings could be seen. Working on the assumption that such a valuable cloth, which was not in fact used for a burial and so was certainly not considered impure, was meant to be reused, we washed it in natural washing-soap water. The colouring remained, but became much lighter. But no imprint could be made out on it. Repeated washings and observations over a period of several months did not change the appearance at all. The cloth image could not have been formed in that way.

In another test the pulverized herbal mixture was strewn over my perspiring body, and a piece of clean, untreated linen fabric was placed on it. John's Gospel does not mention how the herbal ointment was prepared, so this does leave open the possibility that the dried substances were applied directly in this way. The result was much more satisfactory. We could clearly see a body imprint (see Plate 61). At the places where a lot of sweat was secreted, such as in the middle of the chest, we obtained a very strong image, although it was formed by direct contact. The colouring penetrated the sheet and could be seen clearly on the reverse side as well. The image was different at the places where the cloth lay very lightly on the body, and which were not dampened with sweat so much, such as the arms. Here a very faint image appeared. Clumps of the dried herbs remained sticking to the fibres, and the textile took on a slight beige tint around them. These results were encouraging. At least we had shown that the substances applied to the skin can lead to a colouring process on the cloth, even on those areas not lying directly on the body surface.

Encouraged by the results of the second test, we went straight on to do a third. More visits to the sauna for me. Now my body was coated with the substances dissolved in wine. We also placed some towels on top of the linen covering me, to simulate the curative hot pack. Thirty-five long minutes passed. Had we done it right this time? Was this test close to the true conditions of the healing work? Many thoughts ran through my mind. It was certainly a strange feeling to repeat the events which had taken place 2000 years ago in a Jerusalem rock grave, and which to this day remain hidden in the shadows of a secret old tradition.

Removing the towels and lifting the linen from my body, we beheld the astonishing result: a clear imprint of the thorax with the crossed hands in a soft beige tint (see Plate 62). But our cloth still did not match the Shroud picture. At first glance the correspondence was indeed striking, but looking more carefully the matter became more problematic. The dark areas appeared flat and quite sharply bounded. They did not show the smoothly graded shading we find on the Turin Shroud. The body forms were also distorted a little in their breadth and so looked out of proportion.

The linen we used was of a coarse kind, not as fine as the Turin cloth and also not in the same type of weave. And a much longer period lying in the cloth – Jesus lay in it throughout the night at least – might change the effect. Moreover, we could not simulate the ravages of time, whose influence is practically unknown. So the original could not have been formed in this way either, even though the general form and colour of the image did look similar to the Shroud picture. We were just not able to simulate the image formation process precisely enough in our experiment. For one thing I could not remain lying in a sweat without moving for hours – a short period of this and I was near circulatory collapse because of the heat trapped under the cloth. But at least the image could not be removed by washing.

One can assume that some time elapsed before the herbal mixture was applied, covering the entire body of Jesus, including the head, which of course bore the wounds from the crown of thorns. The tincture had probably already dried on the body when Jesus was wrapped in the sheet. Due to the febrile process the tincture was gradually dampened again in the sweat. During evaporation, molecules of the herbal mixture may thus have been transported on to the cloth with the perspiration. Therefore the process must have been a gradual one, which precludes any sudden saturation of the sheet. It remains to be examined whether such vapours do in fact colour a cloth in such a manner. This would be a suitable explanation for the kind of image on the Turin cloth, because fluid vapours tend to rise vertically during evaporation. Thus we would expect a direct projection for the picture rather than a distorted image. These reflections led us to set up one further experiment. We poured a little of the aloe-myrrh tincture into a heat-resistant glass. A piece of linen was stretched over it and the substance was carefully heated on a very low gas flame. Soon small water droplets formed on the surface of the taught cloth, like dew. After about forty minutes a distinct yellowish mark had formed, only visible on the underside of the cloth. The coloured substances had not penetrated through the material to the surface. The colouring[10] could not be removed even by repeated washing.

A human evaporates up to a litre of water in just one night during sleep. If one bears in mind that the body of the 'Man of the Shroud' probably passed at least one whole night under the cloth without moving, an image might well have been formed by evaporation of the substances. The evaporated vapours did not have to travel far. The picture on the Turin cloth is only visible at places where it was directly in contact with the surface of the body or only millimetres from the skin. Where the fabric was further off, no coloration can be seen; for example none of the whip marks were transferred. The process we have suggested here also explains why the picture is not sharply outlined, why the borders slowly merge with the colour of the surrounding cloth. At areas where the sheet lost contact with the body surface, the vapour only made an indistinct impression, because there was a longer distance to be traversed than at the areas of contact. The further the cloth was from the skin, the less distinct is the outline, until finally it becomes lost in the background colour of the cloth, where the colouring substances could no longer be carried far enough. With a very slow and weak but continuous evaporation process, such as may happen on the skin of a man, the picture on the Shroud can be quite rationally explained – *if* the body was still living and perspiring.

A Needle in a Haystack

Besides our own experiments, we pursued another line of investigation in the quest for the greatest possible certainty: we tried to see if we could identify the shroud seen by Robert de Clari in 1203 in Constantinople as the Turin cloth. We knew we could not raise our hopes too high, but it was worth trying to follow even this faint track.

After the Fourth Crusade numerous relics from the treasuries of the city were scattered abroad. Most highly prized were the select relics of the Passion. Very quickly their prices soared. For a single thorn from the crown of thorns, astronomical sums were paid out. When King Louis IX, known as St Louis, procured the circlet alleged to be the 'crown of thorns' from the Venetians, there was not a single thorn left on it. They had all 'walked' to the reliquaries of countless churches. The pious ruler paid out the incredible sum of 135,000 livres for this unprepossessing ring, 21 cm in diameter. By comparison the beautiful Sainte-Chapelle, which was built for him in Paris by the architect Pierre de Montreuil to house it, was really good value – it cost him just 40,000 livres!

Historical documents say that a 'Shroud of Christ' in Constantinople was given out piece by piece to various locations, but we did not know whether the fragments came from the Turin cloth or from copies. Perhaps, we thought, it would be possible to follow the path of such a fragment, track down its present whereabouts and compare the material with the Turin cloth. In this way evidence might be obtained showing that a piece of the genuine Shroud really had been cut off. This would be a solid proof of the presence of the Turin cloth in Constantinople around the year 1200.

Let us have a look at the documents then. According to one

report, Robert de Clari himself brought back a sizeable treasure of relics to his home town of Corbie. It seems he managed to get hold of two small pieces of an alleged shroud relic. They are listed in an old inventory in Corbie.[11]

As soon as the Fourth Crusade was over, highly placed churchmen were the first to set about loading up their ships with the unique relics. Abbot Hugo de St Gilles took a relic containing a shroud piece to Clairvaux.[12] In October 1205 the Bishop of Soissons, Nivelo de Cherisiaco, gave his niece, Abbess Helvis, a piece of the 'pure Sindon' from Constantinople for the Church of Our Lady at Soissons.[13] Konrad of Krosigk, Bishop of Halberstadt, was as we have said one of the more zealous relic hunters. In 1205 he brought pieces of the shroud and *sudarium* from Constantinople to Halberstadt.[14]

In a transfer document of June 1247, Baldwin II, the Latin Emperor of Byzantium, gave Saint Louis, a passionate collector of relics, a 'portion of the *sudarium* in which His body was wrapped in the grave' for the Sainte-Chapelle.[15] Twenty years later Louis bequeathed some of his relics to the Abbot of the monastery at Vézelay, Simon de Brion. Among them was a corner piece from the shroud relic.[16] Simon de Brion then issued an edict on 11 August 1267, ordering that none of the relics left to him and the Vézelay monastery by Louis IX could ever be sold. In 1248 King Louis sent the archbishop of Toledo another piece of the precious shroud relic for his cathedral.[17]

The task before us was to find out if the shroud fragments could still be traced among the sacred treasures of the churches involved. However, some 800 years have passed since then, centuries in which Europe has experienced countless wars, uprisings and revolutions. We knew we were after needles in haystacks. But sometimes it is the church treasures which, well protected as they are, survive the worst times of unrest. It soon turned out that our hopes were unfounded. It was unfortunate that most of the shroud relics had ended up in France. For centuries the country enjoyed a quiet existence, but then the French Revolution swept through the land and the mob showed a special preference for storming church property. Numerous monasteries and churches succumbed to the ravages of the destructive, fire-wielding crowd – irreplaceable artistic treasures and cultural monuments.

In Corbie the two shroud pieces, held in cruciform reliquaries,

were last mentioned in an inventory of the St Pierre church dated
January 1791. After that the atheistic plunderers of the Revolution
ransacked the church treasures in search of valuable objects and
simply threw away the relics which were in the precious shrines.[18]
The cloth relics in Vézelay, Soissons and Clairvaux suffered the
same fate. The monastery at Clairvaux was completely destroyed
during the Revolution, together with the relics. In Vézelay no one
had to worry about Abbot Simon de Brion's edict. None of the
relics had been sold, but during the revolution all of them fell into
the hands of the plunderers.[19] In Soissons the last entry for the
cloth relic is found in an inventory of 1622, prepared for Bishop
Charles de Haqueville. The abbey Notre-Dame de Soissons was
also robbed and partly destroyed at the time of the revolution.
The relic treasures have disappeared.[20] Now our last hope
was Toledo and Halberstadt. But the curator responsible for the
Halberstadt cathedral treasures, Konrad Riemann, informed us
that none of the inventory lists included a piece of the shroud.
They did however have a *sudarium* in Halberstadt cathedral.[21] On
15 August 1991 I was shown the extensive textile collection in the
cathedral by the restorer, Mrs Happach, the sister of Mr Riemann.
It is to her credit that the 300 items have been well stored and
looked after. These include no less than ninety copes from the
eleventh to the seventeenth centuries. The '*sudarium*' is a kind of
small sack made of cotton crêpe, which had probably been fixed
to a bishop's crosier. The cloth bears no similarity to the Shroud.
Again the trail faded in the dust.

We received a reply from the Toledo cathedral chapter, full of
baroque eloquence, and pervaded by the mystical spirit of Span-
ish Catholicism.[22] The only entry which could relate to a shroud
was in an inventory of Archbishop Francisco Antonio Lorenzana
dated 20 June 1790. There under No 10 is listed a crystal reliquary
with gilded pedestal and lid, containing various relics, including
relics of the 'cloths in which our Lord Jesus Christ was wrapped'.
It does not say whether they mean the cloth in which he was
wrapped in the tomb. Another thing one notices is that there is
nothing to say that the reliquary comes from St Louis, although
other shrines are noted which are explicitly described as gifts
from him. It seems that it is a later acquisition and not the piece
among the relic treasures of Constantinople which Louis transferred to Toledo in 1248.

The Italian priest Luigi Fossati, an excellent historian of the Turin Shroud, pursued a course similar to ours. While studying the early icons of the 'Holy Visage' or copies of the Edessa Portrait, Fossati noticed that the pictures were often painted on pieces of cloth stretched on a panel of wood. There would be nothing remarkable in this if the boards were just used as a support for the painting. But in some cases the panel is only partly covered by a small cloth piece. On the 'Holy Visage of Edessa' kept in the Armenian church in Genoa, the canvas covers about two thirds of the board. The material is completely covered by the paint, and is only visable in places where the paint layer is coming off. Obviously the cloth is a *brandeum*, that is an object which had been sanctified by the touch of a sacred relic. The only relic which would have been suitable for this was the Edessa Portrait itself.

On another 'Holy Visage of Edessa', kept by the Vatican in the Matilda Chapel, a cloth can again be seen beneath the paint at places where it has peeled off. The picture was first painted on the canvas and only later fixed to a wooden panel. The cloth appears to be woven in the herringbone pattern. Here too we have to posit a *brandeum*, one reason being the unusual painting surface. To make a *brandeum* as 'authentic' as possible, an article identical in appearance to the relic was normally chosen. The fact that a linen with the herringbone pattern was used would suggest that the Mandylion was on a linen of the same type of weave – that rare and costly twill weave which is the distinguishing feature of the Turin cloth. Unfortunately at the present time neither the cloth of the Genoa icon nor that of the Vatican has been thoroughly examined to determine their similarity to the Shroud.

We felt that both lines of inquiry would be worth examining further, despite the difficulties involved.

A Disturbing Suspicion

On the morning of 16 June 1969 the Shroud chapel in Turin was closed to the public for three days. No explanation for the action was given. The faithful were probably not very concerned, because of the constant need for renovation works in churches. At 8.30 am a small group of people met Cardinal Pellegrino and several other Church dignitaries inside the chapel. The Cardinal celebrated a mass, then as part of the sacred rites the container with the cloth was taken from the shrine, and the cloth itself laid out on a long table covered with a white sheet. For the first time in history scientists were able to carry out a direct examination.

We have referred to this investigation of 1969 in Part I as a very unsatisfactory undertaking. Not enough good scientists were invited. We now understand why this was so. Cardinal Pellegrino could easily have summoned a commission of internationally respected experts. But then the operation would probably have attracted a lot of attention, and this is just what the church authorities wanted to avoid. The expert analysis of the relic was to be kept secret at all costs. Only years later, in 1976, were the members' names released because of public pressure. Before then some quite concrete rumours about the secret operation had trickled out.

Apparently nobody would have taken much notice of these secret events if it had not been for a German sindonologist Hans Naber who brought the obscure affair to the notice of the press and so to the public. Apparently Naber had received a discreet hint about the events in the Shroud chapel from a 'Vatican official'. Who this source was, was never revealed, but the informant wrote in his report, 'They go to work like thieves in the night.' Naber issued a series of press statements in which he claimed that the Church intended to manipulate the sacred cloth in some way or other, to falsify or even destroy it, or to erase the image from the surface, because it represented a serious danger for the continued existence of the entire Christian Faith. Naber was in fact one of the first to announce publicly what many already knew but had kept to themselves for fear of the shattering implications: the blood marks on the Turin cloth prove that Jesus was still living when he was taken from the cross and laid out in the linen.

For the public, unprepared for this disclosure, the claim was simply bizarre, absurd, monstrous. Many authors had already suggested that Jesus did not die on the Cross, but to hold proof of it in one's hands, that was shocking in the extreme for a Western world moulded by Christianity. Naber's assertions were a sensation for the press, and he had no difficulty in attracting their interest. The Vatican was compelled to make an official denial of the accusations. On 20 June 1969 Monsignor Annibale Bugnini, an undersecretary in the Vatican, announced to Associated Press, 'At the present time the Vatican has no intention of dealing with the Shroud question.' Because of his authority it soon seemed as if no one was seriously interested in the case any more.

The opponents who wanted to silence Hans Naber found him easy game, for he is a very peculiar fellow, and his appearances were not usually calculated to inspire confidence. He took a variety of names, calling himself Kurt Berna or (in English publications) John Reban or Nelson T. Bruknear. All the pseudonyms are anagrams of his real name. He also decorated himself with imposing professional titles, such as 'President of the International Foundation for the Shroud of Jesus', of which he was sole member. Naber had previously been a waiter and in 1947 he had allegedly had a vision over a period of days, when Jesus gave him a revelation. According to Naber's story, in the vision Jesus chose him to make known to the whole world that the Saviour of humanity had not actually died on the Cross, but was only apparently dead, that he had survived the Crucifixion and after three days had come out of a coma. Naber drew the proof for this claim directly from the Turin cloth, because it could be seen from the blood marks on the image that Jesus could not have been dead.

Naber felt confirmed in his convictions by the publications regarding the research work and the photographs of the cloth, and he even managed to track down some specialists who supported his views in expert opinions and reports. His primary aim was to use his presentation of the evidence to put an end to the thousands of years of tension between Christians and Jews. If Jesus had not died on the Cross, the Jews could not have been his murderers or be made responsible for his death.

From 1957 Naber continued to publish new tracts, essays, books and illustrated newspapers (*News Flash*), in which he described his mission. In 1963 his book *Resurrected in Flesh and Blood* was published, allegedly in its fifth edition, by a hitherto unknown publisher in the Alpine principality of Liechtenstein. In one *News Flash* with many pompous titles Naber declared his 'world discovery' in red banner headlines like a cheap rag of the sensational press: 'Christ was buried alive'. An obscure company, Interfound Publishers, in Zurich and London, served as publisher;

this too was probably one of the Naber's numerous foundations and enterprises. His *News Flash* reporting how Jesus survived the Crucifixion could be purchased at kiosks in Germany, Austria and Switzerland over a three-month period in 1980. On the last page of the newspaper Naber announced in grand style a forthcoming edition to be available at the kiosks from June 1981. The title 'The "Secret Service" of Jesus at Work – The Shroud as Graphic Record', but the story never appeared.

The pseudonyms and invented societies helped to ensure that Naber's thesis was met with a pitying smile by both dogmatic churchmen and secular scientists, and attracted little attention. But the waves continued to be felt, and all the serious writings on sindonology mention his work. In the opinion of the theologian Prof Werner Bulst, Germany's best-known and competent sindonologist, Naber's publications are 'pure fantasy'. He criticizes him for incompetence, lack of education and the 'absence of any scientific training'.

I briefly mentioned Naber and his story in 1983 in my book about the historical Jesus, and one day he paid me a visit. He was unbelievably corpulent and had difficulty fitting into the back seat of the taxi, with the front seat pushed forward as far as it would go. At the time I had a semicircular sofa some 2 m long, and Naber was almost a perfect fit. This colossus felt constantly threatened and under attack, because hardly anyone wanted to take his thesis seriously. He had borrowed considerable sums of money to carry out his mission, hoping to pay off the debts with the profits from his publications, but he was disappointed to find that hardly anyone was interested in his 'truth'. In every action against him he saw the machinations of the Vatican, who wanted to silence him in any way they could. When he visited me in 1983 he was a wreck, ruined mentally, physically and financially.

He obviously saw in me a comrade-in-arms for his just cause, and he generously offered me the chance of becoming 'world general director' of a new association, the Investigative Commission J, which he had set up in some banana republic. I felt unworthy of such a great honour and declined his offer with thanks. Shortly after this I publicly distanced myself from him during a press conference in New Delhi. From then on he considered me as another one of his personal enemies, and tried to take legal proceedings against me because he claimed

I had not quoted him correctly. Yet again he was off tilting at windmills.

On 28 June 1969, just ten days after the activity of the secret investigating commission in Turin had finished, Naber knocked at the doors of the Vatican. He had a case of documents with him and was accompanied by a photographer. Surprisingly, he was received by the Undersecretary of the Religious Congregation, Monsignor Charles Moeller. With an irked expression the secretary took the folder with the documentation, as Naber's photographer released the shutter. With that Naber had really succeeded in getting what he wanted. The photograph went round the world.

United Press International (UPI) reported from the Vatican:

> Today the President of the Swiss Foundation for the Holy Shroud, Kurt Berna, handed over documents to the Vatican which allegedly prove that Jesus Christ did not die on the cross. Professor Berna describes in the illustrated report his view that the blood marks on the Turin Shroud, in which most probably Jesus was wrapped, could not have come from a corpse . . . This find is contrary to the dogmas of the Roman Catholic Church. If Berna's claims are right, it means that Christ was still alive when he was taken down from the cross, and may then have recovered from his injuries. This would cast a completely new light on the 'Resurrection'. So far we have been unable to obtain any statement from the Vatican about the matter.

Associated Press reported in a similar vein:

> The German author Kurt Berna, who doubts the death by crucifixion of Christ, has called upon the Vatican for a new careful examination of the Turin Shroud. The author of four books about the Turin cloth claims that Christ was still living after being taken from the cross. Yesterday Berna handed the Vatican representative, Charles Moeller, a twenty-page text illustrated with photographs, which he described as a 'documentation' . . . An official comment from the Vatican has not yet been made.

Despite all its sensational appeal the news did not seem to make waves. If the Vatican had reacted, the curiosity of the world public would certainly have been aroused. But the Vatican proceeded with great diplomatic finesse. An official denial often has the opposite effect to that desired – people sit up and take notice – whereas if no response is made, all the excitement is soon forgotten. As it happened nothing more was heard of the affair, until in December that year 'Berna' received a strictly confidential note 'from the highest level', direct from the Vatican. Again no name was given. The secret information was alarming. A high dignitary of the Church, a member of the Curia, wrote that the Church could tolerate no rift. It could not on the one hand teach that Jesus Christ died on the Cross for the salvation of mankind, and on the other revere a shroud in which no corpse ever lay. *A radical and final solution had to be found*.

Naber was beside himself. What was meant by the cryptic statement that a radical and final solution had to be found? He immediately telephoned the news agency Reuters in London and told the reporters that he thought the Vatican was planning to destroy the Turin Shroud. What else could one understand by a 'radical solution'? Besides, he told the amazed journalists, the Church had already tried to eliminate the Shroud once before, but this time there was evidence for the Vatican's intentions. Reuters allowed themselves to be convinced by Naber and on 3 January 1970 shot an announcement round the world. 'The Holy Shroud of Christ may be destroyed.' Days later UPI ran a similar report.

These two news agencies are among the oldest and most respected, and the Church now felt it was forced to make a statement. On 6 January 1970 the Turin Cardinal Michele Pellegrino declared that Naber's assertions were 'unfounded and irresponsible', although he had to admit that the cloth had been taken from its accustomed place in the chapel. But this was purely in connection with the work of a team of experts who were examining it to improve its preservation. Under the pressure of publicity they were forced to reveal things which had been kept quiet or even denied.

From then on the Church authorities had no choice but to keep all the examinations of the Shroud open to public view. There was obviously someone very well-informed among their own ranks leaking the facts. They could no longer be sure what would remain secret and what would come out in public. Nevertheless, they took their time about publishing an official report on the 1969 investigations; it only came out in 1976. A year later the Episcopal Ordinariat published a volume reporting the sampling of 1973.[23] At this time all the studies supported the view that the cloth was genuine, from Palestine and the time of Jesus. If further analysis were to show incontrovertibly that the 'Man of the Shroud' had been alive, the Church would be faced with a tremendous problem. The whole future of institutional Christianity could depend on this 4 m *corpus delicti*, and it would lead to a crisis of tremendous magnitude! Because people in the twentieth century tend to be great believers in science, the first priority of the guardians of orthodoxy in the Vatican was to get scientists to establish beyond all doubt that the body of Jesus was dead, by examining the Shroud. Therefore in 1978 a further volume appeared under episcopal editorship, which attempted to use the Turin cloth to prove Jesus' death by crucifixion.[24]

It gradually became clear, however, that the arguments could not hold water. The Church's situation was critical. They had to change their approach. Then just at the right moment came the interest of scientists in the carbon dating field. The method had proved itself among the experts despite occasional set-backs and spectacular errors.[25] Regarding the errors, we can say that only recently in a study by three scientists of the British Museum Research Laboratory, who figure as authors of the *Nature* article along with Michael Tite, it was found that the entire range of radiocarbon dates published by the British Museum from 1980 to 1984 were wrong![26] This is a striking confession by the researchers about their 'completely reliable' method. Nonetheless archaeologists commonly rely on the C-14 method for contested age measurements.

The progress in the 1970s with new procedures allowed the 'exact' dating of minute fragments of an object. Harry E. Gove, one of the pioneers of the new AMS technique, pressed for a dating of the Turin cloth.

The result of an age measurement by radiocarbon dating, thought the worried churchmen, would be accepted by scientists and public alike. Despite all the inaccuracies the C-14 method has a reputation for providing precise results. Most of the scientists were sure in any case that the Turin cloth had not really held the body of Jesus; they were just waiting for the proof of the forgery. If the radiocarbon dating put the linen in the Middle Ages, the 'problem' could be solved at a single stroke. What meaning could the evidence that the 'Man of the Shroud' must have been alive have then? They could not destroy the cloth now, it was too much in the public eye.

The radiocarbon dating offered an excellent chance to silence the speculations about the cloth once and for all, using a scientific-ally recognized procedure. By acquiring the relic the Vatican had taken the first step. Previously it had still been in the possession of the House of Savoy and only lent to the Turin diocese for safekeeping. As the condition of Umberto II, the ex-King of Italy, grew more serious and his departure from this world seemed imminent, the Pope was asked to personally try and have the rights of ownership of the relic transferred. On 2 March 1983 while on his fourth trip to Latin America, the Pope stopped over in Lisbon for this purpose.

He met the aging Umberto, embraced him, heard his con-fession and received the Shroud as a gift, literally at the last moment. For two weeks later, on 18 March, the ex-King died while still in exile (see Plate 64).

Now the Turin Curia and the Vatican could make a start on the preparations for the carbon test. The Church authorities were probably concerned about arranging the experiment in a way which would avoid any possible loopholes for later critics. It was not without reason that they took years to prepare the test pro-tocol. If scientists were always to allow themselves so much pre-paration and planning for every experiment they performed, they would only complete a few experiments in their careers. At least one cannot accuse the Italian guardians of the cloth of acting hastily and without reflection. On the contrary, they spent such a long time pondering and working away at it, that one has to say the result was a foregone conclusion. So it must have been part of the strategy of the men pulling the strings in the background to overturn the agreed plan of action at the last minute.

In Part I we have described the embarrassing quarrels among the scientists and the peculiar decisions of the Vatican. They seemed perplexing, incomprehensible and silly. But now the way they acted is clear: they were trying to break the flow of scientific evidence which supported both the authenticity of the cloth and the survival of Jesus once and for all. They went to work systematically.

In Trondheim everything had been clearly decided. Obviously they let the scientists discuss the course of the test and decide on the control precautions, while the 'wire pullers' in the Vatican had long agreed on a protocol. But like all undertakings that aim at perfection, there were mistakes – and quite a few of them. One of the first and most noticeable was the withdrawal of the supervisors. Three independent institutions had been discussed to guarantee the proper conduct of the test, the world famous Insituto di Metrologia G. Colonetti in Turin, the Pontifical Academy of Sciences and the British Museum. A multiple check in such a controversial and unique test was not only sensible, it was essential. It would give the impression that a sharp eye was being kept on the selected experts from both the scientific and the ecclesiastical side. This illusion was kept up for some time. Then suddenly and without giving any reasons, both Colonetti and the Pontifical Academy vanished as supervisory institutions! On 10 October 1987 Cardinal Ballestrero wrote to the then seven laboratories, saying that the Holy See had told him about the change and the final procedure.

Doubtless the Vatican had planned this step earlier, because no objection was made by Prof Chagas, the director of the Academy, or his secretary Vittorio Canuto. Obviously everything was to look as if the experts were building a watertight experimental arrangement, until shortly before the actual test date. All the basic arrangements were settled, and if a minor alteration was made by the highest authority, no great objections could be raised. In fact, regarding the Archbishop of Turin's letter Hall merely remarked that some 'details' had been changed.[27] In reality the Trondheim protocol and all the talks already held were shaken by a major earthquake. Nothing was left as agreed.

The radiocarbon laboratories did not react to the exclusion of the Colonetti Institute and the Pontifical Academy of Sciences. For them it was almost a cause for celebration. What scientist likes to have others keeping a sharp eye on him during his investigations, and that by a committee which the dating experts considered to be part of the 'opposing' camp of the Church?

One basic question we have to deal with is the Vatican's motive for withdrawing its renowned Scientific Academy from the experiment of the century. Should not the Catholic 'watchmen' be the first to stand as guarantor for the millions of faithful around the world who would be following the unique test with mistrust? Why this sudden change of mind? No explanation was given.

But the reason is clear: under no circumstances was the Vatican to be drawn into the discussion about the result of the dating test. It had to appear as if the scientists alone were responsible for it.

Should any irregularities be found, then the laboratories alone had to explain them. The Holy See was cleared of all suspicion. It had not checked anything and so it had also not condoned anything which might turn out to be dubious. Such a procedure only makes sense if the inconsistencies were already pre-programmed, and this by the Vatican itself. Otherwise the natural course would have been to ensure a more thorough supervision on their home ground – after all the Vatican is the owner of the cloth. They had to be quite sure to avoid doing any checks themselves. To be on the safe side they 'whistled back' the Instituto di Metrologia G. Colonetti, which had been appointed mainly to check the correctness of the statistical evaluation. Everything was done in a way which allowed them to manage things as they pleased, unobserved. And should inconsistencies still come to light, the Church would be out of the matter.

It is striking how the Vatican pensioned off its faithful servant Cardinal Ballestrero immediately after the announcement of the test results – owing to his age, as the press office tersely said. Chagas too, who probably knew too much, was removed from his post as head of the Pontifical Academy of Science just two weeks after the C-14 results were announced. All the inquiries and correspondence directed to the Cardinal or Chagas by appalled sindonologists and scientists, who had not failed to notice that the whole dating process 'reeked', were left unanswered.

The behaviour of the Vatican staff who gave the commission leaves us with no other conclusion than that they themselves meticulously planned the deception. The result of the carbon test was settled in advance. All they had to do was to find a suitable form of procedure that was as 'shady' as possible.

Splendour and Rot of the Great Experiment

What to a cursory view looks like a well-planned and supervised experiment, actually depended entirely on the honesty of just one individual, Dr Tite. For the Vatican had seen to it that the supervision remained in his hands alone. Tite was the key element in the whole affair. If he were to arrange the manipulations, there would be no one to check up on him. Bruno Bonnet-Eymard and his colleagues, who have done meticulous research on the dubious carbon test, make this very accusation – manipulations directed by Michael Tite. They say that it was Tite who, on the orders of certain circles in the Vatican, was to see that the relic was dated in the Middle Ages. Tite had long been a good friend of the Oxford radiocarbon tester Teddy Hall. Hall belong to the British Museum's team of advisors – a serious conflict of interests. There can be no question of this being an independent laboratory. And after the announcement of the results Tite was made director of Hall's laboratory, while Hall retired. He too followed the example of Ballestrero and Chagas: no replies were given to letters and queries. Tite moved into his new office with gratifying financial reserves of £1 million, which anonymous wealthy 'friends and donors' had given Hall on Good Friday 1989 to secure the position for his friend and successor. Who would have chosen Good Friday of all days for such a financial transaction? 'I leave it to you,' writes Prof David Boyce, 'to guess the origins of these "wealthy friends". But they betray themselves by their actions.'[28] This announcement was even more of a surprise to those who knew the conditions at Oxford University, with many teaching posts left unfilled for want of funds.

One would have thought that in the case of such an epoch-making experiment, with the spotlight of world publicity turned on Turin, one could at least expect precision in the simple task of noting down numbers. But the data for the weights and sizes of the cloth samples began to look like a comedy of errors, although the gravity of the matter stops us from actually laughing. First Riggi claimed that the strip removed from the cloth was 7×1 cm. In his talk at the Paris symposium he gave the weight for the complete cloth piece removed first as 497 mg and then 540 mg.[29] Reading the weight off the balance in the video recording the figure is 478.1 mg. Three different results!

This piece was cut into two halves of about the same size. One of them, according to the textile expert Testore who placed it on the precision balance after it was removed, weighed 144.8 mg. Riggi gave its weight as 141 mg. This piece with the two different weights was kept back and is probably still in Riggi's possession now. ('The Cardinal will see what he will do with it,' was Riggi's terse remark.[30] This too is extremely odd; how is it that a private person was given a piece of the relic? The second piece weighed

154.9 mg according to Testore and was divided into three pieces of about the same size, with weights of 52.0, 52.8 and 53.7 mg.[31] Riggi proudly said that all three pieces cut weighed almost exactly 53 mg.[32] (Teddy Hall was later to report that the pieces had all weighed about 43 mg.) One only has to make the effort to add up the weights given, to obtain a total weight of 158.5 mg. Again the numbers given do not tally.

Confronted with these inconsistencies, Testore and Riggi changed the version they had once given and suddenly claimed that not the larger but the smaller piece was used for the three experimental samples. This statement is even more perplexing, since every laboratory was supposed to have received a sample of about 50 mg. That was simply impossible starting with a piece of 144.8 mg (Testore) or 141 mg (Riggi)! Now Testore says that what happened was as follows: the smaller piece was cut into three parts, producing pieces of 52.0 mg, 52.8 mg and 39.6 mg. The third piece, understandably enough, turned out to be too narrow. So another fragment of 14.1 mg was taken from the second strip. Therefore one of the three laboratories must have received two pieces of the Shroud, which together weighed 53.7 mg. Riggi on the other hand sticks to the version that the three pieces for the laboratories were taken from the larger of the two strips. The third sample at 50.1 mg turned out rather less than the others, and therefore 3.6 mg of cloth was added from the strip which had been kept back.

At least now the confusion is complete. The laboratories were to be given about 50 mg, so the third sample was just right. Why should it be supplemented with a ridiculous 3.6 mg? Obviously the addition only took place in Riggi's imagination, in order to make the figures given tally. But who is giving us the right version, Riggi or Testore? Or are both statements perhaps incorrect?

If we reconstruct the original complete piece from the two strips which provided the samples for the laboratories and the 'reserve piece', then we get 154.9 mg plus 144.8 mg (using the 'higher' weight values), which together make a total weight of 299.7 mg. But the balance showed 478.1 mg, almost twice as much! Can one be so far off?

Testore, again differing from Riggi's statement, says that the freshly removed portion of the relic had measured about 8.1 × 1.6 cm, which makes 13.0 cm^2. From the precise examination of 1978 we know the density of the cloth: it is 23 mg/cm². Thus for 13 cm² we can calculate a weight of 299 mg, again much less than the balance shows. Riggi claims that the cloth piece was reduced slightly. He lifted it with tweezers and triumphantly showed it to the representatives of the laboratories. Then he pulled out a loose thread and cut straight the rather frayed edge. These remnants were put in a separate container. The piece, thus tidied up, had according to Riggi a size of 7 × 1 cm and weighed exactly 300 mg. To reduce a piece with the dimensions 8.1 × 1.6 cm to 7 × 1 cm, Riggi would have had to remove almost half of it. No one claimed they did this, nor was it done. If we consider the density of the cloth again, we see that the 'Riggi sample' cannot possibly have weighed 300 mg; it must have been about 161 mg, again only about half. The weight data show such obvious discrepancies between actual and alleged values, that the authors Orazio Petrosillo and Emanuela Marinelli ask whether the piece which ended up on the balance came from the Turin cloth at all.[33]

Because of the massive inconsistencies in the weights and sizes of the samples, Karl Herbst contacted Riggi. In his letter of 26 February 1990, which he has kindly placed at our disposal along with Riggi's reply, Herbst formulated a series of questions. Riggi dismissed them all with the remark that he did not know who Mr Herbst was, nor what he wanted to use the information for, and referred to the more that 30 eyewitnesses. 'I do not want' he wrote on 6 April 1990, 'conflicting private statements which could lead to more useless polemics in this case, such as we have already had following a letter from France very similar to this document, which I thought I would generously reply to. To conclude then, considering how private replies can lead to many angry polemics, would you take your questions in this letter to persons who are more qualified than myself, for example to those responsible for the sampling operation.'

Herbst commented: 'Obviously nobody is more qualified to give information in this case than the man who wielded the scissors. So someone has forbidden Mr Riggi to tell the truth; someone on whom he depends. Naturally there would be no more effective way to put an end to the "strong polemics about the sampling", than to state the truth.'

After the experiment the investigators constantly made clear that the whole thing had proceeded in a correct and proper fashion. But they watched as bit by bit the evidence began to erode the foundations of their test. More and more inconsistencies came to light, more lies and constant new evidence. The way Willy Wölfli put his view in an article in *Die Welt* sounds like a form of incantation: 'I have always considered this declaration of the radiocarbon results to be the final end to the discussion about the authenticity of the Turin Shroud, because there is no doubt that the correct samples of cloth were tested and the measurements were provably undertaken correctly according to plan. Various control mechanisms ensured this.' He studiously avoids revealing what control mechanisms he was thinking of, as they were non-existent. They had been systematically eliminated long before in the early phases.

Even in the case of the supposedly solid documentation to record the sampling, the Vatican had taken precautions. Riggi reported that there was a complete video documentation of the whole sampling procedure. This arrangement would satisfy even the sceptics. On the film one would openly be able to see which piece was removed from the cloth. But what they did not mention was the scandalous incompleteness of this documentation. The removal of the cloth piece is indeed to be seen on the video tape. But during the most crucial phase when Tite disappeared with Ballestrero and Gonella into the sacristy, to distribute the test and control samples among the containers, the cameras remained switched off. Why undertake the whole outlay for the documentation if the most important part was left out? The argument that they wanted to perform the test 'blind', with even the film crew not knowing which cloth samples were put into which containers, is not acceptable. The whole show was never a blind test. The scientists knew the Shroud very well from macro-photographs, and those who had not seen them could inspect it at their leisure in Turin. Everyone could immediately identify the cloth sample. Therefore not only *should* the video documentation have been complete, simply to avoid violating the test protocol, it *had* to be, to remove all doubt. What fine 'control mechanisms' these are. They become a source of mistrust rather than control. The fact that no pictures were taken in the sacristy casts serious doubt on the whole affair. Everything suggests that this part was intentionally omitted to make a manipulation possible. In this half hour it was possible to take a carefully selected, similar piece of fabric and make it look the same as the original cloth samples by trimming and weighing.

Similarly no verbal protocol on tape, or written record, was made of the events on that notable day. Were the months and years of preparation all to lead to such an amateur procedure? Unthinkable! The omissions can only be understood as well-planned actions.

The dating scientists made light of such details. The speech of Prof Hall of 15 February 1989 in London is an object lesson in academic arrogance. The Oxford scientist started by saying that anyone who still clung to the authenticity of the Turin cloth was 'pathological' and 'automatically prejudiced'. He was going to 'shoot dead' (sic) the critics of the carbon dating. In his lecture he took a typical swing at scientific anomalies and so tried to push the cloth in the direction of parascience, to make it easier to discredit. Of course, he told the audience, even as long ago as 21 April 1988 when he saw the linen for the first time, he saw at once that it was 'too good to be true'. In his lecture he said all the 'certain facts' about the history of the Turin cloth were wrong. For him all the scientific investigations were of no value except the carbon test. He dismissed the medical evidence about the linen out of hand. One has to read Hall's actual words to see how he stamps all those who think differently as idiots: 'There will be some flat-earthers who won't accept this. They're onto a loser. Anyone can take refuge in a miracle.'

Such a scientist, who does such messy research, who ignores the actual history of the object of study in this way, who without being an expert in the field of textiles simply says that the linen is too good to be true, who offends a whole crowd of research colleagues because they have arrived at different results hardly inspires confidence. Who is 'automatically prejudiced' if not Hall himself?

In the article we have referred to, Wölfli stressed the orderly work of the scientists, and the special agreement 'that the three institutes would not communicate among themselves before the complete results were given to the British Museum. This agreement was strictly adhered to.' As this article was being published, it was already known that contact between the laboratories had taken place before all the results had been submitted.[34] Yet Wölfli still made these statements to convince the public that everything proceeded in an orderly fashion. Even the rejected Gove and his scheming famulus Sox were allowed to look over the shoulders of Damon and Donahue in Tucson while they worked! For Sox, the chronicler of the 'radiocarbon Mafia', this was a great privilege. When on 13 October 1988 the results of the dating were officially released by the Vatican, his paperback, *The Shroud Unmasked – Uncovering the Greatest Forgery of All Times*, was already being sold in Britain. The freshly announced results had long been printed in David Sox' book. .... But no one admitted to knowing anything about it, no one told anyone anything. Perhaps Sox received a heavenly revelation, like a certain Richard Luckett, who also announced the result long before the official statement, in the *Evening Standard*.

By asking around we were able to locate Richard Luckett. He is a librarian at the Pepys Library of Magdalene College in Cambridge. In a letter dated 18 September 1989, he told us how he had studied the Shroud a little in connection with his doctoral thesis, but had lost interest after learning that the Savoy family themselves did not believe it was genuine. He was asked by his friend Christopher Hudson of the *Evening Standard* to write a short article about the cloth. All he had to do was draw on gossip overheard in Cambridge during common conversation. 'I was amazed to learn that my article was news, because in Cambridge it seemed to be general knowledge that the carbon dating had confirmed the medieval hypothesis. I heard about it purely by chance. It would be a pointless embarrassment for me to say from whom, but I can say that this person had no connection with Oxford or with Arizona and only an indirect (but important) connection with Zurich.' Zurich of all places, where the 'decent fellows' were sitting silently! Indeed the C-14 stars were so silent that for a long time they let the fourth sample – threads of the cope in Saint-Maximin – go by the board.

Masks of the Conspirators

To reconstruct the events at the sampling we have to rely on eyewitness reports, and these are very unreliable. The video film is no great help either, for everything suggests it was only ordered to provide an alibi. Riggi, who keeps the film as well as the countless photos of 21 April 1988, has it under lock and key. If scientists or journalists want to view it, then an edited version is offered. When we wished to view the complete film, to study the exact course of events and perhaps find out the exact period of time for which Tite disappeared into the sacristy with the Cardinal and Gonella, a few selected sequences chosen by Riggi were all that could be seen, despite his earlier assurances.

Questioning the scientists was a sobering experience. Defective observations were compounded by false statements. The reports of the eyewitnesses differ considerably among themselves and in many details are simply wrong. Thus it was officially claimed that Tite was alone with the Cardinal for the sample distribution in the sacristy. From another source one learns that Riggi and Gonella were also present.[35] Checking with Riggi we confirmed that Tite, the Cardinal and Gonella, but not Riggi, were in the sacristy! Riggi did forbid us to publish his letter, however. We were only allowed to keep to the 'official documents', which 'come from the sole authorized and guaranteed sources'. In the course of our inquiries it has become all too clear what was to be made of these official 'guaranteed' sources. Instead of bringing clarity to the affair, Riggi only adds further mystification.

One thing at least is clear to anyone who knows the facts: a deception took place on the scale of a regular conspiracy. Of course one has to make the effort to untangle all the threads, including those of history and exegesis, to provide the proof for Jesus' survival of the Crucifixion, otherwise the conspiracy theory is unconvincing. No plausible motive would be found.

Depending on one's professional affiliations and world-view, the blame for devious deeds will be put on one or other of the 'traditional' opposing groups. Classical groups targeted here are Freemasons, Jews and Jesuits. Whenever there is something inexplicable and of great significance to make people excited, it is not long before some voices are heard trying to pin the blame on one of these groups. The 'bad guys' are always the secret men behind the scenes, giving orders under cover of darkness. As soon as the first slanders of this nature are heard, we usually have an unmistakable sign that the accusers are at their wits' end and are trying to conjure up a scapegoat.

The question of manipulation was the topic of a short television interview with the German sindonologist Professor Werner Bulst SJ, which was broadcast on German television over Easter in 1990. The reason for the interview was the publication of Bulst's new book *Betrug am Turiner Grabtuch – Der manipulierte Carbontest* ('Fraud Against the Turin Shroud – the Manipulated Carbon Test').

The Professor had already spoken directly about fraud at the Bologna conference in 1989, in his speech before Shroud researchers from all over the world, although without hinting at the possible perpetrator. We received no reply to our written query to Bulst about who he thought was behind it. On television he was unable to avoid the same question: he did not know, he said with a meaningful look, who was really behind the Shroud swindle, but there was mention of a 'Masonic anti-Catholic' conspiracy. Historically the Freemasons represented the traditional conspiracy group for the Jesuit Bulst.

It was the way he said it that gave his words their effect. Everyone was to think that Prof Bulst secretly knew exactly who the wicked deceivers were, for he had already found out their motive: a blow was to be directed at the Christian Faith. But as is usually the case with secret conspiracies, he could not simply come out with it in public. So he was cautious. After all he could be in danger of a strike by the opposition. When it comes to conspiracies, half-concealed slander is used by all parties.

Doubtless he meant the participating scientists, hatching their plot under secret orders. For him the radiocarbon dating was a model example of the infamous working of devilish dark powers, who do everything they can to try and oppose the benevolent, light-bringing work of the divine Christ. The sole existing piece of evidence for the historical Jesus was to be destroyed in a lightning blow.

Let us now seriously ask the question who could really be behind such a monstrous deception. What reason could the Freemasons have had for staging such a thing? Even if we take the widely held (though incorrect) view that the Masons are an anti-Christian secret society combating ignorance, the ones who really hold the reins of world politics. Would the Masons, first among them our 'master Freemason' Tite, have staged the deceptive dating just to damage the Church? I think the effect a group of such convictions would achieve would be quite small.

The dubious carbon dating does not disturb anyone's faith in Jesus. If this was what the mysterious Freemasons were aiming at, one would just have to laugh at their folly. In any case these speculations depend on a common misconception about the Masons. They certainly do not seem to be the right group with sufficient motive to enact this scandal.

Who then could it be? First there are the scientists themselves, rather dubious, impenetrable figures like Gonella, the scientific aide to the Turin Cardinal, whose true role was never quite clear to anyone. Then Riggi, who gave totally false information about the cloth piece he cut off; at first confidently busy with white gloves, but then, curiously enough, taking them off when he actually cut the strip off. Then we have Tite, smiling triumphantly and mischievously about the test result; monolithic guarantor for the entire experiment, who has since settled comfortably to a new living at the Oxford Radiocarbon Accelerator Unit. Teddy Hall, who dismisses all those who differ with the crude language of the arrogant know-all. Vial, the lackey of Tite and procurer of the suspicious fourth sample. Wölfli and Damon, who wanted to make their mark with the dating. The rejected Gove, who had felt sure of gaining fame from a place on the test team, hoping to join with the proselyte Sox in the battle against the sindonologists, making himself heard behind the scenes.

Motives can certainly be found here. But how is one to picture this conspiracy of laurelled heads? Was it the isolated action of one black sheep or a collective plot? Any international intrigue would have led to the problem of keeping a horde of accomplices quiet. Just think of it: reputed scientists, who are recognized authorities in their fields, mostly upright citizens, with a reputation, a career and a regular income to lose – would they have exposed themselves to such a risk? And why? Their fame was secured. If the cloth had been dated to the first century AD, the controversy would have been no less acute. They would probably have had more attacks from their researcher colleagues to fend off, but they would certainly have been the heroes of one camp, and at least they would have been the ones privileged to perform the definitive test of Christianity's most controversial relic.

It is true that scientists are by no means above all suspicion in these matters. There is a long history of deception in the sciences. There always lurks the temptation of quick fame and lasting respect. Every student knows, for example, that statistical data and measurements which obstinately resist the proposed hypothesis can all too often be made compliant by a few sleights of hand at ground level. As chance would have it, at the time when Prof Hall gave his farewell lecture the British Museum was holding a large exhibition called 'Fake: The Art of Deception'. The exhibition included great deceptions in science, such as the infamous Piltdown Man case. At the entrance to the showrooms a slide of the Turin cloth was presented life size. Tite allowed himself this triumph as he turned his back on the museum.

Nevertheless, it is difficult to imagine that a large number of researchers could be involved in what turned out to be such a clumsy manipulation, with such an important assignment which was to take place under the watchful eyes of a whole crowd of sindonologists. Considering these points, we are left with just one option: a few individuals planned the deception and the others just carried it out unsuspectingly.

In our search for the men pulling the strings, we have long been clear about one thing: it must have been the ones who commissioned the experiment, those men in the background at the Vatican, who planned the sensational undertaking. We realize that the idea will look absurd to anyone who does not know our reasoning. Surely in these times, when such store is set by the pronouncements of science, the Church would be especially keen to have tangible proof of the life and Passion of Jesus. But as it turned out the previous scientific analysis of the cloth had undermined the popular idea of Jesus' death. Taken in combination with a precise study of the Biblical and apocryphal texts, it left hardly any doubt that Jesus survived the Crucifixion. Now it was the Vatican alone which had a very strong motive for withdrawing the Church's most important relic from the public eye. The revered and closely guarded shrine had suddenly changed in their eyes, and become a Trojan horse, a timebomb on a church altar behind toughened glass. Some day the bomb would go off and threaten the foundations of institutional Christianity. Evidently the Church had a serious problem. And it still has, especially now.

Investigations by a French 'Detective'

Let us see what form the Church's new problem has taken since the deception.

The French Shroud researcher Bruno Bonnet-Eymard has examined the many inconsistencies during the sampling, and the weights and sizes, together with a fellow brother of the Catholic Counter-Reformation, the 'International Priestly Brotherhood of St Pius X' of the famous Archbishop Lefebvre. While Testore and Riggi each offer a completely different version about the appearance of the main cloth sample and the way it was divided up (the individual weights), they at least agreed on one thing: one of the laboratories was given two pieces of the Turin cloth. Surely this was verifiable. Brother Bruno and his unnamed colleague[36] set out to find which laboratory had received a test sample in two parts. The physicist Donahue of the Tucson team gave the French questioners the following details. He said that at their laboratory they had immediately subdivided the cloth piece into four parts. The total weight was 52.36 mg. There was nothing in their notes about the Shroud sample coming in two pieces. Donahue reacted evasively on the telephone to the request for more details, and ten months after this no reply had come to the same request in writing. On 26 October 1990 Bonnet-Eymard and his colleague flew to Tucson.

There they discovered an odd story. They met with Donahue and his colleague Jull, who had also figured as an author of the *Nature* article. Neither could remember whether the Turin cloth sample consisted of one part or two. In any case there were certainly no photographs or other records of the opening of the containers, Donahue stressed repeatedly. The chemist Toolin, who had signed a paper along with Damon, Donahue and Jull to witness the proper opening of the container, appeared in the office by chance and turning to the Frenchmen said, 'In my opinion it consisted of a single piece.' But Donahue cut in and again stressed that there were no records.

The following day our bold 'detectives' visited Damon, the Quaker as they like to emphasize. He told quite a different tale. Only he and Donahue had opened the seal; neither Jull nor Toolin was present. The opening took place on a Sunday, and their two colleagues only arrived on the Monday. Damon said, 'We set about examining all the samples under the microscope and photographing them.' When questioned about the photographs he added that had they not only taken photographs, but a local television company had recorded everything on film; they had also cut off a piece of the Turin cloth and kept it separate – like Wölfli, to 'be able to show it in the event of a complaint by the ecclesiastical authorities'. So on one hand there were reported to be no records at all, on the other hand, photographs and television film! First there were said to be four witnesses to the opening of the container, then two contradictory witnesses. All this was disturbing and confirmed Brother Bruno and his companion in their suspicions that something had gone wrong.

Their second destination was Zurich and the ETH. The first point they raised was the impossible figure given in the *Nature* article for the size of the main cloth sample, 7×1 cm. Donahue had simply brushed them off with the remark that Tite had measured it exactly. Later Tite told them that he had not measured anything; they had all just relied on Riggi's information. Obviously it was wrong. The cloth piece must have been considerably larger, about 8×1.8 cm. Wölfli admitted that after lengthy discussions among themselves they had come to an agreement about this 'problem'. Throughout this period they had left the queries about it, by Bonnet-Eymard and others, unanswered. Actually they were arguing for weeks behind the scenes to find a 'clean' explanation for the glaring error. An embarrassed Wölfli said, 'Well yes we were under pressure because the article for *Nature* had to go to the printers in February 1989. We did not take the time to check. In the article Tite gave the dimensions which we had agreed on in January 1988 during a discussion in London.' One really had to hear Wölfli's highly embarrassed tone as he gave this explanation, the authors write.

Embarrassing this disclosure certainly was. The exact size of the cloth piece had been fixed three months before it was actually removed – so fixed that Riggi had to stick to it even though he knew he had cut off quite a different size; so fixed, that Tite recorded it in the article. Of course the size was fixed: Tite needed to have the substitute piece ready and obviously would know its measurements.

The story of the two-part sample also appears to have been a cause of concern to the radiocarbon experts. They talked about it at a meeting in Paris during an AMS conference in April 1990. No two-part sample had turned up in Oxford or in Zurich. In Paris, according to Wölfli, Jull admitted that they had been sent the two part sample in Arizona! Why had he not said that to brother Bruno?

The Frenchmen then visited Oxford to talk to Tite. He told them that Hall had already cleared his office and taken his entire archives with him. The figures for the size of the main sample were only an approximation, Tite claimed – a strange approximation which is out by 50 per cent! He shoved the whole problem on to the Italians; they were responsible for the sampling, not him. He was only present in Turin as a 'simple witness'. Now we can see the effect of doing away with the supervisory institutions. The sole 'overseer' Tite was able to push the responsibility on to others' shoulders with impunity. But there was one fact he must have noticed when he put the fragments into the containers in the sacristy: one of them was in two parts. Tite's reply here is typical of many of the answers given by the carbon daters, not only to Bonnet-Eymard, but also to us: 'I can no longer remember.' Astonishing. The man had wrapped the test pieces individually in small sheets of foil and then packed them in the tubes, yet cannot remember that one of the samples came in two sections.

Shortly after this Bonnet-Eymard and his colleague phoned Damon in Arizona. He told them that the photographs had finally been found. Donahue's wife had taken them on the Sunday when the containers were opened. They had ended up in a family album. Asked whether they showed one or two pieces, Damon was very unsettled and replied, 'No, we divided the piece into, er . . . into . . . er . . . er . . . several parts. We have the photographs of this operation.' And, even more unsettled, he added that there were no records on video; they were only made on the Monday, but at the removal itself only he, Donahue and Jull were present, and they had taken poor photographs.

Donahue confirmed the discovery of the photographs and added that they showed that the Shroud sample had come in two parts (see Plate 63). This conjuring up of the second piece was necessary, concluded our French 'detective', because they could not longer support Tite's version and so they had to come to an agreement about Testore's.

Abbé Georges de Nantes, also of the Catholic Counter-

Reformation, explains in his description of the manipulation[37] that the laboratories did have pieces of the Shroud, but they only served as control samples. His reconstruction looks like this.

In the mid-1980s Tite had a number of cloth fragments dated by several laboratories, with the specific aim of designing a procedure for dating the Turin linen.[38] These included a Sample Nr 3, whose age was uncertain; the laboratories dated the cloth with '95 per cent confidence' to 1289–1438. This cloth was especially well suited to be a substitute for the Shroud. It was already dated, was accessible for the British Museum and had an age which was compatible with the one 'desired'. Tite knew from Wilson's book that the first public exposition of the Turin cloth had taken place in 1350. Therefore he wanted to find a 'control sample' from this period. His letter to Jacques Evin of 12 February 1988 proves this. He asked his French radiocarbon colleague to find a piece of textile for comparison, about 6 cm², or 120 mg of linen from the thirteenth or fourteenth century, preferably the fourteenth. Historical knowledge of the precise age was important, and he enclosed photographs of the Shroud weave, to make it easier to hunt out a piece as similar to it as possible. Evin found the right cloth in the cope of St Louis d'Anjou, but it was too late to send the secret envelope with the threads to Tite.

Tite left London for Turin, taking with him a 7 × 1 cm strip of the medieval cloth which had been dated between 1289 and 1438 as Sample 3. In Turin Vial appeared with the threads from the cope. Tite was angry and anxious because he had not been given the pieces before, and now he had already prepared the medieval pieces he had brought along. To avoid explanations, he just gave the laboratories the cope threads to use as Sample 4. He did a double switch in the privacy of the sacristy; in the tubes which were supposed to contain the Shroud, he placed pieces of the medieval sample he had brought with him. The fragments of the Turin cloth were also used; they ended up in the containers which were reserved for Sample 3, supposed to be the linen of an Egyptian mummy.

On 8 June the investigations in Arizona were completed, and the results sent to Tite. The dates were 'a little too recent'; some results suggested late fourteenth/early fifteenth century. That could not be right, because the Turin cloth must definitely have existed by about 1350. Then the results came in from Zurich. They were a bit older, but still not convincing enough to prove the 'correct' date for Tite. To be quite sure, he recommended that Hall, who had waited until last with his measurements, mix in some threads of the cope of St Louis, whose date was just right. The Oxford results were then noticeably 'older' than those of Zurich and especially those of Arizona. With the average value of the three laboratories Tite was able to keep to the 'correct' date. For the cloth sample of the 'mummy', with '95 per cent confidence', a date of origin of 9 BC – 78 AD was obtained. The mummy was a certain Cleopatra, who died at the age of eleven at the time of Hadrian's rule (117–38 AD). Strange, that the shroud she was wrapped in was apparently 100 years old! But in fact the fragment did not belong to the mummy at all, but to the Turin cloth, and the latter was dated precisely.

So runs the explanation of Abbé Georges de Nantes. His thesis is certainly interesting, and contains many elements which warrant further investigation. But what we really miss in the whole analysis is the motive. He makes Tite the villain who was in league with Hall, and would like to leave the responsibility for the whole drama with him alone. Zurich was tolerated because it had come off so badly in the earlier dating attempt and was therefore manipulable, and Arizona was far away. But the Counter-Reformers have to acknowledge that the Vatican stood behind the conspiracy; there is simply no denying it. However they cannot provide the reason. The operation they discovered hangs in the air, inexplicable, without reason or purpose.

Chronology of the Untold Events

We have gone to some length to explain why the Vatican felt it was so desperately urgent to have the Shroud removed from circulation in this way. We have also carried out intensive investigations to find out just how it was done, and so Georges de Nantes's version is in need of revision.

The alleged pieces of the Shroud which arrived at the institutions did not really come from the Turin cloth; the comparative computer analysis has clearly shown this. However, that does not mean that the switching of the relic samples to the containers meant for the Cleopatra mummy did not take place. The brothers of the Counter-Reformation suppose that the textiles given out as Shroud on the laboratories' photographs actually came from the container with the supposed mummy cloth and were included in the statistics as Sample 3. But since the comparative analysis has shown that these cloth pieces are not the same as the cloth piece that was cut off in Turin, it is superfluous to discuss whether the Turin linen was dated as the control sample; it was not. In the No 1 containers there were indeed pieces of linen in twill weave bearing a close similarity to the Turin cloth. But they were only similar, not identical.

The exchange can only have been done in the sacristy. Prof Hall assured me in a letter of 19 April 1989 'that no dishonesty could occur during the period from the removal of the sample from the linen and handing out the containers to the participating laboratories. Dr Tite was present throughout the whole procedure and the lab representatives for 90 per sent of this time. I assure you that you are wasting your time (and that of others) if this is what you mean.' This is a worthless assurance, because it is precisely the fact that Dr Tite was the sole witness which is the decisive point. It is the same Michael Tite who says he can not remember anything, neither the appearance of the cloth samples nor whether he signed a document with the Cardinal expressly guaranteeing that the samples came from the Turin Shroud; who gave flagrantly wrong measurement data in the *Nature* article; who for a long time deliberately left the inclusion of Sample 4 unmentioned; who first lent support to the fantasy of a 'blind test'; who took his supervisory function so lightly that he allowed communication between the laboratories. From the forensic standpoint, one could hardly find a worse referee. It was with this man that the Cardinal disappeared in the sacristy, with the public excluded; Cardinal Anastasio Ballestrero, who was allowed his last great appearance in the dating drama before being sent off into retirement; who, long before the results were announced, declared on television that he had never believed it was authentic anyway; who actually said it would not matter at all if the cloth were shown to be a forgery 'from the Middle Ages', as if he had long known in what period the 'forgery' was going to be dated (a 'forgery' could also have originated in the third, fourth or some other century before the Middle Ages). Also in the group was

Luigi Gonella, the Cardinal's mouthpiece, as interpreter they said. But what was there to translate, with a few pieces of cloth just being packed in little tubes? Gonella is the alibi, the door-keeper, who did not see the procedure from close up at all, other-wise he would have said later in his dozens of rambling lectures that he had seen exactly that the whole procedure was correctly performed. He said nothing of the sort, because he had seen nothing; the sacristy is a large room.

But how did Tite obtain the substitute pieces? Here we have to take another look at the radiocarbon dating results.

A glance at Figure 1 (p. 75) shows the surprising and highly significant way the figures for Samples 1 (supposed Shroud) and 4 (cope of St Louis) match each other. The agreement is so striking that some authors (Marinelli and Petrosillo) have spoken of a 'twin piece'. In fact the dates found for Samples 1 and 4 differed more between the laboratories than within each laboratory. This suggests that we may be dealing with samples of identical material.

I have already described my investigations in connection with the cope in Saint-Maximin in Part 1. It was a strange 'ambush commando' which appeared there on the morning of 12 April 1988 – official bulldozering under the direction of Gabriel Vial and Abbé Boyer of the Laboratoire de Conservation, Restauration et Recherches of the Centre National de la Recherche Scientifique in Draguignan. Abbé Weber, the custodian of the Sainte Marie Madeleine basilica, was appalled at the way the surprise attack happened. It was carried out under the direction of Boyer, a 'scientifique' or a 'scientist written with a very, very small "s"'', as Weber sarcastically put it. The department obtained the mayor's sanction, had the cabinet opened and removed threads from the cope. They had chosen a day on which Abbé Weber was away. I asked the priest if anyone could have known that he would not be there that day. His reply was: 'Someone who knew my habits could certainly have known in advance.' Obviously they had found out and wished to by-pass him. At the time when the commission approached the mayor there was no mention of an immediate operation to take the threads. As Abbé Weber told me in a letter dated 2 March 1990, 'The scientists told me about their visit to the mayor to show him how they planned to take the threads and ask for his authorization. The letter gives the im-pression that they had a later date in mind.' Thus the mayor too was taken by surprise. 'As usual,' the embittered Weber continues in his letter, 'the Curé was not contacted by the scientists. It was a case of a classified object owned by the district council; these people simply ignored the statutes of 9 December 1905 and 2 January 1907 which state that the churches and their contents are excepted from the collective ownership, are juristically distinct, and the curés are the proper administrators and legal authorities for them.'

When Abbé Weber came back unexpectedly, he found that the strange 'commission' had already finished their work. He was horrified at the underhand operation and demanded that they open the sealed envelope, which had immediately caught his eye. Abbé Boyer tried to appease him, telling him not to make a fuss, and two others who were with him assured him that it was only 'about five or six threads each 5 cm in length'. 'I snatched the envelope,' Weber wrote, 'it was almost empty. I thought it could not contain more than a few threads, and I found that acceptable.'

So the strange commission had apparently taken only a few threads. In Turin this sample was divided into four equal amounts. Vial kept one portion, the others were given to the three laboratories as Sample 4. The threads must have been divided into quite similar portions. Hall in Oxford measured 69.7 mg for his set of threads, and Wölfli in Zurich 68.8 mg. In Paris Vial spoke of about 200 mg of threads, divided up in this way. That means the original quantity of threads from the cope must have come to nearly 300 mg. The weight of five or six threads 5 cm long is about 20 mg, and would not even suffice to supply the 68.8 mg of the Zurich sample. How did the marvel of the multiplication of threads come about? This considerably larger quantity (about fifteen-fold) would certainly have been noticed by Abbé Weber when he checked the envelope.

The answer can only be that one of Tite's assistants already possessed a larger quantity of the Saint-Maximin fabric, and made it available to him. The most obvious person for this would be Gabriel Vial. As Technical Secretary of the Centre International d'Études des Textiles Anciens at the Musée de Tissues in Lyons, he had free access to the most important cloth archives in France. All our attempts to find out from the museum whether cloth pieces of the cope from one of the earlier restorations had ended up there, failed, but finally we had some success. Although no one made the effort to look through the archives, they all referred us every time to Gabriel Vial. Obviously he is known as the expert on the cope, and consequently his name was mentioned in connection with it.

The cope was restored for the first time as long ago as the 1930s. In the course of this work the original lining material was obviously removed and replaced with a modern one. As we learned from the second restorer, Mme Classen-Smith, the usual policy was to hand over any original samples to the Ministry for Historical Monuments in Paris. When I visited Mme Maître-Devallon at the Ministry in 1989, she said there was in fact a file on the cope; but during her search in the archives she was no longer able to locate it. I contacted her predecessors, M. Feray, and Mme Odile Bordaz, Curator at the Musée de Gers. But they too were unable to help me further. It was not possible for me to look for the lost documents in the archives on that occasion, and I returned to Paris in February 1992.

In the meantime Mme Maître-Devallon had retired, and her young lady successor turned out to be very helpful. We searched together in the catalogue for the reference number, and we found the thick file in the archive with the reference 3042/3. 1494. In this file everything that had happened in connection with the cope over the past 150 years was recorded. For example there were all the documents about the preparation of the display cabinet with the heavy iron grille in 1921. Thorough records were kept of every detail, from the first sketch, through construction plans, to the invoice. But there was not a whisper about the major restoration in 1965. The staff at the Ministry found this circumstance most unusual and remarkable. Someone or other must have surreptitiously removed these documents. Finally I went to try my luck in the library of the Ministry of Culture.

The inspector, M. Bruno Mottin, had kindly collected the relevant documents from the archives before I arrived. Together we flicked through them to look for references to the restoration. Again the same result: not a single reference to be found! Now the inspector was also convinced that someone must have systematically destroyed all the papers which could have given a clue to the whereabouts of the lining material.

We wanted to know what is normally done with 'remnants' left from the restoration of cultural articles. Mme Maître-Devallon told us that they would normally go back to the owner or be made available to research institutions which were interested. One person who might have a special interest in the cope, she said at the end, was a certain Gabriel Vial in Lyons. The last piece of the puzzle had fallen into place.

Vial's knowledge of the Turin cloth as a textile was practically second to none. He had studied it in depth and published a detailed specialist article about it. It appears that he must have had access to the Turin cloth long before, when the carbon dating was being planned. I talked about this with Prof Raes, because much of the information Vial gave seemed inconsistent. Prof Raes, who had himself become concerned about the goings on at the dating test, decided to pass on information given to him in confidence, because he thought it could play an important role in exposing the truth.

In a letter of 16 November 1989 he gave me some interesting news. 'Since the Paris meeting I have received some information about the piece which I sent back in 1976. Riggi told me they had found a large percentage of amides [sugar] on my piece. That was not the case on the Riggi sample.' By 'Riggi sample' Raes means the half of the main Shroud sample which Riggi had kept back when he gave out the others to the dating laboratories. Raes had sent back his own sample of the Turin cloth in November 1976. Obviously it had come into Riggi's possession, via various routes or stops, as he admitted at our conversation in Turin. It was then that Riggi had made the strangely cryptic remark, suddenly cut short, that he did have a part of the Raes sample but it was not useable. What had happened to the piece to make it unuseable? Did it have something to do with the surprising concentration of sugar in the fibres? Raes never treated his sample with chemicals, which could possibly have explained the concentration of sugar. 'That shows,' Raes continued in his letter, 'that the sample which I sent back to Turin was not just stored away. This was also confirmed by my correspondence with Prof Vial.' Vial again! What did he have to do with it? Gabriel Vial, it suddenly turned out, also had access to the Raes cloth sample.

Prof Raes let us have the letter which Gabriel Vial had written to him on 29 September 1989. One should note here that Raes would never have passed on this personal and confidential letter if he were not himself convinced that the carbon test was manipulated and Vial had possibly played a key part in the affair. In his letter Vial writes:

> I will tell you – in strict confidence – that in order to find this out exactly [whether cotton threads were present among the fibres or only on the surface], I removed some threads from the fragments which you analysed in 1973. I had them examined at the Institut Textile de France in Lyons . . . Because I removed the threads outside the course of the programme, Gonella, Riggi and Testore asked me not to mention them in my report, and I complied.'

So Vial had had a genuine piece of the Turin cloth to examine; therefore he knew exactly what it looked like and was well prepared when it came to finding a comparable textile from the Middle Ages. If he had only removed a few threads, it is certain that the quite substantial Raes sample (about 4 × 1.3 cm) would still have been useable. But Riggi spoke of 'fragments', and these had become unuseable. In his letter Raes refers to the assumption, which he had heard from various sources, that the secret C-14 dating in California which we have mentioned, may have been done on a thread from 'his' cloth sample. If only one thread was taken for this, and Vial only removed a few threads, it is still not clear why there were only some unuseable fragments left. Raes says, 'If tests really were carried out in the USA on threads that came from my piece, they must have been passed on by Riggi or by Vial.'

Perhaps the secret tests in the USA were not the only investigations done on the piece. Would there not have been a strong temptation to date a part of the Raes sample secretly? Perhaps this was even ordered before the official dating to provide certainty. Vial numbers several radiocarbon specialists among his friends, such as Jacques Evin, director of the Laboratoire de Radiocarbon at the University of Lyons.

Let us then sketch the following hypothetical scenario. Tite asked Evin in his letter of 12 February 1988 to find a 'medieval control sample which is as similar as possible to the Shroud in type of weave and colour'. Evin conferred with Vial. He did not have to search long. In 'his' museum in Lyons there were metre-long threads and whole pieces of cloth from the cope, remnants from the restoration work. Tite was informed that the desired cloth has been found. Using the threads, a cloth was woven in the

3:1 twill weave on a small test loom in the institute (assuming that the old lining was not already in this weave). Vial knew the Turin cloth well enough to have the 'control sample' made as similar as possible. For some unknown reason it must have leaked out that parts of the cloth of the cope of St Louis were in Vial's institute and were obviously to be used for the important radiocarbon test of the Turin cloth. Now the cloth could no longer be slipped to Tite and Turin, and it had to be made 'official' in some way. Therefore it was necessary to remove threads from the cope in public, with a large contingent, so that all could clearly see when the threads were collected and where they came from. Vial took the threads to Turin, where they were given out as the fourth sample. But there were a lot more threads than those removed in Saint Maximin. Vial had contributed the rest from his supply at the institute; he had plenty of them. The textile pieces Tite put in the containers meant for the Turin cloth really came from the pluvial of St Louis. No wonder Sample 1 turned out to be identical to Sample 4.

The people at the Vatican giving the orders had, they thought, now achieved their aim: the Turin cloth was dated as medieval by a neutral party. In this way they were able to put a stop to the discussions about Jesus surviving the Crucifixion.

It is ironic that Otlet, a member of the Harwell laboratory – one of those excluded from the test – was to prove correct in the letter of injured pride mentioned in Part I; 'someone in Italy is trying to obstruct the course of Science', and the reduction to three laboratories had as he had foreseen led 'to a scientific catastrophe'.

On 28 April 1989 the journalist Orazio Petrosillo accompanied Pope John Paul II on his journey to Madagascar. In the aircraft he had the chance to question him about various topics. Petrosillo, who was also convinced the dating was not right, asked for the Pope's opinion of the Turin cloth. The Pope's view was quite different from that of Cardinal Ballestrero. The cloth, the Holy Father told the reporter, was definitely a relic. To the question whether the linen was authentic, he replied, 'If it is a relic, then I think it is. If many think it is so, their conviction that they see an impression of the body of Christ on it, is not without cause.'[39] Does the Pope himself then not believe in the result of science? The talk with John Paul II was printed on 3 May 1989 in the Vatican's own journal *Osservatore Romano*. However, his clear opinion about the authenticity of the cloth was the one statement deleted. It is an incredible scandal that even the words of the Pope himself were censored. Is it too far-fetched to see in this behaviour the long arm of a 'Vatican guerrilla', someone who is also behind the radiocarbon dating drama, men in soutanes in the background, whose intentions and intrigues the Pope himself does not know?

Inquiries at the Vatican and the Archepiscopal Ordinariat in Turin are fruitless, like playing cricket in a heavy fog. On 2 October 1990 the Holy See sent us a terse reply to our inquiries about the cloth: although the cloth belongs to the Vatican, it is the Archbishop of Turin who is responsible for it. The secretary to the new Turin Bishop, Morello, told us on 16 March 1991 that they thought the conservation of the cloth was the most pressing problem. Only when this had been dealt with could one think about another exhibition. But there was no urgency at all to arrange further investigations: 'The Church, which is aware of the constant changes, developments and progress of the sciences, is in no hurry to arrive at results which one can never describe as definitive (and does not press for them). Since the Church bases individual faith solely on the "Revelation" and the message of Christ, and not on the value of relics, it does not find it necessary to check their authenticity.' It rather seems as if the cloth should slowly slip into oblivion. Allegedly the chapel of the Holy Shroud in Turin has been in danger of collapse. From 4 May 1990, the feast day of the Holy Shroud, it has remained closed indefinitely.

Part Five

AFTERWORD

'Now if Christ be preached that he rose from the dead, how say some among you that there is no resurrection of the dead? But if there be no resurrection of the dead, then is Christ not risen. And if Christ be not risen, then is our preaching vain, and your faith is also vain.' (1 Cor. 15:12–14). With these words Paul strongly reprimanded his contemporaries, who had great difficulty in following his idea of the salvation of humanity by the death of Jesus by crucifixion. Paul makes the whole purpose of Jesus' activity rest exclusively in this dying on the Cross. Here he has little interest in the words and teachings of Jesus, but he makes everything depend on his own teaching: the salvation from sins by the vicarious sacrificial death of Jesus.

Does it not seem most strange that Jesus himself did not give the slightest hint that he intended to save the entire faithful section of humanity by his death? If he concealed such an intention it would have been a deplorable and misleading act, and would go against the essential, highly ethical stand of Jesus and his love for mankind. Why did Jesus beg in his prayer in Gethsemane, 'Abba, Father, all things are possible unto thee; take away this cup from me: nevertheless not what I will, but what thou wilt' (Mark 14:36), if he intended his death to be the climax of his mission? And what sort of father would that be, who does not hear the imploring appeal of his 'only begotten Son'? As far back as 1917 the theologian E. Grimm wrote in his book *Die Ethik Jesu* ('The Ethics of Jesus') about the Pauline idea of Salvation, 'However much this teaching has become rooted among the Christians, the real Jesus knew nothing about it.' There is widespread agreement in theological research today that the tradition of the story of the empty tomb is historically older than the legend of the resurrected man. At first the report that the tomb of Jesus was empty circulated in the early communities, and only later did Paul tell the story of the miraculous Resurrection of the Lord. In his early accounts Paul only spoke of a revealing, a seeing or appearance of the 'Son of God'. Only afterwards did he formulate his theology of the resurrected man. In other words it is actually an interpretation which Paul puts at the centre of his teaching. It may be that Paul meant well, because it is quite conceivable that this man who, prior to his conversion, had been a fanatic zealot against the Christians, had come across Jesus in the large Essene community of Damascus, where he may have been staying incognito after his recovery. Damascus lay outside Roman jurisdiction, in Syria. Paul had obtained a special authorization from the high priest allowing him to persecute the followers of Jesus beyond the city walls of Jerusalem.

Paul, like the disciples, was convinced of the death of Jesus. The experience of the encounter and the ensuing existential upheaval may have reinforced the idea of a resurrection from the dead. The subsequent developments, however, no longer have anything to do with the message of Jesus.

Although there are several most delightful passages in the texts of Paul, Christianity has his narrow-minded fanaticism to thank for numerous detrimental developments, which are diametrically opposed to the spirit of Jesus: the intolerance towards those of different views (for example, Gal. 1:9; 1 Cor. 16:22; Tit 3:10), the marked hostility to the body and the consequently low view of woman (1 Cor. 6:18, 7:1–2, 7:38, 12:23, Gal. 5:17, Eph. 5:3–5; Col. 3:3, 5–6), and especially the fatally flawed attitude towards Nature (Col. 2:8; 1 Cor. 2:14; Eph. 5:19; Phil. 3:20).

According to Paul all are under the wrath of God from the start (Eph. 2:3) and are lost without exception (Rom. 15; 1 Cor. 15:18), all are without hope and without God (Eph. 2:12), for Satan has power over all (Rom. 3:9; Gal. 3:22; Col. 2:14). There is a judgement of damnation by God against everyone without exception (Rom. 5:16; cf also Rom. 8:1). This wrath of God (which also applies to new-born babes) can, according to Paul, only be averted by the death and the blood of Jesus, and only the death and the blood of Jesus can atone for the 'original guilt' (cf Col. 1:22 and Heb. 9:22): ' . . . and without shedding of blood is no remission'. By adopting this idea of the vicarious sacrifice of the first-born son, Paul slips back to the primitive culture of the prehistoric Semitic religion. He turns Jesus' teaching of Salvation upside down, and opposes his reforming ideas; instead of the original joyous tidings the Pauline message of threats was developed.

According to the teaching of Paul, the human individual is unable to attain Salvation and atonement before God by any good works of his own, or by any change however good (Rom. 3:24, 3:28, 9:11, 9:16; 1 Cor. 1:29; Gal. 2:16): 'For by grace are ye saved through faith; and that not of yourselves: it is the gift of God: Not of works, lest any man should boast.' Consequently the precondition for the action of God's Grace is the acceptance of the Pauline teaching on Grace; that means membership of the Church of Paul.

Based on Paul, the Christian churches today still teach that the Salvation of all was perfectly finished once and for all by the blood sacrifice of Jesus on the Cross, and that men would have absolutely nothing to contribute to it, apart from simply accepting this kind of Salvation in a single act of conversion (baptism). Nothing more is needed to reach the purpose and goal of life, for Jesus has already done all that is needful for us anyway, as our representative. This leads on to the idea that any attempt to participate in Salvation by one's own effort can be taken as a belittling of the service rendered by Jesus, and even as an original sin, as a futile attempt at self-salvation. According to this view anyone holding different beliefs, however exemplary the life he has led (such as Gandhi), is considered to be lost if he does not accept the Cross sacrifice for himself, in other words if he refuses to profess the Pauline Christianity.

Naturally it is an attractive and tempting offer, to be released from all responsibility for one's actions and the consequences of bad acts and thoughts, in a simple and comfortable way, by a few splashes of water. The ominous consequences of this form of Salvation doctrine finally lead to a kind of trade in indulgences, where the offender can count in advance on the annulment of his guilt before God and his conscience. Therefore even the worst misdemeanours against any fellow creatures have no consequence.

But this idea is completely alien to the teaching of Jesus. It was far from his mind, to form a hierarchical bureaucracy with laws and scriptural doctors, with belief in the letter of the law and arguments about interpretations, with cult and image worship, with 'churchianity' and claims to exclusive rights to bless. He wanted to preach the intimacy between the Divine and the human individual, and not self-aggrandising channels of official instances set up by self-righteous administrators of God. Jesus was certainly educated enough to be able to write his message himself, if he had considered it to be a valid method. But instead of this he presented his teaching by living it as an example: the renunciation of egoistic thinking and acting, unbiased care for all living beings, giving and sharing, the greatest possible tolerance towards people of other convictions, taking on the suffering of others and feeling compassion for them, in other words unlimited love in action for all fellow beings.

What we today refer to as Christianity is a misinterpretation and twisting by Paul of the true teaching of Jesus. Knowledge about this misinterpretation, and the doctrine of Salvation by the vicarious sacrifice of Jesus which is given a central place in it, has long belonged to the truisms of modern theological and church historical research. Unfortunately until now these truths have been suppressed by all possible means, and therefore they have not penetrated to the foundations. Even at the start of the eighteenth century the English philosopher Lord Bolingbroke (1678–1751) noticed two completely different religions in the New Testament, that of Jesus and that of Paul. Kant, Lessing, Fichte and Schelling also clearly distinguished between the teaching of Jesus and what the 'apostles' made of it. A large number of reputed modern theologians have come to acknowledge this fact.

One can now ask why it took 2000 years before the Pauline Salvation idea could be shown as absurd by these modern methods, by considering the legacy left by Jesus. One possible answer is that there has never been such an urgent need for an honest study of the heritage of Jesus, to finally get back to the true message of his teaching.

Notes

I. THE OLD RELIC AND MODERN SCIENCE

1 *Historisches Jahrbuch* 24 (1903), p. 340.
2 Cf also Zugibe (1988).
3 Quoted in Wilson (1979).
4 *La S. Sindone* (1976).
5 Tyrer (1981).
6 Frei (1982).
7 Scannerini and Caramiello (1989); Giovanni Riggi has also doubted the value of the pollen studies; Riggi di Numana (1988), p. 141.
8 Bulst (1988).
9 Jackson et al. (1982).
10 Morris, Schwalbe and London (1980). Gilbert and Gilbert (1980).
11 Heller and Adler (1980, 1981).
12 Baima Bollone, Jorio and Massaro (1981).
13 Baima Bollone, Jorio and Massaro (1982). Baima Bollone and Gaglio (1984).
14 Miller and Pellicori (1981), p. 85. A discussion of the various image formation theories can be found in Schwalbe and Rogers (1982).
15 Baima Bollone (1977).
16 Baima Bollone (1981).
17 Riggi di Numana (1988).
18 Sox (1988), pp. 44–51, 56–60.
19 On this, Petrosillo and Marinelli (1990), pp. 33ff.
20 *Our Sunday Visitor*, 13 April 1986, p. 7.
21 Petrosillo and Marinelli (1990), p. 46.
22 Sox (1988), p. 108.
23 Gonella, L., lecture at the Rosetum in Turin, 10 May 1989.
24 Dutton, D., letter to *Nature*, 327, 7 May 1989.
25 *Fidelity*, February 1989, p. 42.
26 Lecture at the Rosetum in Turin, 10 May 1989.
27 The term 'paper' refers to a technical article.
28 Hahn, M., expert opinion of 6 December 1989.
29 Ehrler, P. and Cai, Z., expert opinion of 19 December 1989.
30 Letter of 25 January 1992 from Wölfli to Holger Kersten.
31 Letter of 2 August 1981 from Raes to Holger Kersten.

II. THE CLOTH IN THE SHADOWS OF HISTORY

1 Hieronymus: *De vir. illust.*, cap. II. cf Green (1969).
2 Cf O'Rahilly (1941), p. 59.
3 Scavone (1989).
4 Robert de Clari (1873); English translation (1939).
5 Tixeront (1888).
6 Eusebius: *Historia Ecclesiastica* I, 13; II, 6–8.
7 Pétré (1948); Gamurrini (1887).
8 Evagrius (PG 86). Evagrius' writings derive from the period after 593.
9 Cureton (1864); Philips (1876).
10 *Narratio* (PG 113). English text printed in Wilson (1979), Appendix C.
11 *Narratio* (PG 113), pp. 12f.
12 Tobler and Moliner (1879), p. 116.
13 Kitzinger (1954).
14 Tischendorf (1876), pp. 456f.
15 Cf Dobschütz (1899), pp. 230ff and 157ff. The 'Cura Sanitatis Tiberii' was included in the *Legenda Aurea* of Jacob of Voragine composed in 1275.
16 Matt. 9:20–2; Mark 5:25–34; Luke 8:43–8. Dobschütz, loc. cit. pp. 175f.
17 Wilson (1979).
18 *Narratio* (PG 113), § 16–17. It is recounted along with Evagrius' version.
19 The stone bearing the imprint of the portrait, known as the Keramion, has an important role to play later on. It is quite likely that the discovery of this miraculous copy had some influence on the story of the transference of the Camuliana picture on to Hypatia's robe. Various different versions of the puzzling transfer of the image onto a building stone are known.
20 Wilson (1979).
21 *Narratio* (PG 113), § 15–16.
22 Prokop: *Historikon* II, 12, 26, (Loeb ed., I, pp. 368ff).
23 Tixeront (1888), p. 136; Bayer (1734), p. 95.
24 Tacitus, *Annals*, Book 11, 8–12; Book 12, 10–14.
25 Cf Assemani, *loc. cit.* Vol II, p. 392. It is difficult to say whether Thaddeus did actually die in Edessa. The Armenian version of the *Doctrina Addai* presents the last speech of Addai as that of a man leaving (for the orient) never to return. Cf Tixeront, loc. cit., p. 66.
26 Cureton (1864), p. 34 I. 24.
27 Guriel (1860), p. 148.
28 If Thaddeus really held an episcopate for some ten years himself, as

Cureton supposes (loc. cit., p. 162), then Aggai's twenty-three year term only ended in 63 (or even 66 by the modern reckoning). At this time Ma'nu VI had been at least six years on the throne, and it is not clear why he would have waited so long before dealing his blow to Christianity. The traditions say that the mood swing happened at the time he came to power. If Aggai's leadership really did last twenty years, it was probably only because he had already been made the leader of the community when Thaddeus was still alive, with his express approval.

29 Part I, *Gesta Pilati*.

30 This frightful form of death appears to be of Roman rather than oriental origin. It shows the degree of hatred involved, the king obviously wanting to humiliate the martyr by this form of death.

31 Wilson (1979).

32 Matt. 10:5–6. Another characteristic feature is the repeated admonition to maintain secrecy about his messianic status (Matt. 16:20; Mark 8:30; Luke 9:21) and about the experience of his Transfiguration.

33 Cf Festinger, Riecken and Schachter (1956); Hardyck and Braden (1962).

34 Dobschütz (1899), p. 182.

35 Jackson has demonstrated at least four indications of older folding.

36 Especially good examples of such Mandylion copies are found in the church of Spas Nereditsa near Novgorod, Russia and in the Radoslaw chapel in the Studenica monastery in Serbia. The Mandylion with frilled border is also seen on the so-called Abgar icon of St Catherine's monastery in Sinai, and on a miniature in a fourteenth-century manuscript in the Biblioteca Nacional de Madrid.

37 Grabar (1946), pp. 343ff.

38 Cf Holl (1928), p. 388; Rassart-Debergh (1990).

39 Cf Piper (1867), p. 78.

40 Dobschütz (1899), p. 139. Antoninus speaks of *mensura tollitur* (taking measurements) with cords, and *exinde et circa collum habent et sanantur* (afterwards they wear them round their necks and are healed). The phrase *mensuram tollerare* has nothing to do with wax pressings. This is also confirmed by Kitzinger, loc. cit, pp. 104f. In fact we have here the first reference to the taking of what are called 'sacred lengths': ailing people took the measurements of the corresponding limbs of Christ with cords or a strip of papyrus. Then they wrapped these round their neck and hoped for curative effects. Cf. Kriss-Rettenbeck (1963) pp. 41 & 138; Savio (1985).

41 Koch (1938), pp. 437f.

42 Paris, Bibl. Nat., cod. lat 2688, fol. 77ʳ. Weitzmann (1980), II, p. 77, and Pl. 10 b.

43 Kriss-Rettenbeck (1963), p. 72.

44 Further support for the Mandylion/Shroud hypothesis is provided by the fact that in the art of the sixth century we do not find the full Christ figure of the Turin Shroud, but only the facial features.

45 Vignon (198); Wuenschel (1954). Paul Maloney further reduces the Vignon list from twenty features to just nine which even the most sceptical observer will have to accept.

46 Wilson (1979).

47 Wiech (1990).

48 BSTS 24, 1990, 11–13; Marastoni (1980); Messina and Orechia (1989); Scheuermann (1988); Filas (1982); cf further Hachlili and Killebrew (1983); Meacham (1986).

49 Good examples are the icon of the Ascension from the Palestinian school of the ninth or tenth century in the Sinai monastery of St Catherine, see the plate in Huber (1987), p. 131; and the mosaic of the baptism of Christ in the church of Hosias-Luke (c. 1000) in Phokis, see the plate in Grabar (1964), p. 127.

50 Examples are to be found on numerous Byzantine frescoes and mosaics. Outstanding ones are the frescoes of S Maria del Monacato of Castrociela at Cassino (Italy), where clear forehead symbols following the Vignon-Wuenschel pattern can be seen on a wide range of figures. See the illustrations in Romano (1989), pp. 155–166.

51 A remarkable exception is the image of Jesus on the Emesa vase, to which I have drawn attention for just this reason. Here the hair falls straight to the shoulders, the earlobes are not visible, the right eyebrow is raised, the nose is noticeably long, and the beard is perhaps the most successful rendering from the cloth image.

52 Wilson (1979).

53 The present Salvator image dates back to the twelfth century. During restoration in 1746 it was found that the panel painting, so dearly loved, had been painted anew with great artistry on a fresh canvas, covering the older one. According to a legend, reported by Canonicus Nicolaus Maniacutius (c. 1180), the picture's origins go back to the evangelist Luke, a gifted painter. After long meditation he resolved to paint the portrait of Jesus. When he had drawn only the outlines, the complete face suddenly became finished in a miraculous manner. Cf Dobschütz (1899), p. 66. Concerning other *acheiropoieta* in the West, H. Pfeiffer has recently developed the theory that the Manopello Christ picture is the old Veronica image, and this in turn is the same as the Camuliana *acheiropoieton*. For this cf Zaninotto (1989 b).

54 Piper (1867), p. 249.

55 Latin poem from the Codex Mon. Aug. S. Ulr. 111, ed. Massman, pp. 176f, quoted in Dobschütz (1899), p. 196.

56 Zaninotto (1989 c).

57 Quoted in Green (1969), p. 333.

58 Ordericus Vitalis, *Historia Ecclesiastica*, TI. III, IX, 8.

59 Gervasius of Tilbury, *Otia Imperialia*, III.

60 MS 61, fol. 122. Cf. illustration in Weitzmann (1980), IX, p. 477.

61 MS add. gr. 129, fol. 87. See plate in Weitzmann (1980), p. 478: 'It is difficult to say what made the illustrator use the Egyptian form of mummy wrappings.'

62 On the *epitaphioi*, see Johnstone (1967).

63 Basilius Grolimund, letter of 7 October 1990.

64 Dubarle (1989).

65 Presumably what caused these burn holes was a kind of trial by fire to which the cloth was subjected, most probably at the time when it was being inspected prior to being removed from Edessa. The burn holes are found symmetrically on the dorsal and ventral halves, and originated when the cloth was in folded form. The suggestion of the archaeologist Paul Maloney, that they could be due to candles which were standing on the Shroud, because it was actually used as an altar cloth, is not correct.

66 The text is reproduced by C. Du Cange in his notes about the Alexiade. In: Migne, PG 131, pp. 563–8.

67 All listings of the Constantinople relics that are mentioned here are to be found in Riant (1878), II, pp. 211f, 214, 216f, 223.

68 Scavone (1989), pp. 117f.

69 Ibid., p. 118.

70 Heisenberg (1907), p. 31.

71 Bulst (1990), p. 44.

72 Ibid., p. 49.

73 Regarding the location of the chapel, cf. Ebersolt (1934); Janin (1953), vol. 3.

74 Riant (1878), pp. 175f. Inventory list pp. 197ff. This special case also shows the kind of opportunities which even low-ranking Crusaders had to take sacred objects back home with them, and how unimaginably great the treasure of relics must have been.

75 The picture was kept in the collegiate church of St Pierre at Corbie until 1970, when it was stolen. Afterwards just the frame was found with the reference to Robert de Clari, while the picture remained untraced. I have Dr Robert Caron, Fouilloy sous Corbie, to thank for the reference to the *Sainte Face de Corbie* and a photograph of the painting. Regarding the other portraits of Christ, see the illustrations in Fossati (1982), pp. 19–31.

76 Scavone (1989), pp. 119f, 127. Finally we should refer to a further problem which Bulst ignores. In the relic bequest of Baldwin II to

Louis IX mention is also made of 'part of the Sudarium in which Jesus' body was wrapped in the tomb' (Cf Riant, loc. cit. II, p. 135). How are we to assess this 'shroud' in relation to the Mandylion/ Shroud?

77 Geoffrey de Villehardouin (1938–9), II, pp. 26f.

78 Ebersolt (1934); Janin (1953), III, pp. 9f.

79 Cf Shaw (1963) p. 92; Geoffroy de Villehardouin (1938–9), II, pp. 50, 52; Crispino (1982).

80 Du Fresne du Cange (1826), pp. 30ff. Mansuet (1789), I, p. 226. Cf Epist. Innoc., Migne, PL215, col. 433.

81 Gesta (1874), pp. 118f.

82 Heyck (1886), p. 66.

83 *Annales Ianuenses* (1863), p. 122.

84 Epist. Innoc., Migne, PL215, col. 433f. Cf also Riant (1878), III, pp. 56f.

85 Barber (1978), p. 41.

86 Wilson (1979) claims that the Templars in Paris did put up some resistance. He thus tries to show how they managed to get the Shroud out of the city (where they were keeping it) in this time of extreme oppression. But there is no historical indication of any resistance. Cf Barber (1983), II, pp. 19f.

87 The first reliable study of the Templar prosecution was written in 1654 by Pierre Du Puy (*Traitez concernant l'Histoire de France: Sçavoir la condamnation des Templiers*), who thanks to his position as royal custodian of the archives was able to examine numerous documents which have since been lost. But some caution is advisable when dealing with Du Puy's work, because his aim was to defend Philip the Fair as one of 'the great kings who have held our monarchy' (Lizerand, 1923, p. XIX). The work of Finke (1907) still offers the best analysis of the contradictory prosecution.

88 From the warrant of Philip the Fair for the arrest of the Templars, dated 14 September 1307. Quoted in Lizerand (1923), p. 28.

89 All statements in Michelet (1851), I, pp. 277–280.

90 Michelet (1851), I, p. 212.

91 The Templar Raimundus Rubei stated for the protocol that the superior kissed the *figura Baffometi* and called out '*Yalla*'. One should add that the exclamations '*Yalla*' or '*Selah*' are frequently attested to and are most probably variations of '*Allah*'.

92 Quoted from Du Puy (1751), p. 22.

93 Wilson (1979).

94 Cf Finke (1907), pp. 334–7. Here again Wilson (1979) abridges and alters the description given by Etienne de Troyes in an unjustified manner.

95 Barber (1978), p. 273.

96 Michelet (1851), II, p. 218.

97 According to a legend of the tenth century, Ursula, the daughter of a British king, was killed by the Huns along with her ten companions near Cologne, while returning from a pilgrimage to Rome in 452. These eleven were then transmuted to form the legend of the 11,000 virgins.

98 The Templars probably owned relics like these themselves, keeping them in their churches just like relics in other churches. Cf Sevin, H.: *L'Enigme des Templiers et le Saint-Suaire*. Brussels 1988, p. 112.

99 Michelet (1851), II, p. 218.

100 Lizerand (1923), pp. 46ff.

101 Michelet (1851), II, p. 364.

102 Ibid., p. 366.

103 Ibid., p. 362.

104 Ibid., p. 363.

105 Guillame de Nangis (1738), I, pp. 402f.

106 The genealogy is based on the following texts: Anselme (1730); Bobin (undated); Plancher (1741); Prinet (1920); Courtépée and Béguillet (1968); and Crispino (1990). I am greatly indebted to Mrs Dorothy Crispino for numerous references.

107 Bib. Nat. P. orig., vol. 683, n 6, 9, 10, 11, 13.

108 The best and most comprehensive reference for the historical sources is Savio (1957). Cf also Fossati (1961).

109 *Sibi liberaliter oblatam.* Chevalier (1900), p. 28, XV, p. 32.

110 In the case of documents of Baldwin II of June 1247 we find *sanctam Toellam tabule insertam* and *partem Sudarii quo involutum fuit corpus eius in sepulchro.* Riant (1878), III, p. 135.

111 Crispino (1981).

112 Fossati (1983) presents a thorough treatment of the historical sources in this matter.

113 Currer-Briggs (1984), p. 106, makes things too easy for himself by simply inserting the Templar Geoffroy de Charnay in the family tree as an uncle of Charny. That is pure speculation; there is no evidence for it at all.

114 D'Arcis, quoted in Thurston (1903), p. 26.

115 Fossati (1983).

116 Piaget (1897), pp. 399, 410.

117 Ménestrier (1683), p. 179; Dacier (1777), p. 662; Pannier (1872).

118 Crispino points out that the important role of standard-bearer was normally only granted to senior knights after long service. This could mean that the birth of Geoffroy took place as early as the end of the thirteenth century. However, it is not possible to confirm any precise references to his date of birth. Crispino (1989).

119 Riant (1878), II, pp. 233f.

120 Scavone (1989), p. 121.

121 Rindaldi (1983).

122 Crispino (1985); Vignon (1938), pp. 106ff; Chamard (1902).

123 Bon (1969), p. 110; Morel-Fatio (1895), § 127.

124 Bon (1969), p. 233: '*Les Charny ont dû venir avec le prince Louis.*'

125 The denoting of Dreux as the brother of Geoffroy is an indication that Geoffroy was already an important knight of France at the time when the chronicle was composed. Cf. Morel-Fatio (1895), § 624.

126 Ostrogorsky (1963), pp. 422ff.

III. THE SECRET OF GOLGOTHA

1 Dodd (1963), p. 423; Brandon (1967), p. 16.

2 Lincoln, Baigent and Leigh (1984), pp. 287ff.

3 Ghiberti (1982), p. 43, Fn. 62.

4 Barbet (1953); Bulst and Pfeiffer (1987), pp. 87f; Currer-Briggs (1984), p. 16.

5 Bagatti and Milik (1958).

6 The Mishnah (Baba Bathra 6:8) describes the only correct design for a tomb building.

7 Savio (1957), pp. 33ff.

8 Zaninotto (1989a), p. 148. Of interest in this connection is the text from the *Acta Philippi* (143) where it says, 'Philippus asked that he be buried in leaves of papyrus, and that no linen cloth be placed around him, in order to stay different from Christ, who was pressed in a *sindon* [*en sindoni eneilethe*].'

9 Haenchen (1980), p. 556.

10 The embalming of Jacob and Joseph (Gen. 50:2–3,26) are an exception, but they correspond to the Egyptian custom.

11 Schabbat 23, 5. See also Ketub 20,b.

12 Dessy (1989), p. 42.

13 Boulos (1983), p. 128; Duke (1983), p. 19; Moldenke and Moldenke (1952), p. 35; further cf Reynolds (1950), pp. 394ff.

14 Hepper (1988).

15 Grindlay and Reynolds (1986).

16 Moldenke and Moldenke (1952).

17 Anderson (1957).

18 The teachings of the Ebionites (Epiphanius, *Haer*. 30) were the same as those of the pre-Christian Nasarenes (*nasaraioi*), the only difference being that they believed in Christ. Epiphanius (*Haer*. 18) is careful to distinguish them from the Nazarenes (*nazoraioi*). Cf Simon (1967), pp. 103–5.

19 Cf Geoltrain (1960).

20 Ben-Chorin (1967), p. 41.

21 In the nativity myth of John we find numerous elements from the Old Testament. The Annunciation by the archangel Gabriel is similar to the annunciation of the birth of the judge Simson, and like him John was said to have been a Nasir, a Nasirite (Judg. 13:4,5), who abstained from wine and intoxicating drinks (Luke 1:15). Concerning the Nasirites cf. Num. 6:1–21. The Nasirite group bears elements alien to the culture and for this reason they are compared with the Rechabites (1 Chr. 2:55; Jer. 35).

22 Flavius Josephus, De bello Judaico, II, 8, 3.

23 Plinius, Hist. Natural. V, 17.

24 Even though this was on occasion attributed to him: 'A prophet is not without honour, save in his own country, and in his own house.' (Matt. 13:57).

25 Feuillet (1982), p. 18; Zaninotto (1989), p. 160. The first to point this out was Blinzler (1960). In Matthew and Luke the term eneileo expressing the 'heaviness' of the packing was replaced by the milder entylisso, which simply conveys the fact of 'wrapping up'.

26 Mödder (1950); Zugibe (1984).

27 'The Son of Man came eating and drinking, and they say, Behold a man gluttonous, and a winebibber . . .' (Matt. 11:19).

28 Flavius Josephus, Vita, IV, 75.

29 Petrus de Natalibus (1508) IV, f 72a. Petrus de Natalibus refers to John of Damascus.

30 Lloyd Davies and Lloyd Davies (1991, a,b).

31 Bagatti and Testa (1978), p. 24. The apocryphal Gospel of Peter refers to the place where the tomb was situated as 'Joseph's garden'.

32 Flavius Josephus, De bello Judaico IV, 5, 2.

33 The exegete Haenchen (1980, p. 564) also found it most strange that Joseph had his own tomb built right next to a place of execution.

34 It may have been, though, that John meant the symbolic significance of Christ as the true Passover Lamb. During the Passover a special role was played by hyssop as the sprinkler (Exod. 12:22). The corresponding passage in Mark speaks of the sponge of vinegar being stuck on a cane (kalamos). Has John intentionally chosen hyssopos (hyssop) as an alternative to kalamos?

35 Kennard (1955), p. 238.

36 Cf Thiel (1938), pp. 100f.

37 Evidently Jesus withdrew from the area of his activity at the time of the so-called Ascension.

38 Zaninotto (1989a), pp. 151f. Cf also Feuillet (1982), p. 19.

39 Ibid., p. 162.

40 Bonnet-Eymard (1983), pp. 75–89. Opposing this cf. Pirot (1983), pp. 74ff, who supports the meaning of chin-band.
41 Ghiberti (1982), p. 46, Fn. 67.
42 Lavergne (1979), p. 233.
43 Dickinson (1990), p. 8.
44 Schwarz (1979).
45 Schwarz (1988), p. 27.
46 Cf. also Schwarz (1990), pp. 56ff. Because it is quite evident that the tradition of interpreting the term 'resuscitate' is confused with the theological idea of the actual Resurrection, a clear separation of the meanings in the texts is hardly possible any more.
47 Kühner (1968), p. 53.
48 Cf Gospel of Peter 6:14; Thiel (1938), p. 309.
49 I refer you to just two books which suggest a connection between the Grail and the Turin cloth, even though they both contain major historical shortcomings and have to be taken very critically in consequence: Currer-Briggs (1984) and Sevin (1988).
50 Du Puy (1751), pp. 85f. The treasurer of the Paris Temple, John of Turno, also confirms that the Templars sang this Psalm during the admission rites. Cf. Michelet (1851), II, p. 279.
51 Cf Kopling (1962), I, p. 131.
52 Hirsch (1940), p. 27.

IV. FRAUD OF THE CENTURY

1 Frei (1983), p. 281.
2 Blinzler (1952).
3 Hoare (1978), pp. 50, 52.
4 Letter to Karl Herbst of 16 April 1991.
5 Bulst and Pfeiffer (1987), p. 32.
6 Information given by Prof W. Bonte to Karl Herbst in letter dated 16 April 1991.
7 Hoare (1978), p. 53.
8 Letter of 6 March 1990 to Karl Herbst.
9 Cf Kratter (1921), I, p. 52.
10 Regarding the use of aloe in the history of pigments cf Brunello (1968).
11 'De Sudario Domini in duobus locis'. Cf Riant (1878), III, p. 198.
12 'Continentur iterum in eadem tabula . . . de Sindone . . .' Ex Inventario secundo thesauri Claravallensis, 1504.
13 '. . . de sindone munda'. Cf Riant (1878), III, p. 67.
14 'De syndone eiusdem et de sudario.' Cf Riant (1878), I, p. 20.

15 '. . . *partem Sudarii quo involutum fuit corpus eius in sepulchro*'. Cf Riant (1878), p. 135.

16 '. . . *de ipsius Sudario*'. Cf Riant (1878), III, p. 155.

17 '*De sindone qua corpus ipsius sepultum iacuit in sepulcro*'. Cf *Hispania Illustrata* (1872), II, p. 594.

18 Personal communication by Dr Roger Caron, Fouilloy sous Corbie, of 5 February 1991.

19 Personal communication by Dominique Ferry, Fraternité Franciscaine in Vézelay, of 25 January 1991.

20 Personal communication by Sister Emmanuel Desjardin, archivist for the Espiscopal Ordinariat of Soissons, of 4 February 1991.

21 Personal communications of 8 December 1990 and 7 February 1991.

22 Letter of Pedro Sobrino, Secretary of the Cathedral Chapter, of 27 December 1990.

23 AA. VV. (1977).

24 AA. VV. (1978).

25 One of the most well-known errors of this kind was the dating of the Lindow man. Concerning radiocarbon dating errors cf BSTS 13, p. 7; 14, pp. 2, 5; 22, pp. 8ff; *Shroud News* 50, pp. 26ff.

26 Bowman, Ambers and Leese (1990).

27 Petrosillo and Marinelli (1990), p. 54.

28 Boyce (1991), p. 43.

29 Riggi (1989).

30 Riggi (1988), p. 61.

31 Testore (1989).

32 Riggi (1989).

33 Petrosillo and Marinelli (1990), p. 77.

34 Ibid., pp. 100ff.

35 Ibid., p. 81.

36 The article in which the detective work is described has been published by Bonnet-Eymard's fellow brothers under the pseudonym 'Alter Ego'. Our account is based on this article, '*La traque des faussaires*' (1991).

37 Georges de Nantes (1991).

38 Burleigh, Leese and Tite (1986).

39 *Fidelity*, February 1989, p. 42.

Bibliography

ABBREVIATIONS

AA. VV.	Various authors
BSTS	Newsletter of the British Society of the Turin Shroud
MGH	Monumenta Germaniae Historica
Migne, PL	Migne, Patrologia Latina
Migne PG	Migne, Patrologia Graeca
SST	Shroud Spectrum International

AA. VV.: *L'Uomo della Sindone*. Rome, 1978.

—— *Osservazioni alle perizie ufficiali sulla Santa Sindone 1969–1976*. Turin, 1977.

Ammianus Marcellinus: *Rerum gestarum libri*.

Anderson, A. W.: *Plants of the Bible*. New York, 1957.

Annales Ianuenses. MGH, Scriptores, Vol. XVIII, 1863.

Anselme, P.: *Histoire de la Maison royale de France*. Paris, 1730.

Arculfus: 'Relatio de locis sanctis ab Adamnano scripta.' Tobler, T. (ed): *Itinera et descriptiones terrae sanctae*. Vol. 1, Geneva, 1877, 153–6.

Assemani, J. S.: *Bibliotheca Orientalis Clementino-Vaticana*. Rome, 1719.

Augustinus: 'De moribis ecclesiae catholicae' I, 34: Migne, PL 32.

Aurenhammer, H.: *Lexikon der christlichen Ikonographie*. Vienna, 1955ff.

Bagatti, B. and Testa, E.: *Il Golgota e la Croce*. Jerusalem, 1978.

Bagatti, P. G. and Milik, J. T.: *Gli scavi del 'Dominus flevit'. La necropoli del periodo Romano*. Jerusalem, 1958.

Baima Bollone, P.: 'Rilievi e considerazioni medico-legali sulla genesi delle impronte della Sindone'. *Sindon*, 19, 1977, 10–16.

—— 'La presenza della mirra, dell'aloe e del sangue sulla Sindone'. In Coppini, L. and Cavazzuti F. (eds.): *La Sindone – Scienza e fede*. Bologna, 1981, 169–74.

—— Jorio M. and Massaro A. L.: 'La dimostrazione della presenza di tracce di sangue umano sulla Sindone'. *Sindon*, 23, 5, 1981.

—— Jorio M. and Massaro A. L.: 'Identificazione del gruppo delle tracce di sangue umano sulla Sindone'. *Sindon*, 24, 31, 1982, 5–9.

—— and Gaglio, A.: 'Ulteriori ricerche sul gruppo delle tracce di sangue umano sulla Sindone'. *Sindon*, 26, 33, 1984, 9–13.

Balliani, Camillo: *De' ragionamenti sopra la sacra Sindone di N.S. Gesù Christo*. Torino, 1617–24.

Baluze, E.: *Vitae Paparum Avenionensium*. Mollat G. (ed.), Vol. III, Paris, 1921.

Barber, M.: *The Templars and the Turin Shroud*. SSI, 1983.

—— *The Trial of the Templars*. Cambridge, 1978.

Barbet, P.: *Die Passion Jesu Christi in der Sicht des Chirurgen*. Karlsruhe, 1953.

—— 'Les cinque plaies du Christ'. *Étude anatomique et expérimentale*. Paris, 1937.

Barrett, C. K.: *The Gospel According to St. John*. London, 1978.

Bauer, W.: 'Rechtgläubigkeit und Ketzerei im ältesten Christentum'. *Beiträge zur Historischen Theologie* 10, 1934, 7–43.

Bayer, T. S.: *Historia Osrhoena et Edessena ex numis illustra*. Petropolis, 1734.

Beck, H.-G.: 'Die griechische Kirche im Zeitalter des Ikonoklasmus'. In Jedin, H. (ed.): *Handbuch der Kirchengeschichte*. III/1, 31–61.

—— 'Die Ostkirche vom Anfang des 10. Jahrhunderts bis Kerullarios'. In Jedin, H. (ed.): *Handbuch der Kirchengeschichte*. III/1, 462–84.

Beigent, M. and Leigh, R.: *The Dead Sea Scrolls Deception*. London, 1991.

Belperron, P.: *La croisade contre les Albigeois et l'union du Languedoc à la France*. Paris, 1942.

Ben-Chorin, S.: *Bruder Jesus. Der Nazarener in jüdischer Sicht*. Munich, 1967.

Bennett, R. J.: *Diseases of the Bible*. London, 1887.

Bercovits, I.: *Illuminated Manuscripts in Hungary*, Dublin, 1969.

Bertelli, C.: 'Storia e vicende dell'immagine edessena'. *Paragon*, 217, 1968.

Billerbeck, P. and Strack, H. L.: *Kommentar zum Neuen Testament aus Talmud und Midrasch*. Munich, 1922–8.

Blinzler, J.: *Das Turiner Grablinnen und die Wissenschaft*. Ettal, 1952.

—— *Der Prozeß Jesu*. Regensburg, 1960.

Bobin, É.: *Monographie descriptive, historique et archéologique du Château de Mont-Saint-Jean-en-Auxois*. Paris, (undated).

Bon, A.: *La Morée Franque. Recherches historiques, topographiques et archéologiques sur la principauté d'Achaïe (1205–1430)*. Paris, 1969.

Bonfamiglia, P.: *Storia della S. Sindone*. Rome, 1606.

Bonnet-Eymard, B.: 'Le "Soudárion" Johannique negatif de la gloire divine'. In: Coppini and Cavazzuti (1983).

—— 'Les témoignages historiques surabondent'. *La Contre-Réforme Catholique au XXe Siècle. Numéro Spécial 271*, February–March 1991, 3–24.

Boulos, L.: *Medicinal Plants of North Africa*. Algonac, 1983.

Bowman, S. G. E., Ambers, J. C. and Leese, M. N.: 'Re-evaluation of British Museum radiocarbon dates issued between 1980 and 1984. *Radiocarbon*, 32, 1990, 59–79.

Boyce, D.: 'Les intrigues du British Museum'. *La Contre-Réforme Catholique au XXe Siècle*. Numéro Spécial 271, February–March 1991.

Brandon, S. G. F.: *Jesus and the Zealots. A study of the political factor in primitive Christianity*. Manchester, 1967.

Bréhier, L.: *L'Eglise et l'orient au moyen age: Les Croisades*. Paris, 1928.

Brown, R. E.: *Gospel according to John. The Anchor Bible*. London, 1978.

Brunello, F.: *L'Arte della tintura della storia dell'umanità*. Vicenza, 1968.

Bulst, W.: 'New problems and arguments about the pollen grains'. *SSI*, 27, 1988, 13–17.

—— and Pfeiffer, H.: *Das Turiner Grabtuch und das Christusbild*. Vol. I, Frankfurt, 1987; Vol. II, 1991.

—— *Betrug am Turiner Grabtuch. Der Manipulierte Carbontest*. Frankfurt, 1990.

Burleigh, R., Leese, M. and Tite, M.: 'An intercomparison of some AMS and small gas counter laboratories'. *Radiocarbon*, 28, 1986, 571–77.

Cameron, J. L.: *The Gospel according to Saint John*. London, 1960.

Chamard, F.: *Le Linceul du Christ. Étude critique et historique*. Paris, 1902.

Chevalier, U.: *Le Saint Suaire de Turin est-il l'original ou une copie?* Chieri, 1899.

—— *Étude critique sur l'origine du Saint Suaire de Lirey – Chambéry–Turin*. Paris, 1900.

Chiavarello, G.: *Genesi e storia della Santa Sindone*. Naples, 1978.

Coppini, L. and Cavazzuti, F. (eds): *La Sindone, scienza e fede*. Bologna, 1983.

Courtépée, A. and Béguillet, F.: *Description du Duché de Bourgogne*. Paris, 1968.

Cousin, P.: *Les débuts de l'ordre des Templiers et Saint-Bernard*. Mélanges Saint-Bernard, Dijon, 1954, 42–52.

Crispino, D.: 'Why did Geoffroy de Charny change his mind?' *SSI*, 1, 1981, 28–34.

—— '1204: Deadlock or springboard?' *SSI*, 4, 1982, 24–30.

—— 'Doubts along the Doubs'. *SSI*, 14, 1985, 10–24.

—— 'Geoffroy de Charny's second funeral'. Part II. *SSI* 32/33, 1989, 38–42.

—— 'The Charny genealogy'. *SSI*, 37, 1990, 19–25.

Crone, P.: *Meccan Trade and the Rise of Islam*. Princeton, 1987.

Cuomo, F. 'Gesù è morto cosi'. *Abstracta*, 19, 1987, 58–65.

Cureton, W.: *Ancient Syriac Documents Relative to the Earliest Establishment of Christianity in Edessa and the Neighbouring Countries*. London, 1864.

Currer-Briggs, N.: *The Holy Grail and the Shroud of Christ*. Maulden, 1984.

D'Arcis, P.: 'Memorandum to Clement VII'. In: Thurston, H.: 'The Holy Shroud and the Verdict of History'. *The Month*, 101, 1903.

Dacier: 'Recherches historiques sur l'établissement et l'extinction de l'ordre de l'Étoile'. *Mémoires de l'Académie des Insc. et Belles-Lettres*, t. XXXIX, 1777.

Damian of the Cross: 'The tomb of Christ from archaeological sources'. *SSI*, 17, 1985, 3–22.

Daniel, N.: *Islam and the West: The Making of an Image*. Edinburgh, 1960.

Dausend, H.: *Pilgerbericht der Nonne Aetheria*. Dusseldorf, 1933.

Dessy, A.: 'La sepoltura dei crocifissi'. *Sindon*, 1, 1989, 35–45.

Devastatio Constantinopolitana. MGH, Scriptores, Vol. XVI, 1861, 9–12.

Dickinson, I.: 'Preliminary details of new evidence for the authenticity of the Shroud: Measurement by the cubit'. *Shroud News*, 58, 1990.

Dieten, J.-L. van: *Niketas Choniates. Erläuterungen zu den Reden und Briefen nebst einer Biographie*. Berlin/New York, 1971.

Dobschütz, E. v.: *Christusbilder. Untersuchungen zur christlichen Legende*. Leipzig, 1899.

Dobb, C. H.: *Historical Tradition in the Fourth Gospel*. Cambridge, 1963.

Du Fresne du Cange: 'Histoire de l'empire de Constantinople sous les empereurs Français'. In: Buchon, J. A. (ed.): *Collection des Croniques nationales Françaises, écrites en langue vulgaire du treizième au seiziéme siècle*: Paris, 1826.

Du Puy, P.: *Histoire de l'ordre militaire des Templiers, ou chevaliers du Temple de Jerusalem*. Brussels, 1751.

Dubarle, A. M.: *Histoire ancienne du Linceul de Turin jusqu'au XIII. siècle*. Paris, 1985.

—— 'La date des premières brûlures observées sur le Linceul de Turin'. Lecture at the International Symposium La Sindone e le Icone, Bologna, May 1989.

Duke, J. A.: *Medicinal Plants of the Bible*. New York, 1983.

Durwell, F. X.: *Die Auferstehung Jesu als Heilsmysterium*. Salzburg, 1958.

Dutton, D.: Letter to *Nature*. *Nature*, 327, 1987, 7 May 10.

Ebersolt, J.: *Monuments d'Architecture Byzantine*. Paris, 1934.

Edwards, W. P., Wesley, J. G. and Hosmer, F. E.: 'On the physical death of Jesus Christ'. *Journal of the American Medical Association*, 255, 1986, 1455.

Eliade, M.: *Schmiede und Alchemisten*. Stuttgart, 1980.

Enrie, G.: *La Santa Sindone rivelata della fotografia*. Torino, 1933.

Evagrios: 'Historia ecclesiastica'. Migne, PG 86, 2, col. 2848–9.

Festinger, L., Riecken, H. W. and Schachter, S.: *When Prophecy Fails*. Minneapolis, 1956.

Feuillet, A.: 'The identification and the disposition of the funerary linens of Jesus' burial according to the Fourth Gospel'. *SSI*, 4, 1982, 18.

Filas, F. L.: *The Dating of the Shroud of Turin From Coins of Pontius Pilate*. Youngtown, 1982.

Finke, H.: *Papsttum und Untergang des Templerordens*. 2 vols. Münster, 1907.

Fossati, L.: *La Santa Sindone. Nuova luce su antichi documenti*. Turin, 1961.
—— 'The Lirey controversy'. *SSI*, 8, 1983, 24–34.
—— 'Was the so-called Acheropita of Edessa the Holy Shroud?' *SSI*, 3, 1982, 19–31.
Frei, M.: 'Identificazione e classificazione dei nuovi pollini della Sindone'. In: *La Sindone. Scienza e Fede*. Bologna, 1983.
—— 'Nine years of palinological studies on the Shroud'. *SSI*, 3, 1982, 3–7.
Gamurrini, J. F. (ed.): 'S. Hilarii Tractatus et Hymni et S. Silviae Aquitanae Perigrinatio ad loca sancta . . . ex cod. Arretino depromps'. Biblioteca dell'Academia Storico-Giuiridica. Vol. IV, Rome, 1887.
Gelzer, H.: 'Abriss der byzantinischen Kaisergeschichte: In: Krumbacher's Geschichte der byzantinischen Literatur. 1897.
Geoffroy de Villehardouin: 'La Conquête de Constantinople'. Tr. and ed. by Edmond Faral. Paris, 1938–9.
Geoltrain, P.: 'Le traité de la Vie contemplative de Philon d'Alexandrie'. *Semitica*, 10, 1960.
Georges de Nantes: 'Les trois substitutions du docteur Tite'. *La Contre-Réforme Catholique au XXe Siècle. Numéro Spécial 271*, February–March 1991, 65–71.
—— 'Gesta Episcoporum Halberstadensium'. MGH, Scriptores, Vol. XXIII, 1874, 118f.
Ghiberti, G.: *La Sepoltura di Gesù, i vangeli e la Sindoné*. Rome, 1982.
Gibbon, E.: *The History of the Decline and Fall of the Roman Empire*. London, 1840.
Gilbert, R. and Gilbert M. M.: 'Ultraviolet-visible reflectance and fluorescence spectra of the Shroud of Turin'. *Applied Optics*, 19, 1980, 1930–6.
Gonella, L.: Lecture at the Rosetum in Turin, 10 May 1989.
Grabar, A.: 'Martyrium. Recherche sur le culte des reliques et l'art chrétien antique'. Vol. II, *Iconographie*, Paris, 1946.
—— *Die byzantinische Kunst des Mittelalters*. Baden-Baden, 1964.
—— 'Une hymne Syriaque sur l'architecture de la Cathédrale d'Edesse'. In *L'art de la fin de l'antiquité et du moyen âge*. Collège de France Fondation Schlumberger pour les études Byzantines, Paris 1968.
—— *Christian Iconography: A Study of its Origins*. Princeton, 1980.
Gramaglia, P. A.: *Le ultime "scoperte" sulla Sindone di Torino*. Turin, 1981.
Green, M.: 'Enshrouded in Silence'. *Ampleforth Journal 74*, 1969, 319–45.
Gregory of Nyssa: 'Oratio de deitate filii et spiritus sancti'. Migne, PG 46.
Grindlay, D. and Reynolds, T.: 'The Aloe vera phenomenon: A review of the properties and modern uses of the leaf parenchyma gel'. *Journal of Ethnopharmacology*, 16, 1986, 117–51.

Grolimund, B.: 'Die Darstellung der eucharistischen Realpräsenz Christi in der byzantinisch-slawischen Hagiographie und Ikonographie'. In Goltz, H. (ed.): *Eikon und Logos. Beiträge zur Erforschung byzantinischer Kulturtraditionen*. Halle, 1981, 35, 307.

Guillaume de Nangis: 'Gesta Sanctae Memoriae Ludovici Regis Franciae'. In Bouquet, M. et al. (eds.): *Recueil de Historiens des Gaules et de la France*. 23 vols. Paris, 1738–1876, Vol. I.

Gunther de Paris: 'Historia Constantinopolitana'. In Riant (1878).

Guriel, F. (ed.) *Grammatica chaldaica*. Rome, 1860.

Gutschmid, M.: 'Die Königsnamen'. In *Rheinisches Museum. Neue Folge*. 1864.

Hachlili, R. and Killebrew, A.: 'Was the coin-on-eye custom a Jewish burial practice in the second temple period?' *Biblical Archaeologist*, Summer, 1983, 147–53.

Haenchen, E.: *Das Johannes-Evangelium. Ein Kommentar*. Tübingen, 1980.

Hardyck, J. A. and Braden, M.: 'When Prophecy Fails Again: A Report of Failure to Replicate'. *Journal of Abnormal and Social Psychology* 65, 1962, 136–41.

Hart, G. V., Kvas, I., Soots, M. and Badaway, G.: 'Blood group testing of ancient material'. *Masca Journal*, 1, 1980, 146.

Heisenberg, A. (ed.): *Nikolaus Mesarites, die Palastrevolution des Johannes Komnenos*. Würzburg, 1907.

Heller, J. H. and Adler, A. D.: 'A chemical investigation of the Shroud of Turin'. *Canadian Forensic Society Scientific Journal*, 14, 1981, 81–103.

—— and Adler, A. D.: 'Blood on the Shroud of Turin'. *Applied Optics*, 19, 1980, 2742–4.

Hepper, F. N.: 'The identity and origin of classical bitter aloes (aloe)'. *Palestine Exploration Quarterly*, 120, 1988, 146–8.

Herbst, K.: *Der wirkliche Jesus*. Olten, 1988.

Heyck, E.: *Genua und seine Marine im Zeitalter der Kreuzzüge*. Innsbruck, 1886.

Hirsch, E.: *Die Auferstehungsgeschichten und der christliche Glaube*. Tübingen, 1940.

Hoare, R.: *The Testimony of the Shroud*. London, 1978.

Holl, K.: 'Der Anteil der Styliten am Aufkommen der Bilderverehrung'. In *Gesammelte Aufsätze zur Kirchengeschichte*, II, Tübingen, 1928.

Huber, P.: *Die Kunstschätze der heiligen Berge. Sinai, Athos, Golgotha*. Augsburg, 1987.

Jackson, J. P.: 'Foldmarks as a historical record of the Turin Shroud'. *SSI*, 11, 1984, 6–29.

Jumper, E. J. and Ercoline, W. R.: 'Three dimensional characteristics of the Shroud image'. *Proceedings of the IEEE International Conference on Cybernetics and Society*. Seattle, Washington, October 1982, 559–75.

Janin, R.: *La Géographie Ecclésiastique de l'Empire Byzantine*. Paris, 1953.

John of Damascus: 'De imag. Orat'. Migne, PG 94.

Johnstone, P.: *The Byzantine Tradition in Church Embroidery*. London, 1967.

Jones, J.: *New and Full Method*. Oxford, 1798.

Judah Ben-Zion Segal: *Edessa – The Blessed City*. Oxford, 1970.

Kempf, F.: 'Die innere Wende des christlichen Abendlandes während der gregorianischen Reform'. In Jedin, H. (ed.): *Handbuch der Kirchengeschichte*, III/1, 485–539.

Kennard, J. S.: 'The burial of Jesus'. *JBL* 74, 1955.

Kersten, H.: *Jesus Lived in India*. Shaftesbury, 1986.

Kitzinger, Ernst: 'The Cult of Images in the Age before Iconoclasm'. *Dumbarton Oaks Papers*, VIII, 1954, 83–150.

Klauser, T. (ed.): *Reallexikon für Antike und Christentum*. Stuttgart, 1950ff.

Koch, L.: 'Zur Theologie der Christusikone'. *Benediktinische Montasshrift*, 1938.

Koch, L.: 'Christusbild – Kaiserbild'. *Benediktinische Monatsschrift*, 1939.

Kolping, A., in: Fries, H. (ed.): *Handbuch Theologischer Grundbegriffe*. Vol. 1. Munich, 1962.

Kötting, B.: *Peregrinatio Religiosa. Wallfahrt und Pilgerwesen in Antike und alter Kirche*. Regensburg/Münster, 1950.

Kratter, J.: *Lehrbuch der gerichtlichen Medizin*. Stuttgart, 1921.

Kriss-Rettenbeck, L.: *Bilder und Zeichen religiösen Volksglaubens*. Munich, 1963.

Kühner, H.: 'Die Katharer'. In Schultz, H.-J. (ed.): *Die Wahrheit der Ketzer*. Stuttgart/Berlin, 1968, 50–9.

—— 'La S. Sindone. Ricerche e studi della commissione di esperti nominata dall'Arcivescovo di Torino, Car. Michele Pellegrino, nel 1969'. *Rivista diocesana Torinese*, Turin, 1976.

'La traque des faussaires'. *La Contre-Réforme Catholique au XXe Siècle*. Numéro Spécial 271, February–March 1991, 35–42.

Lafontaine-Dosogne, J., in Volbach, W. F. and Lafontaine-Dosogne, J., *Byzanz und der christliche Osten. Propyläen Kunstgeschichte*, Vol. 3, Berlin, 1968.

Lavergne, C.: 'La protohistoire du Linceul du Seigneur'. In AA.VV.: *La Sindone e la Scienza*. Turin, 1979.

Lincoln, H., Baigent, M. and Leigh, R.: *Der heilige Gral und seine Erben*. Bergisch Gladbach, 1984. (*The Holy Blood and the Holy Grail*. London, 1982.)

Lizerand, G.: *Le dossier de l'affaire des Templiers*. Paris, 1923.

Lloyd Davies, M. and Lloyd Davies, T. A.: 'Resurrection or resuscitation?' *Journal of the Royal College of Physicians of London*, 25, 1991 (a).

—— and Lloyd Davies, T. A.: *The Bible: Medicine and Myth*. Cambridge 1991 (b).

Luchaire, A.: *Innocent III. La question d'Orient*. Paris, 1907.

Magnesia, Macarius of: *Apocriticus*. Blondel, C. (ed.). Paris, 1876.

Malloni, F. D.: *Stigmata sacrae sindoni impressa*. Alphonso Palaeotus. Venedig, 1606.

Maloney, P.: 'The Shroud of Turin: Traits and Peculiarities of Image and Cloth Preserved in Historical Sources'. Lecture at the International Symposium La Sindone e le Icone, Bologna, May 1989.

Mansuet, P.: *Histoire critique et apologétique de l'ordre des Chevaliers du Temple de Jérusalem dits Templiers*. Paris, 1789.

Marastoni, A.: Tracce di scritte sulla S. Sindone di Torino'. *Sindon*, 29, 1980, 9–12.

McCrone, W.: 'Light microscopical study of the Turin Shroud I–III'. *The Microscope*, 28, 1980, 29, 1981.

Meacham, W.: 'On the archaeological evidence for a coin-on-eye Jewish burial custom in the first century AD'. *Biblical Archaeologist*, 3, 1986, 56–61.

Mendelssohn, L. (ed.): *Appian: Translation des Bildes der großen Göttermutter*. Leipzig, 1879.

Ménestrier, F.: *De la chevalerie ancienne et moderne*. Paris, 1683.

Messina, R. and Orecchia, C.: 'La scritta in caratteri ebraici sulla fronte dell'uomo della Sindone: Nuove ipotesi e problematiche'. *Sindon*, 1, 1989, 83–93.

Michelet, M. (ed.): *Procès des Templiers*. Paris, 1851, 2 Vols.

Miller, V. D. and Pellicori, S. F.: 'Ultraviolet fluorescence photography of the Shroud of Turin'. *Journal of Biological Photography*, 49, 1981, 71–85.

Mödder, H.: 'Die Todesursache bei der Kreuzigung'. *Stimmen der Zeit*, 144, 1948, 50–9.

—— 'Die neuesten medizinischen Forschungen über die Todesursache bei der Kreuzigung Jesu Christi'. *Der Gottesfreund*, 3, 1950, 40–51.

Moldenke, H. N. and Moldenke, A. N.: *Plants of the Bible*. New York, 1952.

Moneta di Cremona: *Adversus Catharos et Valdenses*. Ricchini, T. A. (ed.), Rome, 1743.

Morel-Fatio, A. (ed.): *Libro de los fechos*. Genéva, 1895, 127.

Morey, C. R.: *Early Christian Art. An outline of the evolution of style and iconography in sculpture and painting from antiquity to the eighth century*. Princeton, 1953.

Morris, R. A., Schwalbe, L. A. and London, J. R.: 'X-Ray fluorescence investigation of the Shroud of Turin'. *X-Ray Spectrometry*, 9, 1980, 40–7.

Moses of Khoren: 'Histoire d' Arménie' (French tr. by P. E. Le Vaillant de Florival). Livre second. in: Cureton (1864) pp. 125–39, Chap. XXX.

Narratio de imagine Edessena. In Migne, PG 113, 423–454.

O'Rahilly, A.: 'The Burial of Christ'. *Irish Ecclesiastical Record* 59, 1941.

Ohme, H.: 'Das Quinisextum auf dem VII. Ökumenischen Konzil.' *Annuarium Historiae Conciliorum*, 20, 1988, 325–44.

Omont, H.: *Miniatures des plus anciens MSS grecs de la Bibliothèque Nationale du VIe au XIVe siècle*. Paris, 1929.

Onasch, K.: *Liturgie und Kunst in der Ostkirche*. Leipzig, 1981.

Origenes: *Contra Celsum*. English tr. Cambridge, 1953.

Ostrogorsky, G.: *Geschichte des Byzantinischen Staates*. Munich, 1963.

Paleotti, A.: *Esplicatione del Sacro Lenzuolo ove fu involto il Signore*. Bologna, 1598.

Pannier, L.: *La noble Maison de Saint-Omer, la Villa Clippiacum et l'Ordre de l'Étoile*. Paris, 1872.

Panovsky, E.: 'Die Entwicklung der Proportionslehre als Abbild der Stilentwicklung'. *Monatshefte für Kunstwissenschaft*. Geneva, 1961.

Pellicori, S. F.: 'Spectral properties of the Shroud of Turin'. *Applied Optics*, 19, 1980, 1913–20.

Pernoud, R.: *Die Kreuzzüge in Augenzeugenberichten*. Düsseldorf, 1965.

Perret, A.: 'Essai sur l'histoire du Saint Suaire du XIVe au XVIe siècle'. *Mémoirs de l'Académie des Sciences, Belles-Lettres et Arts de Savoie*, 1960.

Pétré, H.: 'Peregrinatio Aetheriae'. *Sources Chrétiennes*, 21, Paris, 1948.

Petrosillo, O. and Marinelli, E.: *La Sindone. Un enigma alla prova della scienza*. Milan, 1990.

Petrus de Natalibus: *Catalogus sanctorum*. A. Verlo (ed.) Lyon, 1508.

Philips, G. (ed.): *The Doctrine of Addai the Apostle*. London, 1876.

Pia, S.: 'Memoria sulla riproduzione fotografica della santissima Sindone, 1907'. Reprinted in *Sindon*, April 1960.

Piaget, A.: 'Le Livre messire Geoffroi de Charny'. *Romania*, 26, 1897, 394–411.

Piano, L. G.: *Commentarii critico-archeologici sopra la S. S. Sindone di N. S. Gesù Cristo venerato in Torino*. Turin, 1833.

Pingonius, F.: *Sindon evangelica*. Turin, 1581.

Piper, F.: *Einleitung in die Monumentale Theologie. Eine Geschichte der christlichen Kunstarchäologie und Epigraphik*. Gotha, 1867.

Pirot, J.: 'Soudárion mentionière'. *Sindon*, 32, 1983, 74f.

Plancher, U.: *Histoire générale et particulière de Bourgogne*. Dijon, 1741.

Prinet, M.: *Armorial de France*. Paris, 1920.

Pseudo-Dionysius: 'De ecclesiastica hierarchia'. Migne, PG3.

Quispel, G.: *Makarios, das Thomasevangelium und das Lied von der Perle*. Leiden, 1966.

Raes, G.: 'Rapport d'analyse du tissu'. In *La S. Sindone* (1976).

Rassart-Debergh, M.: 'De l'icône païenne à l'icône chrétienne'. *Le Monde Copte*, 18, 1990, 39–70.

Rendle Short, A.: *The Bible and Modern Medicine*. London, 1953.

Reynolds, G.W.: *The Aloes of South Africa*. Johannesburg, 1950.

Riant, P.-E.-D.: *Exuviae sacrae Constantinopolitanae*. Geneva, 1878.

Riggi di Numana, G.: *Rapporto Sindone (1978/1987)*. Milan, 1988.

—— 'Prélèvement sur le Linceul effectué le 21 avril 1988'. Lecture at the Symposium Scientifique International de Paris sur le Linceul de Turin, September 1989.

Rinaldi, P. *The Man in the Shroud*. London, 1974.

—— 'Un documento probante sulla localizzazione in Atene della Santa Sindone dopo il saccheggio di Costantinopoli'. In Coppini and Cavazzuti (1983).

Robert de Clari: 'The History of them that took Constantinople'. In Stone, E. N. (ed. and tr.): *Three Old French Chronicles of the Crusades*. Seattle, 1939.

—— 'Li estoires de chiaus qui conquisent Constantinople 1203'. In Hopf, C.: *Chroniques gréco-romaines inédites ou peu connues*. Paris, 1873.

Romanese, R.: 'Contributo sperimentale allo studio della genesi delle impronte della Santa Sindone.' Papers of the Congress of Cultores Sanctae Sindonis. Turin, 1939.

Romano, S.: 'Affreschi da S. Maria del Monacato a Castrocielo (e un'aggiunta da Roccasecca). *Arte Medievale*, 3, 1989, 155–66.

Runciman, S.: *Geschichte der Kreuzzüge*. Munich, 1968.

Savio, P.: *Ricerche storiche sulla Santa Sindone*. Turin, 1957.

—— 'The height of Christ'. *SSI*, 14, 1985, 7–9.

Scannerini, S. and Caramiello, R.: 'Il problema dei pollini'. *Sindon*, 1, 1989, 107–111.

Scavone, D. C.: 'The Shroud of Turin in Constantinople. The Documentary Evidence'. *Sindon* 1, 1989, 113–28.

—— 'A Note on the Name of the Pharos Chapel in Constantinople'. *Shroud News* 61, 1990, 10–12.

Scheuermann, O. 'Amulett-Abbild auf dem Turiner Grabtuch?' *Der Fels*, 19, 2, 1988, 54–6.

Schmidt, J. A.: *Sudaria Christi*. Helmstädt, 1698.

Schönborn, C. v.: *L'Icône du Christ. Fondements Théologiques élaborés entre le 1er et le 2me Concile de Nicée (325–787)*. Fribourg, 1976.

Schwalbe, L. A. and Rogers, R. N.: 'Physics and chemistry of the Shroud of Turin.: A summary of the 1978 investigation'. *Analytica Chimica Acta*, 135, 1982, 3–49.

Schwarz, G.: '*Anhistemi* und *anastasis* in den Evangelien. Biblische Notizen.' *Beiträge zur exegetischen Diskussion*. 10, 1979, 35–40.

—— 'Tod, Auferstehung, Gericht und ewiges Leben nach den ersten drei Evangelien'. *Via Mundi*, 55, 1988.

—— *Wenn die Worte nicht stimmen. Dreißig entstellte Evangelientexte wiederhergestellt*. Munich, 1990.

Sendler, E.: *The Icon: Image of the Invisible*. Redondo Beach, 1988.

Sevin, H.: *L'Enigme des Templiers et le Saint-Suaire*. Brussels, 1988.

Shaw, M. R. B.: *Joinville and Villehardouin: Chronicles of the Crusades*. New York, 1963.

Simon, M.: *Jewish Sects at the Time of Jesus*. Philadelphia, 1967.

—— 'Le Christianisme antique et son contexte religieux'. *Scripta Varia*. Tübingen, 1981.

Sox, D. H.: *The Shroud Unmasked*. London, 1988.

Stroud, W.: *Treatise on the physical cause of the death of Jesus Christ and its relation to the principles and practice of Christianity*. London, 1847.

Symeon Magister, *Chron*. In Bekker, I. (ed.): *Corpus scriptorum historiae Byzantinae*. Bonn, 1838.

Szyszman, S.: *Das Karäertum*. Vienna, 1983.

Tafel, R. and Thomas, F.: 'Urkunden zur älteren Handels-und Staatsgeschichte der Republik Venedig'. *Fontes rerum Austriacum*. Vienna 1856f.

Tamburelli, G. and Oliveri, F.: 'Un nuovo processamento dell'immagine Sindonica'. Papers of the Third Nationalen Kongresses der Sindonologie, Trani, 13–14 October 1984.

—— and Balossino, N.: 'Ulteriori sviluppi dell'elaborazione elettronica del volto sindonico'. *Sindon*, 1, 1989, 137–41.

Testore, F.: 'Le Saint Suaire – Examen et prélèvements effectués le 21 avril 1988'. Lecture at the Symposium Scientifique International de Paris sur le Linceul de Turin, September 1989.

Thiel, R.: *Jesus Christus und die Wissenschaft*. Berlin, 1938.

Thümmel, H. G.: 'Patriarch Photios und die Bilder'. In Goltz, H. (ed.): *Eikon und Logos. Beiträge zur Erforschung byzantinischer Kulturtraditionen*. Halle, 1981, 35, 275–290.

Thurston, H.: 'The Holy Shroud and the Verdict of History'. *The Month*, 101, 1903.

Tischendorf, C.: *Evangelia apocrypha*. Leipzig, 1876.

Tixeront, L.-J.: *Les origines de l'église d'Edesse et la légende d'Abgar*. Paris, 1888.

Tobler, T.: *Itinera et descriptiones terrae sanctae*. I, Geneva, 1877.

—— and Moliner, A.: 'De Locis sanctis quae perambulavit Antoninus Martyr.' In: *Itinera hierosalymitana et descriptiones Terrae Sanctae*. Publications de la Société de l'Orient Latin. Vol. XLIV, Geneva, 1879.

Tribbe, F. C.: *Portrait of Jesus*? New York, 1983.

Tyrer, J.: 'Looking at the Turin Shroud as a textile'. *Textile Horizons*, December 1981.

Vial, G.: 'Le linceul de Turin – étude technique'. *CIETA Bulletin* 67, 1989, 11–24.

Vignon, P.: 'Le Linceul du Christ'. *Étude scientifique*. Paris, 1902 (a).

—— 'Sur la formation d'images negatives par l'action de certaines vapeurs'. *Comptes rendus hebdomadaires de séances de l'Académie des Sciences*, 134, 1902 (b), 902–904.

—— *Le Saint Suaire de Turin devant la science, l'archéologie, l'histoire, l'iconographie, la logique*. Paris, 1938.

Vogt, H. J.: 'Der Streit um das Lamm. Das Trullanum und die Bilder'. *Annuarium Historiae Conciliorum*, 20, 1988, 135–149.

Walker, W.: *All the Plants of the Bible*. New York, 1957.

Weidinger, E.: *Die Apokryphen. Verborgene Bücher der Bibel*. Augsburg, 1990.

Weitzmann, K.: *Byzantine Book Illuminations and Ivories*. London, 1980.

Whanger, A. D.: 'Images derived from the Shroud by the overlay technique'. Lecture to the International Symposium La Sindone e le Icone, Bologna, May 1989.

—— and Whanger, M.: 'Polarized image overlay technique: a new image comparison method and its applications'. *Applied Optics*, 24, 1985, 766–72

Wiech, B. A.: 'The two- and three-lock hairstyles in early portraits of Jesus'. *SSI*, 35/36, 1990, 13–5.

Wilson, I.: *The Turin Shroud*. London, 1979.

Wölfli, W.: 'Keine Spur von einem Wunder'. *Die Welt*, 14 April 1990.

Wuenschel, E. A.: *Self-Portrait of Christ: The Holy Shroud of Turin*. New York, 1954.

Zaninotto, G.: 'GV 20,1–8. Giovanni testimone oculare della risurrezione di Gesù?' *Sindon*, 1, 1989, 145–70 (a).

—— 'L'Immagine acheropita del ss. Salvatore nel Sancta Sanctorum di Roma'. Lecture to the International Symposium La Sindone e le Icone, Bologna, May 1989 (b).

—— 'Il sermone dell'arcidiacono Gregorio il referendario: Un' Antica ricognizione della Sindone?' Lecture to the Symposium Scientifique International de Paris sur le Linceul de Turin, September 1989 (c).

Zugibe, F. T.: 'Death by crucifixion'. *Canadian Society of Forensic Science Journal*, 17, 1984.

—— *The Cross and the Shroud: A Medical Inquiry into the Crucifixion*. New York, 1988.

Index

Picture Credits

31: Bibliothèque Nationale, Paris
47: Bodleian Library, Oxford
17, 19, 63: Frère Bruno Bonnet-Eymard, C.R.C, St.-Parres-Les-Vaudes
13: Prof. Damon, Tucson
2–7, 57: G. Enrie
54–56, 58–62: Elmar R. Gruber, Bretten
12: Prof. Teddy Hall, Oxford
1, 15, 25–28: Holger Kersten, Freiburg
45, 46: Mario Moroni, Robbiate
24: Maurizio Paolicchi
9, 10: Precision Processes Ltd., Derby
11: Gilbert Raes, Gent
14, 16, 20: Giovanni Riggi, Torino
36: S. Bartolomeo degli Armeni, Genova
22, 23: The Max Frei Collection: Association of Scientists and Scholars
   International for the Shroud of Turin, Ltd. (ASSIST).
29: The Pierpont Morgan Library, New York. M. 499, f. 15
43, 44: Alan Whanger, Durham
21, 53: Ian Wilson, Bristol